AMERICAN
COUP

Also by William M. Arkin

Top Secret America: The Rise of the New American Security State
with Dana Priest

Divining Victory: Airpower in the 2006 Israel-Hezbollah War

*Code Names: Deciphering U.S. Military Plans, Programs,
and Operations in the 9/11 World*

Operation Iraqi Freedom: 22 Historic Days in Words and Pictures
with Marc Kusnetz and General Montgomery Meigs

*The US Military Online: A Directory for Internet Access to the
Department of Defense*

Encyclopedia of the US Military with Joshua Handler,
Julie A. Morrissey, and Jacquelyn Walsh

Nuclear Weapons Databook: Volume IV: Soviet Nuclear Weapons
with Thomas B. Cochran, Robert S. Norris, and Jeffrey I. Sands

*Nuclear Weapons Databook: Volume III: US Nuclear Warhead
Facility Profiles* with Thomas B. Cochran, Milton M. Hoenig,
and Robert S. Norris

*Nuclear Weapons Databook: Volume II: US Nuclear Warhead
Production* with Thomas B. Cochran, Milton M. Hoenig, and
Robert S. Norris

Nuclear Battlefields: Global Links in the Arms Race with
Richard Fieldhouse

S.I.O.P.: The Secret U.S. Plan for Nuclear War
with Peter Pringle

*Nuclear Weapons Databook: Volume I: US Nuclear Forces and
Capabilities* with Thomas B. Cochran and Milton M. Hoenig

Research Guide to Current Military and Strategic Affairs

AMERICAN COUP

HOW A TERRIFIED GOVERNMENT IS DESTROYING THE CONSTITUTION

WILLIAM M. ARKIN

LITTLE, BROWN AND COMPANY

New York Boston London

Little, Brown and Company
Hachette Book Group
237 Park Avenue, New York, NY 10017
littlebrown.com

First Edition: September 2013

Little, Brown and Company is a division of Hachette Book Group, Inc. The Little, Brown name and logo are trademarks of Hachette Book Group, Inc.

The publisher is not responsible for websites (or their content) that are not owned by the publisher.

The Hachette Speakers Bureau provides a wide range of authors for speaking events. To find out more, go to hachettespeakersbureau.com or call (866) 376-6591.

ISBN 978-0-316-25124-2
LCCN 2013940401

10 9 8 7 6 5 4 3 2 1

RRD-C

Printed in the United States of America

To Luciana

CONTENTS

AMERICAN COUP

Introduction

We are a nation living with two sets of laws, one public law as guided by the Constitution and a second, invisible text that exists between the lines of that document. The Constitution specifies the ABCs, upholding public welfare and common defense with powers granted to the federal government that are excruciatingly limited and balanced so as to not infringe on the inherent rights of the people or the member states of the republic. Between the lines are the XYZs of the extraordinary, the charter of another realm, one beyond the reach of Congress, the courts, and the people; a system of federal preeminence and an executive preoccupation that possesses self-authored powers to govern in the hereafter, subtly reordering the relationship between the people and its government in the here and now.

This duality—codified through decades of deliberate concealment—purports to merely supplement the two-hundred-year-old doctrine that couldn't possibly anticipate societal vulnerability to man-made and natural threats in an age of weapons of mass destruction and terrorism. But the implementation of the XYZs is not lagging in some legislative queue; it is already in place, the very essence of executive tyranny our forefathers feared.

It is the elevation of common defense above public welfare, expediency turned into necessity, a subtle house of correction offering the illusion of security. This tug-of-war has been ever present during our lifetimes, the shining promise being that someday we will return to the application of the basic principles enshrined in the Constitution. Yet we are not going back. The soul of our nation, the principle of individual rights upheld by the union of constraints on executive and government power, is at risk. At no point in our history have we faced a challenge like the one we face now, a wholly permanent state of martial life hidden in fine print, secrecy, fear, and the dream of guaranteed physical protection.

I became interested in underground government on the day John Hinckley, Jr., attempted to kill President Ronald Reagan in 1981. Then a young Washington analyst and budding expert, I was called upon to comment in the news media about how the country was run amidst chaos. Over the years, I researched and wrote about the world of *what-if*, my heart pumping as hard when I discovered some vague piece of the puzzle buried in budget documents and government reports as when I drove out to some Washington suburb to take a look at an invisible hideout.

I was never seized with a fear of nuclear war during this period, so I fell into the camp that saw "continuity of government" as more comical than sinister—more the latest incarnation of duck and cover and Bert the turtle, much closer to *Dr. Strangelove* than *Seven Days in May*—a waste of money perhaps but not really dangerous. It seemed common sense to me that plans should have been made for managing the nation if a president was murdered, especially in the nuclear age. But I was swept up in the conventional wisdom that there was a twisted and unbalanced militarism behind Secretary of State (and retired general) Alexander Haig's infamous "I am in control here" proclamation, not really able to see or articulate the larger system of emergency procedures that seized greater import.

Three decades later I could adeptly recount both the history and continuity of these preparations for control after catastrophe: priorities and procedures that seemed to persist through Republican and Democratic administrations, conservative and liberal, peacetime and wartime. But there was one huge difference after 9/11: these secret procedures and plans weren't just geared toward the possibility of Doomsday, for some single and distant final event, because Doomsday was now every day.

Something new was going on, much of it explained in *Top Secret America*, the *Washington Post* newspaper series and book that Pulitzer Prize–winning reporter Dana Priest and I collaborated on for three years. The basic premise of that investigation was that the post-9/11 civil defense industry was not only bureaucratically but geographically transforming the nation. The lights had never gone out in many of the facilities that had been used during the Reagan years and before; others were reintroduced, the government urging the news media to keep their locations secret from al Qaeda even though a good number of them, such as Mount Weather and Raven Rock, the primary civilian and military underground bunkers just outside Washington, had been mentioned in numerous books and articles in years previous.[1] And while the old initials and logos remained, there were some notable new acronyms and euphemisms that hinted of secret activities down vaporous paths.

Among the phrases that caught my attention as I dug through documents and spoke with sources after 9/11 was "martial law." Mentioning the possibility wasn't new, yet martial law hadn't been declared on the day of the attacks, nor during the darkest days of the Cold War, and it seemed the stuff reserved for other countries or conspiracy nuts. On the other hand, General Tommy Franks, the commander of wars in Afghanistan and Iraq, gave an interview in, of all places, *Cigar Aficionado*, saying that if terrorists struck the United States with weapons of mass destruction, the country would likely discard the Constitution for some kind of military government.[2] Not exactly the ravings of some 9/11 denier or Internet paranoid.

Then there was the word "extraordinary"—in theory, not exactly something to ring alarm bells; the government throws around terms like "extraordinary" to mean just about everything and anything. But when it came to the classified world, I was increasingly seeing the word attached to something very specific, a term on a very particular continuum (as military briefers like to say) that starts on the left as peacetime (what is sometimes labeled "steady state" on briefing slides, or "temporary circumstances," since technically there is no peacetime anymore) and then moves toward a middle ground of "crisis" and then over to "emergency" conditions three-quarters down the line before becoming "extraordinary" as it scrapes the right edge.[3] Variations found in new homeland security documents and congressional testimony included "rare circumstances," "extreme circumstances," and "gravest possibilities."

Curious, I followed up with a multitude of sources, many high-ranking and some even in positions where they would *have* to know, but got only a lot of vague dead ends. A few dropped hints, others communicated with me in the cautionary and disapproving way I had grown used to when reporting on the secret world, or began to speak in tongues in such a way that placed more dark alleyways on the same grid. Several insider friends, some of whom I had been familiar with for over thirty years, said frankly that they didn't know anything. It was a maddeningly thorny cul-de-sac.

I might have given up on my quest to understand martial law

and the realm of the extraordinary except for one thing: I was also hearing a biased supposition from so many—including many on the inside—that anything as diabolical as plans for martial law and "all that stuff" surely was the creation of the Bush administration and its engagement with the "dark side."[4] Now, that I knew wasn't true: continuity and preparations for the possibility of martial law weren't new and weren't an invention of 9/11. The Reagan team had dusted off Eisenhower programs, renovating and testing plans and procedures as part of their strategy to fight and survive a protracted nuclear war. During the Clinton years, terrorism and weapons of mass destruction and even a society-ending Y2K scare became the new justifications for another flurry of codification. And those convinced that this mentality was peculiar to the Bush administration would have been flummoxed had they realized that Obama and company worked not, as promised, to change course but merely to make the extraordinary perhaps more palatable and friendly for consumption by a nation of *hopers.*

Nevertheless, many intelligent people continued to believe that the dastardly plans for a military takeover were perpetrated solely by Bush and Cheney schemers, or the neocons, or the unbridled work of some evil cabal within the FBI, the CIA, the NSA, or some other three-letter agency. Surely the conspirators were the military-industrial complex—what we now called merely "contractors"—and the corporate greedy; or mysterious men with secret powers and multifarious motives working in the shadows à la *The X-Files.* Given the Obama campaign's refutation of the "Cheney way," any documentary traces of martial law and the "extraordinary" were widely seen, and presented as, the detritus of the previous administration or, more sinister, evidence of a secret government beyond Obama's reach.[5]

Then it dawned on me that my search for proof of some cabal

administering decades-old contingency plans was too narrow. The term "martial law" is alarming and alluring as an ominous story line, but the truth seemed to be that there was some "state of" that we were already "under" that wasn't quite that, and even more, was intentionally and subtly constructed to avoid either direct military rule or the necessary societal recognition and acceptance that constitute the law.

Martial law might someday be implemented, I surmised, but even if what Tommy Franks indelicately referred to did transpire, what would be implemented would surely be far less Hollywood in its drama or even less consequential in a civics sense than whatever unimaginable event would have had to unfold to necessitate it. And martial law as an ultimate and unfortunate possibility really requires no secret preparations. Civil laws, even unclassified military regulations, could carefully define what might trigger its imposition and what would terminate it and set the conditions for a return to normalcy. Surely if Washington can be attacked, the expectation of the citizenry must be that the government prepares? And though there is a hallowed tradition that dictates the separation of a federal standing military from American civil life, who among us is hurt—even aggrieved—if the most respected institution in American society steps forward or takes the handoff in a national moment of need?

If I couldn't answer these questions, any inquiry into the underground and martial law was just pandering to the paranoid or the headline-hungry.

There were other questions, too. If some unlegislated program persists for over sixty years, even if it is under secret rules, haven't Congress and the people *in absentia* made it common law? We live with our nation at war but there is no draft, no wartime rationing, no overt or obvious curtailment of our freedoms; beyond the dollar-

and-cents reality that a good chunk of one's federal income tax payments help fund the troops, people can choose to stay completely uninvolved. In exchange, we go about our lives, giving those who do the fighting license to care for the eventualities. And therein lies the issue: license to what? There are those who are charged with protecting the country from nuclear attack, from a terrorist strike with a weapon of mass destruction, charged with maintaining continuity of government and dealing with national calamity. They are responsible for maintaining the last line of defense. Yet what if a terrorist managed to explode a nuclear weapon, or spread a society-killing virus? What *would* happen? How do we create internal security when we also have immutable freedoms of religion and assembly and speech that are supposed to prevent the government from overtly probing who is a trusted American and who is not? How can there be effective oversight and even journalistic relevance when we are told that the cost of transparency for our society might be greater vulnerability, thus ultimately undermining the very transparency that makes us uniquely American? How can we maintain the distinction between what is military and what is civilian—possibly the most important task of all, since the scourge of terrorism gleefully ignores that very distinction? Indeed, how can we maintain the distinction between who is a combatant and who is not when *everyone* is needed, whether in uniform or not, to be part of the forces of vigilance and order? (Meaning that whoever chooses *not* to be involved in the security of the homeland is also potentially suspect—including those who might dare to criticize the military and intelligence communities.) How do we have a civil society when the presumption is that the order and hierarchies associated with the military are needed for our very survival? And how do we adhere to the Constitution's crucial distinctions between federal and local rights and powers—particularly police power—in an age when purported threats are considered all-encompassing?

When I took all of these questions into account, I realized that thinking strictly of some imposition of booted martial law had made me oblivious to the fact that such an appropriation had already occurred—not martial law, but martial *life*. We live in such a state characterized by an underlying ambiguity regarding what is military and what is civilian, what is federal and what is local, what is external and what is internal security, what is public and what is private, what is war and what is peace. It did not come into being with 9/11 or the Clinton-era war against al Qaeda or even the second Cold War under Reagan. Instead of being tied to a single incident, martial life is more the product of political accretion than diabolical edict—something akin to too many greenhouse gases in the atmosphere, too many hormones or chemicals in the food, national obesity. It is not written down somewhere as a specific plot, a step-by-step guide to deposition and seizure; and it is not the intentional product of the accumulated consent of the governed. Even among experts, it is not generally seen or acknowledged. On some level, it is the product of ignorance—and manufactured complexity.

When we think of a coup, the image that comes to mind is a general standing behind a podium, his country's flag as backdrop, explaining that for the sake of the nation the military has been forced to step in, that *as soon as law and order have been restored*… This is the nightmare but also a figment of the imagination for America; it would and could never work and would never happen. The government—and here I mean the executive branch of the federal government—can't overtly sweep aside the Constitution, and those responsible know it. But an unelected elite that cares for secret law, what I refer to as the executive agents, instead administers a dual system, one that they think is fully justified to deal with extreme contingencies. Their system is designed to comport with the requirement that the XYZ and exceptions to the Constitution not interfere with the ABCs of American law. Yet over the years, the XYZ has changed how we live day-to-day, the ABCs.

Only rarely does America get to meet its executive agents. Powerful deputies like Oliver North and John Poindexter have publicly emerged in scandal and others like Robert Gates or Colin Powell have risen through the ranks to serve in executive agent positions before becoming the principals themselves. Most are wholly invisible civil servants and retired military and intelligence officers, men and women who toil away for years out of the spotlight.

Today and any day, all across the government, these executive agents—one step down, one step away—hold the innocuous titles of counsel, special assistant, principal deputy, assistant administrator, executive secretary, secretarial officer; and they are just one door behind the front office, their power established by direct access—*I work for the secretary, I work for the president*—and confirmed by being read into the special-access programs, by membership in certain committees, by inclusion on certain lists, all with the mightiest of speed dials.

The presence of such men (and they are almost always men) is noted from time to time, sometimes with a raised eyebrow, even a shiver. To mollify a cantankerous and suspicious citizenry, the government goes on a binge of reassurances: privacy and civil liberties offices constellate officialdom, presidential decrees and directives enforce this or that right of the people, promote transparency and all the other do-goods of government. Enhanced training of police and security monitors and record keepers is undertaken to teach the legions and their auxiliaries not to profile, not to pay attention to political views, race, ethnicity, or religion when considering dangers. The intelligence community promises it is not spying on innocent Americans. The FBI pledges that it does not act without reasonable suspicion and a legal predicate. The military goes out of its way to reassure that it operates *always* in subordination to civilian authority, that it has no real interest in being in charge.

And here's the thing: I believe them.

The vast majority in government have the best of intentions and perfectly follow all of the ABCs of American law and life. Yet they are not part of the Program. The Program is the overseer of this world between the lines, an entity and group, but neither conspiracy nor secret puppet master. To conceive of what the Program is, think Wall Street. It is a place, but it is also allusively the entirety of interests. It is made up of the equivalent of banks and financial institutions—departments and agencies of government—but it is not ruled by one man or even one committee, yet it acts in unison and with united purpose according to written and unwritten rules. That is the Program.

The Program oversees the chronic state of preparation for the national XYZ, a safeguard and mirrored system where command is not held by an elected official, nor a general, nor a public figure of the president's Cabinet, but instead a now-permanent and between-the-lines governing continuum—that is, above and beyond the elected. There are actual secret plans, and there are men and women charged with the task of carrying them out, a uniquely American Coup, carefully constructed to avoid the stain of military rule.

This is a regime change justified—as undemocratic regime changes usually are—on the basis of national security and necessity, and those in favor of it make sense if you put aside the fundamental basis of American freedom. For example, on some level national and standardized responses and communications protocols during conditions of emergency and survival are the most practical and neutral of measures: it would be pretty ridiculous if an out-of-town firefighting crew arrived to save your house only to find that the hydrant didn't fit their size hose. But "local" is also not just some cookie-cutter term vacated by national homogenization. "Local" is first and foremost the very project of federalism. The term "martial law" has such an ominous ring to it precisely because this is *America*, a country founded upon notions of civil government, of civil liberties and individual rights. So then "martial life" also has to comply with the American design and Constitution, guaranteeing all of those rights.

There is no American image more powerful than the constitutional defender, whether suspendered and stentorian with well-thumbed little book in hand, or bandana-and-camouflage-clad with gun rack and DON'T TREAD ON ME bumper sticker. There is also likely no greater political expletive in America than "unconstitutional." Every president, every Cabinet and sub-Cabinet member, every member of Congress, every judge, every state official, every officer of the law, every sheriff, every commissioned and noncommissioned officer of the United States of America swears allegiance to the Constitution: to preserve, defend, and uphold it. And though amended a number of times and itself a living document, the Constitution embodies an undeniable set of ideals, with literal (if not sometimes outmoded and conflicting) rules cherished for their ability to protect immutable rights and constrain government power.

While the government swears and pursues constitutional adherence, the Program and its executive agents care for *the nation*. After five decades and many trials, the Program is steeped in lessons learned, the most essential of which is the peculiar paradox of its own existence and survival: the nation will survive, constitutional government will persist, *no matter what*, even if that means that an unconstitutional, extralegal system must be kept apart, and often hidden, from the nation's lawmakers and the people, a system that itself alters the very laws of the nation. The Program can't be allowed to alarm or activate a freedom- and Constitution-loving citizenry by openly taking away rights or codifying something as nightmarish as martial law, yet it needs at the same time to shepherd the very citizenry it protects into a state of voluntary thralldom and permanent duty so that the citizenry will accept living in more pleasing equivalents.

It is for now an exaggeration to say that we have destroyed the country in order to save it, and it is way too simplistic to merely argue that if we spent less—or more—that security would be within reach and the executive agents would be out of a job. Similarly, the issue is not simply the enemy or the nature of warfare; the state of martial life is in some ways postenemy and postwar, requiring neither for its sustainment; the blurring of borders, the loss of true distinctions between military and civilian, define a very tangible state of being that, because it is based on uninterrupted fear, is uninterrupted regardless of actual threat.

The very real predicament—and the danger—of a nation permanently at war is not just that there is no room for anything else, that there is nothing else of priority, but also that a nation constantly at war is just that, one perpetually awaiting and thus preparing for the next battle.

Perhaps the only bright spot is that the obsession with and need for continuity make the executive agents fearful citizens as well, and though they are searching always for a promising and functional model, they are also uneasy with the unchanging state of being and the constancy of war. It is that personal and family vulnerability that is the key to change: if all of society is vulnerable, if America is an undifferentiated battlefield, if there is no safety even for their own, given all of their efforts, perhaps a different paradigm of safety will emerge. If we can rebalance military and civilian with a new distinction between the two, then we can also start to make a stab at weakening terrorism while strengthening the nation.

This book is the story of how we arrived at this moment, and of the system that maintains this dangerous status quo. It focuses on several events in recent years that have acted as X-rays, revealing the internal organs hidden by the corpulent flesh of federal bureaucracy and pronouncement. That hidden system is populated by many good people who care deeply about America, but in the course of their work they have changed what that "America" actually means. In the end, theirs is not the America spelled out by the Constitution. Their America is not rooted in the fundamentals of democracy and freedom. And while their America may protect its infrastructure and workings, the disregard for the lives and aspirations of the people contributes to the corrosion of its soul.

CHAPTER ONE

Between the Lines

The powers not delegated to the United States by the Constitution, nor prohibited by it to the States, are reserved to the States respectively, or to the people.
TENTH AMENDMENT TO THE CONSTITUTION

T he sealed outer envelope identifies the sender: the Executive Office of the President. The name of the addressee—a Cabinet officer, an agency head, or one of their deputies—along with a unique number in the top right-hand corner, augmented by an unclassified short title of the contents, is on the bottom right. A second opaque envelope inside has a prominent security classification stamped on top and bottom, front and back, and the notation: "TO BE OPENED BY THE _____ [designated official]." Inside the double-sealed wrapping is a government Standard Form (SF) cover sheet: SF 706 for Top Secret and SF 712 for Sensitive Compartmented Information, clipped to the enclosures. If the contents are associated with an even more secret Special Access Program, or SAP, as it's called in the supersecret world, a specially colored and printed card stock is used.

Scores of such envelopes are scattered throughout the federal government, from the Pentagon to the Environmental Protection Agency, locked away in briefcases, in personal safes and office vaults, with duplicates located in bunkers and emergency relocation sites. The master index is cataloged at the office of the White House Counsel and at its subordinate Program Coordination Division.[1] Every first Monday of the month, the sets of envelopes are inspected and inventoried. Once a year, the entire contents are reviewed and authenticated, any new, expired, or modified ones replaced.

The most sensitive correspondence is made up of one-of-a-kind letters written to the vice president, Cabinet members, agency heads, and even some private citizens—"Emergency Designees"—each document (affixed with the president's signature and seal) expressing the president's wishes and assigning the bearer some specific delegation of responsibility under circumstances of national calamity.

A level down on the hierarchy, the remaining envelopes contain Presidential Emergency Action Documents (or PEADs), similar yet more broadly written delegations and orders to government agencies and military commands. They include standby legal authorities and not-yet-issued executive orders prewritten to guide the nation during an emergency.[2] One step below the PEADs in sensitivity are emergency action packages (EAPs), and one step below the EAPs are major emergency actions (MEAs)—both commonly called "emergency actions"—each in turn subject to wider and wider circulation but still as tightly controlled.[3] All of these, too, are collected and processed at the Program Coordination Division. Regardless of acronym, none of these instructions are meant for either public consumption or legislative affirmation and codification.

They do, however, presumably have the public in mind: what is formally known as "emergency action" was first introduced during the Truman administration in 1952,[4] but what is the antecedent of today's Program was really created by President Eisenhower, the first president to grapple with the real possibility of rapid global annihilation. The Program was never one place or one person, one administration or one party, or one side of the political spectrum.

If, it was posited, Washington were wiped out in a Soviet nuclear attack, with presumably the federal government gone as well, implementation of the Program would be essential if the United States was to survive. In fact, the Soviet Union might forgo a first strike in the first place if it couldn't guarantee itself a crippling blow on America. At least that was the Cold War theory. The scores of secret presidential instructions were a start in preassigning the responsibility for decision-making, mobilization, and constitutional governance. But there was no way then, and even less way today, that letters from the Oval Office could cover all contingencies and complexities.

Preventing a Soviet strike was predicated on the fact that even if Washington lay in ruins, administration would continue—if not "the Administration." Regardless of who is president or the political status of the nation, regardless of ongoing visible or invisible wars, regardless of the likelihood of attack, the Program would endure, a living organism of documents and envelopes continually being drafted, reviewed, redrafted, approved, signed, and distributed, a hush-hush back-and-forth played out by a select class of national security professionals—executive branch elites, some known officially, others unofficially, as "executive agents"—a system of governance that exists to preserve constitutional government while at the same time existing between the lines of the Constitution.

From Eisenhower to George H. W. Bush, the Cold War meant massive amounts of resources devoted to civil defense. In practice, this entailed not just military buildup but the development of a class of government experts outside public institutions and beyond constitutional rules. The fact that these men were unelected was seen by many of them as a plus: they were above the political fray, rationalists in an age of equilibriums and zero sums. And because the arrow of history meant ever-increasing complexity, their expertise made them ever more essential. Surely America would want its most experienced, most prepared, most practiced citizens at the controls come disaster.

Providing for the common defense is so basic a government obligation that the framers explicitly said so in the Preamble to the Constitution.[5] When George Washington became the first president in 1789, "common defense" meant defending against Native Americans or foreign invasion. Military forces—and this included various state militias—were raised to defend the country against England, France, and Spain, the latter two holding claim to huge tracts of what is today the United States. When the threat of an external enemy disappeared, "common defense" became "national defense," a term that persisted until 1945, when Congress decided that the word "security" connoted an activity more expansive than just military affairs.[6]

And it did. The National Security Act was passed just two years later, creating the underpinning of today's federal organization. There were already a multitude of nonmilitary agencies—the FBI, the Coast Guard, the Secret Service, the Central Intelligence Group (predecessor of the independent CIA), and the Atomic Energy Commission—with a hand in the constitutionally invisible. The new legislation expanded the cloak; lines like "such other functions and duties as assigned" in the National Security Act of 1947 would be used to codify CIA covert action without ever mentioning a mission, yet while academic and policy volumes galore explored the nuclear chokehold and covert operations abroad, the implications for domestic action and the domestic exceptions were hardly even noticed.

As "common defense" and even "national defense" as terms

disappeared, "civil defense" lingered on.[7] Ironically, the first government office created, even before Pearl Harbor, was called the Office of Civilian Defense, but that soon changed. In the words of one official history, from the very beginning three sets of enduring conflicts colored the discussion: the place of civil defense in the national security; the division of responsibility (and the relationship) between the federal government and state and local governments; and the question of extraordinary powers.[8] Truman's National Security Resources Board initially asserted that state and local governments would become the "field army" of civil defense,[9] but the states balked and big-city mayors decried the absurdity of mass evacuation.[10] Subsequently, a Forty Years' War began over the value and loci of civil defense in the nuclear age. Schemes of fallout shelters and mass evacuation and "highways for the national defense" barely survived spates of disgust at the national icon of government absurdity. In the twenty-five years between passage of the 1950 Civil Defense Act and the end of the messiness of Vietnam, "little firm agreement on, or widespread understanding of, the most appropriate ways to organize either the functions of planning and preparation or the emergency operations that would be required in the event of an attack" was concluded.[11]

Civil defense as a concept, then, has muddied the waters from the beginning of the modern era because "civil defense" has always been meant to boost public morale and mobilization, in the process mixing what is practical and mystical, what is military and what is civilian, a fuzziness accentuated in the heightened mania of the post-9/11 world.

The declaration of martial law in New Orleans probably helped to save the United States of America.

Not in 2005 during Hurricane Katrina, but in 1815, when Louisiana, barely three years young as the eighteenth state of the

Union, became the final battlefield in the War of 1812. Superior British forces who were emboldened after repeatedly triumphing against militia and federal troops alike, after successfully attacking the nation's capital and torching the Capitol and the White House, and now reinforced by battle-hardened men with the end of the Napoleonic war, were headed for New Orleans. Believing that the odd mixture of whites, Creoles, and free blacks in New Orleans would prefer independence or even a return to colonial rule to staying part of the United States, the British plan was to move up the Mississippi River from the Gulf of Mexico, severing the north-south supply route and separating the west.

General Andrew Jackson—Old Hickory—arrived on December 2, 1814, to command the city's defenses. When the Louisiana legislature hesitated to suspend the writ of *habeas corpus* (the legal right to be brought before a judge after arrest),[12] and fearing that they might capitulate to the British, Jackson proclaimed "strict martial law," placing all policing and civil matters under his authority. Jackson forbade the legislature to convene and ordered the governor of Louisiana to take field command of the militia in federal service. Everyone entering the city had to check in with Jackson's adjutant general, and no one was allowed to depart without his or his staff's approval. No vessels were permitted to leave the surrounding waters without approval. Streetlamps were to be extinguished at 9 p.m., and a strict curfew was imposed.[13]

Jackson cobbled under his command the most unlikely collection: US Marines, two regiments of federal infantry, navy vessels and gunboats; Louisiana, Kentucky, Mississippi, and Tennessee militia; New Orleans riflemen and volunteers; French exiles from Napoleon's army; "free men of color" from Santo Domingo and Haiti; a company of Choctaw Indians; even pirates from Jean Lafitte's Baratarians, until then enemies of the United States but now partners in its defense. Under martial law, every able-bodied man except British subjects was called to do his duty; even the old and infirm were formed into reserve units or compelled to join the police force. Some out-of-state volunteers arrived without arms or uniforms; under martial law Jackson directed the mayor to have houses searched for arms, taxing the population to buy woolens to clothe the newcomers.

In fierce fighting from December 24 through January 8, thousands on both sides were killed and wounded. Peace between the two nations was actually negotiated in Belgium in the middle of the battle,[14] but official word did not reach Jackson and he kept the militia and the city of New Orleans under martial law until March 12, 1815.[15] The war now over, Louisiana state legislator Louis Louaillier questioned the continuation of martial law. Jackson would hear none of it, still wary of a British return and not completely trusting the loyalty of the local Creole population. He ordered "French subjects" to leave New Orleans. Louaillier fired back in a newspaper article: "It is high time that…the citizens of the state should return to the full enjoyment of their rights…we are indebted to Gen. Jackson for the preservation of our city and the defeat of the British, we do not feel much inclined…to sacrifice any of our privileges.…"

Jackson ordered Louaillier arrested on charges of inciting mutiny and disaffection in the army. A federal judge ordered him released, but the general refused. Louaillier's lawyer obtained a writ of *habeas corpus*, and a US District Court judge hearing the case ruled that martial law was no longer authorized. Jackson responded by having the judge arrested and jailed for his alleged complicity in aiding and abetting mutiny. Louaillier was later acquitted, the final taste of martial law coming when the court ordered Jackson to pay a $1,000 fine for contempt. Once revered, Old Hickory was now in such poor repute that the Louisiana legislature's resolution thanking the troops for their defense of New Orleans did not even mention the commanding general.[16]

One hundred and twenty-six years later, martial law looked much the same. On December 7, 1941, after the Japanese attack on Pearl Harbor, Hawaii's territorial governor, Joseph B. Poindexter, declared martial law on the islands and suspended the writ of *habeas corpus*. Under Poindexter's order, approved by President Roosevelt five days later,[17] military courts were given the power to decide cases without following the rules of evidence or sentencing laws in determining penalties. Walter C. Short, commanding general of the territorial command, issued a proclamation announcing that he was assuming the position of military governor of all of Hawaii. Around the territory's main islands, army troops took up positions, airports were occupied by the military, beaches were covered with obstacles, blackouts and curfews were extended; there was even censorship of news and mail. All courts were closed, and military personnel were authorized to arrest, try, and convict civilians in all matters of what was formerly civil law. And of course Japanese-owned businesses and publications were shut down completely; residents considered dangerous or suspicious were detained; citizens of Japanese descent were required to register. (Only the presence of over 100,000 Japanese-Americans in the Hawaiian territory stood in the way of a plan to expel them all.) The period of martial law that the governor assured everyone would only last a short time continued until October 24, 1944—three years—and Hawaii was designated a military area with limited civil law until July 11, 1945.[18]

As in New Orleans in 1815, though, the judiciary was quick to question the extent and duration of martial law and particularly the application of military courts to civilians. In the case of Lloyd Duncan, a civilian shipfitter charged and sentenced for assaulting two military guards at the Pearl Harbor naval shipyard, the

United States Supreme Court later heard his challenge under *habeas corpus.* The court held that extension of martial law so long after the threat of invasion ceased was intrinsically illegal; indeed, Chief Justice Harlan F. Stone stated in a concurring opinion that if the bars and restaurants could reopen within two months after the attack on Pearl Harbor, it was hard to see why the courts could not also reopen.[19]

Martial law was declared again in New Orleans during Hurricane Katrina. Mayor C. Ray Nagin signed an executive order officially giving the city government the authority to commandeer or use any private property; to direct and compel evacuation; to suspend or limit the sale of alcoholic beverages, firearms, explosives, and combustibles. "It…empowered us to take all necessary steps to ensure that no looting or arson occurred and it gave me the power to suspend any ordinance that was in effect," Nagin later wrote, giving power as well "to the police chief to take command and control of all law enforcement and military officers in the city."[20]

Of course it did nothing of the sort. The mayor of New Orleans didn't have the authority to command any military officer — National Guard or federal — and no mayor can lawfully order martial law in America. Soon enough, however, the news media reported that "martial law" had indeed been declared,[21] a tidbit picked up by watch officers at the befuddled Homeland Security Operations Center in northern Virginia, who rushed to inform the White House Situation Room. Two hours later, the watch officers came back with their tails between their legs.[22] A law enforcement emergency had been declared, not martial law. The mayor could order closings, set curfews, and suspend liquor sales, but civil law persisted.

Then White House press spokesman Scott McClellan further confused matters, telling reporters that "at least in parts of Mississippi and Louisiana, there has been [sic] declarations of martial law in certain areas."[23] That evening, Louisiana governor Kathleen Blanco stoked the fires even more, announcing the arrival of 300 soldiers from the Arkansas National Guard. The troops, she said, were "fresh back from Iraq, well trained, experienced, battle-tested, and under my orders to restore order in the streets. They have M-16s and they are locked and loaded. These troops know how to shoot and kill and they are more than willing to do so if necessary and I expect they will."[24]

"Do we need to impose martial law?" President Bush asked the active-duty Katrina Joint Task Force commander, Lieutenant General Russel Honoré, in a morning videoteleconference after Blanco's locked-and-loaded remark during what seemed like the worst of Hurricane Katrina. "No, sir," Honoré replied. "We can handle the situation as we have it."[25]

Nevertheless, martial law continued to be bandied about as either fact or the next step along a continuum of federal action. Speaking to reporters at the Pentagon on September 3, Lieutenant General H. Steven Blum, head of the National Guard Bureau,[26] tried to clarify matters: "Martial law has not been declared anywhere in the United States of America. That keeps continually being erroneously reported," he said. "An emergency condition exists in parts of the states and there are curfews that are being enforced by the existing civilian law enforcement agencies."[27]

Compared with FEMA's dismal performance—and that of so many other civil agencies—the military looked mighty organized and decisive. Yet the universal assumption of a need for greater military command or a federal takeover was contrary to what every military commander who was on the ground—National Guard and active-duty—believed. Honoré later told congressional investigators he didn't need any more authority.[28] In fact, Honoré thought a large-scale federal military deployment would only complicate an already complicated logistics puzzle, just in receiving, housing, and sustaining the incoming soldiers, given the particular geography of New Orleans. General Bennie Landreneau, head of the Louisiana National Guard, said at the same congressional hearing that "there were over 8,500 National Guardsmen on the ground performing operations....Changing this process would have only stalled current operations...and not have provided any additional boots on the ground."[29] Blum later admitted that he didn't think that what some in the Bush administration were pushing was a necessity "at that time."[30]

Speaking at the Department of Energy a month later, President Bush promoted the idea of the military playing a primary role in responding to future disasters:

> I...want [Congress] to think about a circumstance that requires a lot of planning and a lot of assets immediately on the scene in order to stabilize. And so what I was speculating about was a scenario which would require federal assets to stabilize the situation, primarily DOD assets...and then hand back over to Department of Homeland Security, for example. And I think it's very important for us as we look at the lessons of Katrina to think about other scenarios that might require a well-planned significant federal response right off the bat to provide stability.[31]

A week later, Bush was asked at a White House press conference whether there was anything that he "personally, could have done, or would have done differently...?" "Well," he answered, "one area where I hope the country takes a look at is the responsibility between federal, state, and local government when it comes to catastrophic events, highly catastrophic events.... [Is] there a need to move federal assets more quickly, in spite of laws on the books that may discourage that."[32]

Scott McClellan added that Bush felt "we need to establish some sort of a trigger that would automatically say the federal government, and specifically, the military, is the one that will be in charge of stabilizing the situation."[33] Homeland security advisor Frances Townsend, appointed to lead the Bush administration's internal examination of Katrina, agreed, saying she was considering whether there was "a narrow band of cases" in which the president should seize control.[34] NORTHCOM commander Admiral Timothy Keating followed, recommending that the Defense Department be given "complete control" for response to disasters like Katrina: "We have to think the unthinkable may be possible, even probable."[35]

The odd thing about the calls for automatic triggers was that the unthinkable was hardly invented with Katrina, and the Bush administration already had revised its own policies with an eye toward doing everything possible to keep the federal military out of catastrophic response. The National Response Plan, a draft of which had been kicking around the bureaucracy since 2003, was signed by the president eight months before Katrina. The Plan contained a Catastrophic Incident Annex, and *it* contained a separate and more sensitive Catastrophic Incident Supplement laying out exactly what needed to be done without the Defense Department.[36] According to the Plan, a catastrophic incident was

> any natural or manmade incident, including terrorism, that results in extraordinary levels of mass casualties, damage, or disruption severely affecting the population, infrastructure, environment, economy, national morale, and/or government functions. A catastrophic event could result in sustained national impacts over a prolonged period of time; almost immediately exceeds resources normally available to State, local, tribal, and private-sector authorities in the impacted area; and significantly interrupts governmental

operations and emergency services to such an extent that national security could be threatened. All catastrophic events are Incidents of National Significance.[37]

The supplement, stamped "For Official Use Only," posited "tens of thousands of casualties (dead, dying, and injured)" necessitating support from outside, certainly not on the scale of Katrina.[38]

All combined, including annexes and supplements, it was a dense 692 pages of what civil government should do. Apologists for FEMA and the Department of Homeland Security argued that if everyone had just followed the Plan, the civil response to Katrina would have been fine. And, indeed, everyone should have been familiar with it and followed it: every agency and state had redlined and commented on multiple drafts; hundreds of briefings had been held with federal, state, and local authorities; pages were practically laminated so that they didn't get soggy in the rain. Yet here was revealed the universal variant that no plan survives first contact with the enemy: even as President Bush designated Louisiana a "major disaster" on August 27 and then upgraded that designation to a federal emergency on August 29,[39] Secretary of Homeland Security Michael Chertoff, a lawyer and the Cabinet member responsible for the National Response Plan, didn't know what to do. Two days later, criticism mounting, Chertoff declared Katrina an "incident of national significance," a label that Congress, the White House, and even his own inspector general later declared redundant and legally incorrect.[40] And though Katrina met the criteria to be a "catastrophic incident" under the Plan, Chertoff never made that designation.[41] Chertoff also made the mistake of appointing FEMA head Michael Brown the principal federal official, not realizing until weeks later that the law—not just some federal *plan*—required designation of a federal coordinating officer to authorize the expenditure of federal funds.[42]

A DHS-run Joint Field Office, the federal hub and integrator of "whole of government" also called for in the Plan, wasn't activated until two weeks after the storm.[43] The House committee investigating Katrina later said it found the Plan an "alphabet soup" of indecipherable elements.[44] Homeland Security's inspector general concluded that the Plan "fell far short of the seamless, coordinated effort that had been envisioned."[45] Even the White House report on the response to Katrina suggested that the National Response Plan should be revised, though the initial intent was to create conditions in which the military—or at least the federal government—would automatically take the lead in future catastrophes and supplant state and local authority.[46]

If only a catastrophic incident had been declared[47]—that claim became the new argument: if only the Plan were better and clearer and everyone followed and trained for it—all clearly doable—then, then…There was really only one piece of unfinished business: the archaic laws like *Posse Comitatus* and the Insurrection Act that stood in the way of the holy grail of true unity of effort, laws that supposedly impeded a rapid and effective response on the part of the federal government, and specifically the federal military during Katrina.

The aftermath of Hurricane Katrina is far from the only instance of official confusion regarding martial law. Official army history says that martial law has only ever been declared once in the United States,[48] a puzzling claim given that the army's own 2010 *Field Manual*[49] says martial law has existed four times. And even this enumeration is in error: martial law was also declared on parts of the West Coast in 1942 after the Japanese attack; and there are other cases where governors have lawfully declared a state of martial law: during labor strikes in the 1800s and early 1900s; in San Francisco after the 1906 earthquake; in 1933 after the North

Dakota capitol was burned down by protestors; and in Phenix City, Alabama, in 1954 after the murder of a reform-minded candidate for state attorney general.[50]

And it's not just the military that is confused; the Department of Justice in a 2003 briefing says that there have been two cases of martial law being "imposed on U.S. territory."[51] On US territory, *not* on US territory, during wartime, or in limited and temporary instances, declared by the federal government or declared by a governor? There seems to be no rhyme or reason why some instances are included and others are not.[52]

Perhaps one reason that historians and writers can't agree on a specific number of martial law cases is that there is no constitutional definition. There is no direct reference to martial law in *the book*, and though the Supreme Court has interpreted Article I, Section 8, Clause 15 — Congress has the power "[t]o provide for calling forth the Militia to execute the Laws of the Union, suppress insurrections and repel Invasions" — and Article II, Section 2, Clause 1 — "[t]he President shall be Commander in Chief of the Army and Navy of the United States, and of the Militia of the several States, when called into the actual Service of the United States" — to allow for a declaration, and though the courts have generally accepted the premise of martial law, every presidential declaration that has ever been made has been controversial, questioned, or legally challenged.[53] Even in July 1861, when Congress ratified some of the martial law provisions declared by President Abraham Lincoln at the beginning of the Civil War, the suspension of the writ of *habeas corpus* was disputed. The Supreme Court ruled that only Congress had that power, and though it approved Lincoln's suspension of the writ in 1863, even then, Union forces were authorized to arrest and detain Confederate soldiers and sympathizers, but only until they could be tried by a court of law.[54]

After 9/11, the army attempted to define the parameters of martial law in the Code of Federal Regulations (32 CFR §501.4): Title 32—National Defense, Chapter V—Department of the Army, Subchapter A—Aid of Civil Authorities and Public Relations, Part 501—Employment of Troops in Aid of Civil Authorities, Sec. 4—Martial Law, and it is worth quoting in full:

It is unlikely that situations requiring the commitment of Federal Armed Forces will necessitate the declaration of martial law. When Federal Armed Forces are committed in the event of civil disturbances, their proper role is to support, not supplant, civil authority. Martial law depends for its justification upon public necessity. Necessity gives rise to its creation; necessity justifies its exercise; and necessity limits its duration. The extent of the military force used and the actual measures taken, consequently, will depend upon the actual threat to order and public safety which exists at the time. In most instances the decision to impose martial law is made by the President, who normally announces his decision by a proclamation, which usually contains his instructions concerning its exercise and any limitations thereon. However, the decision to impose martial law may be made by the local commander on the spot, if the circumstances demand immediate action, and time and available communications facilities do not permit obtaining prior approval from higher authority (Sec. 501.2). Whether or not a proclamation exists, it is incumbent upon commanders concerned to weigh every proposed action against the threat to public order and safety it is designed to meet, in order that the necessity therefore may be ascertained. When Federal Armed Forces have been committed in an objective area in a martial law situation, the population of the affected area will be informed of the rules of conduct and other restrictive measures the military is authorized to enforce. These will normally be announced by proclamation or order and will be given the widest possible publicity by all available media. Federal Armed Forces ordinarily will exercise police powers previously inoperative in the affected area, restore and maintain order, insure the essential mechanics of distribution, transportation, and communication, and initiate necessary relief measures.[55]

There was nothing particularly new or ominous in this,[56] though one study done for the Defense Department pointed out that the new articulation was "rife with ambiguities about the authority and procedures for and the limits of martial law. There is an inadequate amount of legal guidance regarding invoking martial law in the event of a WMD attack on the United States that results in the disintegration of social and legal structures."[57] What the study didn't say, what the study *couldn't* say, was that such a state of martial law would not be found in, or predicted by, the Code of Federal Regulations.

On one level, then, martial law has simple meaning that in some ways requires no elaboration and no lawyers: it is military rule. As an American phenomenon, it also has unique, specific, and nation-threatening meaning. After a Confederate sympathizer was sentenced to death by a military commission during the Civil War, the Supreme Court ruled, "Martial law ... destroys every guarantee of the Constitution." The court said: "Civil liberty and this kind of martial law cannot endure together; the antagonism is irreconcilable; and, in the conflict, one or the other must perish."[58]

"Martial law" is bandied about so much in the news media, in political rhetoric, and over such a large corner of the Internet that there is a greater impression of substance than really exists. The stark truth is that in the American form of government, "martial law" is an oxymoron; it is as much about what does not exist as what does—as one military officer says, it is the absence of order, courts, and the Constitution that defines the environment of martial law. "If the courts are open then martial law is not appropriate."[59]

While there are hardly any public-domain materials on the subject, little bursts of radiation from the black holes of the Program have given definition to the XYZ conception of martial law and revealed three subtle historical shifts in executive agent thinking on the subject over the years.

During the post-Vietnam period, when "public necessity" connoted some postnuclear catastrophe, necessitating military intervention, martial law lingered as a consequence of nuclear war or foreign attack, civic cheerleading promising that civil authority would be rapidly restored. The 1983 "Basic Planning Directive for Land Defense of the Continental United States and Military Support of Civil Defense" (still only partially declassified a quarter-century later) closely held with the Supreme Court view regarding the declaration of martial law in Hawaii, that is, that the objective "is to create conditions wherein civil government can be rapidly reconstituted." In every case, the formerly classified Joint Chiefs of Staff directive states, "control will be returned to civil authorities upon receipt of notification from a recognized civilian authority, at an authorized level, that civil authorities are prepared to exercise control."[60]

Watergate and the era of congressional assertion that followed created reform and forced the Program further underground. Gerald Ford and Jimmy Carter carried out the largest number of revisions to presidential directives since Eisenhower, carefully rewriting each of the emergency documents, aware of changes in the Cold War (and the country) since Ike's time, and the recent massive unlawfulness on the part of the secret services. The Reagan team came in and rewrote again, fully embracing end-of-the-world possibilities, pumping up Doomsday procedures for the nation to endure, endowing the executive agents with new power.

A second martial law era — a revival when terrorism started to become *the* national security threat — lasted from the mid-1990s until well into the Bush administration. The Clinton administration at first made a tentative stab at some post–Cold War strategy, declaring a "domestic imperative" in its National Security Strategy, announcing that something that had previously only been defined in purely military terms now had to be viewed in the context of the nation's well-being.[61] The Pentagon issued new civil support regulations, formally handing the related mission — "in both peacetime disasters and national security emergencies" — to the National Guard, stressing that any response would have to follow specific requests for assistance from civil authorities. The Pentagon also codified the notion that civil support was always a "secondary priority" to "military operations," pledging that the military would "not perform any function of civil government" unless "absolutely necessary on a temporary basis."[62]

During both administrations, even through 9/11, WMD catastrophes became the almost exclusive domestic focus of any anticipated military intervention. A broader assessment of the need for martial law stayed deep underground, but as executive agents became far more concerned about dealing with terrorists using WMD on American soil, their search for ways around constitutional limits increased. And what characterizes the third era — definitely post-Katrina, but also one where public wariness of post-9/11 life has begun to influence the executive agents — is seeming constitutionality and return to normalcy, that illusion being the very definition of the state of martial life.

*   *   *

Richard Reeves tells the story of John F. Kennedy's introduction to the Program on January 19, 1961, when he met privately with President Eisenhower on the eve of his inauguration:

> Ike talked about being President. He began with the black vinyl satchel, "the Football," which contained nuclear options, commands, and codes, officially called "Presidential Emergency Action Documents." It was carried by military officers who handed it off to each other in eight-hour shifts, like quarterbacks and halfbacks. The President carried a laminated plastic card in his wallet to identify himself to electronic systems and begin choosing among deadly options outlined in the thirty thick loose-leaf pages in the Football....
>
> "Watch this," Eisenhower said, picking up a telephone and ordering: "Opal Drill Three!" They were standing by the French doors behind the President's desk. Three minutes later a Marine helicopter settled on the lawn behind the Oval Office. Kennedy loved it.[63]

When he triggered OPAL, Eisenhower set in motion a series of procedures known as continuity of government—or COG, as it has commonly come to be called. It's an apt acronym: the gears that grind on, no matter what.

Eisenhower is generally credited with being the grandfather of the Program: emergency procedures, continuity, relocation, bunkers, and survival. His approach from the very beginning had the practicality of a military man commanding large pieces on a huge battlefield. There was a plan that followed a strategic thrust—civil defense and even civil government preparations for disaster preparedness, evacuation and sheltering in the rear area—and then there was *the* plan, one built around the assumption that no plan survives the first shot, that all combat takes place on the seam between two map sheets, that on the front lines something different and less manicured would be needed.

Nothing symbolizes the duality that would define America's national security policy more than the series of survival exercises called Operation Alert (thus the nickname OPAL) that the Eisenhower administration instituted between 1954 and 1960. The Federal Civil Defense Agency opened the multiyear OPAL series on June 11, 1954, identifying twenty-seven possible target cities for Soviet atomic attack and enlisting the local governments and population to take cover at the designated hour and minute. The government furiously went through its motions and the media was brought in to report on the results, the number of bombs dropped, the number of cities hit, and the number of casualties.[64]

That's what made the papers. Underground, though, a coterie of select federal officials met for the first time within the rudimentary conditions of a Mount Weather just starting to be hollowed out, and there they sat around, under mock Soviet attack with no information, no policies, no communications, and no feedback. It was the first of hundreds if not thousands of simultaneous and supplemental secret meetings and drills that would develop between the lines over the next six decades, the very first appropriately called Operation Minuteman to coordinate army action if all else failed. A Deputy Assistant Director for Plans and Readiness at the Office of Defense Mobilization, one Innis D. Harris, a retired army colonel and Eisenhower's chief of intelligence for the Office of Military Government, US Zone (Germany), chaired the highest-level Emergency Action Task Force. In a world of nonexistent history, Harris was probably the first executive agent.

On June 15, 1955, more than 200 members of the news media

were invited to the follow-on three-day OPAL II, an even larger-scale nuclear drill. Eisenhower himself evacuated the White House—along with some 10,000 federal government employees instructed to move from their offices to field sites—the president shuttling from bunker to relocation camp, every location given a coded name for reporters to use in their stories: Highpoint, Newpoint, and—no kidding—Lowpoint. Desiring to truly test the system, Eisenhower threw an unscripted wrench into the well-prepared machinery and unexpectedly declared martial law from his Cadillac on the way out of Washington. No one knew what to do next. "The lawyers were running for the books to draft an appropriate proclamation," Innis Harris later recalled.[65]

Then, on September 24, while visiting his in-laws in Denver, Eisenhower had a heart attack. Meeting in his hospital bed with his attorney general, Herbert Brownell, Jr., he asked: "What happens under the Constitution if my illness is prolonged and emergencies arise requiring immediate action?"[66] No one knew the answer—the Constitution was vague on the question; it would take ten years and the assassination of John F. Kennedy before the Twenty-Fifth Amendment was ratified.

In the interim, though, "what happens" also had a direct urgency. Uncertainty as to who was in charge with the possibility of nuclear war hanging overhead made it clear that the Program needed to exist and it needed to do better. Eisenhower directed that emergency orders be prepared that would organize the nation in the case of a nuclear war or other "matters of supreme national importance." Emergency Action Papers were prepared for the Cabinet's review, ratified into Emergency Action Documents and lesser Emergency Preparedness Orders. They covered every conceivable scenario, from creating a national food authority, through detention of security threats and suspicious aliens, to the maintenance of civil "law and order";[67] as one government document says, "the full range of powers" that might be utilized by a president "during an emergency,"[68] including all of the extraordinary powers that might be needed if the best of plans failed.

In 1957, Eisenhower approved Federal Emergency Plan C, dealing with mobilization for general war, the first comprehensive prewar (and peacetime) national domestic defense plan and one that would persist through the Reagan years.[69] Its twin, Federal Emergency Plan D, was issued soon thereafter; it dealt with government actions to be taken in the case of "a crippling nuclear attack on the United States," setting out in hundreds of pages the pursuit of five objectives from the routine to the grandiose: "to ensure the continuity of government and order, to support military operations and military alliances, to ensure survival of the remaining population and recovery of the nation, to ensure the most effective use of resources, and to maintain free-world unity."[70] Annex A of Plan D contained the original twenty-two Presidential Emergency Action Documents, or at least the titles and the classification and distribution of each, some so sensitive that they were shared only among a small circle of high-level officials in the affected departments and agencies and then secreted away under sealed envelope, each PEAD given a specific codename—BANANA, GOLDEN, FINANCIAL, COMEX—that would have to be invoked in order for it to be implemented.[71]

OPAL VII in May 1960 was the last of the Eisenhower series. The smallest unexpected act in the exercise proved that, despite all previous efforts, little had changed in real-world implementation of the most carefully laid plans: Eisenhower decided to convene a no-notice meeting of the National Security Council at the underground command center at Raven Rock on the Pennsylvania border. The Cabinet was called by White House Signals (the predecessor of today's White House Communications Agency) at 7:20 a.m. and told to report to an emergency NSC meeting and that military helicopters would transport them. Secretary of Defense Thomas Gates was so surprised by the call that he couldn't get official transportation from the Pentagon to the site of the helicopter takeoff; without official driver or identification, marines at first wouldn't let him inside the gate at the Anacostia naval base. Secretary of State John Foster Dulles got official transportation, but his car broke down on the way. The chairman of the Joint Chiefs of Staff, General Nathan Twining, was left behind in Washington, while Atomic Energy Commission director John McCone had a conflicting engagement and never showed up.

Somewhat absurdly, OPAL was seen as a resounding success, pointing to what still needed to be done and what could never be achieved. The ABCs were better plans, better communication, new relocation sites, and practice, practice, practice, but just as necessary was a parallel XYZ system of exceptions and extraordinary powers for the inevitable when things didn't work out as planned. Desperate times call for desperate measures—and the room to improvise was seen as crucial. The main elements—preserving continuity of government, preparing for a breakdown in the country internally, thwarting and responding to WMD—identified by the Eisenhower team would be reconfirmed and bolstered through subsequent administrations and major reviews, through wars, assassinations, and assassination attempts, through blackouts and Y2Ks and storms, and, of course, through 9/11.

By the time George W. Bush became president in 2001, almost every trace of the envelopes and the PEADs had disappeared from public view. The Department of Justice inadvertently revealed in its 2001 budget that there were forty-eight existing Presidential Emergency Action Directives, twice as many as in the Eisenhower days;[72] the Department of Commerce let it slip that three PEADs were applicable to its department.[73] A pandemic response plan of the Nuclear Regulatory Commission discussed the need for PEADs to be completed before any crisis because during a calamity, getting the attention of the National Security Council would be most difficult, given demands on its time.[74] A Bush White House staffer later blabbed about her work with PEADs in her online résumé.[75] But that was it.

When President-elect Obama arrived in Washington, the marine helicopters were still at the ready, many of the outlines of COG and the Program little changed from Eisenhower's days. Officials from the Program came—and spoke to the president-elect to brief him on the highly classified rules of what would happen if something catastrophic occurred in the days before the inauguration, when he was still president-elect. Obama was fully "read into" the compartmented measures beyond top secret—measures that as senator he was not cleared to know about—and some that, once he was president, many of his top advisors would not be privy to.

Obama then received *the* briefing, a thorough rundown of US nuclear capabilities and the nuclear war plans and procedures that were meticulously maintained by the Joint Chiefs of Staff and the US Strategic Command in Omaha, as they always had been. As the exclusive authority to order nuclear weapons into battle, the president would take possession of the "gold" card (albeit no longer just a card and not even gold), his one-of-a-kind authenticator that uniquely identifies him as the commander in chief. As president, Obama would never be without his gold card and never be far from his military aide, still carrying the football, now an eight-inch-wide trial bag stuffed with way more than just thirty loose-leaf pages of nuclear options, as well as a host of communications and computing devices befitting our information era.

The night before his 2009 inauguration, Obama and his incoming national security advisor, retired marine corps general

James Jones, sat down with their Bush administration counter-parts to go over the *what-ifs*. Secretary of Defense Robert Gates, whom Obama had decided to retain from the Republican admin-istration, would sit out the inaugural away from Washington, a natural choice as the traditional Cabinet member to absent him-self, given that he was in a very real sense the bridge between two administrations.[76] But "natural" to whom? The constitutional order of succession as of January 2009 was: vice president of the United States, speaker of the House, president *pro tempore* of the Senate, secretary of state, secretary of the treasury, and then sec-retary of defense. This meant that constitutionally, Gates was sixth in line to succeed to the president. In inaugurals before 9/11, some minor secretary was chosen to symbolically represent conti-nuity, but now that the US was at war, Gates's selection meant he—and what he stood for—was effectively number one.

Behind Gates was a man named Louis E. Caldera, a lawyer from New York and an incoming Obama appointee who knew more about COG than anyone else on the new political team. Caldera had served as secretary of the army in the Clinton admin-istration, where he'd been the Pentagon official with direct responsibility for the Program.[77] Technically, Obama had appointed Caldera incoming director of the White House Military Office (WHMO), an obscure agency at the center of the Program but an organization normally headed by some mission-driven cyclone of one-star rank. (Those in the know might well have found it an amusing coincidence that the man in charge of coordinating the procedures to be followed in case of cataclysm had a last name that was also the technical term for the basin left behind by a massive volcanic eruption.)

Obama's retention of Gates and his appointment of such a heavyweight as Caldera to oversee the transition reflected not just caution regarding a specific terrorist threat but also a continuity demanded by a nation at war. Other national security titans also took up positions working for Obama—his White House national security advisor and the director of national intelligence were both initially retired four-stars—continuity slowly and subtly thwarting many of the promised foreign policy and government changes, while completely insulating the Program.

Today some Presidential Emergency Action Documents still bear the same designation they were assigned in the 1950s, and many deal with the most basic (and in some ways, uncontroversial) matters of national calamity and industrial-age mobilization: instituting a draft, cranking up war production, stockpiling commodities and supplies, and rationing foodstuffs. Others are a direct result of that attempt on President Reagan's life, procedures that spell out presidential intent and the rules of temporary and permanent transfer of power as well as specific authorities to grant private individuals access to highly classified government information in an emergency.[78] Some of these directives involve the commandeering of private-sector electrical power and communications, or the quarantining of contaminated areas of the United States. Presidential Emergency Action Document 20, created under Eisenhower and thoroughly revised and signed by President Jimmy Carter on October 13, 1978, for instance, addresses martial law and precisely directs the secretary of defense or his alternates and designated successors—including the military itself if no civilian leadership exists—when and how to take charge and restore and maintain law and order. Another PEAD deals with the institution of full-fledged government censorship of the press and of free speech; a third deals with the detention of certain American citizens considered security threats. A fourth addresses executive powers between a period of constitutional rule and a new democratic election. Nothing is really known about the contents today.

As dangers to America and domestic tranquility have become more widespread, and as a predominantly urban society has become more vulnerable, the Program has gained greater and greater sway in day-to-day America. Threats arise against any place and every place, in shoes and underwear, by nuclear bomb and nasty virus. They are external *and* internal, spreading from the earthly to the cyber, and no amount of intelligence information or physical security or defense spending, law enforcement, or even targeted killing is guaranteed to stop the last determined enemy. That next catastrophe might never occur, but if it comes, if a terrorist nuclear strike or a deadly pandemic or some unimaginable calamity is so off the charts that it shuts down government and even civil society, the executive agents who survive will be ready. And no president during the past several decades has had any real interest in changing this. The Reagan team practically invented counterterrorism and critical infrastructure protection, putting in place programs that wouldn't gain much public exposure (or traction) until after 9/11. Bill Clinton threw himself into the Program, mastering the obscurities of biological weapons and Y2K and the development of the national mission force,[79] overseeing a rewrite of almost all of the basic presidential directives, complete with a political pretension of discovery and originality.

George W. Bush hardly had much time to experience peacetime before 9/11. We think we know what happened *that day*—the communications glitches between the president and the White House, Secretary of Defense Donald Rumsfeld running around outside the Pentagon rather than inside on command at a crucial moment, air defenses that were looking the wrong way, uncontrollable rumors of more attacks—but while numerous books, articles, and films have dissected the gaps in airport security and agency coordination, less understood was how badly the XYZ plan for the *what-if* floundered: communications unavailable or spotty, evacuation random, civil and military command confused. So, in the wake of this disarray, Bush, too, put on his stamp, becoming a punctilious taskmaster of the invisible, focused particularly on maintaining foolproof communications to the president, intent on having the decider see the country through to its very end.

The Obama team valiantly followed; a *summa cum laude* student council fully intent on returning the country to normalcy, smoothing Bush's knife to eliminate any jagged edges. The team's review undertook the largest number of revisions to the Program since the Carter administration, a thorough rechecking of all of the wartime exceptions to affirm legalities, to reform what the incoming team assumed were anomalous years of lawlessness and excess. Yet from even before day one, Obama had no real intention of disrupting the Program, worried about the electoral consequences of appearing critical of the "war on terror," but more important, accepting the Bush practice of appointing a political insider—in Obama's case Caldera—to oversee the XYZs, which had become ever more extensive and independent.

The image of the dark-suited, sunglasses-wearing, wire-hanging-out-of-the-ear government agent has become synonymous with the protective elite—"elite" meaning not only the best of the best, but the influential and privileged. There is some truth to this: few reach the heights of executive agents like Gates and Caldera who have been in and out of national decision-making. Yet the Program is full of such men who are decidedly unfantastic in their bearing and demeanor, whose only weapons are their pens and expertise, their specific rank and power secured in envelopes. They are also a brand of constitutional defender, neither Bible thumpers nor aggressive flag wavers, more actual caretakers who operate in the shadows, keepers of a flame, even if that flame is underground. In secret briefing after secret briefing, they

reinforced to the incoming president in specific detail and via ter-
rifying hypotheticals that the country existed in permanent
extraordinary mode. The Program doesn't govern, nor purport
to interfere in the day-to-day ABCs of the nation. But it possesses
exclusive ownership of the secret survival text, the fundamental
basis for certainty in a world no longer certain.

And the "enemy"? Also everywhere. After 9/11, the Program
retooled not for missiles or bombers but for two almost uncontrollable certainties of our day: the first a massive system breakdown, whether from an act of God or from terrorism; the second
the internal threat of extremism. Nuclear weapons maintained
their preeminent cachet, followed by enemy nations and armies,
but now the extreme—man-made and natural—was assumed
able to wreak comparable havoc.

So who are those extremists? Here it is important to think
well beyond "terrorists," since enveloped in the word are a diverse
bunch of nonconformists who tend to reject the forces of moder-
nity, globalization, and the uniformity of everything. On right
and left, foreign and domestic, they hate McDonald's and mono-
culture, they deny the notion of universal human rights, and they
fear the dominant civilizing vision of a globe destined toward one
standard, one government, one law, one language, and one religion. At least, so says the Program, with no single country, people,
or group fully encompassing this potential enemy.

Terrorism is but part of the story, one facet of this most American of coups, one evidenced not just in Washington-area offices
and secret compounds, but also increasingly on the streets of our
cities and towns. In such cases, conventional narratives speak again
and again to the competency of federal assistance over futile local
efforts. A closer look reveals something much more complex—and
disconcerting—at work.

CHAPTER TWO

High Water or Hell

*The Privilege of the Writ of Habeas Corpus shall not be
suspended, unless when in Cases of Rebellion or Invasion the
public Safety may require it.*
ARTICLE I, SECTION 9 OF THE CONSTITUTION

T he entire unit — 315 strong from the 1st Battalion, 148th
Infantry of the Ohio National Guard — loaded onto
Blackhawk helicopters for the final leg of their mission. Five days
earlier, on August 29, 2005, Katrina had slammed into the Gulf
Coast,[1] wreaking havoc over an area almost as large as Great Brit-
ain, obliterating 300,000 homes, forcing an estimated 1.2 million
people to evacuate and leaving millions more homeless.[2] Eighty
percent of New Orleans, America's thirty-fifth-largest city, was
underwater, and more than 100,000 of its citizens were stranded;
electricity and all forms of communications were gone. The fresh
troops from Ohio didn't quite know what to expect: television was
a horror show and even official reports repeated every imaginable
gumbo of human stink: thousands stuck on roofs, in trees and
attics, starving; rampant looting, riots, massive civil disobedience; arson; random killings, snipers, assassinations, armed gangs
and mobs; drug addicts were going crazy; there were running gun
battles with the police, people were shooting at hospitals and rescue helicopters; and, according to New Orleans mayor Ray Nagin,

the Superdome had become a snake pit of murder, assault, sexual violation, animalistic behavior of the basest sort; Nagin had even heard stories of babies being raped and their throats slit, and that bodies were stacked up everywhere.

Battalion commander Lieutenant Colonel Gordon Ellis, a twenty-five-year army veteran and in civilian life a small-town police chief from near Youngstown, commanded the first boots on the ground from outside Louisiana. His Ohioans were to move to the Superdome to augment and relieve their Louisiana brethren, many of whom had been on the job for six straight days, dealing with the accumulated 15,000 to 30,000 stranded citizens—it didn't seem as if anyone could give a firm figure of how many there were. The situation was critical and hundreds were reported in various states of medical emergency. Under the operational command of the Louisiana Guard,[3] Task Force Buckeye was to restore order, triage those most in need, and get the remainder peaceably onto buses and out of the living hell within the hell.

The men and women of the 148th assembled by flashlight at the blacked-out Belle Chasse naval air station, ten miles from downtown. New Orleans police on the scene feared a full-scale riot; a National Guard soldier had been shot in the leg, a new report said.[4] Ellis stressed in his predawn September 2 run-through with his company commanders that he expected soldiers to be professional and courteous, just as they had been during Kosovo peacekeeping duties less than a year earlier. They weren't there to put the city under siege or make things worse, Ellis said, but they needed to be ready: every soldier was issued body armor and a shotgun and eight rounds of buckshot. Weapons were to be kept on safe and chambers empty with muzzles pointed down. Soldiers were directed to sling their weapons in front and not over their backs, just in case.

As the lead element moved from the landing zone through the

plaza onto the Superdome grounds, the mass of humanity was more disturbing than anything they'd ever encountered: old and young were crowded together in stifling heat; some were standing in their own waste; garbage was strewn knee-high, the temperature hovering at ninety-five degrees, the stench overwhelming. As the troops made their way forward, their boots frequently slipped in human waste, the artificial turf as soggy as a kitchen sponge. The reconnaissance element peered over their respirators at first, fighting the urge to gag, until officers ordered them to remove their masks—they were scaring people.[5]

A foul-smelling, rain-soaked, uninhabitable hellhole, Lieutenant General Russel L. Honoré later called the Superdome. Katrina's island prison was surrounded by temporary retaining fences, movement restricted by guards and floodwaters beyond. Yet despite media reporting and abundant official panic from bottom to top, the place hardly reeked of civil disturbance. For days on end the people there mostly stood quietly behind the flimsy barricades, waiting "with a patience that only the poor knew," Honoré said; a human tragedy both breathtaking and appalling in its enormity.[6] "These were...people who were used to having nothing but patience," says the general. "Their tolerance for these horrible conditions and their calmness while waiting for help were amazing. There was never a harsh word for us, never a sense that we were going to be attacked."[7]

That wasn't how everyone saw it. In fact, back in Washington, another word had been bandied about in discussing the shattered residents of New Orleans. That word was "insurgents."

On Tuesday morning, the day after Katrina made landfall on the Louisiana coastline and three days before the Ohioans arrived, Honoré telephoned his good friend Major General Bennie C. Landreneau, head of the Louisiana National Guard, to tell him that he had been appointed commander of something called Joint Task Force Katrina, a Defense Department command created to oversee the overall rescue effort, and that he would be coming to Louisiana.[8]

"The door swung open and General Russell [sic] Honoré strutted into the building," Ray Nagin recalled. "This tall, brown-skinned, confident man marched in with an imposing presence that said he was all business."[9] Indeed, in a drama begging for a leading man, Honoré became it. The tall and handsome Creole with the clipped mustache, just by coincidence a native of rural Louisiana, spoke plainly, snapped orders, and exuded competence, almost instantly becoming everyone's symbol and honest broker. The general later modestly said he just tried "to present a voice of calm and reason when the politicians could not."[10] Nagin labeled him a "John Wayne kind of dude."[11] The news media gushed and anointed him as *the* man in charge.[12]

Honoré huddled with the mayor and his staff and the men from FEMA, everyone in a near-panic, the blame game howling at full gale force. As commander of the First US Army, one of two remaining continental armies of a once-celebrated era when the entire United States was divided into military regions, Honoré had his headquarters in Atlanta. His territory extended from the Atlantic Ocean to the Mississippi River, the command responsible for overseeing the training and certification of active-duty and reserve troops for combat duty overseas. Since 9/11, though, First Army also picked up a secondary mission of providing support to civil authorities—when asked.

As Katrina gathered strength long before landfall, Honoré's headquarters started pulling together its standard package of assets most needed in the first twenty-four to forty-eight hours after a hurricane—helicopters, boats, medical support, and communications equipment—things that from experience they knew the states might ask for if they asked for help. Honoré had commanded through the 2004 hurricane season and was the first national post-9/11 homeland defense task force commander before being promoted to command First Army. He also had his own bases to look after and out-of-state troops training in Mississippi for Iraq deployments, many of whom he knew had never been through a hurricane before.[13]

Honoré watched the news, got his briefings, moved from his gut, spoke to Bennie Landreneau, picked up the phone, and called various other "brothers" in arms, many of whom were already saddling up, at one point so many commands and units moving on their own initiative without formal orders that the operations director at Northern Command (NORTHCOM) in Colorado called it a "wide open barn door" and said he couldn't keep up with tracking them all.[14] Honoré recounts, almost as a point of pride, that despite being subordinate to NORTHCOM, "I did not want to be controlled by Northern Command because I would have ended up being told what to do and where to do it rather than doing the things that needed to be done at any particular moment."[15]

The general blew through Baton Rouge on his way to New Orleans on August 31 to take a look for himself, the governor and her staff visibly despondent that the army general hadn't brought an army with him.[16] "Send me everything you've got," the Louisiana governor had pleaded with President Bush after landfall, asking for 40,000 federal troops, a number she picked out of thin air.[17] But Honoré knew that such numbers didn't materialize out of nowhere — *it's the logistics, stupid* — and he also wanted to get a look for himself: "That personal view, one that was not filtered through staff officers or the amplified emotions of the television reports, put into context the number and severity of the problems we were facing."[18]

One learns at the lowest level of nothingness in military or government service that there is one universal falsehood that can be uttered by any institution: "Hi, I'm from headquarters and I'm here to help you." The reason for Honoré's annoyance with NORTHCOM was simple: those in distant commander centers tend to have both sky-high perspectives and self-centered priorities, whether it's the demand for more information or tidy paperwork or a proper budget line item or some favorable news to make the bosses look good. Hardly ever are those priorities doing what needs doing to help the people who need helping.[19]

The higher one goes in any hierarchy, whether it's in a corporation or a school system or the most secret recesses of government, a sameness of human indifference often kicks in; the stricter the rules become, the thicker the regulations, the more punctilious the checkers, the more grandiose and remote the priorities. As for those doing the actual work on the Louisiana ground—soldiers, police, firefighters, EMS crews, or emergency managers; federal, state, or local; National Guard or active duty; coast guard, army, navy, air force, marine corps; professional or volunteer; and who knows from where—well, they didn't really care who was in charge as long as someone was, didn't have time to check the law or policy and doctrine manuals, didn't have time to watch TV or listen to the radio. There weren't enough helicopters, enough boats, enough people, enough shelters, and, largely oblivious to the reasons why, those in the midst of the disaster just wanted what they needed now.

Honoré, as good as he was at exuding control and navigating through what would turn out to be *the* American quagmire, was never actually in charge—indeed, he wasn't even the senior-ranking federal official on the ground: that honor belonged to the tragic Michael Brown, the totally outmatched FEMA director, a political appointee with hardly any emergency management experience before joining the administration, "a cowboy hat with no cattle," as Honoré labeled him.[20] Brown was appointed the principal federal official by the secretary of homeland security—a position for which congressional investigators later found he had not even completed the requisite training.[21] Once America discovered his skill set (or lack thereof), the preening, cavalier, and petulant Brown was unappointed and fired a week later.[22]

Brown's boss was Secretary of Homeland Security Michael Chertoff, former head of the Justice Department's criminal division and a quintessential archetype of the Washington executive agent made good. In the post-9/11 flowcharts, he was the federal official in charge of disaster management, and the president's principal disaster advisor; his new department was the civilian agency that all military support was supposed to flow through.[23] Yet even by his own admission Chertoff was not a specialist on domestic matters or natural disasters and at the time was focused on more important issues, which to him and Washington meant terrorism. (When Katrina was battering the Gulf Coast, Chertoff stayed at home working on a speech on national preparedness in the case of a pandemic; he would actually fly to Atlanta amidst the disaster to deliver it.[24]) Congressional investigators later concluded that the secretary of homeland security executed his responsibilities "late, ineffectively, or not at all."[25]

And the Bush national security dream team? Despite the team's chaotic, and at times incompetent, coordination that sunny Tuesday four years earlier, once again nearly everyone essential was oblivious or out of town—a lapse worse than 9/11 in the sense that, unlike al Qaeda's attack, Katrina's arrival was known to anyone who had been watching the Weather Channel. White House chief of staff Andrew H. Card, Jr., was on vacation in Maine; Vice President Dick Cheney had escaped sweltering August Washington at his mountain lair in Wyoming. On the day the storm hit,

President Bush celebrated Senator John McCain's birthday in Arizona before speaking to a group of seniors about Medicare prescription drug benefits at a luxury RV park. Bush and Rumsfeld then went to San Diego to celebrate the sixtieth anniversary of the end of World War II, time off from the president's own monthlong vacation at his ranch in Crawford.[26] The president's homeland security advisor, Fran Townsend, was on vacation overseas and then went on a previously scheduled trip to Saudi Arabia (so much for the homeland), the agenda being counterterrorism.[27] Condoleezza Rice went shopping in New York and took in a Broadway show. Each had their protection details, their aides and briefers, their communications teams at the ready for a secure videoteleconference, all backed up by command centers and bunkers just in case, but to an astonishing extent the most powerful people in the world seemed to think that a disaster that would end up costing approximately $81 billion in damage (let alone any loss of human life) was not worth skipping curtain calls and Western sunsets.

Cascading downward from the willfully departed crowd was a seemingly endless list of federal actors and agencies, the echelons above and around Honoré a practically indecipherable legion of military officialdom. Locally, however, the chain of command was crystal clear, given the Constitution: in Louisiana, the military man in charge was the Louisiana National Guard's Major General Landreneau, and he, in turn, reported solely and only to the commander in chief for the state: Governor Kathleen Babineaux Blanco.

That hierarchy would have made sense to the Founding Fathers. The president is the commander in chief of the armed forces, but the governor of each of the fifty states commands the state's own National Guard. These "Militia of the Several States," as the Constitution refers to them, are distinct from federal "troops," as they are formally called, and were created by the Founding Fathers specifically to serve as a counterbalance to a national standing army.[28] Importantly and quite sentimentally, they are direct descendants of the volunteer citizen militia formations predating the American Revolution and therefore even predating the United States.

Though most Americans would never know it, the National Guard is not "the military," and it is not national, and it isn't even uniformly synonymous with the reserves. And yet it is also all of those things: guardsmen and -women wear the same uniform as those in the army and air force, comply with the same broad directives, receive the same pay, and compete for similar promotions; the Air and Army National Guards are even two of the seven reserve components of the armed forces. Unique among soldiers and airmen, those in the Guard swear an oath to the Constitution as well to their states, and officers are commissioned by their states.[29]

After 9/11, the National Guard basked in this unique domestic status: first on the scene because they were there—at the World Trade Center, at American airports and train stations, even guarding the skies. Because they are local, because they aren't the federal troops of some faraway dictatorship, the National Guard likes to say that they are the preferred military responders during emergencies, natural or man-made.[30] Though most people are completely mixed up as to the difference between the national army and the National Guard, let alone the nation's history around the role of a small standing army and an ever-present and potentially expanding citizen militia, that sense of being local—and the prohibition on federal military forces being involved in law enforcement—allows the country to crawl with soldiers without fear of a military coup.

While the unique status of the National Guard preserves this protection, the Guard's domestic duties are diluted and even undermined by conventional military responsibilities. Hundreds of thousands of guardsmen and -women were federalized for duty in Afghanistan, Iraq, and elsewhere overseas after 9/11, states practically bragging about who was shouldering the greatest weight, who was taking the greatest number of casualties per capita. When Katrina hit the Gulf Coast in August 2005, despite the heavy deployment of Guard to Iraq and Afghanistan—79,000 were in federal service and committed to the war on terrorism—and despite the Louisiana Guard's being down to fewer than 2,500 available for state duty,[31] nearly 58,000 Guard from every state and territory poured into the stricken area, the largest and fastest disaster response in the National Guard's 369-year history and more than three times the number of Guard members deployed to any previous natural disaster.[32] It was impressive, showing the power of the confederation, but it was hardly local.

A bedrock assumption of federalism is that the federal government may not overrun the states' police powers unless authorized by the Constitution and the laws. The federal government has limited, explicitly granted powers under the Constitution and the laws, while state governments retain primary responsibility for "protection of life and property and the maintenance of law and order." Federal troops can be employed domestically if invited by the state; and the president can act in the case of obstructions to the enforcement of law that cannot be overcome by ordinary judicial proceedings, his authority being Article II, Section 2 of the Constitution, charging him with the "faithful" execution of the laws.[33]

But to be clear, federalism also means that Congress cannot restrict presidential constitutional authority merely by enacting a law. The Guard was never meant to be entirely independent, as the Constitution also allows for it to be federalized—"called into the actual Service of the United States." Perhaps the most famous example of this was Eisenhower's federalizing of the Guard in order to desegregate Central High School in Arkansas, an action he justified as necessary to avoid "anarchy." But in terms of the ABCs of America, the entire structure of disaster response is based upon respecting the state's role and opinion in determining when it is overwhelmed and the assistance it wants from the federal government.[34]

Yet disasters have a way of sweeping away more than just homes and bridges. The conventional wisdom that came out of the Katrina disaster and persisted through later storms such as Hurricane Sandy and beyond—that the Gulf Coast didn't heed warnings, that the governor and mayor were at each other's throats and delayed in ordering an evacuation, that New Orleans was dysfunctional and corrupt and had one of the nation's highest crime rates anyhow; that the New Orleans Police Department disintegrated, that Governor Blanco and Mayor Nagin were in over their heads, that some archaic law with a Latin name impeded an effective federal response, that FEMA was poorly led or that it had become "too" political or that the Department of Homeland Security was youthful, underfunded, and understaffed; that the National Response Plan that everyone should have followed was new and had never been tested; that Chertoff and his Department of Homeland Security were too focused on protecting the nation from terrorism; that the watch centers and the intelligence people were slow to recognize the gravity of the event; that Donald Rumsfeld guarded and delayed Defense Department assistance; that the military didn't respond fast enough even when called because it had its own cultural aversion to domestic duty; that the Louisiana National Guard was unable to respond because it was depleted due to so many of its people serving in wars in Iraq and

Afghanistan; that civil unrest and security concerns in New Orleans, real and perceived, impeded rescue and response; that it was all the media's fault; or, most obscene, that it was New Orleans's fault for being where it was, that those who lived there were responsible because they didn't evacuate or because they expected government handouts should things go bad—all contain tiny kernels of truth and yet completely fail to even come close to the true lessons that need to be learned.[35]

As the hours and days went by, in the wake of the Bush administration's inept and tactless response to the disaster, Washington should have been grateful for Honoré's salvaging at least some sliver of respect for the federal government, being a front man for the initial rescue effort, which almost exclusively was made up of local police and other emergency services, National Guard from scores of states, and the Coast Guard. Instead, many would later criticize the general for cutting too many corners, for getting too far out in front of the federal paperwork, grousing that he was just making up stuff as he went along. Nevertheless, anointed as he was by the news media and locals, political concerns dictated that no one was going to order the hero of New Orleans to stand down. The army leadership certainly warned him not to become a celebrity and urged him to take a lower media profile, in particular to promote the National Guard and the States of Louisiana and Mississippi as being in charge; such was the institution's overall reluctance to get sucked into domestic affairs.[36]

Not everyone had the same reluctance. While the people on the scene were doing the best they could and National Guard and (per the governor's request) federal troops were flowing in, the president and his advisors contemplated next steps, namely that Washington would take over the relief and rescue effort—and not just Washington, but a particular class within the country:

the envelope bearers and the executive agents of what is commonly referred to as the national security establishment. It wasn't that anyone argued the benefits of involvement in such a mess, nor even was it some political precedence that the executive agents wanted to establish, it was just that Washington couldn't imagine not being in charge, especially after decades of practicing being in charge for the big one.

Though Louisiana governor Blanco is presented by federal sources and most histories as everyone's goat: in over her head, too slow to respond, panicked, baffled, hostile Democrat to a Republican administration, playing politics,[37] in fact, three days before the storm made landfall, before the National Hurricane Center adjusted Katrina's track as definitively bearing down on New Orleans, she made all the necessary moves, including requesting a disaster declaration from Washington, the first time that one had ever been requested and approved before a hurricane actually hit.[38] She also activated more National Guard than the state had ever activated prestorm and ten times more than did neighboring Mississippi, at that point still the presumed main target of the eye.[39] And she did this despite the fact that the majority of Louisiana's Guard *was* in Baghdad on federal duty.

Bush and Blanco first spoke on Sunday morning, August 28, the day before Louisiana landfall, the president urging the governor to issue mandatory evacuation orders for New Orleans.[40] "My people tell me this is going to be a terrible storm," he said, and he asked Blanco what else she needed from the federal government, her reply being "We've got it under control."[41] But because Katrina roared in with unexpected fury, the levees holding back the waters of Lake Pontchartrain and the Mississippi River failed, flooding the city. Chaos reigned, the Superdome filled, and another 25,000 congregated at the nearby Ernest N. Morial Convention Center; the reports and the images from the city truly suggested anarchy, precisely the conditions that might compel a forcible federal takeover.

The official record shows that as early as Tuesday, the day after landfall, federal contingency plans assuming the inadequacy of constitutional norms were already unfolding: the White House warned the Pentagon that it might federalize the disaster and bring in federal troops.[42] Andrew Card called Blanco on Thursday morning, formally proposing to take the response away from the state. The governor responded that she did not want to give up authority, so Bush decided to make his case to her in person the next day.[43]

Meanwhile, Honoré, flying here and there in his helicopter, observing for himself and talking to everyone, could see that most of the news media reporting was exaggerated, and that some of the high-level sources for the media, particularly the New Orleans Police Department leadership, were given to "wild statements and overexaggerations" that quickly went viral.[44] Honoré pleaded with Mayor Nagin to get the clearly unhinged chief of police to stop talking: people in Washington were watching television, he said. Guardsmen and rescuers and volunteers preparing to deploy were also watching—and Honoré felt that maybe they were holding back, hesitating to deploy, thinking "maybe these people are running around taking over the city and that the city is out of control."[45]

At first light on Friday morning, September 2, Honoré finally heaved a sigh of relief for the first time since his arrival in the destroyed city. Though "the noise level about crime and rapes far exceeded what actually was happening,"[46] under Nagin's command, New Orleans police had shifted from rescue duties to law enforcement, and Honoré concluded that "nothing indicated that riots or a citywide insurrection were imminent."[47] At an early-morning videoteleconference he told President Bush as much:

evacuations had commenced and New Orleans was turning a corner.

Air Force One and the grand apparatus of the presidency of the United States of America flew into Louis Armstrong International Airport that afternoon, and in the presence of Bush; Chertoff; Brown; national security advisor Stephen J. Hadley; White House deputy chief of staff and Bush number one fix-it man Joe Hagin; Lieutenant General H. Steven Blum, chief of the National Guard Bureau; other senior staff unidentified and ominous; *and* the entire Louisiana congressional delegation—but not Honoré[48] and not Rumsfeld (nor any other high-level Pentagon official, for that matter)—the lone Kathleen Blanco was treated to the protocol equivalent of waterboarding. "After four days of chaos," Bush said, "it was clear the authorities in Louisiana could not lead."[49] The meeting was as blunt as you can get without the Secret Service becoming involved, *Newsweek* reported,[50] but even after Bush made the one-on-one case for her to give up power, she wouldn't agree, asking for twenty-four more hours.[51]

"We don't have twenty-four hours," Bush snapped.[52] He was as frustrated as he'd ever been in the presidency, he later said, and though White House lawyers and Cheney's office were cheering him on to invoke exceptional constitutional authorities and take over anyway, they neither had a cooperative military man on the ground nor the secretary of defense in their camp, and Bush thus was not inclined to override the governor.[53]

But that was hardly the end of it.

One of the common arguments made by those who watched the disaster unfold in Louisiana was that everyone involved was, to some extent, improvising. Bush administration officials would later claim that weather forecasts and flooding predictions had been incomplete and inaccurate. Indeed, had anyone in the administration had an inkling of but a fraction of the damage to be inflicted by Katrina, surely vacations would have been canceled.

And yet a week before the nightmare began, at 8:41 in the evening on August 28, ten hours before Katrina even made landfall and before the impact of the storm was even known, Vice President Cheney's senior counsel, David S. Addington, wrote to his Pentagon counterpart and good friend William J. ("Jim") Haynes—the top lawyer in the Defense Department.

"Given the potential massive size of the problem there could be civil unrest during the aftermath," Addington (described by *U.S. News & World Report* as "the most powerful man you've never heard of"[54]) said in his e-mail. "You might want to have an [Insurrection Act] proclamation...in the can in case it is needed." Legally, Addington reminded Haynes, the proclamation should include the appropriate language to constitute a lawful cease and desist order whereby the president would "immediately order the insurgents to disperse," thereby authorizing the "use of militia and armed force to enforce Federal authority" if they did not.[55]

Insurgents? As if the people of New Orleans were the enemy in Iraq? And *insurrection?* The term used in the Constitution was "domestic violence."[56] And a *cease and desist order*, as if Katrina were the Whiskey Rebellion of George Washington's day, when the first president justified the use of federal troops in western Pennsylvania because, as he wrote, "acts of treason were committed against the United States"?[57]

What Addington was proposing was a pure implementation of the core principle of the Program: the executive is preeminent; no matter what, someone has to be there; there can be no ungoverned spaces. That he was doing so before Katrina hit was further revealing: this was not poststorm improvisation. Bush might not have known which way the weather was blowing, Mike Brown might not have known whether rain fell up or down, but there were some in Washington who recognized an opportunity.

Just before midnight, with a frustrated Bush back from his visit to insurgent territory, Andy Card faxed a draft document to the governor's office including a Memorandum of Understanding and a draft letter from her to the president surrendering: a federal general—undoubtedly Honoré—would have "dual command status," the White House now offered, somewhat confusingly reporting both to Blanco and to the president, with the federal chain of command prevailing only *if* there was a conflict between the two officials.[58] Card rousted the governor's chief of staff from sleep, urging that Blanco sign fast because an announcement of the new arrangement was all ready to go out the next morning in Washington.[59] "I'm not signing anything in the middle of the night," Blanco told her advisors.[60] The next morning she called the White House and said no.

An hour later, flanked by Rumsfeld, Chertoff, and General Richard Myers, the chairman of the Joint Chiefs of Staff, President Bush strutted out to the microphone and announced he was sending 7,200 federal troops to the Gulf anyhow: humanitarian relief.

Subsequently, the official lore became that the 82nd Airborne Division saved the day.[61] Yet even the 82nd's division commander later said it was the division's presence that promoted the appearance of order—"that sense of assurance that everybody is there to help you."[62] Indeed, while everything seemed so urgent, the command element of the division wasn't even scheduled to arrive until late afternoon Saturday, and the actual soldiers wouldn't arrive until Tuesday, when the immediate storm after the real storm had largely passed. It was just a federal show: the maroon-bereted paratroopers were carefully staged to conquer the never-flooded French Quarter, a fresh and friendly set of extra hands to be sure, but pawns, too.[63]

CHAPTER THREE

Critical Conditions

*DOD has responsibility to provide a rapid and effective response
and recovery from domestic catastrophic event. Specifically, the
Department must maintain continuity of operations, save lives,
prevent human suffering and mitigate great property damage. This
responsibility involves capabilities to provide mission assurance
(internal support) and Defense Support to Civil Authorities
(external) utilizing active duty, Reserve, National Guard, DOD
civilians and DOD contractors.*
DOD PRIMARY MISSION ESSENTIAL FUNCTIONS, 2012

A fter less than twenty-four hours on the ground, while
moving thousands of tired, filthy, and sick American ref-
ugees from the Superdome to buses and to safety, Task Force
Buckeye of the Ohio National Guard had received a secret "squir-
rel" mission assignment to protect Washington's assets.

The order came in a circuitous way, neither from the Guard's
headquarters back home in Columbus nor from the Louisiana
National Guard task force the Ohioans were assigned to in Baton
Rouge. Instead, it came from the Pentagon, in a SPECAT—special
category—message, meaning very limited distribution. A squad
was to be volunteered to provide security for a high-water dump
truck commandeered by the Central Intelligence Agency. Mission: wade into the muck to retrieve sensitive papers and codes
from the Agency's little-known and abandoned New Orleans

office. Not surprisingly given that it was the CIA, it was all very hush-hush.

And then another national security mission assignment came in: the State Department sent a "high-priority message" to the Joint Chiefs of Staff announcing that "national security documents of the highest level" were located on the twelfth and thirteenth floors of the federal building at 333 Canal Street in the Central Business District. "Soldiers must secure building. No one will enter the building once secured, until authorized personnel arrive to retrieve documents," the cryptic message said. A team of National Guard infantry was dispatched. "National security of the highest level" turned out to be a few hundred blank passports.[1]

And that wasn't all; the Secret Service was readying its own nighttime special operation with a SWAT team for a mission right out of a Hollywood movie: Louisiana National Guardsmen were to support the black-suited civilian commandos and go into the Federal Reserve Bank building on Lafayette Square and rescue $50 million in cash.[2]

As to why National Guard troops were tasked with such missions instead of working on something like, say, saving lives—well, David Addington hadn't been the only one among Washington's leading ranks who watched the Weather Channel in the days before Katrina made landfall. The CIA, State Department, and Secret Service had all bugged out of New Orleans before the storm, as had all of the other federal law enforcement agencies—FBI; Bureau of Alcohol, Tobacco, and Firearms (ATF); DEA; US Marshals Service; Immigration and Customs Enforcement (ICE); Customs and Border Protection; Border Patrol; Federal Air Marshals—hundreds of their staff and families skedaddling out to safety, only skeletal crews left behind to watch over federal buildings, valuable equipment, and classified information.[3] Even the agency that one might think would stay and even augment itself for the worst—FEMA—had just one employee in New Orleans when the hurricane made its Louisiana landfall, and he was a PR guy from Michael Brown's office in Washington, there to prepare for the expected VIP photo ops that would follow from rubbernecking federal officials.[4]

Before the storm hit, the military was equally focused on its own. The navy moved ships out of harm's way, the air force flushed aircraft north, marine corps reserve headquarters in New Orleans were evacuated and shuttered.[5] At Louisiana and Mississippi military bases, special airlifts were laid on to evacuate critical patients and pregnant women in their third trimester to Texas;[6] military retirees living in the area were air evacuated to Maryland.[7] Those military personnel who stayed behind focused inward. The old naval base in the Algiers section of New Orleans was sealed up tight, so much so that the officers in charge there later turned away stranded civilians seeking shelter, at gunpoint.[8]

New Orleans after Katrina would offer tons of examples of true heroes—military included—pilots, the rescuers and aid workers, the Louisiana police who worked day and night despite their own homes being destroyed and their own families and relatives becoming part of the calamity; the Coast Guard; the Louisiana National Guard and the guardsmen and -women who came in from all over the country, the hundreds if not thousands of citizen volunteers, both organized and spontaneous. But while chaos reigned for the five days after landfall, federal law enforcement was effectively absent—by choice.[9] From hundreds prestorm, about forty-five federal lawmen remained in New Orleans when the hurricane hit.[10] Instead of a massive restocking, the Departments of Justice and Homeland Security then fought over who was in charge of law enforcement. (At one point, things became so tense between the two agencies that some in Homeland Security proposed that their tactical teams take up positions around the city and mount a show of force rather than relinquish law enforcement powers to the men from Justice.[11])

The federal argument about jurisdiction wasn't solved until September 4, when Governor Blanco finally filled out the right paperwork agreeing to credential federal agents to allow them to enforce local laws and be deputized under the State.[12] *Then* the federal flood began: over 2,300 federal law enforcement officers swarmed, the system primed for both redemption and possible takeover, in just one week growing to a force nearly equal to the total of the New Orleans and state police officers in the entire state of Louisiana before landfall;[13] they grew to more than 3,000 strong in two weeks.[14]

On the evening of August 31, when he was in Baton Rouge on his way to New Orleans for the first time, General Honoré was approached by an FBI supervisor with another secret mission: "We've got some shooters we need to put on a building we have to protect," the supervisor whispered, asking if they could hop a helicopter ride back into town. Seven black-clad snipers piled into Honoré's Blackhawk; "They never said a word from the time we picked them up until we dropped them off atop a building downtown," he later wrote. "To this day I don't know what building they were on, why they were there, or how long they stayed."[15]

In fact, it was the BellSouth main exchange on Poydras Street (separating the French Quarter from the Central Business District), the regional hub for multiple commercial carriers—what's called a telecomm hotel. Though damaged, the main exchange was still operating at diminished capacity. The corporation wanted to send in a team to refuel the diesel generators, which were running low, but were fearful of all they were reading and seeing on television about the anarchy in the city. Corporate executives called the Justice Department in Washington seeking help.

Since the Kennedy administration, private property like the

BellSouth facility holds a special status in the XYZ world. Communications problems during the Cuban missile crisis, extending to links from Washington to its own military forces, let alone to the Soviet leadership, drove the president and the executive agents to seek a single unified communications system for command and control.[16] In 1984, the Reagan team expanded the mission of what was now called the national communications system to encompass prewar responsibilities as well, including coordinating the emergency plans to help the government—and the American economy—survive a nuclear war. In some ways, it was a change necessitated by advances in technology; a centralized government-only system of closed circuits and links needed to be updated to keep pace with the far more robust decentralized commercial networks and technologies that were emerging.[17] But it also meant a further need for constant oversight that extended well beyond the federal government.

For the national security establishment, communications were merely one of the newest of its private-sector concerns. Long before the information age, the military had systematically identified what it called key assets—strategic materials, factories, and transportation links—that would be vital in war production and mobilization. It was all pretty straightforward, though nuclear weapons and the era of mutual assured destruction made the notion of mobilization of large numbers of anything seem obsolete if not wasteful. Yet ever-nimble nuclear strategists proposed that protection of key assets was linked to the deterrence of a Soviet attack: if the economic survival of the nation could be assured, the theory went, then this would reduce the possibility of postnuclear-war coercion and thus of attack.[18] With enough shovels, America would survive and endure: COG flourished, civil defense (dormant with the passing of bomber and missile gaps) revived, billions were poured into "command, control, and communications." The military's ARPANET—the nuclear-war-surviving packet-switched network that was the seed of today's Internet—emerged.

When years later the Clinton administration inherited the burgeoning World Wide Web, the attempt to strategically unite all of the old pieces—continuity, national security communications, enduring and protectable key assets—was already well under way. There was understandable logic to this, but the "civil" in "civil defense" began to take on a broader meaning than it had for the beginning of the Cold War. For example, when the Reagan administration tasked FEMA to examine how "various critical US infrastructure elements (e.g., the computerized banking system, power grids, and communications networks) are vulnerable to acts of terrorism," it was the first time a national security directive explicitly identified as critical private-sector infrastructure not directly part of the military-industrial complex.[19] A decade later, Clinton's National Security Strategy for 1997 stated that the US "must be prepared to respond effectively to protect lives and property and ensure the survival of our institutions and national infrastructure" in the event of natural disasters, terrorism, WMD, and sabotage of information systems.[20] Presidential Decision Directive 63 followed in May 1998, setting out government responsibilities. "Critical infrastructures are those physical and cyber-based systems essential to the minimum operations of the economy and government," the directive said. "Non-traditional attacks on our infrastructure and information systems may be capable of significantly harming both our military power and our economy."[21]

In February 2000, President Clinton announced the "first-ever" public-private partnership for protecting the nation's communications: "stakeholders in the critical infrastructures," they were called.[22] That was still on the books, as it were, when Katrina hit, so it made perfect sense that, following orders, the SWAT team came in with Honoré to secure the place, followed later by US marshals to protect the building.[23] Snipers would enforce the private-public infrastructure partnership, putting the focus on security from needy civilians who might disrupt federal working.

In the end, the BellSouth's Poydras Street central office never completely failed, but so many poles, relays, and towers were damaged or destroyed that whatever phone service remained was not only sporadic but completely inadequate. With the loss of electrical power and the flooding, almost all of the communications lines in and around New Orleans went down as well; the city's main communications tower was destroyed and two others were damaged, causing catastrophic cascading failure. In total, almost three million customer phone lines were knocked out, telephone switching centers were flooded and damaged, and over 1,475 cell towers were incapacitated.[24] The rescue effort and the general welfare were disrupted, but the experts in Washington concluded that the loss of communications didn't really affect the rest of the nation.

Oil was a different matter, though, and here corporate and government devotion coincided. Washington's expression of priority came in the amount of intelligence resources thrown into assessing the impact, activity undertaken even without an industry lobbyist knocking at the door.

More than 10 percent of the nation's imported crude oil entered through the Louisiana Offshore Oil Port.[25] Two days before Katrina made landfall, energy companies were already estimating that the approaching storm had reduced Gulf of Mexico oil production by more than a third.[26] Katrina forced the evacuation of more than 75 percent of the Gulf's 819 manned oil platforms.[27] It was enough of a concern that national reconnaissance satellites were diverted from wartime duties to begin imaging important installations.[28]

Whereas virtually no attention was paid at the federal level when it came to making sure lives were protected, pursuant to the federal government's priorities, before the storm, the entire oil infrastructure on the Gulf was mapped and lists of factories and infrastructure critical to the executive agents were also compiled. Intelligence analysts at multiple agencies in Washington were assigned Katrina-related tasks concerned with infrastructure. Well before landfall, the National Geospatial-Intelligence Agency created customized charts and maps of critical infrastructure and government facilities.[29] A special Defense Department team cataloged potential hazardous materials.[30]

The hurricane damage proved huge: most crude oil and natural gas production in the Gulf of Mexico was shut down. Eleven petroleum refineries, or one-sixth of the nation's refining capacity, were damaged or destroyed by Katrina.[31] Once the storm passed, the National Reconnaissance Office again diverted satellites to assess flooded areas and identify industrial and environmental hazards;[32] and what followed was a massive and hidden government intelligence collection effort: the air force deployed Eagle Vision teams to pull down commercial satellite imagery that was already being purchased in bulk for the two foreign wars.[33] Fourteen different types of reconnaissance and surveillance aircraft were called in: National Guard RC-26B Condor aircraft started flying reconnaissance missions from Texas on August 30,[34] followed by the high-flying U-2 Dragon Lady, the first domestic service by the California-based planes.[35] Three different types of auxiliary aircraft from the Civil Air Patrol provided a continual stream of digital imagery.[36] OC-135 Open Skies aircraft, normally used for nuclear arms treaty verification and monitoring, were pulled in.[37] So were C-130 Scathe View aircraft, normally used for counterdrug surveillance.[38] Navy P-3 Orions intended for maritime surveillance and antisubmarine warfare were tasked to image, as were clandestine DC-3 Shadow Harvest reconnaissance aircraft of the Defense Intelligence Agency.[39] Even special-operations AC-130H gunships and fighter jets flew overhead, providing imagery and full-motion video from various pods and internal sensors.[40]

In, too, came the unmanned drones,[41] high-flying Predators and a swarm of other aerial vehicles filling the skies of the battlefield laboratory, taking pictures and producing live video of selected locations.[42] Reconnaissance experts even duct-taped unmanned aerial vehicles to the bottom of helicopters to improvise in delivering video; another experimental drone was mounted on the thirty-eighth-story roof of the Hyatt Regency hotel to provide real-time surveillance.[43]

Good intelligence is never a bad thing, and in this situation any kind of intelligence was sorely needed. But in reality, the Katrina-related intelligence collection and analysis ended up being little more than bomb damage assessments that merely transposed wartime methodologies to the United States. Some of what was obtained was laughable, some of it downright ominous, but most of it focused on the conditions of critical infrastructure rather than on human needs, and all of it was rather boilerplate and thoughtless, feeding the voracious appetites of gigantic, competing, and overlapping headquarters far, far away.

Take, for instance, the initial "damage assessment" issued by Honoré's higher headquarters, US Northern Command in Colorado: "Analysis of 2 September U-2 optical bar camera imagery along the United States Gulf Coast showed areas of light to extensive damage to infrastructure, residences, and businesses along the I-10 corridor between Pascagoula, Mississippi and Mobile, Alabama," the report declared, as if the American Gulf Coast were distant Indonesia after a tsunami, as if anyone didn't already know the broad outlines.

If NORTHCOM thought it was breaking ground with such pronouncements as "Heavy damage was observed around Gulfport and Biloxi," it was far from alone in stating—and ignoring—the obvious.[44] "Spectral analysis of the I-10 causeway between New Orleans and Slidell indicates sections of the bridge are missing," announced another carefully annotated imagery report produced *three weeks* after the fact, as if complex spectral analysis were needed to know what everyone knew in the first hours.[45]

"Technical Image analysis of the Chalmette Petrol Storage Facility indicates presence of flood-water surface refraction indicative of petroleum contamination throughout the facility," said one typical infrastructure report, proudly using similar hyperspectral imagery and analysis, long after the workers had already been back to make an on-the-ground assessment.[46] And just as would have been done for a bombing survey, the national intelligence agencies calculated percentages of damage to factories, power plants, and petroleum facilities—levels of damage classified as limited, moderate, extensive, and "catastrophic," each with precise definitions laid out in additional reports. Elaborate maps of the Gulf region were prepared showing percentages of damage to communications, energy infrastructure, electrical production, airfields, highways, bridges, the petroleum industry, ports, defense plants, etc. The National Geospatial-Intelligence Agency in Washington created hundreds of intelligence products (as they are officially termed) a day;[47] 2,300 imagery and mapping products were produced by air force intelligence alone;[48] scores of special graphics were prepared in response to federal needs, such as one aerial reconnaissance study that showed various views of the FBI field office near Lake Pontchartrain, as if it were a behind-enemy-lines target, even though skeletal FBI staff had stayed right there all along.[49]

The graphics and images used for the constant briefings were rich and expertly prepared. But intelligence didn't inform any decisions on the ground, not intelligence from Washington, not from *the system*. When Honoré arrived at the Superdome on August 31, he thought the total head count there might be around 16,000 to 17,000; he soon discovered that the estimate was low by half;[50] none of the intelligence gathering had anything to say to explain the error. No imagery or intelligence reports informed any of the federal watch officers of the existence of a second gathering place at the convention center—in all the collection of information on buildings and infrastructure, 25,000 people were missed.[51]

There is no indication whatsoever that any of this intelligence effort provided people on the ground with what they needed, informed one decision, or made one iota of difference—that is, except one, and it was the most important one: the federal government's view of crime and governance on the ground, where there was an utter absence of any official intelligence. The ensuing panic, overreaction, power struggles—and federal takeover—were all fed by this enforced ignorance. The Homeland Security Operations Center—designed to be "the nation's nerve center for information sharing and domestic incident management"—completely failed.[52] The operational director, a retired marine corps brigadier general and a man known for loudly demanding the latest intelligence and then rolling up his sleeves to scrutinize the satellite photography with his own eyes, didn't at first realize that the Superdome and the convention center were two different buildings.[53]

Gordon R. England, Rumsfeld's deputy and perhaps the most active official in Washington urging military commands to provide assistance regardless of FEMA's incompetence, later said he had no accurate information whatsoever in the first twenty-four hours, "except what was on the news."[54] At NORTHCOM, the deputy director of intelligence, navy captain Brett Markham, said that the Colorado headquarters relied heavily on "national technical means"—satellites—in the immediate aftermath, but also that none of the intelligence yielded "a sufficiently clear picture" of what was happening.[55] The divide between what Honoré could see on the ground and what was perceived in Washington was so large that the Pentagon actually believed it had to plan for a far more complicated military operation, "one in which federal soldiers might have to kill American citizens."[56]

All of the now-too-familiar intelligence failures discovered on 9/11 recurred: parties not talking to each other, overclassification of information, limited distribution—and this despite billions invested in intelligence and information sharing, despite an entirely new homeland security apparatus, despite hundreds of thousands of man-hours put into the mapping efforts in Washington.[57] And if the priorities weren't crystal clear amidst the destroyed city, they would eventually become a bit less opaque: Congress later found scant evidence that any satellite imagery was used to *any* advantage to target relief, nor was information resulting from aerial damage assessment flights ever distributed.[58] Honoré had to have his people develop their own aerial grid system from scratch to guide door-to-door searches.[59] So if rescuing the residents of New Orleans was not the priority, if, despite rhetoric, the federal government was willing to devote astonishing resources to gathering intelligence that had little to nothing to do with human needs, what was the purpose of all of those satellites and clandestine activities? (And no: it wasn't to help prevent the environmental disaster that followed.) A hint came buried in the intelligence advisories issued to federal troops: amidst the human catastrophe, Northern Command simply reminded "commanders" that

THE REAL WORLD TERRORIST THREAT STILL EXISTS AND TO REMAIN VIGILANT....RE-MAIN AWARE OF POTENTIAL TERRORIST AND EXTREMIST THREATS AND CONTINUE TO REPORT SUSPICIOUS ACTIVITY.[60]

*　　*　　*

On September 7, NORTHCOM and the FBI—jointly with Department of Homeland Security "intelligence"—issued advisories warning of the upcoming anniversary of 9/11 and the domestic dangers that needed tending because terrorists might take advantage of the hurricane and conduct another strike.[61] The next day, Joint Force Headquarters National Capital Region, the newly created military command responsible for defense of the nation's capital, added its own intelligence warning of suspicious activity; a second report called for "increased vigilance during the 9/11 memorial period."[62]

One reason that federal assistance in New Orleans was such a failure was that the executive agents who tend to love such seizures of power from local authorities also have little to no interest in locals, period. Of course, nobody wants dead bodies, but the overarching priority is for a macro-level web of infrastructure—communications, military, economic—not things like old ladies dying in apartments without air-conditioning, children drowning in floodwaters, and young men gunned down in the street violence that so often accompanies social breakdown. In a very real sense, theirs is a calculus not unlike those of nuclear-age theorists who considered millions of deaths simply part of the equation; the crucial thing was *America's* survival, not the survival of Americans.

The long state and federal cleanup was just beginning, but national security instantly lost interest in the human drama. Katrina had been a useful proving ground for the Program and its executive agents to evaluate continuity, critical infrastructure, command lines, and takeover. But now it was time to get back to business.

CHAPTER FOUR

Posse Comitatus

The powers reserved to the several States will extend to all the objects which, in the ordinary course of affairs, concern the lives, liberties, and properties of the people, and the internal order, improvement, and prosperity of the State.
JAMES MADISON, "THE FEDERALIST NO. 45"

B lanco had said no, the military had been a reluctant accomplice to executive agent coup, homeland security was disorganized and befuddled, and federal law enforcement was on autopilot. President Bush flew away from New Orleans seething. "I was as frustrated as I had been at any point in my presidency," he recalled.[1]

Posse Comitatus — Latin for "force of the county" — is easy to cite and hard to comprehend. The term has its origins in fifteenth-century England and is simply defined in common law to refer to all able-bodied men on whom a sheriff can call to assist in carrying out his duties.[2] Yet there is nothing simple about *Posse Comitatus* as a US statute and an American legend; it has come to be a ubiquitous political touchstone, a perennial favorite of right and left, from survivalists and states' rights patriots to civil rights and antimilitary activists, all of whom argue similarly and simply that the Civil War–era law prohibits "the military" from domestic duties. And not only that, but that it "is a pillar of freedom designed in complete accordance with the views expressed by the founding fathers."[3]

Posse Comitatus, however, was never the codification of some American ideal. All during the period preceding the Civil War, "governors, sheriffs, US marshals, revenue agents, and other persons in authority frequently requested and received the assistance of detachments of troops, employed as a posse, to assist in carrying out their duties," both in the North and in the South.[4] The law is a post–Civil War law, infused with racist overtones and emblematic of a country searching for a uniting center.

After the Confederacy was defeated, the Union Army—the federal US Army—occupied the South, where it quelled violence against free blacks and Unionist whites alike and operated military tribunals where civil courts failed or refused to enforce civil law.[5] As Reconstruction dawned, recalcitrant Southern states started to pass "Black Codes," effectively enforcing exclusion; Congress passed a weak civil rights law in 1866, followed by the Fourteenth Amendment to the Constitution, which provides all citizens equal protection of the laws. Ratification of the amendment became the provision for readmission of states to the Union. What followed then was true martial law. Army General Order No. 44, issued in July 1866, empowered federal troops to arrest anyone involved in crimes aimed at "citizens and inhabitants of the United States" when local law enforcement failed to do so;[6] and the occupying army was authorized "to suppress insurrections, disorders, and violence, and to punish, or cause to be punished, all disturbers of the public peace and criminals."[7]

Martial law lasted for three years, only relinquished after most of the Southern states pledged adherence to the Constitution and were readmitted to the Union.[8] Yet the postwar battle didn't abate, and after the Ku Klux Klan emerged and undertook an unprecedented terror campaign in South Carolina and Georgia, federal troops were again called in to suppress waves of violence, and the army played a significant role in vanquishing the Klan.[9] As the presidential election of 1876 approached, radical Republicans contested the influence of states' rights Democrats, and violence again increased: blacks were harassed and flogged, elected officials were assassinated. In South Carolina, Democrats proclaimed they would triumph against Republicans "if we have to wade in blood knee-deep."[10] The army was again called out as a *posse comitatus*, and troops were stationed at polling places.

Democratic Party candidate Samuel J. Tilden, governor of New York, won the popular vote and was leading in the electoral vote, with the exception of Florida, Louisiana, and South Carolina, heavily occupied by federal troops and under Republican control. The official count finally put Republican Party candidate Rutherford B. Hayes up by one electoral vote. Both sides claimed victory, and voting in the three states came under closer scrutiny. A special congressional commission was created to resolve the impasse. Meanwhile, President-elect Hayes negotiated a backroom deal: he would be named president; in return, he promised to remove all federal troops from the South and not interfere in their internal affairs in the future.[11] It was the end of any kind of Reconstruction and the beginning of an almost century-long battle for voting and civil rights for blacks.

What also followed was a vow by the Democratic-controlled House of Representatives to pass a law prohibiting federal troops from ever again getting involved in local law enforcement, one Southerner calling the use of such troops "tyrannical and unconstitutional." At first the Democrats failed to get an amendment through a Republican Senate in the 1877 army appropriations. The next year, though, with more Democrats in Congress and an alliance forged with Northern legislators who bristled at the use of federal troops to crush labor riots, Congress passed an amendment to the 1878 appropriations bill placing restrictions on the use of the military as a *posse comitatus*. It became known as the *Posse Comitatus* Act, and provided that:

> It shall not be lawful to employ any part of the Army of the United States . . . for the purpose of executing the laws, except on such cases and under such circumstances as such employment of said force may be expressly authorized by the Constitution or by any act of Congress. . . . [12]

The law turned the concept of *posse comitatus*, meant to bolster the nation's ability to uphold the law and democratic ideals, into the symbol of oppression and tyranny. (As one comprehensive army historical study says, it was "almost certainly intended as one last bulwark against federal meddling in the internal affairs of the white supremacist South."[13]) A violation of *Posse Comitatus* and the image of the federal government as a tyrannical oppressor has become one of the most powerful myths in the nation.

Like the Bible or the Constitution itself, *Posse Comitatus* invokes outsize emotions. "Most individuals think they know what the *Posse Comitatus* Act allows and disallows; most of them are wrong," says the foreword to the most comprehensive post-Katrina military study of the subject.[14] "Not only is the law confusing to pundits and commentators," another military officer writes, "it is confusing to soldiers of all ranks, as well as political leaders in Congress and the executive branch. Even military lawyers, who have the luxury of spending time in academic settings studying the Act, have found it to be confusing."[15] "The complication of PCA [*Posse Comitatus* Act] requires volumes of exceptions and DOD instructions to cover all of the dos and don'ts as we tap dance around the law," says another.[16]

The truth is that the president has wide constitutional authority to take military action to do almost all of what is restricted in *Posse Comitatus;* the law itself makes provision for presidential powers granted in Article IV of the Constitution, to "call into Federal Service such of the militia of the other States, and use such of the [federal] armed forces, *as he considers necessary* to enforce the laws and suppress the rebellion." *Posse Comitatus* also allows for the use of federal troops as otherwise authorized by statute, and over the years Congress has not been shy about passing subsequent legislation giving the president many powers. Today, federal troops are authorized by law to conduct domestic law enforcement under the disaster relief and protection of public health and safety provisions of the Robert T. Stafford Disaster Relief and Emergency Assistance Act of 1988.[17] Other legislative authority provides for certain assistance to customs officials, as part of the so-called war on drugs; in response to acts of terrorism involving weapons of mass destruction; in the execution of quarantine laws; in the protection of designated individuals, including members of Congress and foreign dignitaries; and during designated "National Security Special Events," which can be as diverse as a presidential inaugural, the Democratic or Republican Party's nominating convention, or a Super Bowl game.[18]

An intrinsic exception to *Posse Comitatus* is also called military purpose doctrine, which "allows the military to enforce civilian laws on military installations, to police themselves, and to perform their military functions...."[19] Commanders have the right to protect themselves, their properties, military interests, guests of the military, and classified information; protect and enforce law and regulations on military property; authorize military criminal investigators to conduct investigations, even of civilians; and they can assist civil law enforcement, regardless of the direct benefit, if there is a foreign policy or military connection to such action.[20] There is also the doctrine of "immediate response," allowing military commanders to act "to save lives, prevent human suffering, and mitigate great property damage" in imminently serious conditions.[21]

Each of these allowances comes with restrictions. Defense Department regulations say that immediate response can only be invoked if local authorities are unable to handle the situation, or if some incident involves chemical, biological, radiological, nuclear, or other high explosives.[22] Military commanders can make emergency decisions in the course of immediate response to assist local law enforcement in suppressing civil disturbances, but again, only "if the commander has exhausted all resources to obtain prior authorization" from the president.[23] And there are constraints on *what* federal troops can do even if they do become involved, including restrictions on active participation in search and seizure except under extraordinary circumstances, and there are stringent rules for the use of force, the domestic equivalent of overseas rules of engagement. Still, the Constitution, Congress, and the courts have granted so many exceptions to *Posse Comitatus* that the Army War College teaches prospective general officers "that the law essentially gives the President all the authority he needs to employ DOD forces inside the US."[24]

The most significant statutory concession is the Insurrection Act mentioned by David Addington in his e-mail to Jim Haynes, which is actually a set of statutes predating *Posse Comitatus* that originally codified the president's constitutional authority to see to it that the laws are faithfully executed. Found in its earliest iteration in the Uniform Militia Act of 1792, a law that permitted calling forth the militia to execute the laws of the Union, it was relied upon by President George Washington to suppress the Whiskey Rebellion despite the opposition of Pennsylvania's governor.[25]

The current statute was enacted in 1807 and remained in effect on the books, with very little change, for exactly 200 years.[26] (President Grant used his authority under the statutes to send federal troops to restore order in Louisiana, Alabama, Arkansas, and South Carolina before the presidential election of 1876.) It authorizes the president to order the use of federal troops to suppress domestic violence that hinders execution of state or federal law or otherwise deprives citizens of their constitutional rights in three circumstances:

The first (Section 331) permits use of federal troops to suppress an insurrection in a state upon the request of that state's governor or legislature, and is meant to fulfill the federal government's responsibility to protect against "domestic violence." This provision was used during Hurricane Hugo in 1989 to suppress widespread looting in the US Virgin Islands, and during the 1992 "Rodney King" riots in Los Angeles.[27]

The second (Section 332) permits the president, on his own initiative, to suppress rebellion or enforce federal laws if he believes that "unlawful obstructions, combinations, assemblages, or rebellion against the authority of the United States make it impracticable to enforce the laws of the United States in any State by the ordinary course of judicial proceedings."

The third (Section 333) permits the president to take such measures as he considers necessary to suppress an insurrection, domestic violence, unlawful combination, or conspiracy, if such disturbances hinder the execution of the laws of that state. It also applies to the laws of the United States within the state particularly when some of, or a class of, its citizens are deprived of a right, privilege, immunity, or protection named in the Constitution and secured by law, particularly if the constituted authorities of that state are unable to, fail to, or refuse to protect that right, privilege, or immunity, or to give that protection. This provision was the basis for the use of federal troops during the civil rights era, such as Eisenhower's actions in Arkansas, as mentioned earlier.

Section 334 of the Act, the fourth provision, requires the

president to issue a proclamation ordering insurrectionists to "disperse and retire peaceably to their abodes" before he can employ any of the previous three sections.[28] This was precisely the draft proclamation being prepared by the executive agents before Hurricane Katrina made landfall, not to subvert or suspend *Posse Comitatus*, as many, including many in the military, would argue. That is because the Insurrection Act enforces constitutional executive authority. Even if, against the wishes of the governor, federal troops were sent to New Orleans to restore order, to see to it that no one's civil rights were being infringed by the temporary breakdown in governance and law enforcement, many would no doubt have howled about federal tyranny, but it was unambiguously within the president's lawful power even if it would have been a very questionable call.[29]

Hurricane Katrina was one of the largest and most destructive natural disasters in modern American history. In the end, though, considering the 120,000 or more trapped in the floodwaters, given the gravity of the reports of chaos and violence, and given the muddle of federal response, the official death count was surprisingly low—1,096 in Louisiana, 228 in Mississippi, and two in Alabama[30]—low, that is compared to, say, the Galveston hurricane of 1900, which claimed 8,000 lives, which at the time was 20 percent of the entire population of the city.[31] A majority of the Louisiana deaths—roughly 80 percent—came from the New Orleans metropolitan area. As many as 10 percent of those 800 died in nursing homes, some allegedly abandoned by their caretakers; throughout the state, approximately 70 percent of the victims were older than sixty.[32]

More than 1,000 deaths is hardly a welcome statistic. But Katrina is not the test case for the executive agents to use to affirm that the Constitution suffocates disaster response and survival, or that antiquated rules stand in the way. "When you can get helicopters there within twenty-four to forty-eight hours of the event, that makes you virtually a first responder," says Paul McHale, the homeland defense assistant secretary during Katrina[33] and a former member of Congress.[34] Over a twelve-day period, more than 72,000 men and women in uniform participated in the Katrina response—the largest in-country use of forces since the Civil War, the military proudly claimed. Just over 51,000 National Guardsmen responded under state control.[35]

Digging deeper, other than the Coast Guard, the federal presence becomes increasingly irrelevant. Over 60,000 people were physically rescued after landfall.[36] A little more than half were rescued by the Coast Guard; the Louisiana National Guard rescued more than 25,000. FEMA claims to have rescued some 6,500, the rescuing done by volunteer urban search and rescue teams that came in from around the country.

More specifically, the Department of Defense says it rescued 2,911 people,[37] two-thirds of them by the helicopters of the USS *Bataan*, a navy amphibious ship that moved on its own initiative and coordinated rescues locally with the Coast Guard from the earliest days.[38] By the morning when President Bush announced the deployment of the 82nd Airborne Division, Louisiana general Landreneau said that his National Guard forces had successfully taken down the last bastion of civil unrest in the city.[39] Honoré agreed.

Twenty thousand federal troops eventually served under Joint Task Force Katrina, but in addition to the 7,200 soldiers and marines whom the president mustered for humanitarian duty after the worst had passed, that number included every pilot and crewman, everyone on a navy ship, every communicator and logistician, every staffer, and in fact everyone in the five-state "joint operating area" assigned to the effort, most of them high and dry. It would be a mistake to imagine that the federal military saved the day. And it would be an even more pernicious error to accept the conventional wisdom of anarchy, insurrection, or insurgency. The pre-landfall evacuation from New Orleans, despite all the criticisms, was twice what the metropolitan area had ever produced.[40] While the city was far from peaceful, its occupants were safer and more disciplined than anyone reported or imagined at the time; some 90 percent of the New Orleans police force stayed on duty, despite the loss of their own homes and concerns about their own families, despite police sleeping in their cars, exhausted, physically and mentally, and 911 operators who attempted to organize assistance despite virtually no communications or support.[41] For all of the horror stories, there were six deaths at the Superdome; none were crime-related. And after a week of hell on earth, there was only one confirmed incident of an attempted violent crime.[42] Four bodies were found at the largely unsupervised and unguarded convention center nearby.[43] The New Orleans coroner estimated eight gunshot victims in the storm and its immediate aftermath; "that's not even a good Saturday night in New Orleans," he said.[44]

"The third provision of the [Insurrection] Act," academics Michael Greenberger and Arianne Spaccarelli later wrote, "is of particular interest in the context of a catastrophe such as Hurricane Katrina, during which a State is unable to provide the basic guarantees of government and public safety to a large number of its residents. In addition to the widespread looting and privations experienced by ordinary citizens left behind in New Orleans, the legal system in the city and state was so devastated by the shortage of police, prison guards, attorneys, and resources that thousands of individuals detained in its jails were deprived of even the basics of constitutional criminal process. Such a governmental collapse arguably deprives citizens of their constitutional right to equal protection of the laws and, if so, justifies unilateral federal intervention under the Insurrection Act."[45] Were it only the case that this was Washington's motivation.

At about 3:30 in the afternoon on Tuesday, March 10, 2009, twenty-eight-year-old Michael McLendon of Kinston, Alabama, started an insane killing spree, shooting his mother before burning down the house they shared, then getting into his red Mitsubishi with an arsenal of guns, heading east to the nearby town of Samson, where he drove up to the front porch of an uncle's house, killed him and two cousins, then killed a young woman and her daughter who were visiting from across the street and critically wounded the woman's four-month-old child. He followed that up by walking next door and killing his seventy-four-year-old grandmother before getting back in his car and driving through the town of 2,000, shooting randomly out the window with two assault rifles, killing a pedestrian and a woman as she walked out of a gas station.

Chased by police, McLendon drove twelve miles farther east on Alabama Route 52 to Geneva, population about 4,400, where he shot and killed a random driver who got in his way on the road, shot at an Alabama state police vehicle, striking it seven times, sprayed bullets at Geneva town police who attempted to set up a roadblock, then turned north on Alabama Route 27 in the direction of Reliable Metal Products, where he had once worked six years earlier. As he ran into the building, McLendon fired an estimated thirty rounds at the police vehicles now congregated in pursuit. After shots were heard from within, police found McLendon lying dead from self-inflicted gunshots.[46]

It took all of one hour: eleven were dead, including McLendon; six were injured, including four officers of the law; Alabama was in shock after the truly senseless killings; cable news had its usual feeding frenzy—and twenty-two soldiers from nearby Fort

Rucker were brought up on charges of violating the *Posse Comitatus* Act.

The 1878 *Posse Comitatus* Act is every government official's favorite excuse: the legal constraint that gets blamed by executive agents and their allies whenever the wishes of the *what-if* crowd are thwarted, a dastardly albatross that explains away failures of responsibility and execution. And it is a political football of the military, thrown around when partisan domestic duties are ordered, and a convenient whipping boy whenever homeland security falters. Military officers, frequently taking their cue from leaders, military and civilian, are just as happy to pay homage to its legendary restrictions whenever they want to limit what they consider mission creep. Meanwhile, in the National Guard's own domestic operations handbook, *Posse Comitatus* has come to "symbolize the separation of civilian affairs from military influence—that is, federal troops."[47] This is a critical point, for the Guard, as a state militia, is exempt from the restrictions of *Posse Comitatus*, and zealously guards that institutional identity—and accentuates its uniqueness, especially when it is fighting for budgets and recognition.

Between these rigid and intransigent battle lines, *Posse Comitatus* is consistently invoked by executive agents as pernicious. This position is often justified by claims that only the federal government has the resources and infrastructure to guide the country through a disaster like Katrina or 9/11. But the more fundamental rationale has much less to do with boots and tarps: executive agents believe that because America is an irrational partisan tinderbox, the archaic law impedes rather than enhances common defense. In an age of constant vigilance, then, *Posse Comitatus* is the enemy.

"The *Posse Comitatus* Act of 1878 prohibit[s] active-duty military from conducting law enforcement within the United States," states President Bush in his memoir *Decision Points* to explain how his hands were tied during Hurricane Katrina.[48] Every fact of American history contradicts Bush's articulation. Even right after the Civil War, even in the face of the act, the army often engaged in disaster response,[49] and it often enforced law and order—sometimes not without controversy, but hardly ever rebuffed when it was available and willing to help.[50] Three successive presidents then used federalized National Guard troops from 1957 to 1963 to enforce civil rights laws against the will of recalcitrant governors. In addition to Eisenhower's September 1957 dispatching of federal troops to Little Rock and federalizing of the entire Arkansas National Guard, under Section 333 of the Insurrection Act, President Kennedy federalized the Alabama National Guard six years later when Governor George Wallace pledged to prevent black students from attending classes at the University of Alabama. Kennedy again federalized National Guard units and used federal troops to assist US marshals at the University of Mississippi from October 1962 through July 1963. Indeed, the record of *Posse Comitatus* is that the very enforcement of civil law that the post-Reconstruction Congress sought to prevent by passing the act *occurred anyhow*,[51] a not-inconsequential affront to many who seek refuge behind the act.

In the years after Kennedy's interventions, federal troops—and the National Guard—not only enforced civil rights but were liberally used for riot control and to suppress political dissent, from Detroit in 1967 through the Democratic National Convention in Chicago in 1968 and into the 1971 riots in Washington, DC.

After a long hiatus, in 1992, Bush's father also federalized the California National Guard and used federal troops—more than 15,000—to quell the Los Angeles riots, upon the request of the Republican governor. Executive agents advised President Bush (and his then secretary of defense, Dick Cheney) to invoke the Insurrection Act. As during Katrina, though, the state's National Guard had already largely stabilized the situation. While it was clear to those on the ground that such stability was precarious, "bewildered and perplexed military attorneys" filled the heads of federal commanders with all sorts of confusing and conflicting information about *Posse Comitatus*. Almost immediately the federal Joint Task Force commander Major General Marvin L. Covault declared that federal troops wouldn't do any policing. "It was not the military's mission to solve Los Angeles's crime problem, nor were we trained to do so," he said.[52]

For the federal military, a lot had changed since the civil rights era: all-volunteer armed forces had been created; the assumption of the counternarcotics mission (and the segregation of that mission) in the 1980s had sharpened the inherent bias against domestic mission creep; civil defense and the Program had gone underground. A decade and a half later in New Orleans, though, the civil disturbance, counternarcotics, and civil defense specialties had congealed into a homeland security constituency. *Posse Comitatus* and some other apparently irrational law prevented a necessary response, the new constituency argued, allies now to those in favor of extraconstitutional intervention. In fact, without someone or some organization standing in the way of order and unity; without chaos and fear (which in the cases of both Los Angeles and New Orleans meant images of blacks "looting" and repeated and amplified rumors of snipers and roving gangs); and without the public's civic ignorance, executive agents have no chance.

On March 18, 2009, in the wake of the McLendon shooting spree eight days earlier in Alabama, the army initiated a formal inquiry to determine whether federal troops had violated the *Posse Comitatus* Act. Twenty-two military policemen led by the base provost marshal had come from Fort Rucker, the 63,000-acre home of army aviation nearby, to assist in traffic control and crime scene security pursuant to a mutual aid agreement signed two years earlier by the Fort Rucker garrison commander and the Geneva

County sheriff. The town of Samson's tiny police force and county officers were stretched to the limit after the shootings, working without a break, without food. However, an inspector general's investigation found that the military personnel had violated the *Posse Comitatus* Act. "The historic tradition of limiting direct military involvement in civilian law enforcement activities, and the requirement of applicable law, do not appear to have been analyzed or considered," the August IG report stated. By establishing traffic control points, the IG concluded, the MPs had "regulated the freedom of movement of civilian persons which served to prohibit those persons from going to where they might desire to go."[53] The local police chief said that he didn't think anyone was actually stopped from doing anything and that the federal troops never had any intention of doing wrong and that no abuses of power had occurred, and even the IG conceded that "the intent was to be a good Army neighbor and help civilian law authorities facing a difficult, unique tragedy affecting the local community."

"One of the creepiest details to emerge in the shooting rampage [in Alabama]," the liberal digital news service Alternet whined about the McLendon case, "were reports that troops from nearby Fort Rucker were brought into Samson and other surrounding areas to patrol the streets." Alternet called this "a clear violation of the *Posse Comitatus* Act, every freedom-loving American's worst nightmare."[54] Yet the criticisms came not only from the left: "Congress has been clear that the use of U.S. troops for civilian police purposes is forbidden," Cybercast News Service—"The Right News. Right Now"—agreed.[55] "Free from Constitutional restraint…military commanders deployed US Army active duty combat troops into the small civilian community of Samson, Alabama last week in a demonstration of their newly received despotic, domestic police power," the equally exercised *JAG Hunter* blog claimed.[56] Bloggers spewed that Obama was treasonous; birthers, survivalists, Tea Party activists all came out of the woodwork to condemn the occupation. (It's all part of the Civil Assistance Plan with Canada to circumvent *Posse Comitatus* by preparing to bring in foreign troops to suppress the American people, wrote Jim Kouri, fifth vice president of something called the National Association of Chiefs of Police.[57])

Asked to comment about the IG's conclusions in the Alabama press, Geoffrey Corn, a retired army lawyer and professor at the South Texas College of Law in Houston, muddled things even more by agreeing with the inspector general and calling the Rucker incident "a slippery slope." Controlling traffic is one thing, he said, "but if you keep going down that daisy chain, you have a soldier that may not be trained with the same practical restraint as a civilian law enforcement officer."[58] This "not trained" argument—that the US military exists to fight the nation's wars and needs to be prepared for that task, not for domestic police work—is the seemingly neutral expression favored by the modern military to justify avoiding getting sucked into imposed domestic tasks. Donald Rumsfeld, notoriously resistant to *his* military being used for anything other than what he wanted, employed a similar argument after Katrina: "Our military had not been organized, trained, or equipped to conduct law enforcement in American cities."[59]

There is some truth to this, but just a little: patrolling the hills of Afghanistan is obviously a different task than piling sandbags or directing traffic. But the specifics of what troops have actually been called upon to do hardly require years of schooling in Arabic dialects or coursework in how to fix reactors on nuclear submarines. Federal troops have always been intended for—and are increasingly being prepared for—both foreign wars and domestic law enforcement. The question asked by Washington's executive agents is not whether federalization *can* be done, but whether such federalizing might help further the argument that a successful government is one that swerves around the Constitution.

CHAPTER FIVE

The Garden Plot

*Widespread civil violence inside the United States would force
the defense establishment to reorient priorities in extremis to
defend basic domestic order and human security. Deliberate
employment of weapons of mass destruction or other catastrophic
capabilities, unforeseen economic collapse, loss of functioning
political and legal order, purposeful domestic resistance or
insurgency, pervasive public health emergencies, and
catastrophic natural and human disasters are all paths to
disruptive domestic shock.[1]*
KNOWN UNKNOWNS: UNCONVENTIONAL "STRATEGIC SHOCKS"
IN DEFENSE STRATEGY DEVELOPMENT, NOVEMBER 2008

The executive agents who have decided that the Constitution is an impediment have shown great awareness of the fact that, at the end of the day, the primary tool for ensuring their preferred outcomes is the military. The evolution of the internal (as opposed to foreign) role of federal troops is complex and often intentionally confusing. One way to obscure who's in control is to make certain it is obscure who's in control.

On August 25, 2005, when Hurricane Katrina was just crossing the state of Florida, four days before it made landfall in Louisiana, while the Bush administration was still on vacation, the 3rd Brigade of the 82nd Airborne Division at Fort Bragg received a warning order: be prepared to move to New Orleans.[2]

The selection of the "All-Americans" wasn't by chance, and it had nothing to do with President Bush's later call for them to take up humanitarian duties. Since the Korean War, the 82nd has been designated the vanguard of a "strategic reserve," the force that would be called out in a crisis or for missions other than big wars, which it was: in the Dominican Republic, Nicaragua, Grenada, Panama.

The 82nd was also part of a very special quick-reaction force with unique duties on American soil.[3] Known as the Civil Disturbance Task Force,[4] over the years it has also gone by the names Joint Task Force 250, Joint Task Force 140, Task Force Washington, and Joint Task Force MACDIS, the last an entity with an inscrutable acronym standing for "Military Assistance for Civil Disturbances." The task force has no permanent headquarters and formalizes and expands as the situation demands. Furthermore, the Civil Disturbance Task Force is actually five task forces: one responsible for maintaining two federal brigades in readiness for an incident in the continental United States; one responsible for action solely in the nation's capital; a third held in reserve for both reinforcements and the possibility of multiple events occurring at the same time;[5] and two additional and separate task forces, one each for Alaska and Hawaii.[6] Under this arrangement, a domestic quick-reaction force has been on 24/7 alert every day of the year for more than five decades, with a subunit of 300 to 500 men required to move in less than six hours if a civil disturbance seems likely.[7]

Today, the 82nd isn't the only active-duty military unit assigned this mission—other brigades and battalions from the XVIII Airborne Corps at Fort Bragg; from the III Corps at Fort Hood, Texas; and from the marine corps[8] are also assigned task force duty,[9] but the 82nd—"America's 911 Force," as they've dubbed themselves—is the unit that is most widely known and visible, and one of the few that speaks openly of its otherwise sensitive tasking. Like all of the units earmarked for action under the

Civil Disturbance Task Force—and completely contrary to the utterances of Donald Rumsfeld and others during Hurricane Katrina—the 82nd receives specialized civil disturbance training and is issued special equipment to carry out its domestic mission, from nonlethal weapons to pepper spray and tear gas.[10] These are hardly just nineteen-year-old marines with guns.

The task force is also completely lawyered up. As duty in New Orleans approached, specialized attorneys drafted the language of the 82nd Airborne's formal orders so that the mission, regardless of any confusion in Washington or fighting between the president and the governor, would fully comply with the Constitution and the law. "The situation in the areas affected by Hurricane Katrina has exceeded the capabilities of State and Local Authorities," the unit's orders said, creating the conditions to preempt a state request and providing the legal wording that might accompany a presidential decision. Justifying self-defense, the orders added, "Civil unrest/disorder presents a clear and present threat to troops deploying into the area of operations." And the Fourth Amendment was covered as well: Paragraph 3.E.1.M of the orders made it crystal clear that: "Unless specifically authorized, personnel will not participate in activities that constitute search, seizure or arrest of individuals, participation in pursuit or surveillance activities, investigation, interrogation, evidence collection and/or security functions or crowd control."[11]

General Honoré added his own admonition in a fragmentary order ("FRAGO") that made it clear that forced evacuation of anyone from their home, if they didn't want to leave, was a law enforcement action and thereby prohibited: "No JTF Katrina task force service member will perform or assist with any type of forced evacuation of any citizen in the AO [area of operations]."[12]

National security was covered, too: use of force was authorized to protect and defend the full panoply of assets designated by the president as "vital to the national defense," including the vague catch-all of critical infrastructure.[13] The orders also required every battalion to deploy an antiterrorism officer just in case they encountered al Qaeda in New Orleans.[14]

The modern-day civil disturbance mission emerged in 1967, when domestic orders for federal troops shifted from enforcing legislation—as they had done from 1957 to 1963 in the South, forcing states to implement decisions made by federal courts—to, at least in theory, protecting states against internal domestic violence, which was the constitutional justification to call out National Guard and federal troops.

Organizationally, the army, as the dominant military service, had been assigned "primary responsibility" for the United States as a theater of war in 1956. In what was probably one of the strangest bureaucratic moves ever to happen in Washington, where claiming control is as involuntary as breathing, the Joint Chiefs as a body even expressly "dealt themselves out of a role" in domestic matters, giving the army as executive agent wide military latitude, no small expression of an attitude among the other services—and of plenty within the army—that policing America was beneath the modern fighting man.[15] The secretary of the army was designated the "executive agent" for domestic missions and given overall Defense Department responsibility, despite contrary fighting doctrine, retaining that power even after the service secretaries were stripped of their operational duties in the 1958 statutory reorganization of the department, retaining the function even after passage of the 1986 Goldwater-Nichols act, which required *all* military forces to fall under a joint combatant commander. In the early years, the four-star army vice chief of staff was personally engaged as the "action agent" for the executive agent, a man of sufficient rank to deal with his civilian counterparts in government.

The army created a Directorate for Civil Disturbance Planning and Operations to handle the mission, an organization renamed the Directorate of Military Support on September 1, 1970.[16] Though the name change was intended to make the organization seem more innocuous, DOMS, as it became known, sounded suspiciously domestic, maybe even a bit taboo.

The military *plan* for quelling civil disturbance was originally Operations Plan 563, which was issued soon after military commanders sent to Mississippi reported back that they were blindsided by a lack of intelligence (or indeed a lack of plans) when they were ordered to take up arms in support of civil rights. OPLAN 563 was replaced by a second plan, nicknamed Steep Hill, which was approved on September 4, 1963, creating a standard for having specialized units, rather than the nearest unit to any event, assume the job as civil disturbance first responder. The Steep Hill plan was refined and renamed Garden Plot in June 1967.[17]

The Detroit riots of 1967 were the transitional point,[18] "the first time that federal troops were deployed to assist in a racially motivated disturbance outside the South in a quarter century,"[19] the first time a governor had *requested* federal troops since 1943.[20] The riots broke out in the early-morning hours of July 23 following a Saturday-night police raid on a black club. Michigan's Republican governor (and presidential hopeful) George Romney brought in state troopers and mobilized the state's 46th Infantry Division to augment the police. Romney instructed the Michigan National Guard to use whatever force was necessary to restore order. As one study recounts:

> Guardsmen were issued ammunition and were ordered to fire when fired upon and to shoot looters if they could not find an alternate means of stopping them.... As instructed, the untested and fearful soldiers of the Michigan National Guard took to the streets and, literally, executed their

orders. Detroit was soon a veritable battle ground in which supposed representatives of law and order—the Michigan National Guard—acted as if looters were a foreign enemy. What transpired was comparable to the legendary vigilantes of Dodge City of the 1860s—lawlessness, chaos, and a total disregard for restraint by the National Guard.[21]

There was considerable back-and-forth between Michigan and Washington over the deployment of federal troops to stabilize a situation evidently made worse by the police and the National Guard. President Johnson finally agreed to call in the 82nd Airborne Division and federalized the Michigan Guard under the provisions of the Insurrection Acts, but not without considerable hesitation. The combat-experienced troops of the 82nd Airborne immediately proved far more capable than their National Guard counterparts, who also happened to be 98.7 percent white, compared to the (relatively) integrated active force.[22]

Garden Plot (like DOMS, its name could be interpreted as homey or as a grand conspiracy) emerged just a month before the riots in Detroit, defining every *this* and *that* of who was responsible and making it clear that the military was always subordinate to civil authority, going into details on who would pay for what and what reports needed to be submitted. As for what the troops would do on the ground, well, it was a plan but not a military strategy, because, well, there was no military strategy.

Detroit made that clear. From the very beginning of deliberations, President Johnson set up his own command structure and ordered minimal force, selecting Lieutenant General John L. Throckmorton, commander of the XVIII Corps at Fort Bragg, because, as he put it, he did not want a "hero" of the Douglas MacArthur type "riding…on [a] white horse."[23] Throckmorton also had the most unusual chain of command, reporting to the president through his explicit and direct representative on the ground—Cyrus Vance, the future secretary of state who was former general counsel at the Pentagon, secretary of the army in the Kennedy administration, and deputy secretary of defense in the Johnson administration. Executive agent Vance was a private citizen, having left government service a month earlier, before being recalled to XYZ service, now officially called the "presidential emissary."[24]

When Throckmorton arrived in the Motor City, he immediately ordered the National Guard to unload its weapons and only fire if ordered to by an officer (an order that met considerable resistance from local police and Michigan guard leadership). It was better to let a looter get away with some goods than to shoot a man, the general said. It was clear right from the beginning that reports of snipers were wildly exaggerated, and every random shot or car backfire had provoked a fusillade from the police and National Guard. Throckmorton's cool head and the 82nd troopers' restraint stabilized the situation, that is, after the rioting exhausted itself.

Throckmorton later had to defend his approach of maximum restraint to members of Congress, many defending the Guard and bellowing that soldiers should never be put in a position where they are left defenseless, that they were trained to kill. The general responded that the situation in Detroit had not been, contrary to media reports, "red hot" and that he had no intention of "having any of those soldiers shoot innocent people, or small children," describing the very nonmilitary bearing of the Michigan guardsmen and justifying his decisions. "I considered the best way to handle the situation, which to my mind was not red hot at all—was to have them not load their rifles."[25] In the end, the expenditure of bullets was 700 shots fired by National Guardsmen to every one shot by the regular army, a number that speaks volumes.[26]

Every potential and actual domestic use of federal troops over the next four years of racial and political unrest was equally ad hoc and equally charged,[27] especially because the performance of the Vietnam-era Guard left so much to be desired. "After the Guard's poor showing in Newark and Detroit during the summer of 1967 numerous questions arose about the professionalism of the National Guard," one scholar says. "It was believed that not only were they poorly trained, but they were also too close to the problem to be separated from it. In other words, they, for the most part, shared the prejudices and discriminatory practices of the local populace. Thus, they were an extension of the segregated society, with vast arsenals and permission to impose as much force as was deemed necessary."[28]

As the Vietnam War waned, though, the regular army started an important transition to professionalism and an all-volunteer force; for the professional fighting man, that meant an increasing wariness of anything that might tarnish the image. Not much was heard again about the domestic role for almost a decade—that is, until 1981, when Congress passed the Military Cooperation with Civilian Law Enforcement Agencies Act, stating that "the rising tide of drugs being smuggled into the United States...presents a grave threat to all Americans," one that civilian law enforcement could not effectively deal with.[29] Caspar Weinberger, then secretary of defense, opposed Pentagon involvement, arguing that drugs were not a vital American interest—that is, that they didn't threaten the common defense in the way the framers of the Constitution meant when consenting to a federal military—and additionally making the war-fighting argument that conducting such operations would diminish the military's ability to provide for the common defense. "Reliance on military forces to accomplish civilian tasks is detrimental to both military readiness and democratic process," he said, succeeding in at least imposing some resource limits on the extent of Defense Department participation but overall losing the war.[30] Over time, Paul McHale has said,

"Many senior DOD leaders—civilian and uniformed military alike—believed that providing support to civilian authorities was a mission of secondary importance. Yes, it had to be done, but only if forces could be spared from more important overseas combat missions, and even then with remaining doubt that DOD should be doing it at all."[31]

Fully embracing the so-called Weinberger doctrine, the Defense Department fenced off drug missions and the residual Garden Plot tasking as a special and separate activity, establishing a Joint Task Force solely responsible for lending counterdrug support and segregating civil disturbance and other domestic intervention missions. (These would, not surprisingly, be the very organizations, and the very people, who would take up the homeland defense and domestic involvement flag after 9/11.)

From the early 1960s through 9/11, there were five different domestic "joint" commands, every one headed by an army general, but every one also so anomalous and controversial with the military at large that each lasted no more than a few years.[32] The composition and flowchart placement of the various army organizations responsible for the domestic missions also shifted and changed, almost as if those directing the effort needed to burrow underground to survive.

But while the Big Army generally distanced itself from domestic duty, it was also big enough that a domestic-oriented constituency separately developed. By the time terrorists struck the World Trade Center and the Pentagon, the army had plans and units to provide civil support to states when requested, to support the war on drugs, to assist with emergency federal needs and continuity of government efforts, and to provide "consequence management" and emergency civil defense in the aftermath of a disaster. The employment of special operations forces to thwart the use of weapons of mass destruction on domestic soil was part of a search for a way to competently conduct missions that inevitably would be ordered, while at the same time adhering to the ideal of making certain that the federal military did not have undue influence over domestic affairs.

The terminology used to describe such missions evolved and devolved countless times, from insurrection to rebellion and unlawful obstructions, to domestic violence, to riots and disorders, to violence and disorder, to obstruction (in the case of a recalcitrant state), back to domestic violence and to civil disturbance again.[33] There was the mission of disaster relief[34] and military assistance to safety and traffic[35] and military support to civil defense,[36] which begat cooperation with civilian law enforcement,[37] which begat civil emergency assistance[38] and then support to disasters[39] and then civil emergency management[40] and then domestic support operations[41] and then national security emergency preparedness,[42] only to beget military support to civil authorities[43] and then military assistance to civil authorities[44] and then military assistance to domestic consequence management[45] and then military support to civilian operations[46] and then defense support of civil authorities. Dealing with civil disturbances[47] begat employment of military resources in the event of civil disturbances,[48] which begat defense support for civil disturbances[49] and finally settled at civil disturbance operations. Each riot, each natural disaster, each new piece of legislation, each new administration, each new secretary, each new commission—all of them added to an alphabet soup of diverse missions and doctrines—CAAP, MACA,[50] MAST, MSCA, MSCD, MACDIS, and MSCLEA—on and on, each with its own regulations and specialized training and its own plan (in the stovepipe, as the military likes to say) separate and coequal, known and understood only by those tasked to do each obscure job and ultimately fully overseen and controlled only by executive agents.

In the immediate aftermath of 9/11, Rumsfeld designated Secretary of the Army Thomas White as the "interim executive agent for homeland security" to extend his duties.[51] Of the mission, White said: "I define and view homeland security as having two principal elements. First there is homeland defense, a Department of Defense–led task involving protection of the United States in every dimension—land, sea, aerospace and protection from computer network attack. Second is civil support, where DOD provides assistance to a lead federal agency, which can range from the FBI for domestic counter-terrorism tasks to [the Department of] Health and Human Services for biological attacks."[52]

Though the Pentagon didn't yet have an officially approved definition of "homeland defense,"[53] later elaborations made it clear that the phrase meant defending the United States against *external threats*.[54] As for the second mission, White was referring to those XYZ circumstances in which ground operations might be required for homeland defense inside the United States as well, but still it was against external attack. So in fact his description "civil support" was completely mistaken: the use of federal troops as a backup when state and local capabilities are overwhelmed—officially called military support to civil authorities (MSCA) and renamed defense support to civil authorities (DSCA) after 9/11 to obscure the word "military"—is an ABC mission within the legitimate confines of the Constitution, requiring either a state governor or a legislature to make a formal request for help. Secretary White, though, was talking about something else, where different rules applied. Homeland defense thus acquired a dual—and rather unfortunate—connotation, amalgamating the actual defense of the United States against an *external* enemy with the various and confusing internal XYZ tasks, some of which fell under Garden Plot, some of which did not.[55]

When the joint Northern Command was activated in 2003 to

tend to the new homeland defense mission, it began the long process of bringing the Garden Plot plan[56]—along with a slew of
obsolete defense policy directives on ABC and XYZ military
intervention relating to domestic law enforcement, spying, and
command—up to date.[57] A newly created assistant secretary of
defense for homeland defense in the Pentagon at the same time
took over executive agent duties from the secretary of the army;
and DOMS became JDOMS, the Joint Director of Military Support, moving to the Joint Staff.[58] The army's long traditional connection and responsibility were officially severed, except that
almost every aspect of *the doing* fell back upon the army, just where
it had always been.

A year before Katrina, NORTHCOM held a planners' workshop to discuss Military Assistance for Civil Disturbances (MAC-
DIS), the central question being how to harmonize the decade-old
Garden Plot plan with the public's "recently acquired" reluctance
to use troops for law enforcement.[59] Even after 9/11, none of the
basic precepts were in question: MACDIS was still predicated as
support of civil authority, and the lead federal agency in law
enforcement was considered to be the Department of Justice (which
had designated the FBI for terrorism-related matters). The participants of the workshop weren't afraid to address the post-9/11 conditions and the "twenty-first-century" challenges they now faced: what
to do if there was a large-scale anti-Muslim backlash in America, or
violence directed against the population along the Mexican border,
or civil disobedience or domestic violence following a quarantine of
nuclear or biologically infected areas. The clear consensus was that
the National Guard would be the first responder and that federal
troops would only step in when the National Guard was inadequate
or exhausted. Strategies were openly discussed for how to minimize armed confrontation with the civilian population. In one presentation, "old think" was labeled as "stomp and drag, confrontation,

intimidation and pursue." "New think," forged by 9/11 and the transformation of the professional force as well as years of combat experience, was defined as "stand-off (shape battlespace), avoid confrontation, security, and cordon." Other new terminology was batted about: "containment" over "quarantine," "preresponse" to describe sensitive actions, the more neutral "civilian response" instead of "civil disturbance."

The workshop participants concluded that MACDIS now encompassed four specific and separate contingencies: unplanned response to domestic civil disturbances, heavily prepared actions during special events (i.e., protests), actions during domestic terrorist events, and protection of "DOD Key Assets," both on and off military bases. MACDIS would exist within a hierarchy of sorts: non–law enforcement and pure civil support duties one step below, pandemics and maritime security in the middle, and the full-blown homeland defense mission triggered by an invasion or during any of the lesser missions if "enemy forces" appeared.[60]

That November, NORTHCOM issued its Planning Order for MACDIS. The stated mission was:

> Military support to the Department of Justice, enforces federal authority, suppresses in a State, any insurrection, civil disorder, domestic violence, obstruction, unlawful combination, or conspiracy, and assists civil authorities to restore law and order as directed by the Secretary of Defense in consult [sic] with the Attorney General.

Deployment of federal troops would "deter opportunistic terrorist attacks" during domestic crises, the order declared. Under "Commander's Intent," it said that the military should deploy and enforce civil law, all while maintaining public trust and confidence in the armed forces.[61] Involving federal forces in thwarting an armed invasion—"homeland defense"—was undoubtedly an ABC mission; the fine print was what and when a terrorist attack (or even a threat) crossed that threshold, and how much XYZ preparations were needed in day-to-day America. The three missions of counterdrugs (law enforcement), civil disturbance, and counterterrorism overlapped, the sequential steps undertaken to deal with each—and stay within legal and constitutional constraints on the role of the military—becoming the American Coup.

The following July, a month before Katrina, Secretary Rumsfeld signed new Standing Rules for the Use of Force (SRUF)—consolidated rules of engagement for domestic contingencies—canceling the Rules for the Use of Force (RUF) contained in the old Garden Plot plan and other previous plans and regulations.[62] The new Joint Chiefs of Staff order covered "fundamental policies and procedures," from routine military functions of antiterrorism and force protection, to counterdrug operations, to military assistance to civil authorities in nonthreatening environments, to Civil Disturbance Operations (CDO)[63]—another proposed name change for MACDIS—and extending all along the spectrum of domestic missions through protection of critical infrastructure and "land homeland defense." A series of classified appendices dealt with specific actions to take under different circumstances.[64] And the directive made clear that despite its comprehensiveness, it negated none of the mission-specific rules for the use of force that had already been established for special operations, all of which continued to exist between the lines.[65]

There was a significant internal debate regarding the wisdom of combining the "permissive" overseas rules with the "restrictive" domestic ones, the danger being that the latter's restrictions on the use of deadly force—indeed, the overall concept of applying "minimum force"—might lead to overcompensation on the part of commanders—and thus added dangers—in universal situations of self-defense.[66] Dense and impenetrable, the rules were exactly the opposite of what was intended through their rewriting.[67]

As a result, after so much careful consideration, the basic conundrum of martial life could not be resolved. Rules of engagement for combat overseas were the military bread and butter of how to fight and kill the enemy, based on the Law of Armed Conflict and common international law. Rules for the use of force against civilians on US territory, on the other hand, were based on domestic law, specifically the Fourth Amendment.[68] Whatever the Standing Rules for the Use of Force said, whatever operations plans said, whatever special directives from the secretary or even from the president himself, even whatever was in the most secret of envelopes, federal troops had to be "grounded in the Constitutional role of the Executive Branch of government, and tempered by the constitutionally protected civil rights as listed in the Bill of Rights," as one military officer wrote.[69]

The most confusing element of the new Standing Rules for the Use of Force inside the United States was the decision by the Pentagon lawyers to apply the language of international law to the domestic mission.[70] Such was the product of decades of debate and intrusions, the path trod from the Detroit riots to the present day. And the major obstacles to this subversion of the Constitution had been cleared away by the constant, increasingly loud blaring of alarm Klaxons by the executive agents of the national security community. An urban riot was a problem, but more or less a local one, containable. But a terrorist attack that caused massive damage—well, that was a different story, at least to them. In a matter of decades, America had literally become an undifferentiated battlefield. The forever war had arrived.

Chapter Six

All Hell Breaks Down

The Federal civil defense law was written before the advent of the hydrogen bomb and the recent striking advances in methods of delivering modern weapons. This law must be realistically revised. Plans to meet post-attack situations are, of course, essential, but the Federal Civil Defense Administration needs authority to carry out necessary pre-attack preparations as well. It must be enabled to assure adequate participation in the civil defense program. It must be empowered to work out logical plans for possible target areas which overlap state and municipal boundaries....
President Dwight Eisenhower, 1956[1]

I n the beginning, it was just germ weapons, gas, poison gas, biological weapons, bioweapons, and chemical weapons; then came Gadget; Trinity, Little Boy, the fission bomb, the atomic bomb, the A-bomb, the plutonium bomb, the nuclear bomb; Super; the fusion bomb, the hydrogen bomb, the H-bomb; atomic weapons; nuclear weapons, hydronuclear weapons, thermonuclear weapons; warheads, nukes, bunker busters; bombs with the explosive power of one thousand tons of TNT, of one million tons, of ten million tons, of megatons; backpack-sized special atomic demolition munitions; improvised nuclear devices; radiological weapons; tactical nuclear weapons; enhanced radiation (ER) weapons, neutron bombs, nonstrategic nuclear weapons; radiological dispersal devices; atomic, biological, and chemical (ABC) weapons; nuclear, biological, and chemical (NBC) weapons; chemical, biological, and radiological (CBR) weapons; chemical, biological, radiological, and nuclear (CBRN) weapons; chemical, biological, radiological, nuclear, and high-yield explosives (CBRNE); biological, nuclear, incendiary, chemical and explosive (BNICE) weapons; weapons of mass destruction (the Soviet epithet for America's arsenal); weapons of mass destruction (the American epithet for everyone else's arsenal), weapon of mass effect, and on and on. They are bad, all bad; real bad. So we need to be ready—but how much preparation for preventing WMD do we need if we are neglecting greater dangers?

The first incident: on October 18, 2001, three days after an anthrax-laced letter arrived in Senate offices and after others were opened at the *New York Post* and NBC News at Rockefeller Center in New York, Dick Cheney thought he might die. As he was on his way to visit ground zero in New York for the first time since 9/11, the White House Situation Room called to report that biological sensors installed around the White House grounds detected botulinum toxin. "If the result was confirmed, it could mean the president and I, members of the White House staff, and probably scores of others...had been exposed to one of the most lethal substances known to man," Cheney recalls. "A single gram, evenly dispersed and inhaled," he said, could kill a million people.[2]

The filters from the aerosol sensors were carefully bagged and rushed to a Lawrence Livermore National Laboratory outpost that had quietly moved into space at the Walter Reed Army Medical Center, literally a mile up 16th Street from the White House. There the scientists would determine the nature and origin of the triggering pathogen.[3]

President Bush was on a state visit to China, and it fell to the vice president to inform him via secure videoteleconference that he and others might have been exposed. "Mr. President," Cheney intoned, "White House biological detectors have registered the presence of botulinum toxin, and there is no reliable antidote. Those of us who have been exposed to it could die."[4]

Secretary of State Colin Powell, who was traveling with the president and was in the room during the call, sank back in his chair, calculating his time left on Earth.[5]

"I didn't particularly want to die in China," National Security Advisor Condoleezza Rice later wrote of her thoughts at the time.[6]

The second incident: almost a year later, the 708-foot M/V *Palermo Senator* motored into New York harbor as the midnight hour approached, its twenty-four-man crew eagerly awaiting dry land after completing a 3,800-mile transit from Spain. The Liberian-flagged container ship was finishing its usual circuit from the Far East through the Mediterranean Sea and across the Atlantic Ocean, laden with a hodgepodge of products for the American market.[7] A coast guard law enforcement team boarded the *Palermo Senator* to conduct a standard inspection—standard except that it was also September 10, 2002, the day before the first anniversary of the World Trade Center attacks, and President Bush was scheduled to appear at a memorial service the next day at Ellis Island, just six miles away from where the *Palermo Senator* was to dock.

Tom Ridge, the head of the Office of Homeland Security in the White House, declared the anniversary observances a "national security special event"; for public consumption, the homeland security alert level was raised from yellow to orange: "The US intelligence community has received information, based on debriefings of a senior al Qaeda operative, of possible terrorist attacks timed to coincide with the anniversary of the September 11th attacks on the United States," the White House said in a statement.[8]

The Coast Guard boarding went off without incident, and the

vessel was authorized to proceed into New York harbor for an 8 a.m. arrival at Berth 92 at the Port Newark/Elizabeth Marine Terminal. The boarding report—coast guard form 4100—noted unexplained sounds coming from a container below and recommended further investigation in port: perhaps it was stowaways, a common enough event. The Captain of the Port for New York—the senior federal official—ordered a joint boarding by the Port Authority Police; US Customs, Immigration and Naturalization; and the FBI Newark office. Since the Department of Energy had a radiation detection team in New York for the 9/11 anniversary, it was also invited to participate; it would at the least be a good opportunity to test equipment.

The radiation team arrived from Manhattan at midmorning and took its readings. At 1 p.m., the team leader told the on-scene commander that the instruments indicated abnormal levels. FBI and military watch centers in Washington were immediately notified, and the FBI special agent in charge of the Newark Field Office called his boss, an assistant director, who reported the anomaly to the White House. Executive agents on duty there immediately slid into crisis mode, automatically designating the FBI as the "lead federal agency" and automatically triggering the crisis management contingency plan.[9]

It was the day before the first anniversary of 9/11, and a radiation alert in New York City was a scenario that could have come right out of a movie. But it wasn't quite the stuff of Hollywood, with some dashing G-man combining brilliance and biceps directly updating the president while nimble fingers hastily coaxed desperately needed information from computer systems and databases. However, watch officers did pick up real-world versions of red phones and did alert some specialized team, whose heroes promptly hopped into waiting vehicles to be shuttled to rotor-whirling helicopters.

The third incident: as the floodwaters of Hurricane Katrina were receding in 2005, a mysterious figure known only as Akhtir, from the Baluchistan region of Pakistan, finished developing the final components of two radiological dispersal devices—"dirty bombs"—and readied them for shipping. The shadowy Akhtir's college degree and background in science made him especially worrisome to American intelligence.

It took months of negotiations and preparation, and a ton of money, but a man named Cherrad, one of the senior operatives of the Islamic terrorist organization known only as EZ, arranged the delivery of the two nuclear cores stolen from the arsenal of the former Soviet Union. They were moved by truck through Iran to the Pakistani coast, where Akhtir's job was to fabricate the uranium spheres into improvised explosive devices. Once two senior operatives known as Ebrahim and Husseini finished their training, the EZ plan was to transfer the devices to Mexico and then on to the United States for simultaneous detonation, one on the West Coast, one in Washington, DC. Cherrad arranged for a Greek freighter captain to be bribed, and Ebrahim accompanied the deadly cargo to a small port in southern Mexico, aided by the Sinvergüenza Cartel and its established drug-smuggling channels. While the two weapons were stored in a warehouse—one called New Dayton and the other Landport—Akhtir calculated just how much plastic and water were needed to shield radiation emissions while the weapons were in storage and how to mask the emissions altogether when crossing the American border. Two months later, after meticulously packing a truck-trailer with bags of kitty litter to mask New Dayton, a Sinvergüenza operative drove the bomb-laden eighteen-wheeler across the border between ports of entry in Texas, meeting up with Ebrahim on the other side, smuggled in by a *coyote* known for his skill and his high prices. Once Husseini arrived, he would take possession of Landport and accompany the device across Mexico to a charter vessel headed for Oregon.

The recruited suicide martyrs, Abbas Fahim and Badi Al Tayyib, arrived in the United States from Pakistan on student visas, clearing immigration without suspicion. New Dayton was safely stowed away in a suburban Maryland safe house, and once Ebrahim met up with the bombers, he sent an e-mail to EZ Central Command notifying them that the "reception" was ready. A day later, he received a response: detonation was to take place at 9 p.m. East Coast time on July 4, simultaneous with Husseini's arrival on the West Coast.

False alarm?

From the dawn of the nuclear era, scenarios of a nuclear or biological attack have been the driving force of both those committed to the ABCs and the executive agents of the XYZs, a *what-if* burrowing deeply into the American psyche. It doesn't really matter at what point you enter the theater—the Soviet explosion in 1949, China, bomber and missile gaps, the brink in 1962, Israel's boldness or Pakistan's counter, Iraq's genocide; South African, Libyan, North Korean, or Iranian defiance, al Qaeda, Iraq's demise—the nightmare never ends. Indeed, the only tangible medication ends up being the science of size, lethality, detection, and protection. The rest is just psychology and terror.

The incident on October 18, 2001, was real; the *Palermo Senator* alert was real; the EZ conspiracy was a fictional scenario for a national preparedness exercise held in 2007. Each plays its part in the drama and each tells a tale of between-the-lines.

Here's how the real world works: on the first anniversary of 9/11, the *Palermo Senator* was ordered to return to sea once radiation was detected, but it had to wait for the next high tide to make it through the Kill van Kull, the waterway between Staten Island and Bayonne, and that wasn't going to be until 11:30 p.m. The ship was then escorted back out to sea to an exclusion zone off-shore, with FBI sharpshooters and a coast guard maritime security team on the scene, but pretty much nothing else to be instantly done. The reason was that the *Palermo Senator* held about 1,200 metal shipping containers, some forty feet long, in fifteen rows of thirteen containers each, some stacked ten deep, some above deck and some below.

Once back out in New York harbor, the coast guard cutter *Escanaba*, together with New York and New Jersey state police boats, provided overwatch while plans were put together to transport twenty-five people and two tons of equipment in eight-foot seas to the target ship (the *Palermo Senator* had no helicopter deck). Even though the Department of Energy had radiation specialists on the scene, a "PDD-39" event (one of several secret presidential directive types) meant mobilization of a tailored domestic emergency support team, including the FBI's hazardous materials response unit from Quantico, Virginia; the technical specialists would initially deal with whatever was found.[10] Responders also included the Nuclear Emergency Search Team—called NEST—the main components coming from New Mexico and Nevada. Armed support was provided by a military weapons of mass destruction "render safe" team and an *in extremis* unit called JSOTF (pronounced j-so-tiff), the Joint Special Operations Task Force, which was made up predominantly of navy SEALs, who deployed from their Norfolk-area base. The Los Alamos NEST members were the last to arrive, at 10 p.m. on the night of the eleventh.

Eight federal departments, nine local agencies, and a dozen local police departments had their work cut out for them. The search would begin at first light the next morning, just as soon as a unified command meeting oriented the intergovernmental gaggle and all the paperwork and coordination was complete. Lawyers in Washington were contacting the German owner of the ship and the South Korean shipping company that operated it.

At 12:30 p.m. on September 12, the DEST and the Coast Guard commenced boarding, at least according to statements released to the press. The news media gave the incident its usual treatment, heightening the gravity of the danger and massacring most of the facts before dropping the story altogether when details at eleven fizzled: TV and radio and Internet reporting said an intelligence tip had alerted the Coast Guard, that the ship had been boarded as it approached New York because it had already been identified as a "high threat vessel" with known cargo from the Middle East, that Iraq was somehow involved—thus confirming that Saddam had nuclear weapons. The deployment of navy SEALs, never officially mentioned in any government statement but quickly leaked, was particularly headline-worthy, partly demonstrating America's fascination with its secret operators, partly providing hopeful imagery that the military (or somebody) had arrived to save the day, but in the end even the SEALs were not enough to sustain attention.[11]

Sixty hours and thirty minutes elapsed from the moment when the *Palermo Senator* was initially boarded and its entrance into New York harbor and its inspection. By then President Bush had come and gone from New York and the 9/11 anniversary had passed as well. Technicians—some moon-suited and taking nothing for granted and others in their normal uniforms—worked through most of the day and night, finally isolating the radioactive source: a shipment of ceramic roofing tiles emitting natural ionizing radiation from trace elements of thorium. The *Palermo Senator* was cleared at noon on September 13 to proceed once again into port and unload its cargo: mission accomplished.

The "hot wash" of the incident—the government's afteraction report—produced a long list of deficiencies: despite all of the information-sharing and dot-connecting that supposedly blossomed after 9/11, data on tracking and identifying the shipping containers already in the hands of the customs service was never passed along; there was little real-time intelligence on ships entering New York despite the 9/11 anniversary, the national alert status, and the national security special event that had been declared; the FBI, though in the lead, was only one of a dozen agencies reporting simultaneously to Washington, each agency's situation report contradicting others, creating a confounding picture; the Coast Guard was wholly unprepared for the scenario and neither the FBI nor the Coast Guard had the assets to perform a forcible boarding of the ship at sea; there were no protocols for radiation assessment before the ship entered port; detection equipment meant for land use was too bulky to get onto the ship and too sensitive to use at sea. Despite clear instructions from the attorney general placing the FBI in charge and a classified presidential directive implementing plans, there was confusion regarding who was in charge and way too many agencies became involved; state and local officials lacked security clearances and could not be let in on the full operation; it was unclear to those on the scene who was in the lead at the city and state levels; and communications between state-level responding agencies was lacking, particularly in the seam between New York and New Jersey.

One might ask how such an incident could happen a *year after* 9/11, nine months after the customs service unveiled its Container Security Initiative, which promised that ships would be inspected at foreign ports to thwart these very possibilities. One might ask how a foreign ship was allowed to sit in the middle of the nation's largest metropolitan area for eighteen hours before radiation was even detected. And then, one might ask how it took almost three days from arrival before a full inspection took place; and even then, how a ship that authorities thought might have a nuclear weapon on board could be taken less than ten miles offshore.

Indeed, one might ask, and it would be an uncomfortable grilling. Nevertheless, presumably all the asking would result in an orgy of improvement: rewriting directives and plans, beefing up response teams, enhancing equipment and training. The failure, in fact, would be treated like most other government bungles, as an opportunity to do better, and it was: America is so vast, with its largest city on one coast and the second largest on another, that preparing for this "no fail" weapons of mass destruction mission requires not just supernatural logistics but a far more massive blanket than was available that day. If terrorists manage to obtain or crudely build and smuggle a nuclear device into the country; or if they prepare a biological agent to spread in the middle of Washington or at a teeming sports stadium or through a city water system, the government has to get the warning in enough time to deploy to any location from Maine to Florida to Hawaii, and then it has to perform miracles. There are the imponderables that can't be resolved merely through spending more money or reorganizing and rewriting: what if that specific ship *were* carrying some kind of nuke hidden in a shipping container, one with a timer? Could the FBI, military explosive ordnance disposal experts, or the navy SEALs have prevented an explosion, had there been a nuke, had they found it in time?

The EZ scenario was written by FEMA and an intergovernmental team for exercise TOPOFF 4—TOPOFF standing for Top Officials—held from October 15 to 19, 2007. TOPOFF 4 is one of thousands of exercises and war games constantly running, the scenarios right out of the movies, but each meant to test the government in realistic ways, to find flaws and inconsistencies and thus serve as platforms for improvement.[12] Most of the TOPOFF 4 exercise ran at the unclassified level and involved practicing communications and mobilization, and indoctrinating the various cleanup crews and first responders in the procedures to be followed after a WMD detonation or spread. As the State of Oregon announced reassuringly to its citizens, "This full-scale exercise will give state and local emergency management and response agencies the opportunity to test plans, procedures and equipment, while focusing on the following capabilities: evacuation/shelter-in-place, mass care, mass prophylaxis and communications. State and local participants will also benefit from close interaction with the federal government, voluntary organizations, international partners and the private sector."[13]

The publicly released and official scenario for TOPOFF 4 included three dirty bombs, one in Oregon, one in Phoenix, and one on the island of Guam, all slated to be detonated. But hidden from public view was also a fourth, EZ's New Dayton in Washington, the star of separately running and overlapping war games—Vigilant Shield, Positive Response, Global Lightning, Forward Challenge—each sponsored by the people at NORTH-COM, the Joint Chiefs, Strategic Command, and the Program to practice a little corner of the extraordinary.

As Washington's exercises reached their eleventh hour, an EZ member conducting surveillance around the intended target was apprehended. Things then moved fast: At 0530 on June 21 exercise time, the FBI "confirmed" from the apprehended suspect that there was a WMD near Washington. The federal government went to Continuity of Government Condition (COGCON) 3, and then COGCON 2, and then 1, seamlessly implementing evacuation and relocation procedures for a select set of role-playing Program workers and civil servants. At 0730, the FBI players learned the specific location of the suburban Maryland safe house where the mock device was being kept (all set up at Andrews Air Force Base for the players to assault); the DEST and national "assets" were deployed, exercise style within two hours, defying both physics and reality. Nine hours later (exercise time), the safe house was stormed, the radiological device disarmed, the place secured, the bomb evacuated.

Everything in Washington unfolded like clockwork and ENDEX (end of exercise) was declared a huge success, the ghost of the *Palermo Senator* exorcised—that is, until the next Tier I national-level exercise, scheduled for 2009, which would again put the executive agents to the test. Meanwhile, across the country, the fictional EZ operative Husseini made it to the notional city of Landport ("Portland" rearranged). At 10 a.m. on the same morning when the FBI was swatting the terrorists away in DC, Husseini's charter boat arrived in port, only to be boarded by Customs and Border Protection officers. But it was too late: Husseini detonated his radiological dispersal device precisely at noon, 3 p.m. East Coast time. Washington had satisfactory ENDEX; Oregon, together with Arizona and Guam, which were similarly "attacked," had a whole lot of work to do in terms of consequence management and cleanup.[14]

Yet for the executive agents, that was in some ways a perfect outcome. A postulated nuclear attack on Washington has always been the gift that keeps on giving, from before Eisenhower and with every successive administration before and after 9/11. The scenario, whatever era it is revised for, whoever the perpetrator, justifies emergency measures, physical redundancy, and, of course, an equation in which the Constitution becomes secondary to "survival" between the lines. Post-9/11, though, the singular nightmare scenario of the first strike was transformed into a day-to-day never-ending limbo in which catastrophic attack was seen as inevitable—and thus necessitated all of the exceptions of the XYZs.

It isn't enough for four planes to be hijacked on the same

morning, for two to crash into the World Trade Center towers while the third almost simultaneously crashes into the Pentagon on a random sunny Tuesday in September, to test the government and justify the creation of a system of exceptions. The way martial life is imposed and then sustained necessitates weapons of mass destruction—the unimaginable and the fantastic. That's why the TOPOFF failures were also victories for the executive agents. If it seems that safety is guaranteed, panic will cease. Always there must be lit fuses, evidence of a breeze drifting toward a house of cards, rumors of infiltration. And yet if there's no evidence of burgeoning competence, power will shift away from the executive agent community. And if the XYZs are to define American life, that cannot be allowed to happen.

CHAPTER SEVEN

Enough to Make You Sick

*Existing disaster plans may include provisions for mass fatalities
but should be reviewed and tested regularly to determine if these
plans are appropriate for the relatively long period of increased
demand which is characteristic of a pandemic, as compared to the
shorter response period required for most disaster plans. There are
currently no national plans to recommend mass graves or mass
cremations. This would only be considered under the most extreme
circumstances. The use of the term* mass grave *infers that
the remains will never be re-interred or identified. Therefore,
the term* mass grave *should never be used when describing
temporary interment.*
Pandemic Influenza Mass Fatality Response Plan, 2007[1]

Amonth before 9/11, scientists from Livermore and its sister Los Alamos laboratory conducted a test using live microbes in a sealed chamber at the West Desert Test Center of Dugway Proving Ground, eighty-five miles from metropolitan Salt Lake City.[2] Dugway is a huge, remote high-desert military installation surrounded on two sides by mountains and the Great Salt Lake Desert to the north, acoustically and electronically quiet and free of light pollution, about as remote as one can get in the continental United States. Since 1942, through ups and downs, the post has hosted development and testing of and countermeasures to biological and chemical weapons. Until the United

States renounced its own biological weapons in 1972 and destroyed its inventory, ten different biological agents were tested at Dugway.[3]

Since the Nixon years Dugway base has served as the off-the-books black hole of the weapons of mass destruction national mission forces, the commando, SWAT, and technical arm of the Program. Dugway is where secret lethality tests are performed to gauge foreign and terrorist capabilities but also American equipment, protective clothing, detectors, and destroyers. If not literally the birthplace of the guinea pig, then it is certainly the place where the executive agents can play out their darkest fears and fantasies with humans and animals alike; it is the only US facility equipped to test with aerosolized Bio-Safety Level 3 agents, the most deadly.[4]

Once past Access Control Point #2, deep within the Dugway base and into the biological warfare testing area, no weapons and no cameras are allowed. This is the territory of the Special Programs Division, which supports the national laboratories, homeland security, the FBI, the intelligence community, the WMD response community, and the blackest of the black Joint Special Operations Task Force for all matters relating to weapons of mass destruction. It was here, one month before 9/11, that scientists from California and New Mexico completed a compartmented project started during the Clinton administration to develop and emplace biological agent detectors around the White House (the very ones that would later spook Cheney and company).[5] Biological Aerosol Sentry and Information System (BASIS), the name of the program, collects air samples within well-defined locations and at specified time intervals. The samples were then hand-carried to laboratories, where technicians look for indications of potentially lethal bacteria and viruses. Lawrence Livermore and Los Alamos laboratory scientists developed BASIS to achieve "a virtually zero rate of false-positive detections," according to the principal investigator, false alarms having the potential to cause both official disruptions and public panic.[6] BASIS sampling units were deployed around the White House right after 9/11, in Salt Lake City for the 2002 Winter Olympics, and in New York City for the first anniversary of 9/11. At the Olympics, 2,200 air samples were analyzed and the performance of BASIS was reported to be flawless in its early warning of an al Qaeda biological warfare attack.[7]

Just as anthrax had been supplanted by botulinum toxin in October 2001, highly classified intelligence around the time of the first anniversary of 9/11 warned the Bush inner circle of the possibility of terrorists wielding smallpox,[8] a disease that had been eradicated in America and was therefore considered particularly virulent if clandestinely reintroduced. This was actionable intelligence of a different sort—not a connecting of the dots to target some high-level al Qaeda leader or suicidal martyr, but early warning for the executive agents and the XYZ to take action. "We were each informed individually of whether we'd be vaccinated but not told who else was on the list," recalls Condoleezza Rice. "We were all convinced that it was al Qaeda's second wave."[9] Exactly who in the administration and the federal government would be inoculated was known by the executive agents alone.

Now tested, BASIS needed to be transformed into an actual warning system. In a most unusual organizational arrangement, but one identical to its various hidden command lines of warrantless surveillance, torture, and secret prisons, Vice President Cheney's office[10] oversaw the creation of a new system called Bio-Watch, a network of detectors in Washington, DC, and other high-risk metropolitan areas.[11] The government called it "detect-to-treat," and it was to provide insight and warning in large cities and at indoor events such as presidential political conventions; the system was to alert law enforcement and public health officials whenever it recognized a biological agent that was not of natural origin, ideally before any exposed individuals developed symptoms of illness.[12] What would actually happen then was unclear, but the greatest concentration of sensors was to be around the White House;[13] BioWatch was not actually focused on saving millions of lives so much as on serving as part of an executive-agent early-warning system to take action. After all, only Washington, only the executive branch, only the White House, and then only select elements of the Program have the actual trained and ready capability to do anything should the system sniff out danger.

The idea of domestic samplers got its original shot in the arm in March 1995 when a Japanese cult called Aum Shinrikyo—an organization never previously heard of by US intelligence—released sarin gas into the Tokyo subway system, killing 12 and sickening another 5,000.[14] A month later, Timothy McVeigh walked away from an explosives-filled truck parked outside the Alfred P. Murrah Federal Building in Oklahoma City, the explosion killing 168 and injuring 851 others. And there were other events that year: also in March, four members of the Minnesota Patriots Council, an illegitimate militia organization, were convicted of conspiracy charges under the Biological Weapons Anti-terrorism Act of 1989 for planning to use ricin, a lethal biological toxin, to assassinate federal agents. In May, a member of the neo-Nazi Aryan Nations was arrested in Ohio on charges of mail fraud and misrepresenting himself when attempting to order three vials of freeze-dried *Yersinia pestis*, the bacteria that causes bubonic plague, from a Maryland laboratory. In December, an Arkansas man was charged with possession of ricin in violation of the same bioterrorism act; he was arrested and hanged himself in his jail cell the next day.[15]

When Aum Shinrikyo appeared, Presidential Decision Directive 39 (the previously mentioned PDD-39) was already in draft;

at the eleventh hour its focus and priority were taken over by weapons of mass destruction.[16] In its finished form, that secret directive, since declassified by the Clinton Library, reaffirmed the FBI's lead role in the United States, directing the Defense Department to ensure that its "counterterrorism capabilities" were well managed, funded, and exercised in support. "We shall have tailored, robust and rapidly deployable counterterrorism teams capable of incident management, intelligence collection, law enforcement, military operations, technical expertise and disaster relief activities," the directive said. The FBI and DOD were directed to maintain "robust plans and capabilities rapidly to remove or destroy weapons of mass destruction in the hand of terrorists," and the Defense Department was directed to examine "the command and control structure that would be applied in domestic military employment (given *posse comitatus* exemptions)" without further elaboration.[17]

Though it would later be picked apart by committees and pundits for all that it didn't do to prevent 9/11, what PDD-39 did do was sanctify the marriage of terrorism and weapons of mass destruction. "The United States shall give the highest priority to developing capabilities to detect, prevent, defeat and manage the consequences of nuclear, biological or chemical materials or weapons used by terrorists," the classified directive stated. The protocols for a so-called PDD-39 event were established—the very protocols applied in the nuclear scare with the *Palermo Senator* in New York harbor seven years later.[18]

Bill Clinton became a particularly prolific directive issuer after the events of 1995 and the emergence of al Qaeda. While the ABCs of foreign policy were humanitarian intervention and peacekeeping and even leftover dreams of a peace dividend, WMD and terrorism anchored the XYZs—Congress passed the Defense Against Weapons of Mass Destruction Act of 1996, its

own word on the subject, levying a number of domestic requirements for greater readiness to respond to nuclear, chemical, and
biological terrorism, particularly greater involvement by state-
based National Guard teams.[19]

While summering on Martha's Vineyard in 1997, Clinton
also read *The Cobra Event*, a bioterrorism novel by Richard Preston,[20] and grew ever more obsessed with the possibility of a biological warfare attack. He talked incessantly with his advisors and
with outsiders about the potential for an out-of-control clandestine terrorist attack upon a US city. Speaking to the graduating
midshipmen at the Naval Academy, Clinton warned that American enemies "may deploy compact and relatively cheap weapons
of mass destruction—not just nuclear, but also chemical or biological, to use disease as a weapon of war."[21] Clinton's second secretary of defense, William Cohen, made a dramatic appearance
on ABC's *This Week* during which he placed a five-pound bag of
sugar on the table and said that that amount of anthrax "would
destroy at least half the population" of Washington. "One breath
and you are likely to face death within five days," he said.[22]

BioWatch thus came into being on a clear continuum from a
previous administration deeply enthralled—the initial aerosol
detectors funded by Clinton. The list of possible culprits in the
anthrax letters—al Qaeda, Iran, Iraq, even the Taliban, Tom
Ridge says[23]—and the October 18 scare and the later smallpox
scare all had an impact on biological warfare preparedness in the
same way that 9/11 changed counterterrorism: the program went
from peacetime to wartime. A month after the smallpox intelligence, the White House held a conference call with thirty-three
selected metropolitan areas, declaring that a countrywide biological agent threat was now considered tangible and immediate.[24]
Two weeks later in his 2003 State of the Union address, President
Bush alluded to BioWatch, stating that the US had begun "deploy-

ing the nation's first early warning network of sensors to detect a biological attack."[25]

In a period of just eight weeks, scientists installed a network of sniffers in the nation's most populous cities, a half dozen federal agencies now involved, some of them active participants in national security matters for the first time.[26] It would be the responsibility of the cities to manually collect the filters daily, transporting them to one of 160 laboratories within the National Response Laboratory Network—later the Integrated Consortium of Laboratory Networks—the majority lodged in universities now also enlisted in the country's daily defense.[27] The ability of BioWatch to detect three of the six top agents—anthrax, tularemia, and smallpox—was made public with the beginning of the war against Iraq in 2003, but the Washington-area monitors were also able to detect more than twenty different agents,[28] some of them highly classified.[29]

Biological warfare never came, and the Bush administration—at least many in the administration—even grew to accept that the WMD justification for the Iraq war was exaggerated (if not downright deceptive); the FBI determined that the anthrax mailings were the work of a domestic crazy (and incidentally a US government employee); and now the Taliban and al Qaeda were also on the run, unlikely to ever develop their own "program." Yet none of that ended the nightmare.

In April 2005, the Homeland Security Council published fifteen national planning scenarios, each meant to represent the "scope, magnitude, and complexity" of catastrophic events that might occur in the United States. The scenarios would guide future exercises and would help federal, state, and local agencies identify "core prevention and response requirements" to aid in preparedness planning. Five of the fifteen scenarios dealt with biological weapons and six others dealt with chemical and nuclear weapons; one dealt with a hurricane (Katrina being less than four months away).

Scenario Number 1 posited a ten-kiloton terrorist attack with an improvised nuclear device à la the *Palermo Senator;* estimated casualties: "hundreds of thousands." The assumption of this nuclear calamity for homeland security planning purposes was a detonation in Washington, DC (at the corner of 17th and H Streets NW, to be precise),[30] a variation on TOPOFF 4.

BioWatch was getting a baby brother: the Domestic Nuclear Detection Office was opened, jointly manned by military, FBI, customs, and scientific specialists from throughout the government and under the new Department of Homeland Security. The office would integrate all government research, development, testing, evaluation, acquisition, and operations of an integrated radiological detection system.[31] DNDO's network would "improve the Nation's capability to detect and report unauthorized attempts to import, possess, store, develop, or transport nuclear or radiological material," according to its mission statement.[32]

When DNDO opened its doors in 2005, the customs service already managed 552 radiation portal monitors at land and sea ports of entry into the United States. Now they and others would be incorporated into a Global Nuclear Detection Architecture—a domestic portion and an overseas network.[33] Congress newly authorized spending for radiation portal monitors that trucks would have to pass through at all points of entry along the US border, a project that was scheduled to be complete by September 2009.[34]

Little brother grew bigger: a radiation detector program for truck weighing stations throughout the country was added in 2008.[35] DNDO also funded development of dozens of projects to develop long-range domestic detectors. Roadside Tracker was one, a 300-foot-range device designed to detect and identify radiation sources in vehicles over five lanes of traffic at speeds up to seventy miles per hour. Another conference call to the states, more memoranda of agreement, pilot programs in the Southeast, and soon a national network of nonfederal partners in WMD preparedness emerged.[36]

Then came the beating of food into swords. The Bioterrorism Act, passed by Congress after the anthrax letters, dragooned the Food and Drug Administration into service with authorities to detect and respond to the possible adulteration of food products.[37] A month later, the *National Strategy for Homeland Security* elevated the standing of the food sector overall.[38]

One of the fifteen national planning scenarios produced in 2005 addressed food contamination—liquid anthrax bacteria delivered to terrorist accomplices in a meatpacking plant who would lace a shipment of ground beef before it was shipped off to local stores. The resulting illnesses posited—500 fatalities—was pretty small potatoes given the size and scope of the biological and nuclear calamities, plus there had been only three domestic incidents of intentional food contamination in twenty years, the worst causing 751 illnesses and no deaths.[39] Still, food constituted the largest civilian sector by far, and thus the planning scenario served to give the national security establishment the doctrine to begin to intrude into almost every corner of the economy, all under the name of WMD.

The FDA reported to Congress that there was a "high likelihood, *over the course of a year,* that a significant number of people will be affected by an act of food terrorism or by an incident of unintentional food contamination that results in serious foodborne illness."[40] The President's Council of Advisors on Science and Technology even came up with an argument that said that success in the war on terrorism *increased* the terrorist threat of biological warfare or food contamination, writing that "attacks on the food supply...could become a preferred means of attack in an environment where terrorist networks have been 'decapitated' and their ability to communicate and raise funds significantly diminished."[41]

In Homeland Security Presidential Directive 9, President Bush laid down the policy that the government would protect the food system from "terrorist attacks, major disasters, and other emergencies." A successful attack on the nation's agriculture or food system, the directive said, could have "catastrophic health and economic effects."[42] "I, for the life of me, cannot understand why the terrorists have not attacked our food supply because it is so easy to do," Secretary of Health and Human Services Tommy Thompson blurted out in 2004 on his way out the door.[43]

The writers of the national planning scenarios gave it their best shot, but soon enough 500 fatalities were overtaken by an expanded and elaborated menu of *what-ifs*. One scientific study concluded that over 100,000 could be poisoned if a single milk truck was contaminated with one gram of botulinum type A toxin.[44] The FDA estimated that 300,000 individuals could be debilitated in a national attack, saying that "a concerted, deliberate attack on food could be devastating, especially if a more dangerous chemical, biological, or radio-nuclear agent were used."[45]

When a National Infrastructure Protection Plan was published in 2006, food defense blew every other element of the so-called critical infrastructure away.[46] A 2007 inspector general's report discussed the enormity of the task: "The post-harvest food industry accounts for 12% of the nation's economic activity and employs more than 10% of the American workforce." It went on to point out that the nation's $460-billion food retail business consists of more than 34,000 supermarkets, 13,000 smaller food markets, 1,000 wholesale club stores, 13,000 convenience stores, and, it calculated, 28,000 gas station food outlets. Restaurants added another 925,000 US locations serving over 70 billion "meal and snack occasions" during the year.[47] Protection of all of this, the IG said, was impractical in the extreme. A food defense program wasn't out of the realm of government imagination; the problem, as seen through the eyes of the executive agents, was that much of the food-WMD critical infrastructure was privately owned and therefore outside regulatory control. "Vibrant cooperation and support between government and the private sector are needed," the IG concluded, if the United States was to fully master and build its defenses.[48]

BioWatch, DNDO, food defense—merely three more envoys of the apocalypse: nightmarish vulnerabilities turned into homeland security make-work and dogmas to indoctrinate the private sector into the primacy of defense and the need to standardize everything. In just two years after 9/11, federal government spending in preparation for biological warfare increased by a factor of fifteen.[49] The biological and chemical weapons workload at the Dugway Proving Ground increased almost eight times.[50] BioWatch's annual budget is more than $125 million a year;[51] DNDO's is triple that.[52] Over the decade after 9/11, spending—federal, state, and local—on programs relating to biological, chemical, and nuclear defenses in the United States totaled as much as $25 billion a year, according to an independent strategic analysis firm.[53] Spending to address just possible biological terrorist incidents during this stretch was about $57 billion, equal to about 10 percent of what the federal government spent during the same period on public health.[54] Warren Stern, director of the Domestic Nuclear Detection Office, told Congress in early 2011 that countering nuclear terrorism was a "whole-of-government challenge" and that his office was working with federal, state, local, international, and private-sector partners. "In every layer and pathway we will seek to increase detection coverage and capability and deter terrorists from planning or attempting nuclear terrorism," he said.[55] Particularly challenging were scenarios including "threat pathways" that involved noncommercial general aviation, maritime craft under 300 tons, and the borders between the official ports of entry.[56] More investment was needed, DNDO said, because "False alarms can be onerous for the many legitimate transporters of radioactive materials on America's roadways, at its ports, and in its storage facilities, not to mention bulk transporters hauling scrap metal, granite, bananas, and even kitty litter—all of which emit isotope signals that sensors can pick up as 'hot.'"[57]

"The threat is determined and patient, will attempt to use our freedoms against us, will search for any path to produce violent events, and harbors no qualms about killing innocent men, women, and children to achieve its objectives," said Admiral James A. Winnefeld, Jr., the Obama-selected commander of Northern Command and later Obama's vice chairman of the Joint Chiefs of Staff. WMD was first on Winnefeld's list of domestic concerns.[58]

They were destroyers in more ways than one, these weapons of mass destruction. They threatened everyone, or so it seemed, and thus were the perfect accompaniment to a lifetime of extraordinary response. But they were also phantoms, purveyors of fear that allowed a permanent and unassailable shift from the general welfare to national security. Warning mechanisms and special preparations could blanket the land, but even there, true security was unattainable, the treadmill of inertia thus another tool to benefit a select few who toiled between the lines, going through the motions of safeguarding the ABCs.

CHAPTER EIGHT

Pathways

*If you try to protect everything, you'll succeed at defending nothing.
We can't defend everywhere all at once, so we have to identify nodes
and systems that are critical to mission assurance. We've got to
carefully prioritize what assets, what data, which data path, we
will protect* in extremis.
GENERAL WILLIAM L. SHELTON, COMMANDER OF THE
AIR FORCE SPACE COMMAND, SPEAKING DURING THE 11TH
ANNUAL AIR FORCE IT DAY AT TYSON'S CORNER,
VIRGINIA, OCTOBER 11, 2012

O n May 18, 2012, the federal government was back in
New Orleans, ignoring the certainties of nature and
hoping to prepare city, state, and local officials for the enduring
calamity that trumps all others: a terrorist attack with a weapon
of mass destruction. The FBI was sponsoring a daylong tabletop
exercise starring a ship weighted with 12,000 tons of ammonium
nitrate (and two terrorist crew members) belatedly discovered to
be on watch lists, all bound for the Big Easy.[1]

The FBI is assigned responsibility to deal with managing such
crises—"crisis management" being a term with a very specific
meaning beyond the colloquial in order to distinguish it from the
equally precisely defined "consequence management": the FBI, as
the nation's premier law enforcement agency, is in charge of *pre-venting* terrorist attacks, while the Department of Homeland

Security and FEMA—and local authorities—are left with clean-ing up afterward.[2] More specifically, if there is any suspected domestic violation of any WMD statute, it is the FBI's domain.[3]

The FBI's preeminence in domestic counterterrorism goes back to a classified Reagan directive, Managing Terrorist Incidents, in 1982,[4] reaffirmed by Clinton, Bush, and Obama. The FBI is delegated "a host of specialized technical resources so that it can investigate, contain and minimize any weapon of mass destruction," according to a Joint Chiefs of Staff directive.[5]

The New Orleans exercise writers did what exercise writers do—they piled it on: someone suspicious photographing a chem-ical plant, multiple shootings at sensitive facilities, a chemical leak, hostage-taking, even the release of nuclear radiation.[6] The effect was strikingly similar to a mind-numbing action movie with too many car chases, shootings, and subplots—a heart-pumping ride that compensated for a weak story line. But the exercise was not without objective—it was so evident as to be explicit: overwhelm New Orleans's responders and investigators, thus teaching them how to prepare for the ultimate disaster, which meant asking for federal assistance. The scenario was a trap that no locality could escape. Indeed, state and local governments and private-sector businesses thus indoctrinated as to the contin-uance and gravity of WMD could only win by recognizing the need for an early surrender—the only outcome approved by those administering the hundreds of other traveling road shows customized for each community.

One might think that the storm-primed first responders in Louisiana would balk at participating, not predisposed to waste their time in some speculative exercise involving terrorism and weapons of mass destruction when hurricane season was just around the corner. An immediate incentive for participation, though, was that New Orleans was hosting the 2013 Super

Bowl—one of those national security special events that government takes to be the magnet for the worst of all possibilities. Such occasions always bring feds swarming, and there is the promise of grants and financial support from Big Daddy, financial assistance elevated beyond partisan sniping and made more politically immune because it goes under the subject heading of national defense. Plus all the other states and local communities were participating in WMD exercises, equally shepherded by the special call. Thus New Orleans EMS Deputy Chief Ken Bouvier obediently yammered to local TV that the big lesson from Katrina was to "know how to work within a unified command," rationalizing federal rules, preparedness, and a WMD threat.[7]

In East Lansing, Michigan, two months later, the FBI Weapons of Mass Destruction directorate set up another PowerPoint sensation, another local show, this time positing an attack on food and water supplies. The scenario writers piled on signs of suspicious activities at food processing plants, hardware stores, pharmacies, and pool supply businesses, even throwing in newfangled cyberattacks on digital control systems to concoct terrorist—or even foreign government—capability and intent to contaminate the American lifeblood. "At the end of the day, any response to a situation regarding the safety of our food supply will require a multiagency response," said Jeff Muller, assistant section chief for countermeasures in the WMD Directorate.[8] That was exactly the learning objective intended: a multiagency response means the deferential involvement and surrender to the federal government. So it would be in exercise after exercise.

As part of its post-9/11 reorganization to focus more on proactive counterterrorism, the FBI established the WMD Directorate in July 2006.[9] The directorate, the bureau says, created "a unique combination of law enforcement authorities, intelligence analysis capabilities, and technical subject matter expertise that exists nowhere else in the US government."[10] Once intelligence information comes in indicating a WMD connection to any potential domestic goings-on, or if local authorities suspect something related to hazardous materials and a crime, national protocols are for the closest FBI office to take charge of the event (no longer called a PDD-39 event but almost identical in its unfolding). Since April 2008, all fifty-six of the bureau's field divisions have assigned a full-time WMD coordinator; and the larger offices all also have emergency response teams, special agent bomb technicians, and hazardous materials response teams.[11] If a potential terrorism nexus involving weapons of mass destruction is determined to have any validity, the local FBI WMD coordinator then calls on the Weapons of Mass Destruction Operations Unit in Washington for reinforcements.[12] "If we get something unusual on the radar, we immediately jump on it to determine whether it's WMD and possibly linked to terrorism," says Special Agent Michael F. Varacalli, former chief of the unit.[13]

The unit is responsible for convening all the relevant agencies to oversee every aspect of any WMD-related criminal investigation. Inside the FBI, there are more than a dozen biological, chemical, radiological, and maritime technical teams to assist with credibility and safety assessments, some under the WMD Directorate, some under other FBI components.[14] The FBI national-level units include:

- Aviation and Surveillance Operations (ASOS)
- Behavioral Science Unit 1[15] (BSU 1)
- Biological Countermeasures Unit (BCU)
- Bioterrorism Risk Assessment Group (BRAG)
- Bomb Data Center (BDC)
- Chemical, Biological, Radiological, and Nuclear Science Unit (CBRNSU)

- Chemical Countermeasures Unit (CCU)
- Explosives Unit (EU)
- Hazardous Devices Response Unit (HDRU)
- Hazardous Evidence Analysis Team (HEAT)
- Hazardous Materials Operations Unit (HMOU)
- Hazardous Materials Response Team Unit (HMRTU)
- Hazardous Materials Response Unit (HMRU)
- Hazardous Materials Science Response Unit (HMSRU)
- Hostage Rescue Team (HRT)
- Weapons, Tradecraft, and Tactics Unit (WTTU)
- WMD Countermeasures Unit (WCU)

Once the existence of a WMD is affirmed by scientific verification or intelligence, the attorney general authorizes the activation and movement of the multiagency Domestic Emergency Support Team (DEST) to support the FBI.[16] The DEST, today organized by the FEMA administrator, is the consequence management side of the federal response.[17] The FBI's Critical Incident Response Group, an independent organization that is akin to military special operations forces, is the gateway to the black side. CIRG specializes in crisis management[18] (or incident management, as it is sometimes called)—that is, stopping a terrorist attack. CIRG also conducts what the FBI euphemistically calls tactical operations, in essence military operations performed by the FBI, a civilian organization, on American soil.[19] According to the FBI, the Tactical Support Branch of CIRG "provides the FBI with a nationwide, three-tiered tactical resolution capability that upon proper authorization can be activated within four hours of notification to address a full spectrum of terrorist or criminal matters."[20] Four 150-man rapid-deployment tactical support teams are located in Los Angeles, Miami, New York, and Washington, DC, for Tiers 3 and 2. For Tier 1, the most exceptional missions, the National Assets Response Unit calls upon the fully militarized FBI Hostage Rescue Team (HRT), hardly only a hostage rescue team,[21] and/or the defense department's Joint Special Operations Task Force; both are part of the national mission forces. If WMD and terrorism are actually involved, it is literally and officially deemed "extraordinary" and a green light snaps on, allowing federal responders to do anything to prevent use: spare no resources, take initiative if laws or the Constitution are in the way, and shoot to kill.

Outside the FBI, the network of those who can hypothetically join in the DEST is gigantic: more than 1,000 local bomb squads, SWAT teams, fire departments, EMS and hazardous material (HAZMAT) response units, half of them specially trained for various types of WMD, all of them FBI exercise partners and affiliates.[22] In federal departments and agencies outside the FBI, there are more than fifty specialized biological, chemical, radiological, nuclear, and high explosives teams—the most famous being the NEST of the national laboratories under the Department of Energy. Each federal team has separate response protocols and capabilities, depending on the location, the timing, the toxin, and the tier of the crisis.[23] Then there are a host of military capabilities, from the lowliest explosive ordnance disposal units at the garrison level—many of whom are also specially trained to deal with WMD and improvised devices—to fifty-six National Guard WMD civil support teams, at least one in each state that can act as federal first responders,[24] a Defense CBRNE Task Force, the Joint Task Force Civil Support, and the Joint Task Force Elimination, an accumulating multitude stuck somewhere in limbo between crisis and consequence management. And at the tippy-top are those Tier 1 national mission forces.

Tens of thousands of WMD first responders across the nation are assigned the incredible domestic mission, aided by multibillion-dollar detection systems and the highest intelligence and physical security priorities. The numbers are more a reflection of the absolute deference paid to biological and nuclear consequences than to the likelihood that some terrorist incident might occur in real life. In a way, that's why there's so much practicing. FBI data shows that from fiscal year 2005—the year the WMD Directorate was established—until fiscal year 2009, at least 936 WMD exercises were held around the country.[25] In the first year of its existence, the directorate hosted and participated in 16 exercises and provided instruction to 1,200 participants. Just two years later, that number had jumped to 90 FBI-hosted exercises and training for almost 7,000 people in law enforcement and private industry.[26]

When the FBI isn't indoctrinating and training its army of WMD warriors, it is also more tangibly snooping around America for signs of vulnerabilities of WMD stocks and ingredients. Though the FBI has been responsible for familiarity with the vulnerability of the US critical infrastructure since before 9/11,[27] in September 2008, headquarters began requiring that each field division conduct a "WMD domain assessment" to identify and prioritize the most important of all threats and vulnerabilities in their districts,[28] as one national laboratory report says, looking at the vulnerability of "sensitive and high value targets" that terrorists might attack or infiltrate.[29] The local FBI offices collect and analyze information regarding "the most pressing WMD threats and vulnerabilities," preparing a list of the "top 10" and a WMD vulnerability assessment used for outreach and training of local WMD soldiers and private-sector draftees.[30]

A field division's WMD domain can include thousands of different "WMD domain entities," defined as government and private-sector interests such as transportation hubs, nuclear power plants, laboratories, hospitals, and manufacturing firms. And according to an FBI document, the WMD domain entities also include parks, houses of worship, shopping malls, beauty salons, farms, and even "residents."[31] The WMD license is virtually unlimited.

Only since President Clinton's PDD-39 have high-yield explosives—what we used to call conventional weapons—been included in the official definition of weapons of mass destruction, and only since 9/11 has *any* type of weapon "capable of killing a lot of people and/or causing a high-order magnitude of destruction" been included.[32] And that doesn't just mean specifically crafted weapons, since airliners and "disease organisms" and other "nonweapons" have been added to the mix as "weapons of mass effect."[33] (During the Republican National Convention in St. Paul in 2008—a national security special event—the FBI even threw Molotov cocktails in there as well, citing eleven arrests "with respect to WMD," all involving soda bottles filled with gasoline.[34]) And not only that: the *National Military Strategy* statement produced after 9/11 uses the term "WMD" to describe what it calls "asymmetrical weapons," those that "may rely more on disruptive impact than destructive kinetic effects. For example, negative psychological effects on people may be more severe than the numbers of lethal destruction or the degree of economic damage."[35] And as one FBI document says: "Note that the [legal] definitions include words such as 'designed' and 'intended,' indicating that an attack does not need to be carried out for a successful prosecution,"[36] nor as a predicate for wide-ranging investigations. Thus WMD is everything, anything, and always.

What results is an enormous dragnet. The FBI's "countermeasures" program, begun in 2007, follows what the bureau calls a "threat mitigation strategy" to educate the agricultural, biological, chemical, nuclear, and related academic and industrial sectors to detect terrorism.[37] FBI WMD coordinators work with biological, chemical, and nuclear specialists from state and local government—and the private sector—to keep abreast of scientific and technical developments that terrorists might exploit.[38] The FBI's agroterrorism partnership program, its biosecurity program, its synthetic biology tripwire program, and its joint "Crim-Epi" (criminal-epidemiological) initiative open doors to the private sector and justify an enormously elastic predicate for reporting, intelligence collection, and investigation.[39] FBI training and outreach materials promote collaboration of law enforcement and public health, encourage businesses to report suspicious customers and purchase inquiries, and seek to instill alertness (i.e., sow suspicion) amongst experts to prevent "exploitation," reaching far into the academic community and private entities in the name of WMD.[40] The bureau even manages to have the authority to perform background and database checks on private individuals being considered for access to a select group of biological agents and toxins.[41]

"The threat of weapons of mass destruction (WMD) is the FBI's most pressing concern," outgoing WMD Directorate head Vahid Majidi told Congress in October 2011. "Dozens" of international and domestic terrorist organizations have announced their intention to use WMD, he said, citing an "increased threat," boasting that since the establishment of the directorate in 2006, the FBI had successfully managed "hundreds of cases involving biological substances and suspicious powders"—successfully managing to suggest cases that in reality number only a handful since 2006, with an even smaller number involving international terrorism.[42]

Even after the death of Osama bin Laden and a decade of security efforts at home, WMD is portrayed by government officials, members of Congress, the newspapers, the pundits, and the experts not only as real, but as ever growing. WMD is a magic wand, an ever-present license. In fact, Majidi glossed over the reality that the majority of the directorate's investigative workload is responding to hoaxes. To keep busy, moreover, the bureau conducts investigations of "criminals" involved in "materials and knowledge related to WMD"—particularly in the biotechnology field—and "the attempted or actual transfer of materials, knowledge, and technology needed to create a WMD," even if no connection to weapons of mass destruction is present. The FBI is particularly concerned with the insider threat in US biological and medical laboratories, Majidi said, "based on several recent incidents involving the illicit acquisition of bacterial and viral cultures."[43] If anything, the hundreds of cases Majidi refers to represent a monumental improvement, since in just four months after the anthrax letter mailings in October 2001, the FBI says, it responded to over 8,000 "reports" of the use or threatened use of anthrax or other hazardous materials, most of them also hoaxes and bogus copycats.[44] Indeed, in New Orleans, FBI agents chatted with the news media about the fabulous bananas Foster they'd had at their real tabletop in the French Quarter the night before and where to get a good cigar at the end of their WMD war game. "While Perren would not give specifics to how tripwires would preemptively recognize a WMD maritime related threat," one news blogger posted, "…he did say he enjoyed Emeril's last night."[45]

None of this is meant to suggest anything nefarious on the part of the FBI; I'm sure the G-men and the Weapons of Mass Destruction Directorate believe that WMD is indeed the ultimate threat and want nothing more than to prevent an attack. So they cycle through every possibility and method, try and retry every technique, and eye every location to keep one step ahead; they adapt for greater and greater vigilance and unification of the nation, working their exercises and outreach and countermeasures to propagate everyone's part. The FBI not only wants to believe that its work "deters" and "prevents" but also that following the latest methods of counterterrorism, intelligence, and law enforcement—introducing everyone to everyone else, standardizing communications, screening out bad elements and suspicious persons, enlisting the private sector in identifying critical infrastructure and initiating protection, perfecting the procedures and protocols of responding to an alert—not only staves off a possible WMD attack but also forestalls a potentially lawless descent. If everyone can be brought together in harmony, a certain societal unity might help to defeat terrorism. And if not...

What if? What if an attack—a real, large-scale society-changing biological or nuclear attack—were actually detected beforehand? All of the preparations, whether they be the passive efforts of Bio-Watch and DNDO or the proactive FBI measures, certainly suggest that this possibility is taken seriously and prepared for. But where in all of this is the real capability to stop a terrorist attack in its tracks?

CHAPTER NINE

In Extremis

The Army is not composed of lawyers, capable of judging at a moment's notice of just how far they can go in the maintenance of law and order....
PRESIDENT ULYSSES S. GRANT, LETTER TO CONGRESS,
JANUARY 13, 1875

In congressional hearings in May 2002, Secretary of Defense Donald Rumsfeld hinted at the secret hierarchy of government operations and plans, another continuum where the left side of the spectrum is "missions or assignments that are limited in scope" and the far right side of the spectrum is those missions pertaining to the most "extraordinary circumstances."

The hearings' context was discussion of a new homeland security department, and Rumsfeld—showing his reluctance to use the military for domestic tasks—instantly laid down the law regarding when the military—his Department of Defense—might be in charge in the United States, particularly given the new interloper. In "emergency circumstances of a catastrophic nature," he said, the military would operate in support of civil agencies, but "under extraordinary circumstances," those in which the department would execute what the secretary promiscuously labeled "its traditional military missions," the military "would take the lead." Rumsfeld called this "homeland defense" and included examples like "combat air patrols and maritime defense operations," making the extraordinary sound wholly ordinary.[1] In follow-up testimony, Rumsfeld elaborated that plans for extraordinary contingencies "would be coordinated, as appropriate, with the National Security Council and with the Department of Homeland Security...," again creating a picture of normalcy but saying in effect that when inappropriate, they wouldn't be.[2]

Deputy Secretary of Defense Paul Wolfowitz followed with testimony in July, adding vaguely that "the category of extraordinary circumstances are [sic] cases in which the President, exercising his Constitutional authority as Commander in chief and Chief Executive, authorizes military action. This inherent Constitutional authority may be used in cases, such as a terrorist attack, where normal measures are insufficient to carry out federal functions."[3]

Normal measures, of course, stem from *Posse Comitatus* Act restrictions — the general prohibition on the use of the military for civil law enforcement — but it was Wolfowitz's use of the inscrutable phrase "insufficient to carry out federal functions" that transcended emergency circumstances Rumsfeld had already referred to in which temporary conditions might demand military intervention. In fact, since the passage of an obscure 1996 law, if weapons of mass destruction actually were used in the United States, *Posse Comitatus* could lawfully be waived and the Defense Department could "take the lead" under statute anyhow.[4]

Almost nothing in the public domain discusses what would happen in a crisis involving a threat to use a WMD. "Under extreme circumstances," a 2009 directive of the Joint Chiefs says, "the President may unilaterally direct the Department of Defense to assist State and local civilian authorities after a domestic CBRNE [chemical, biological, radiological, nuclear, or high explosive] incident, on or off a military installation."[5] Vice

Admiral James A. Winnefeld wrote to Congress in 2010 in support of his nomination to be the next homeland defense commander that: "In certain rare circumstances, the NORTHCOM commander may be asked to assume overall command and control due to the nature or scope of an incident."[6] In both cases, though, the reference is to what happens *after* an incident, not to the extraordinary crisis management rules that would take effect during a terrorist threat and before a detonation.[7]

National Security Decision Directive 30, "Managing Terrorist Incidents," signed by Reagan in April 1982 and the first presidential directive ever on counterterrorism, makes no mention of the Defense Department in discussing domestic responses. Even in this secret directive, now fully declassified, there is one sentence, without any elaboration, that hints of something that lurks in another realm: the "White House Operations Group," chaired by the director of the White House Military Office, it says, has "responsibility for issues relating to threats or acts of terrorism directed against the President or the Vice President or senior US officials and protectees as directed by the President."[8]

Two years later, President Reagan issued NSDD 138, a top secret/sensitive directive entitled "Combating Terrorism," also now declassified. It stated: "Domestic programs to deal with terrorist activities in the United States must be continuously reviewed and assessed in order to identify useful improvements." The secretary of defense was directed to "continue improvements in the US capability to conduct military operations to counter terrorism directed against US citizens, military forces, property, and interests," but with no explicit discussion or direction whatsoever on the domestic mission or whether US citizens and interests extended to the United States proper. The attorney general was directed to develop "streamlined operational plans for deterring and responding to terrorist threats against prominent locations/events in the United States which could be likely targets for terrorist attack," without any mention of the FBI, the *national mission forces*, or what is known by insiders as the "render safe" mission.[9]

Ever since the 1985 seizure of the *Achille Lauro* cruise ship, every theater military commander in the US military has developed an *in extremis* force, preferably a Green Beret or a marine corps special operations unit. *In extremis*—a Latin phrase that means "in the farthest reaches" or "at the point of death"—has a very particular meaning in the military, referring to the conditions in which a military man or woman would feel compelled to take grave risks in order to accomplish a critical mission or save lives: Medal of Honor territory.[10] There is even an official Defense Department definition: "a situation of such exceptional urgency that immediate action must be taken to minimize imminent loss of life or catastrophic degradation of the political or military situation."[11] Such *in extremis* forces are commonly called CIFs (pronounced "sifs"), for the Commanders' In-Extremis Force.[12] Such 24/7 alert units are the first to arrive in almost every imaginable emergency situation, their quick-response duty to perform reconnaissance of the situation and to stabilize, isolate, and contain.[13] The CIF might even take violent action if the circumstances demand, but in the most extreme cases—the takedown of terrorists involving civilian hostages or the defusing of a bomb suspected of being a weapon of mass destruction—the CIF, as elite as it is, waits until the *national* forces arrive.[14] The national forces train for hostage rescue and the extraction of a downed airman in hostile territory, and would also assume, if time allows, the render safe mission from the normal CIF—a meticulously prepared extrajudicial mission, a ticking weapon of mass destruction always and forever the highest priority.

Nothing better exemplifies the very non–martial law conditions of our uniquely American Coup than the national *in extremis* forces, for they represent the disciplined yet reluctant assumption of power, rather than the four-star grab for it.

Less than a week after 9/11, the General Accounting Office released a report on general counterterrorism matters that stated: "If an exceptionally serious terrorist threat or incident is beyond the FBI's capabilities to resolve, a military joint special operations task force may be established to respond in accordance with contingency plans developed by DOD." Statutory exceptions to *Posse Comitatus*, the GAO said, "would require a request from the Attorney General and concurrence by the Secretary of Defense." The report went on to say that "if military forces are required to restore order as a result of an act of domestic terrorism that renders ordinary means of enforcement unworkable or hinders the ability of civilian law enforcement authorities, the President must issue an executive order and a proclamation." Such documents, the GAO said, were maintained in draft form and are ready for the president's signature, if needed.[15]

A "military joint special operations task force" had never been acknowledged, and the GAO was not only referencing it but also making a rare allusion to the existence of prewritten extralegal directives: the envelopes. With 9/11 any public discussion or even hint of such a task force disappeared from public view, the potential for national mission forces to swing into action now a real possibility and a very active contingency.[16]

So what were the extraordinary missions or the "federal functions" that needed to be carried out beyond *posse comitatus* exemptions? The answer partly lies hidden decades earlier, when efforts on the part of the executive agents to increase the security and safety of US nuclear weapons (of which there were an obscene abundance located at hundreds of domestic and overseas sites) led to the predecessor units of today's national mission forces that work on mechanisms to "render safe" a tampered, stolen, or lost nuclear weapon, as well as to ensure that the physical security of such weapons is sufficient. Military special operations forces established "red teams" to test and gauge such security, and the Departments of Defense and Energy put enormous effort into providing "technical expertise" on the design and workings of nuclear warheads and weapons.[17] In fact, when the FBI was first assigned the counterterrorism mission in 1982, it depended completely on the military "to perform the render safe procedures on a nuclear device," which was considered the ultimate *in extremis* mission.[18] One reason for all the secrecy, then, is that it was not only foreign enemies that were contemplated *in extremis* when it came to weapons of mass destruction. Before 9/11, the exercise scenarios and contingency planning included rogue officers and antinuclear protestors getting their hands on a nuclear weapon, and many of the XYZ contingencies pit the *in extremis* force against American civilians.

It took five years after 9/11 for the Bush administration to formally replace PDD-39 with its own directive—called National Security Presidential Directive 46 (NSPD-46)—signed by the president in March 2006 and still classified top secret. That sweeping directive, "United States Policy and Strategy in the War on Terror," changed little relating to domestic WMD, reaffirming the attorney general, acting through the FBI—"in cooperation with other federal departments and agencies"—as responsible for law enforcement activities to detect, prevent, preempt, and disrupt terrorist attacks against the United States.[19] All of the previous exceptions of military takeover are included if the FBI is overwhelmed, but the Joint Special Operations Task Force was also given extraordinary "homeland defense" missions. According to Admiral Winnefeld, "the President may determine that a terrorist incident rises to the level of an armed attack against the United States and therefore direct that DOD take the lead in the defense of the Homeland."[20]

Tom Ridge describes how when he was the first director of the new office of homeland security, even after he had been Pennsylvania governor and had dealt with nuclear threats, he learned of the national mission forces for the first time—something to do, he later wrote, with "Delta Force and Seal Team Six" involved in domestic nuclear weapons disablement.[21] The work, according to Richard Clarke, linked up "the scientists at the department's [Department of Energy] nuclear labs with the commandos of the Joint Special Operations Command, and focused on "what you do when you have to get a nuclear bomb away from terrorists."[22] Yet no one outside the circle of national mission forces executive agents quite knows for sure when they would be called forth, what they are, what authorities they truly have, let alone what they are supposed to do when confronted with a WMD.[23] Amidst the seemingly endless bureaucratic thicket is a plan both for military special operations forces—special special operations forces—to step in when the executive branch determines that doing so is the best way to impose an adequate state of civil law enforcement, and for the command and control of such efforts to be willfully obscured not only from the public but from government officials at the most elevated levels.

Both Ridge and Clarke neglected to mention the FBI's National Assets Response Unit (or NARU), the on-scene support headquarters of the national assets commander[24] and the custodian of the highly classified national WMD plans.[25] NARU is distinguished from other FBI units in that it is the coordinator of the overall national mission force, not the operational unit itself. Most in the know say on the simplest level that the military element of the national mission force is the elite special mission units of the Joint Special Operations Command (or "jay-sock")—the so-called Tier 1 Delta Force or SEAL Team 6 units or others—but this characterization is too narrow, too obvious, and too broad all at the same time, ignoring the FBI's authorities and the very extraordinary WMD mission; kind of like saying "army" in referring to all things military.[26] In the same way, though, that the design for the operation to kill Osama bin Laden was highly irregular, with a hand-picked collection of black special operators nominally under the command of the CIA director, in the domestic world of weapons of mass destruction, the command relationships and the composition of the national mission force follow no known military doctrine or even legal framework: as the presidential directives say, "modules" are pulled together for specific circumstances under the FBI's command and control, except when, under the most extraordinary circumstances—specified in the most highly classified and compartmented directives in existence—the White House Military Office or some other between-the-lines task force commander or executive agent takes over.

The *national mission force*, then, like the Program itself, predates 9/11; it shifts and expands to meet the imagined contingencies of the executive agents: one incident, two incidents at the same time, three simultaneous attacks, up and up, never down. Beyond the thousands of WMD-focused specialists in the ABC who effectively exist only as feel-good disaster response crossing guards,[27] beyond the Domestic Emergency Support Team, is the true national mission force—the FBI and its various special units, the Joint Special Operations Task Force and its various specialized subunits or modules,[28] the NEST of the Department of Energy and its various special units, specialized military and transport units that are not directly a part of the Joint Special Operations Task Force, and the tactical and technical units of other agencies, including the Department of Homeland Security, which has established what it claims to be its own classified "Tier 1" law enforcement unit.[29]

The national mission forces have domestically deployed countless times over the years, in preparation for—and response to—both the real and the trivial. They were there, secreted away in a Manhattan armory, to prepare to assault the New York offices of Aum Shinrikyo in 1995;[30] they were standing by on 9/11;[31] they deployed for the *Palermo Senator* incident in New York harbor in 2002; they've been there for all inaugurals since 2001 and for State of the Union addresses and summits and other national security special events when continuity of government has been at stake.

They have also been there just to practice, such as at the May 2004 National World War II Memorial dedication in Washington, a celebration that precipitated the activation of a Joint Task Force, mobilization of specialized ABC consequence management task forces, positioning of a domestic disturbance Garden Plot quick-reaction force, standby for continuity of government, and the *national mission force* to stop a terrorist attack, one involving WMD.[32]

The evidence also suggests that they were even there in New Orleans in the aftermath of Hurricane Katrina, ready, according to an FBI briefing, for potential "special missions."[33] Or maybe they weren't there; for the enduring enforcers of XYZ governance, granted special authorities and an extraordinary status during an age of different danger, the point isn't to be seen until there is a need to be seen—but the firm assumption, their guiding principle, is that the time is coming when the invisible will be the salvation of the visible.

Can the possibility of a terrorist attack with a weapon of mass destruction still justify all of this, a day-to-day existence now so normalized that it feeds even preemptive and accelerated preparations for martial rule? The army under Obama, in a 2010 manual, obediently issued an official definition of martial law for the first time in years, saying it "involves use of the military to exercise police powers; restore and maintain order; ensure essential mechanics of distribution, transportation and communication; and conduct necessary relief measures." The manual continued, "In such cases, the ordinary law, as administered by the ordinary courts, is superseded for the time being by the order of a military commander."[34] Additionally, it cautioned that "federal military commanders shall not take charge of any function of civil government unless absolutely necessary under conditions of extreme emergency," instructing its commanders who undertake such function to "strictly limit military actions to the emergency needs, and . . . facilitate the reestablishment of civil responsibility at the earliest time possible."[35] And in September 2012, the Defense Department issued a new directive on civil support, appearing to restore the post-Bush ABCs to legality.[36] One regulation would replace those old ones feeding Garden Plot, all of the pre-9/11 regulations that lacked the "correct" language of terrorism, and all the pre-Katrina regulations that didn't comport with the real-world possibility of disagreement between a governor and the federal government over what to do. Most important, though, the Defense Department needed to articulate policy in a world where relentless alerts and seemingly stratospheric stakes had made the prospect of military involvement in domestic matters the norm yet also red hot in terms of political and public sensitivity. For the bureaucrats at the Pentagon—they wouldn't have to actually implement martial law; that was the army's job if worst came to worst—any mention of martial law was to be avoided. Instead, the new directive explained that immediate-response authority "does not permit actions that would subject civilians to the use of military power that is regulatory, prescriptive, proscriptive, or compulsory"; the military could never and would never push civilians around.

When martial law was twice imposed in America by the federal government during external wars (in 1815 and after Pearl Harbor), the courts later found that its application fundamentally infringed on the rights of the citizen. The litmus test in both cases related not to the declaration but to the length of time during which military authorities felt it necessary to impose it and the effects it had on enduring and immutable rights of the citizen. It was clear that martial law *can* be declared in America—if a number of theoretical and catastrophic circumstances are met—but that it also has the potential to destroy the most fundamental individual guarantees of the Constitution. It simply cannot exist as part of the ABCs of American governance. That's why secret government preparations for martial law, while inevitably at the very heart of the XYZs, are a taboo gingerly avoided and so forbidden that even consideration of such contingencies cannot be hinted at. The terrified mayor of New Orleans can declare martial law when he doesn't even have an army to enforce it, congressmen can pepper their speeches with the term when they really mean executive excess or just legislative displeasure, survivalists and "patriots" can warn that we are inches from tyranny or already deep in the muck, netizens and civil libertarians can decry its presence, but military rule, actual military rule à la Andrew Jackson New Orleans 1815, martial law in America today—no way. Martial life is the way of life, subtle and nonmenacing. The very triumph of governance by ABCs and XYZs is that the actual threat of martial law is literally ABC.

CHAPTER TEN

The Program

We will defend America while protecting the freedoms that define America. Our strategies and actions will be consistent with the individual rights and liberties enshrined by our Constitution and the Rule of Law. While we seek to improve the way we collect and share information about terrorists, we will nevertheless be vigilant in respecting the confidentiality and protecting the privacy of our citizens. We are committed to securing our nation while protecting civil rights and civil liberties.
DEPARTMENT OF HOMELAND SECURITY STRATEGIC PLAN, 2004[1]

D ay-to-day, as president of the United States, Barack Obama lives between the lines. Like all modern presidents before him, but increasingly and inexorably more so, he lives in a bubble, working and residing at 18 Acres, as the insiders call the White House complex. The residence, the family quarters upstairs on the second floor, has its own kitchen and the requisite trappings of normal life; there is even some modicum of privacy. But this is no normal life.

Discreetly yet intimately one step away is the president's protective detail. For the Secret Service, presidential duty is the job of the very best, with an attitude of protection to match: "Presidents are only people who live and breathe like anyone else," one former agent writes, "but they are worth dying for if necessary due to the office they hold. The office of the presidency must be protected at all cost."[2]

The president is the man in the middle; it's not exactly a pyramid that he stands on top of, as there are so many equal partners directly subordinate to him that the shape seems inappropriate. Yet the disparity in importance between him and everyone else is almost astronomical. In service with this mission, the Secret Service builds a bubble wherever the president travels, whether to Camp David for a weekend getaway or on a state visit to China. Since 9/11, the Secret Service has hired hundreds of new agents, doubling in size since the days of the Reagan assassination attempt, its budget growing in that time from a few hundred million dollars to $1.5 billion. Whenever the president goes, the Secret Service takes control of an additional reserve of local and state police (trumping all other activities), other federal law enforcement officers, and dedicated intelligence watchers who have a priority call on the most sensitive intercepts and agent reports; also included are military specialists in radiation detection, explosive ordnance disposal, weapons disablement, and more. And lurking behind these men in the sunglasses is the shadow team, the crisis action team of snipers, and an *in extremis* force, always at the ready.

The next ring around the president is made up of the operational units of the White House Military Office, also one step away and just as intimate, but with a different mission and task. Established in 1957, the WHMO was originally fewer than fifty people taking care of President Eisenhower's communications, transportation, and medical care. Through 2001, that number grew to some 800 strong, and since 9/11, it has more than quadrupled in size, reorganizing into seven operational units made up of almost 2,500 individuals, mostly military personnel but heavily influenced by a permanent cadre of civil servants of the gray man variety. These days they are also supported by over 2,000 civilian contractors from more than a dozen private companies, the majority of them technicians in communications, IT, and other basic services; but also others deeply involved in the counterterrorism and continuity tasks created and expanded in the past decade.[3]

The WHMO is Air Force One and the other coded and numbered conveyances, the famous armored limousines (nicknamed "the beast"), and the exclusive Presidential Emergency Operations Center under the East Wing (the aboveground White House Situation Room belongs to the National Security Staff). The White House Military Office provides support, in its own words, for the "President of the United States (POTUS) in his role as Commander in Chief (CINC), Chief Executive Officer of the United States, and Head of State; and other elements related to the President" including the vice president, the First Lady, the First Family, the Secret Service, the White House staff, the White House Press Office, the National Security Council, "and others as directed," a complex topology that opens the way for the Program and the envelope bearers.[4]

The worker bees of the WHMO are the technicians of the White House Communications Agency, the crew of the airlift and helicopter units, the doctors and trauma specialists from the medical unit, and the drivers of the White House Transportation Agency. The top of the top, the elite of the elite, are the five military aides to the president, one from each service, field-grade officers of major to lieutenant colonel and commander rank—"fast burners," as military types like to say, officers on their way to becoming admirals and generals. They work directly for the man himself, always there, impeccably uniformed, carrying the football in hand. They among all the staff—indeed, among everyone on the planet—exclusively carry the decision documents and the emergency checklists and, these days, digital copies, of all the laws, the letters and envelopes of the secret world, the directives, the findings, the plans, and the predicted consequences—as well as the unique set of codes that would be used if the president issued emergency orders, implemented contingency plans, authorized continuity actions, or approved the use of nuclear weapons.[5]

Only bits and pieces are known about what really goes on with the football today, what "the biscuit"—the president's codes—really looks like and how it works, how Obama's BlackBerry is tied in, or how the contents of the football—computers, modems, radios, cell and satellite phones, and other modern accoutrements—have been modified for today's threats and today's technologies; and that's the way the American government and military like it.

The military aides to the president are formally assigned to the WHMO, but the organization that formally works the procedures and technologies behind nuclear control orders and emergency action messages is actually something called the Center for National and Nuclear Leadership Command Capabilities, a Pentagon-run conglomeration of seven federal departments and agencies, which is itself just a staff organization reporting to the Strategic Command in Omaha, which in turn reports to the secretary of defense, who ultimately reports to the president or one of his constitutional successors, *except* in cases where the secretary—as one-half of the National Command Authority[6]—is authorized to take independent actions, presumably only when the United States is under nuclear attack. In such instances, the secretary of defense can call upon his own football carrier, with his own central locator system identifying the status and location of every successor,[7] and then he can open the symbolic final envelope, follow the guidance from the president, and push the figurative button, all on his own.

The secretary in theory *can* do this all by himself, with no discussion with the president, though the assumptions of this extralegal world—and even the mechanisms involved (there is no literal button to push)—demand that they consult, which is to say that the assumption is that if the secretary had to take independent action, no one down the chain of command would question why, so obvious would be the reasons. Since the assassination attempt on President Reagan's life, the vice president also has his own military aides and football, and constitutionally can only act if sworn in upon the president's death or disability, but again, though he has the accoutrements of independent action, the Program serves as the fail-safe. In other words, an extralegal governing mechanism to preserve constitutional sanctity makes the Constitution irrelevant.

The closest thing to any consistent headquarters of the Program is the White House Military Office, itself quasimilitary, quasicivilian, and practically off the books, partly funded and peopled by bits and pieces of the Pentagon and intelligence budgets but also host to multiple special-access programs of supersecrecy and limited access and enormous privilege.[8] The working-class stiffs who make up the Program—even if they are elite Category 1 personnel and wearers of the proper lapel pins that give them access to intimate events—are meant to be seen and not heard. If that sounds like a comment about class, it is. They have a job to do and are distinguished from the president's people, who are the temporary and temperamental dwellers who come in (and then go) with each election. From the chief of staff and the national security advisor all the way down to the gofers and interns, these guests might also be an inner circle, but it is the Program staff that clears and approves their presence; who gets to be a "tan badger," the privileged one with unescorted access.

An enormous mass backs up all of this and is never many steps beyond: thousands (and ultimately tens of thousands) who toil away at the White House and Camp David and the top command centers and the government bunkers and emergency relocation sites, each with a role to play in the XYZ contingency plans: the WHMO Operations Plan, FUNCPLAN 2400 and the Joint Emergency Evacuation Plan (or JEEP), the Rescue and Security of the Occupants of the Executive Mansion (RESEM) Plan, the White House Emergency Action Plan, the Continuity of Government Support Plan, the Nuclear Incident Contingency Plan, the Chemical/Biological Incident Contingency Plan, the National Cyber Incident Response Plan, the national mission force's Power Geyser WMD render safe plans; and OPLAN 8044, *the* offensive nuclear war plan. The outlines, designs, and authorities to implement these contingency plans are only vaguely known outside the Program and the executive agent class—the important point being how many simultaneous plans there are and how many people it takes to tend to their care and feeding.

When President Obama came into office and announced that his administration would cease using the term "global war on terror" in favor of the bureaucratic mouthful "overseas contingency operations," the city that fights to the death over the differences between phrases like "homeland security" and "homeland defense" took it to be merely a marker that a new team was in town, a hopeful bunch intent on lowering the national volume. Obama followed up with a promise of abandoning the dark side, with pledges of transparency, and with a call for nuclear disarmament.

Obama's new homeland security secretary, the tough-talking Janet Napolitano, followed suit, avoiding the word "terrorism" in speeches and congressional testimony, saying "man-caused disasters" and threats "natural and man-made," prompting some partisan scolding. Terrorism "can't be the evil we don't speak about," said New York Representative Peter King, then chairman of the House Homeland Security Committee. "Any testimony on homeland security should be centered around the threat of terrorism and what we're doing to combat it."

Not to worry, Napolitano's spokesman shot back. "Anyone who doesn't understand that she's talking about terrorism when she says her mission is to protect the American people from threats both foreign and domestic clearly needs a study guide."[9]

For the former Arizona governor, border control loomed large in all risks. "I have walked, flown over, and ridden horseback along our southwest border," she said. "I appreciate its vastness, as well as the grave consequences of our broken system."[10]

The executive agents were all about grave consequences. They briefed the new secretary about natural disasters, infrastructure protection, transportation security, intelligence sharing, consequence management, risk analysis, weapons of mass destruction, money laundering, human trafficking, continuity, and essential fodder for the second decade of the forever war, cybersecurity. Presented with a flood of action directives ordering dozens of reviews of these areas,[11] Napolitano got into the spirit, publicly musing about the threat from a pandemic, later warning the country about "a big influx" of swine flu cases, nattering on about cyberthreats. A reporter asked her if somehow the department—founded with the very justification of needing a federal lead to fight terrorism—was straying. Homeland Security, Napolitano responded, had "a very broad mission"—multitasking, she sarcastically called it.[12] In the view of the executive agents, she done good.

And the president, he done even better. Obama appointed the former secretary of the army—and hallowed executive agent—Louis Caldera as his political man at the top (just as Bush had designated his own political man, Joe Hagin). Obama declared national security and homeland security one—even combining the different White House staffs,[13] ranking the greatest risks to the "security of the nation"—acts of terrorism, cyberattacks, pandemics, and "catastrophic natural disasters," in that order.[14] "A potential game changer would be a nuclear weapon in the hands of terrorists, blowing up a major American city," Obama said in an early interview. "Or a weapon of mass destruction in a major American city...and so when I go down the list of things I have to worry about all the time, that is at the top, because that's one area where you can't afford any mistakes. And so right away, coming in, we said, how are we going to start ramping up and putting that at the center of a lot of our national security discussion? Making sure that that occurrence, even if remote, never happens."[15]

A year into the new administration, the bipartisan WMD Commission released its second report, "The Clock Is Ticking," concluding that the United States was *closer* to a possible attack than it had predicted even in 2008. The commission gave the government a failing grade on bioterrorism preparedness,[16] concluding that BioWatch wasn't good enough, nor were general disease surveillance efforts, which equated to a failure of collective awareness and preparation in either the medical establishment or the university public health systems. The Obama administration agreed: more would be needed, improvement was promised.[17]

The National Security Strategy prepared for and signed by Barack Obama in May 2010 conformed to the continuum: the United States faced "no greater or more urgent danger" than a terrorist attack with a nuclear weapon. Effective dissemination of a lethal biological agent within a US city, it went on to say, would endanger the lives of hundreds of thousands of people and have unprecedented economic, societal, and political consequences.[18] In just the first two years of the Obama administration, three new plans were added to the WMD lineup: the Federal Interagency Improvised Nuclear Device Concept Plan, the Federal Strategic

Guidance Statement for Chemical Attacks in the United States, and the Planning Guidance for Response to a Nuclear Detonation in the United States.

Invisible to the public and with Congress oblivious, as head of the WHMO Caldera oversaw the Program: initiating the legal reviews, intimate with the president behind the scenes, traveling with him on almost every out-of-town trip. Until April 27. Barely three months into the Obama administration, a Boeing 747 airframe painted in the colors of Air Force One and accompanied by two F-16 fighter jets appeared in the skies over New York harbor, making an otherwise routine publicity flight to take a picture of the plane with the Statue of Liberty in the background. At about ten o'clock on a brilliantly sunny morning, the giant airliner dropped down to 1,000 feet. The immediate reaction of those who saw it in the skies over New York and New Jersey was to envision another terrorist attack, with the fighter jets streaking to shoot down the plane. Buildings were evacuated, people flooded into the streets in panic. New York mayor Michael Bloomberg fumed, and a "furious" Obama accepted Caldera's resignation on May 8.

When the administration announced that Caldera's deputy, George D. Mulligan, Jr., would become the new director of the White House Military Office, the media reported the Statue of Liberty incident as some cuckoo PR scheme gone bad, oblivious to the fact that Caldera was there to beef up the XYZ because of the ever present threat of another 9/11 and completely out to lunch about how his replacement put the running of the Program back in the professional ranks of a real gray man. The media applauded that Caldera's replacement wasn't some political hack. As did the president. "George brings decades of experience and has served with integrity and a deep commitment to his country—not just in his role at the White House Military Office, but throughout his distinguished career," Obama said.[19] Mulligan, a retired naval officer, had been deputy director since 2005 and had served in various WHMO positions since 1994. He was the classic invisible man who would become the new first among equals, the new number one executive agent.[20]

Then, in June 2013, Obama appointed trusted insider Emmett S. Beliveau to replace Mulligan, who was going back to the Pentagon. Beliveau had been with the president since day one at the White House, director of advance and deputy in the chief of staff's office. Obama's man would take his training wheels off and follow in the footsteps of Hagin and Caldera as the executive agent extraordinaire, political overseer of a Program crying out for supervision by the elected but one still wholly between the lines.

Meet the new boss, same as the old boss—or perhaps more accurately: new boss, meet the old boss.

CHAPTER ELEVEN

First Family

*Safety from external danger is the most powerful director of
national conduct.... The violent destruction of life and property
incident to war, the continual effort and alarm attendant on a
state of continual danger, will compel nations the most attached to
liberty to resort for repose and security to institutions which have
a tendency to destroy their civilian and political rights. To be
more safe, they at length become willing to run the risk
of being less free....*
ALEXANDER HAMILTON, "THE FEDERALIST No. 8"

Mary Cheney, the vice president's youngest daughter,
was scuba diving with her partner, Heather Poe, on
the tiny Caribbean island of Bonaire on 9/11, seemingly another
American citizen a world away.

As she tells the story, the two emerged from an "amazing
dive" to a minivan tearing down the beach road filled with Secret
Service agents, one of her protective detail jumping out and saying something had happened and "we've got to go." Given the call
sign Alpine by the Secret Service because of her love of skiing,
Mary was one of an exclusive thirty or so—the president and his
wife, the vice president and his wife, their children, even their
grandchildren—who are the First Family of the XYZ.

They were taken back to their hotel, where a protective screen
of agents and encryption was established; Mary spoke to her

mother—call sign Author—who had been rushed back to the White House from an early-morning meeting blocks away.[1] Then she spoke to her father—call sign Angler. A little more than twenty-four hours after that, Mary and Heather were exclusive passengers on a specially laid-on US Customs Service jet. The skies were still closed to commercial and private traffic; people were stranded everywhere and anywhere; but not the vice president's adult daughter and her partner.[2]

Elizabeth Cheney (call sign Apollo), the elder daughter, was in her car on her way to work at the State Department when the first plane hit.[3] After she heard the news on the radio, she also called her father, still in his office; he assured her that he was safe but said he had to go.[4] The Secret Service informed Liz that her husband and *her* toddler children, the vice president's grandkids, were already being whisked away from their upper Northwest Washington home in a hush-hush maneuver, with the nanny.[5]

Vice President Cheney relocated behind the heavy steel doors inside the Presidential Emergency Operations Center (PEOC, pronounced "pea-ock") underneath the East Wing of the White House, perhaps the most exclusive command bunker of all.[6] A military officer there that day describes the facility as plain and functional, with a large conference room at its center and living accommodations for the chief executive off to one side. Adjacent to it and accessed from a separate entrance is the emergency apparatus of the White House Military Office, a thirty-by-twenty-foot operations center with desks, computers, telephones, and televisions.[7] Among those joining Cheney: Condi Rice and her deputy Steve Hadley;[8] Cheney's chief of staff, Scooter Libby; one of his national security advisors, Eric Edelman; his counselor Mary Matalin; deputy White House chief of staff Josh Bolten; economic advisor Lawrence Lindsey; director of media affairs

Tucker Eskew; assistant to the president Nick Calio; Transportation Secretary Norman Mineta; and Cheney's wife, Lynne.[9]

Others were summoned. Cheney's counsel and bureaucratic doppelgänger David Addington (he of the "insurgents" label during Hurricane Katrina) had fled the building, only to be called back by the vice president.[10] The vice president also gave authorization for presidential counsel Karen Hughes to be brought in by military drivers; she was late for work that day because she was with her son Robert at school.[11] There was also the PEOC operations section day shift on duty, Cheney's Secret Service agents, the White House communications team, and various military officers of the White House Military Office and the National Security Council staff who had gone to the PEOC bunker after the Pentagon was hit and served as go-betweens, with the White House Situation Room literally overhead.[12] At one point the oxygen in the overcrowded bunker dropped to such a dangerous level, all but the most essential senior officials were asked to leave.[13]

First Lady Laura Bush, call sign Tempo, was on Capitol Hill when the news came in, scheduled to meet with the Senate Education Subcommittee. Senators Edward Kennedy and Judd Gregg of New Hampshire met her as her limo pulled up, making small talk and playing it cool in Kennedy's office as they waited to either carry on with the hearing or implement some kind of emergency procedure. Then the Pentagon was hit. Mrs. Bush's Secret Service detail hustled her to Senator Gregg's hideaway office on the lower-level interior of the massive Capitol until a heavily armed emergency response team from the uniformed division arrived. The head of her protective detail wanted to take Tempo to a secure location, leaving the staff behind, but the First Lady stood firm and they all ran behind black-clad men with guns drawn through the Capitol basement and the Russell Senate Office Building garage to waiting limos and vans and were taken to a Secret Service building less than a mile away. There Tempo waited in an underground conference room for most of the day, watching television and trying to get her husband, daughters, and parents on the phone. One of the First Lady's aides was sent back to retrieve a few days of clothes for her just in case; her advance man retrieved Spot, Barney, and Kitty, the Bushes' two dogs and cat.[14]

Turquoise, the code name for the president's nineteen-year-old daughter, Barbara, was shuttled from her classes at Yale University to the New Haven office of the Secret Service. Twinkle, the call sign for her twin sister, Jenna, a freshman at the University of Texas in Austin, was awoken in her dorm room and taken to the downtown Driskill Hotel.[15]

In Sarasota, when President Bush—call sign Trailblazer—was told of the attack by his communications officer on the way to Emma E. Booker Elementary School, his first words were "I want to talk to my wife." It was the most human of reactions; it took almost until noon before a reliable line could be established.[16] *"Take care of my wife and daughters,"* he snarled at his supervisory agent as he was hustled away.[17] "I couldn't believe that the president of the United States couldn't reach his wife in the Capitol Building," Bush later wrote.[18]

When it comes to the government's survival, there's both a white and a black system. The white system, the ABCs of continuity, is the one that is open to federal agencies and emergency responders (and even states and private businesses) and is contained in federal budgets and government regulations; it complies with the laws, promotes cooperation and uniformity, provides incentives—even if one of them is merely access and membership—for participation from everyone. The black system appears in no public budget, does not follow any laws, and merely commandeers power in the name of continuity, of doing "its job," and of providing key services.

Internally, this multibillion-dollar enterprise[19] is deeply striated, with at least four different programs and four different lists. At the very bottom is continuity of operations—called COOP—which is the noncaloric pabulum doled out to civil departments and state and local governments. Every agency, every command, every base has a COOP plan, the outlines directed by higher headquarters and vaguely compliant with openly published plans and laws: backed-up computers and alternate headquarters and set procedures for devolution of authorities.

Next higher up is continuity of government—or COG—often used as a catchall but really representing the *contingency plans* for survival of government in the case of a national emergency. Like DEFCONs—the Defense Readiness Conditions—that guide military readiness, executive branch departments and agencies operate according to centrally declared Continuity of Government Readiness Conditions (or COGCONs). These establish response levels for government agencies, in theory running what remains.[20] ("In theory" because FEMA is in charge of COG;[21] but since FEMA doesn't include the national security agencies or the White House under the Program, COG is not the primary focus of executive agent survival.)

Enduring Constitutional Government is COG's cousin, the effort that reaches beyond the executive branch to the legislative and judiciary as well. This is not to say that everything dealing with Congress or the Supreme Court falls within ECG; they each have their own COOP plans at lower levels that are also uncontrolled by the executive, and higher plans as well for those parts that conform with the Program dealing with succession to the presidency.

The third-highest level—for want of a better term—is

national security continuity. Though also officially COG, this is the realm of military command, nuclear command and control, intelligence continuity, and the extraordinary plans of the national mission force all above and beyond the COG of FEMA and the civil agencies. And one assumption of national security COG is the active involvement of some enemy (or at least the threat of terrorist attack), thereby necessitating protective and preemptive measures because some entity is assumed to be intent on thwarting the best-laid plans.

There is something even higher, something rarely spoken about and the realm of the most secret plans of government: it is called Continuity of the President. COP is the true domain of the executive agents and governs the existence of the First Family and a chosen few. Unlike with COOP, COG, or ECG, though encompassing them all, no one declares continuity of the president; it is just the day-to-day automaticity. Following the attack on the Pentagon, President Bush was urged not to return until Cheney and Rice could "find out what the hell was going on."[22] The essential staffers traveling with the president that day crammed into five hardened Secret Service cars and Suburban support vehicles and roared down Route 41 to Sarasota-Bradenton airport, where Air Force One was waiting, destination literally unknown. With the president were Andrew Card, White House chief of staff; Karl Rove, senior advisor; Harriet Miers, the presidential staff secretary; Dan Bartlett, deputy assistant to the president; Ari Fleischer, press secretary; Gordon Johndroe, assistant press secretary; and Brigadier General Mark Rosenker, director of the White House Military Office.[23] In addition, there were Representatives Dan Miller and Adam Putnam of adjacent Sarasota districts, back in Florida that day because of the president's visit; and Matt Kirk, the White House congressional liaison.[24]

Air Force One also carried the men and women who make up

what is commonly called "the package," the administrative, security, intelligence, and military support structure that travels with the chief executive, a group that both protects him and isolates him from any chaos that is going on feet or heartbeats away:[25] There was Colonel Mark Tillman, the presidential pilot and commander of the Presidential Airlift Group and the rest of the crew of Angel, the call sign for the plane; Bush's military aide with the football, the President's Emergency Satchel; there was Blake Gottesman, one of the president's "body men," or personal aides; the president's Secret Service protection detail; Navy Captain Deborah Loewer, director of the White House Situation Room and the presidential communications officer that day; and the president's CIA briefer, who that day was just coincidentally Mike Morell, a man who would himself become director in 2012 after David Petraeus's indiscretions.[26] Also present were the nameless audiovisual specialists, communicators, and IT experts and the drivers from the White House; the galley stewards, flight attendants, engineers, mechanics, and security for Angel itself; the official White House photographer; and the fourteen members of the White House press assigned to the primary pool that day, who get to fly in the back of the plane.[27]

It was a lot of ballast, and as soon as the plane landed at Barksdale Air Force Base in Louisiana, the superfluous press and the congressmen were dumped. The original plan, once the Pentagon was hit, was to fly directly to Offutt Air Force Base near Omaha, the headquarters of the Strategic Command, but according to the head of the White House Military Office, Andrew Card felt that that would take too long. "It was very important to the President to address the nation and make sure that the people could see that he was safe and in total control of the situation," Rosenker said.[28] So they landed at Barksdale so the president could make a public statement.[29] Then it was on to Offutt.

Once Air Force One landed in Nebraska, the Secret Service was still adamant about the president not returning to Washington; they wanted him to hunker down at Offutt for twelve hours or more. Bush argued with his handlers and with Cheney, who was also urging him to stay away. "Unless they tell me something I haven't heard," Bush seethed, "this ass is going back to Washington."[30] So after less than an hour on the ground, Colonel Tillman was told that he'd better get ready to move again; the decider had decided to be the decider. The Program went through all of the motions, requiring who knows what strings to be pulled and what superhuman feats to extend the bubble, launching the Strategic Command's Airborne Command Post, a plane reserved for nuclear war that looks much like Air Force One, as a decoy a few minutes before Air Force One took off.[31]

One of the reasons the executive agents exist is that on any random Tuesday, and with all of the live scenarios swirling, plans are sure to fail, things are sure to go wrong. But on this Tuesday, one of the oddest of things that went wrong was that the head of the Program—the chief executive agent—wasn't where *he* was supposed to be.

Joe Hagin, officially deputy White House chief of staff in charge of operations, former body man for Bush I and a man who had become part of Bush II's inner circle on the campaign trail—"part of the family," Andrew Card later said[32]—was the president's man who oversaw the Program. But on that day, Hagin was with an advance team scouting an upcoming presidential visit in New York City, uncharacteristically separated, neither with the apparatus of the presidency nor at the White House. A testament to Hagin's abilities (or his power), the NYPD assigned a set of squad cars to rush him and his crew across the Hudson River, where they were handed off to New Jersey state troopers, who roared with them down the Jersey Turnpike to Dover Air Force Base in Delaware, where they boarded a waiting military jet, destination Omaha and President Bush. Halfway to Nebraska, in the air over Missouri, Hagin learned that Air Force One was unexpectedly returning to Washington, so he ordered his plane turned around as well: destination Andrews Air Force Base in Maryland, where a flashing-lights convoy of Secret Service, military, and police awaited to drive them all to the White House.[33]

At about 10 a.m., almost an hour and a half after the first plane hit the World Trade Center and twenty-five minutes after the Pentagon was hit, the Program kicked in with an announcement: "By executive order of the President of the United States, Continuity of Government and Continuity of Presidency programs are now in effect."[34] Up to that point, executive agents and protective details all across the government had been operating in precautionary mode, but now everything was official, mandatory, and automatic. The plans would be implemented. An aide even informed the vice president that he had to evacuate; but Cheney looked at him like he was insane and said he wasn't going anywhere.[35]

That day, third in line to be president was House Speaker John Dennis "Denny" Hastert of Illinois, a man *Rolling Stone* magazine named one of the ten worst members of Congress *ever* and the weakest House speaker in history.[36] Cheney at first had trouble reaching him on the phone, but when he did, he suggested that Hastert go to a secure location—Mount Weather in Bluemont, Virginia.[37] Hastert was taken to Andrews Air Force Base and from there was helicoptered to Mount Weather, arriving by 11 a.m.[38] Hastert went to the bunker with other senior legislators, only to return to Washington that afternoon before the official all-clear was given, joining others members to sing "God Bless America" on the Capitol steps.[39]

The next in line for the presidency, the president *pro tempore* of the Senate—the longest-serving member, Senator Robert Byrd of West Virginia, then eighty-three years old—refused to move anywhere and was taken to his Capitol Hill home instead.[40]

Following Byrd on the constitutional succession chart was Secretary of State Colin Powell, who was in Peru; airborne and headed back to the US by 11:58 a.m.[41] At 3:30 p.m., an impromptu National Security Council meeting was held in the White House, now with Cheney, Rumsfeld, and CIA director George Tenet present, Powell still in the air on his way back.[42]

Left on the tarmac in Sarasota that morning to fend for himself was Secretary of Education Rod Paige, the sixteenth in line for the presidency. Paige, a constitutional successor, drove back to the nation's capital in a rental car with his chief of staff.[43] An argument could be made—if anyone noticed—that it was a good idea to separate the various constitutional successors to the presidency, leaving one in Florida just in case. But it wasn't intentional and it wasn't part of any plan. Don Evans, secretary of commerce and tenth in line for the presidency, sat in his office all morning on 9/11 awaiting some kind of order or word, even after Continuity of Government measures were implemented; those in charge had completely forgotten about him and his department. Evans finally had an aide drive him home to McLean, Virginia, and sat around at home for the rest of the day watching television.[44] After almost fifty years of preparations and practice, after constructing an elaborate and foolproof edifice, the executive agents had overlooked a major branch of the executive office, or were too busy—or had their own plans.

Attorney General John Ashcroft, eighth in line for the presidency, was also in the air when he learned about the Twin Towers, ordering his government plane to turn around and return to Washington. ESCAT had been declared by the Pentagon—Emergency

Security Control of Air Traffic—a kind of martial law in the skies, which meant that no plane could now fly without military authorization. Evidently Ashcroft wasn't important enough to clear his own way through, and he had to wait for a military fighter escort to come and accompany him before proceeding into Washington airspace: the attorney general, the chief law enforcement officer of the United States, on a government plane.[45]

Within twenty-four hours, an army of some 4,000 serfs had taken care of the family—Trailblazer and Tempo, Twinkle, Turquoise, Angler and Author, Alpine, Apollo, the grandkids, the nanny, and their pets—driving and flying them here and there, protecting them and feeding them. Former President Bill Clinton, who was in Cairns, Australia, got his Secret Service detail to falsely invoke a threat to him so that he could get clearance (and a government plane) to fly home that night.[46] President Bush's parents—former President George H. W. Bush and his wife, Barbara—were also away from home, on their way from Washington, DC, to Houston for a speaking engagement, when their commercial plane was ordered to the ground in Milwaukee; the former First Family were secured at a nearby motel by their Secret Service detail. After the harrowing experience of eating dinner at an Outback Steakhouse, the next morning Timberwolf and Tranquility somehow also got the okay—and a government plane—to fly back to Kennebunkport. "Flying from a totally closed-down airport, through a total [sic] empty sky, to a totally closed-down airport was eerie. But it was nice to be home," the former First Lady recounts.[47]

While the First Family was being catered to, what's called the survivors' core was evacuated, with just enough time to notify their families and loved ones, who were given a toll-free phone number to contact them but were otherwise left behind.[48] General Dick Myers, then vice chairman of the Joint Chiefs of Staff, recalls that once Continuity of Government was declared, the core—a rotating staff of around 150 senior officials from every Cabinet department, each with orders to join up with the envelopes at underground bunkers to implement continuity plans *if* Washington is decimated—went into action.[49] Sort of. Myers, who normally would be in the survivors' core, stayed at the Pentagon—the Joint Chiefs chairman, Army General Hugh Shelton, also being out of the country that day—leaving survival to a third-ranking army reserve three-star general who later publicly bragged that for a while he was the ranking military man at the bunker on 9/11.[50]

Many of the survivors' core did evacuate, and some were indeed in some official chain of command and confirmed by the Senate: because Secretary of Defense Donald Rumsfeld also refused to move, Deputy Secretary of Defense Paul Wolfowitz was driven to Davison Army Airfield, not far from the Pentagon, where he was then helicoptered to Site R—commonly known as Raven Rock—on the Maryland-Pennsylvania border.[51] Secretary of the Army Thomas White, the top executive agent in the Pentagon hierarchy, not just the coordinator of continuity for the Pentagon but also the middleman for military support to civil authorities, insisted on staying at the Pentagon but was forcibly herded out of the building and off to Site R by his handlers, leaving Army Vice Chief of Staff General Jack Keane in charge of the army (and of decisions relating to military support to civil authorities) for the day, until the Program implementers recognized that they had operated contrary to their own plans and brought White back.[52]

Many other midlevel officials who worked at the White House—some of whom were also supposed to be part of the survivors' core—also declined to evacuate, pulling in information and feeding it to Cheney and Bush, acting as the intermediaries to

Air Force One and the underground bunker. There was an awkward moment when gas masks were brought into the White House Situation Room and there weren't enough to go around for all who stayed; one executive agent also compiled a "death list" so that if the building was destroyed there would at least be a record of who was there in the national rubble.[53]

Had the worst come then, the men and women in the aboveground White House Situation Room would have been gone as well, as might have the vice president, national security advisor Rice, and her deputy, Hadley, both of whom stayed in the underground bunker. In other words, the survivors' core that day was whoever it ended up being, who happened to be in or out of town, who evacuated or who was superfluous, who was wherever they were at the moment they were there, because other than Cheney, who stayed in the imaginary safety of a hole in the ground, everyone else was hypothetically vulnerable.

At about 4 p.m., President Bush had had enough with "this continuity-of-government thing," as he called it, the faceless and nameless authority that was implementing plans and purporting to help but also, in his opinion, making the country and the presidency look like a horse's ass. Enough with going along with these self-declared rules, Bush said, telling the White House additionally that he now wanted every effort expended to bring the Cabinet home, highest priority. The president listened to the arguments of the Secret Service one more time, and to Cheney and Rice, about how it was much wiser to let the system remain in charge and about the need for him to stay away. Bush thanked them for their input and announced that he was canceling the executive order for Continuity of the Presidency. He was returning to Washington.[54]

Six hours later, back in the White House, address to the nation delivered, orders given to get the entire Cabinet home for a morning meeting,[55] rescues and cleanup under way, panic *some-what* subsided, Vice President Cheney, his wife, his military aide with the football, his vice presidential communications officer, his doctor, three Secret Service agents, and his two top staffers—Scooter Libby and David Addington—got into Marine Two, embarking from the South Lawn, from which only the president had ever before taken off previously, for a helicopter trip to Camp David, that night's "undisclosed location."[56]

In his autobiography, Cheney tersely says only that "the Secret Service evacuated Lynne and me to Camp David, a secure location apart from the president."[57] He strangely makes no mention of the mountains moved on behalf of his broader family. By September 13, Aspen Lodge filled with the Cheney clan, the kids and spouses, the grandkids, and the nanny, with an invisible cadre in the background doing the dishes and doing the laundry—no doubt an elite, but still made up of men and women who all kissed their own families good-bye to serve *the* First Family.

Chapter Twelve

Executive Agents

*The powers not delegated to the United States by the Constitution,
nor prohibited by it to the States, are reserved to the States
respectively, or to the people.*
TENTH AMENDMENT TO THE CONSTITUTION

I n the spring of 2012 two very strange local government appointments were made in the nation's capital. In May, Mayor Vincent Gray nominated Christopher Geldart, a resident of Maryland and a former Republican political appointee in the Bush administration, to direct the District of Columbia's Homeland Security and Emergency Management Agency.[1] A month later, President Obama appointed Brigadier General Renwick Payne, a thirty-eight-year veteran of the New York National Guard and a longtime resident of Fredericksburg, Virginia, to be the adjutant general of the District of Columbia National Guard.[2]

A Democratic mayor from the bluest of the blue portions of the American map hiring a Republican homeland security apparatchik? And a New Yorker and resident of Virginia to be head of what purports to be the successor to the citizen's militia connected to the local population—the people's guard against federal tyranny? One might argue that the District of Columbia is the reason for the exceptionality. The DC National Guard is the only guard organization that is not under the control of any governor, as there is no governor; so only the president—but in practicality the secretary of defense—can activate it during natural disasters or civil emergencies, militia legacy be damned and community connection secondary.[3] District government and the District's own homeland security agency similarly might be fine for dealing with snowstorms or the needs of the residents of the city who are unaffiliated with the federal government, but in national matters, and not just in national security matters, the local government must give way to 250-plus federal agencies, over 100 foreign embassies, and dozens of federal police departments.

This is what the country will someday look like: executive agents in charge who are conversant in and reverent toward national security, none of them elected, none of them public men or women whose nominations were submitted to the Senate for its advice and consent. Regardless of feeble residency requirements, they are decidedly not locals, let alone pillars of the community. That is, unless you consider that the local community is national security and the state is martial life.

For the executive agents, the District of Columbia is today merely a pimple on what the government calls the National Capital Region,[4] a statutory entity and national security domain that describes the city and the surrounding Maryland and Virginia counties, but one that for the purposes of the XYZ is itself wholly too narrow, given the needs of continuity and homeland security and all of the "interdependencies of the critical infrastructure"[5] that transcend even this sweeping entity. Thus, despite the law, for the XYZ the region additionally includes eight surrounding counties[6] and a host of additional outposts extending to the second, third, and fourth lines of federal defense in West Virginia, Pennsylvania, Delaware, New York, South Carolina, and beyond.[7] It is a virtual state that only exists in the designs of the executive agents, endowed with Clausewitzian hyperbole—"the political and military center of gravity of the US with an infrastructure vital to the global interests of the nation"[8]—befitting all of the legal and constitutional exceptions.

At the center of governance for this entity—it could be called the State of Mass Destruction or Continuity Land—is not a mayor. The two governors of Maryland and Virginia are similarly discharged, politely treated by the executive agents like doddering grandparents, accorded all of the politeness but dismissed by the Department of Homeland Security as unable to provide the "comprehensive and coordinated regional focus" that between-the-lines demands.[9] There is also something called the Office of National Capital Region Coordination, created after 9/11, but by now we should recognize from our civics lessons that coordination means just that: not in command of anything, and even there coordination is wholly irrelevant because should a catastrophe occur, the Program takes charge.[10]

One could say that local control thus falls to the commander in chief, and if not the president serving in his constitutional role, then at least one of the successors, should *what-if* ever come to pass. In this state of hyperpreparedness and sealed envelopes, though, the president has already delegated to extraordinary authorities the most important tasks: continuity and stasis to the Program and the White House Military Office; the world of terrorism and WMD to the FBI and the national mission force; and the Doomsday instructions to the military aides and the National Command Authority. The Potemkin village falls to the Department of Homeland Security and FEMA and Congress.

For the actual defense of the capital, the secretary of defense is in charge. He has additionally delegated particular responsibilities for the governance of the National Capital Region: to the Defense Continuity Program Office and other special offices, the Joint Staff, the nuclear people, his own Pentagon Force Protection

Agency, the secretary of the army, the Colorado-based commander of NORTHCOM, the Army North commander in Texas; and to the Air Forces North in Florida to run the integrated air defense system around Washington. The entirety merges at the Joint Force Headquarters National Capital Region, the military command once known as the Military District of Washington, which resides at Fort McNair on the Potomac River. This Joint Force Headquarters National Capital Region is small and largely unknown and the closest thing to any one military entity (as opposed to an individual) being in charge, responsible, as it says, for "full spectrum" operations in innocuous-sounding official-speak for situations regarding "land-based homeland defense, defense support of civil authorities and incident management" in the National Capital Region.

The idea of one single headquarters came out of the attack on the Pentagon and, on June 20, 2003, Donald Rumsfeld signed the Joint Force Headquarters order; its day-to-day mission is to take operational control of whatever military forces might be assigned to protecting the government in an emergency.[11]

But for all of the talk of national unity and clarity in chains of command, there is no single general in command of Washington, and never could be. There is a commander of the Joint Force Headquarters, a two-star flag officer who rotates through the command assignment like all other generals every eighteen months or so. Under him is a man named Egon F. Hawrylak, deputy commander since 2007.[12] Hawrylak, a retired colonel, is a civilian, so his designation as deputy *commander* of a military organization makes the assignment particularly exceptional. The title—and the official job description—suggests that he could step up to be *the commander*—that is, to command military forces and issue orders—even though he is no more than a member of the civil service. And even there, civilian deputy commander

Hawrylak's job—"to ensure proper alignment of strategic initiatives," according to his biography and job description—requires a special reading of what lies between the lines. The Joint Force Headquarters National Capital Region oddly professes to be "a willing, subordinate partner and advisor" to civil authorities and is so resolutely subordinate to the governors and mayor and the county commissioners located in its joint operating area, that it is the only military command in existence to reassure on its website that its very existence is legal.[13] The headquarters, it says, "operates within the scope of the law. It will not engage in direct law enforcement activities, but when requested by civil authorities and approved by the civilian leadership of DOD, it supports civil authorities in their public safety missions. Existence of a JFHQ enables better planning by all parties, to the benefit of the public."[14]

Across the river in Virginia are Steven E. Calvery and Jonathan H. Cofer, director and principal deputy director of the Pentagon Force Protection Agency (motto: "Protecting Those Who Protect the Nation"). Calvery, a retired Secret Service agent and between the lines for three decades, is a career lawman who came to the Pentagon in 2006. Cofer, a retired brigadier general, is the number two responsible for securing the infrastructure of the Pentagon with a police force of 850, another seemingly straightforward task, except that his gerrymandered territory includes all the "roadways, walkways, [and] waterways" of dozens of Defense Department facilities in addition to the Pentagon, ranging well into Maryland, Virginia, and even Site R and its surroundings in Pennsylvania.[15]

If the Defense Department itself looks like a patchwork of European principalities ruled by heads of intermarried royal families, consider in addition that Defense is not the only department at play. The military must be careful not to step on the Department of Homeland Security's toes when it comes to civil government COG and COOP, which is under FEMA; or to get in the way of the "maritime defense" of the capital—no kidding—which is the responsibility of the Coast Guard; or the Department of Justice, through which the FBI holds the ultimate reins of law enforcement, crisis management, and incident response; or even the Maryland and Virginia National Guards, which indeed answer to their respective governors and might be unavailable for federal service during a nation-changing catastrophe because, well, they might have their own needs and requirements. If that's not complicated enough, there's also the North American Aerospace Defense Command, an international command, so when it comes to defending the skies of the American capital, Canada also has a say (which of course it does not), as do other international organizations that have a presence in Washington, all of which the United States has security and treaty responsibilities for, and for which security falls under the Secret Service and the State Department's Bureau of Diplomatic Security, who somehow think their missions are a priority. That's a lot of players for the executive agents to brush aside.

And there's more! The executive branch, moreover, coexists with the sovereign duchies of the legislative and judicial branches. Everyone in this exceptional geography is and has their own jurisdiction; Congress controls a twelve-block square in the center of the city and has its own three sovereign police forces—the US Capitol Police and the House and Senate Sergeants. The US Supreme Court Police is the same: Enduring Constitutional Government—of all three branches—makes special provisions for survival of the courts, or at least of *the* court.

This sort of impenetrable murk of organizations and exceptions serves two purposes for those of the XYZs. Given the level of sheer bureaucratic brilliance and memory required just to fig-

Lieutenant General Russel Honoré, commander of the federal Joint Task Force Katrina, with Vice President Dick Cheney aboard the USS *Iwo Jima* in the aftermath of Hurricane Katrina, September 8, 2005. Behind Honoré's back, Cheney's counsel, David Addington, prepared a statement to enable the president to declare an "insurrection" in New Orleans, with a forcible federal takeover. At the eleventh hour, Bush declined to force Louisiana to submit, lacking the military's support. (US Navy)

Paratroopers with the 82nd Airborne Division "patrol" Bourbon Street in the French Quarter of New Orleans after Hurricane Katrina, September 13, 2005. President Bush announced the deployment of federal "humanitarian" forces after Louisiana governor Kathleen Blanco thwarted federal pressure to take over the relief effort. By the time the 82nd Airborne arrived, military commanders on the scene knew that the worst of the crisis and the need for security provided by infantry troops had already passed. (US Army)

An experimental unmanned aerial vehicle (UAV) camera on a pedestal atop the thirtieth-floor roof of the Hyatt hotel in downtown New Orleans—the highest vantage point in the area. Air force intelligence officers set up links from the camera to the same kind of ROVER laptops being used by ground targeters in Iraq and Afghanistan to give them a constant overview of the area downtown and for miles around. Congressional investigators and internal Pentagon reports later found that none of this "intelligence" was used to aid the rescue efforts directly. (US Air Force)

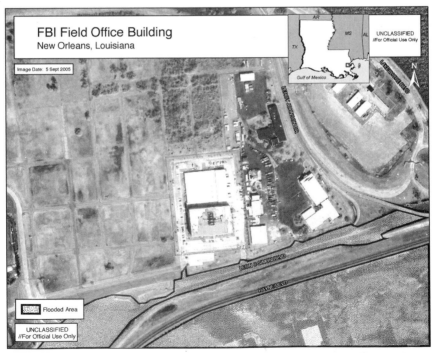

U-2 reconnaissance photograph prepared after Hurricane Katrina of the FBI New Orleans Field Office building and surrounding neighborhood. A small group of FBI personnel stayed behind at the field office, but the intelligence community still imaged the building and prepared multiple annotated graphics in anticipation of a possible need to either defend or assault the area. (US Northern Command, prepared by National Geospatial-Intelligence Agency)

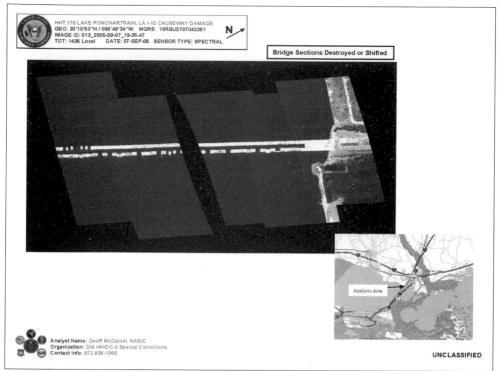

A special spectral image of the I-10 causeway across Lake Pontchartrain prepared by the Defense Intelligence Agency after Hurricane Katrina. The DIA and other intelligence agencies prepared hundreds of similar studies, treating analysis of so-called critical infrastructure in the Gulf as if it were a collection of bombed-out targets in Iraq and Afghanistan, applying the same damage assessment methodologies. (US Northern Command, prepared by National Geospatial-Intelligence Agency)

The container ship M/V *Palermo Senator* in New York harbor being watched over by the coast guard cutter *Escanaba*. The ship was suspected of carrying a possible nuclear weapon or radiological device into the port of New York on the first anniversary of 9/11. It took federal WMD specialists sixty hours to clear the ship, which anchored just ten miles from shore. (US Coast Guard)

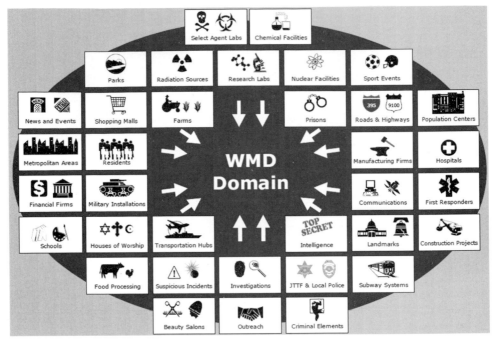

FBI portrayal of the domestic "WMD Domain" in the United States. Fifty-six WMD coordinators are charged with cataloging (and spying on) everything from nuclear, biological, and chemical factories and laboratories to beauty salons and houses of worship. (Department of Justice)

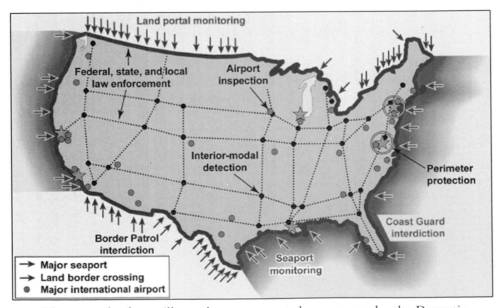

The network of surveillance detectors operated or overseen by the Domestic Nuclear Detection Office in the United States. (Domestic Nuclear Detection Office)

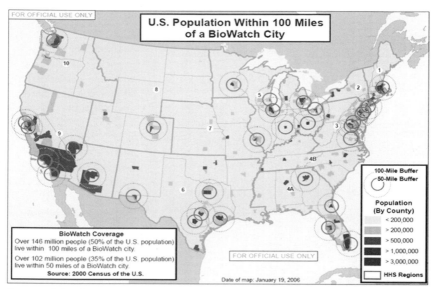

U.S. Population Within 100 Miles of a BioWatch City

100-Mile Buffer
50-Mile Buffer

Population (By County)
< 200,000
> 200,000
> 500,000
> 1,000,000
> 3,000,000

HHS Regions

BioWatch Coverage
Over 146 million people (50% of the U.S. population) live within 100 miles of a BioWatch city.
Over 102 million people (35% of the U.S. population) live within 50 miles of a BioWatch city.
Source: 2000 Census of the U.S.

Date of map: January 19, 2006

A map of the domestic coverage area of BioWatch biological agent detection sensors throughout the United States. The crash program was directed by Vice President Cheney's office after 9/11, growing to a $100-million-plus annual program locally managed by health departments, universities, and emergency departments. (Department of Homeland Security)

BioWatch monitors in a Washington, DC, Metro station, similar to the one that detected an anthrax attack on the White House in October 2001. While President Bush was in China, scientists rushed to analyze the "hit," and a small circle prepared for the possible death of the president and vice president. It was a false alarm. Today, the heaviest concentration of nuclear, biological, and chemical agent detectors in the country surrounds the nation's capital. (Department of Homeland Security)

Above the Law, illustration by Art Young, published in *Puck*, October 1907. "A dark and gloomy landscape where the police have imposed martial law conditions on the laboring class and punish violators with impunity, while, at the top, those responsible for the deplorable working and living conditions stand on a cloud labeled 'Immunity.'" (Library of Congress)

A meeting of the Council of Governors takes place at the Pentagon, March 1, 2011. The council was established by the National Defense Authorization Act in 2008 to strengthen national security partnerships between federal and state governments. Governors serve two-year terms and are appointed by the president, one representing each of the ten FEMA "regions." The council has become the main negotiating body between the states and the Defense Department. (Department of Defense)

California National Guard soldiers from the 270th Military Police Company and 49th Military Police Brigade assigned to the 49th Homeland Response Force practice against rioting role-players at Camp Roberts, California. The 270th and 49th were ostensibly testing and being evaluated on their capabilities as part of the HRF's response to chemical, biological, radiological, nuclear, and high-yield explosive incidences. (National Guard Bureau)

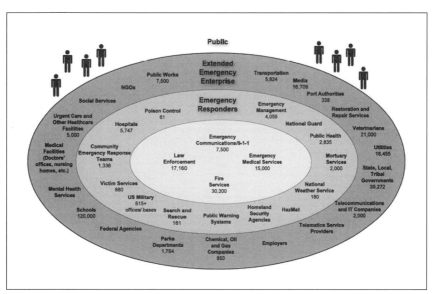

The universe of pseudosoldiers and martial-life volunteers who need to be vetted and credentialed, according to the Department of Homeland Security, stands at close to 60 million Americans. (Department of Homeland Security)

One of the lesser-known federal continuity of government facilities outside Washington, DC. It has been buzzing with activity since 9/11, serving the emergency needs of the Program. (William M. Arkin)

President Obama meets with the director of the White House Military Office, commanders of various White House military units, and his military aides, the men and women who carry the "football," in the Oval Office, June 28, 2012. In the center is George D. Mulligan, Jr., director of the WHMO and head of the Program from May 2009 to June 2013. (White House)

ure out who does what, it makes sense to want Cabinet officers and presidential staff and military commanders and political appointees to stay in charge, but just in case, there are the executive agents—real people like Messrs. Geldart, Hawrylak, Calvery, and Cofer, even uniformed interlopers on special assignment like General Renwick Payne; powerful precisely because each is a possessor of actual knowledge, able to implement when scenarios don't suffice, when the political system falters or plans inevitably break down.

These are Darwinian survivors. It was really only after 9/11 that such a dominant species could be so clearly characterized. Executive agent Richard Clarke emerged first, author of the landmark PDD-39 counterterrorism directive and armchair general of the pre-9/11 "war" against al Qaeda. Clarke was a savvy Washington operator who deftly became a celebrity via the public apology ("your government failed you") before the 9/11 Commission. Clarke had held every policy-making position in Defense and State on his way up, but was also a fine storyteller who could speak of the government as if it were some distinct and different entity from him, happily blaming his bosses for any decisions made or not made, because, well, when it came to the ABCs, he didn't officially make decisions. And when it came to the XYZs, his involvement and duties were secret.

Clarke became a liberal and 9/11 "truth movement" darling after the Bush administration finally disposed of his services, but that then left the vice president's men in the spotlight, and a massive misunderstanding that whatever didn't appeal, or was legally questionable, had been purely a partisan political undertaking of the Bush administration. At the center swirled the infamous lawyers Scooter Libby, David Addington, John Yoo, and Jim Haynes, all fighting on behalf of executive power and each with enormous reach and clout in the XYZ inner councils.[16] Jim Haynes was the first person David Addington—the two of them being the pair who later conspired to invoke the Insurrection Act even before Hurricane Katrina hit, before any directive went out or any discussion was had—called from the White House on 9/11 to discuss emergency authorities and procedures.[17] Still obsessed with the threat of "insurgent" uprisings, Addington even authored a White House signing statement in 2008 claiming that the president's ability to respond effectively to "public emergencies" at home was inadequate, apparently hoping to pry open the door in case of some future Katrina-like challenge.[18]

Like other temporary residents, Addington and company were gone with the electoral cycle, replaced by the new gray men of the Obama administration, such as Louis Caldera and a set of new desk warriors picked from the Democratic Party–leaning roster of executive agents. And of course the new president's staff would consort with and rely upon the permanent Geldarts, Hawrylaks, Calverys, and Cofers.

The key to martial life is, in a very real sense, a perpetual sense of inadequacy. A mountain carved out of impenetrable Appalachian granite on the Pennsylvania-Maryland border and built to survive a nuclear blast is vulnerable: if not the mountain itself, its phone service, electricity, and water and air supplies. Without some system of deterrence to dissuade terrorists from attacking, no fortification, however strong, is beyond terrorism's reach; and without distinction between what is military and what is civilian (such as is conferred in "normal" international law and wartime dealings), the workings of civil society are equally and gravely vulnerable. Security is thus only possible if there are redundancies: redundant communications paths, a plan and a backup plan, a chief and a successor, an ABC and an XYZ, redundant presidents, even two Constitutions.

That means that there really isn't any local anymore, either: there are Washington and the alternate Washingtons, major metropolitan areas becoming their own republics with their own survival dependent on being tied to Washington and not a state. Such adjusted geography isn't just the product of 9/11, nor is it evolved response to modern-day cybervulnerabilities, but instead it is tried and true from the earliest days of planning for nuclear war, when "target and damage zones" never followed state boundaries—in the words of one history of civil defense: "Of the cities which had populations greater than a half a million in 1950, for example, one-third are located at the boundary of two States; of the fifty cities which had the largest populations in 1960 (each, over a quarter of a million), more than one-fourth are located at State boundaries. The Federal Civil Defense Act of 1950 provided for mutual-aid compacts to be entered into by neighboring States; and there have been major efforts, such as followed the 1955 Project East River Review, to stimulate planning based on metropolitan target complexes which cross State lines. But the fact that State boundaries do not coincide with target and damage zones continues to be a major reason for proposals to federalize civil defense more completely."[19]

As nuclear weapons accumulated in the thousands, the Program gave up on civil defense altogether; grandiose programs were proposed but never funded.[20] Civilian "mobilization"—other than public mobilization through fear—was less and less practical for either the national defense or national security. Mobilization was supplanted by emergency planning[21] and largely isolated from the nuclear business. The state National Guards went off in their own directions, preferring to develop as military organizations (with access to Pentagon funding), ceding the responsibilities of both nonmilitary preparedness and the aftermath to civil government (which, of course, is not civil government at all, it is government, because for there to be civil government there would have to be military government and there is no military government).

Civil defense as an act of submission and volunteerism persists, if not in terminology, then in the aggressive public enlistment and national uniformity that are hallmarks of homeland security. There are no outward manifestations of civilians having to do anything (or anything for them *to do*); but intellectually, civilian defense, the original term, remains a uniquely American concept: who ever heard of a nation being founded and structured around the precept of arming the people? As such, then, civil defense has a place of distinction separate from *big* defense or national security or homeland security, even if the original intent of the framers was to prevent government tyranny and more precisely to constrain the long arm of the national government.

At the end of the Johnson administration, a series of natural disasters hit the nation: Hurricanes Hilda and Betsy caused tens of millions' worth of damage in the Southeast, an Alaskan earthquake caused a damaging tidal wave in California, and a lethal tornado swept through Indiana on Palm Sunday in 1965. Hurricane Camille then ripped through the Gulf of Mexico in the first year of the Nixon administration, exposing serious shortcomings in large-scale disaster response.[22] With each succeeding year, the magnitude and cost of damage from natural disasters increased. Everything was conspiring to make it so: more and more people were living in coastal and urban areas, more vulnerable to weather and natural disasters. Rapid and unplanned urbanization in flood-prone regions and the ubiquity of concrete, which collects water, together contributed to bigger and bigger floods. While the number of deaths generally declined due to better preparedness and prevention, more and more people were being affected, with a greater requirement to aid the injured and displaced.[23] An urbanized and modern society was more vulnerable to the loss of basic utilities and thus more dependent on government.

By the time the Federal Emergency Management Agency was created in 1979, civil defense had gone through dozens of revisions, each to accommodate changes in nuclear strategy or as a result of government reorganizations and political power struggles that dispersed more and more specialized aspects of preparedness to more and more specialized professionals throughout the federal government.[24] FEMA in many ways brought the turmoil and fragmentation of services to an end at the federal level; and the director of the independent agency was even at one point made a part of the Cabinet. Yet this in no way resolved the classic tension between military and civilian, between providing for the general welfare and martial emulation, between the dominating vision of the federal government and the practical needs of the civilian population. Indeed, the true precipitant for FEMA was another event that signaled vulnerability and unlimited geography and the death of distinction resident in "critical infrastructure" and all the XYZ that followed: the nuclear accident at Three Mile Island in March 1979.

CHAPTER THIRTEEN

Pull to Push

*American democracy is rooted in the precepts of federalism — a
system of government in which our state governments share power
with federal institutions. The Tenth Amendment reserves to the
states and to the people all power not specifically delegated to the
federal government. Our structure of overlapping federal, state, and
local governance . . . provides unique opportunities and challenges. To
meet the terrorist threat, we must increase collaboration and
coordination. . . . Each level of government must coordinate with the
other levels to minimize redundancies in homeland security actions
and ensure integration of efforts.*
NATIONAL STRATEGY FOR HOMELAND SECURITY 2002

O
n September 14, 2005, before Katrina's floodwaters had
receded, Virginia senator John Warner, chairman of
the Armed Services Committee and one of the longest-serving
members of Congress, sent a letter to Donald Rumsfeld proposing "a thorough review of the entire legal framework governing
a President's power to use the regular armed forces to restore
public order in . . . situations involving a large-scale, protracted
emergency. . . ."

The president, Warner wrote, "should not have to worry
about misperceptions by the public based upon outdated wording
that does not accurately describe what the armed forces may be
doing in a particular emergency," referring to the Insurrection

and *Posse Comitatus* Acts. "The only entity in the United States that has the personnel, the equipment, the training, and the logistical capacity to lend support to the National Guard and other State entities in an emergency of this scale is the Department of Defense."[1]

Asked about the letter, Pentagon spokesman Lawrence Di Rita responded that *Posse Comitatus* indeed was a "very archaic law" and that it consequently limited the Pentagon's ability to defend against twenty-first-century threats.[2]

The next night, in front of a meticulously prepared and lighted backdrop of St. Louis Cathedral on Jackson Square in New Orleans—a stage that Mayor Ray Nagin called "better than Cinderella's castle at Disney World" for the work the White House advance team did to fabricate it amidst a blackout[3]—President Bush declared: "It is now clear that a challenge on this scale requires greater federal authority and a broader role for the armed forces—the institution of our government most capable of massive logistical operations on a moment's notice."[4]

Less than a week later, Rumsfeld, the supposed dissenter in the Katrina coup, wrote to Dick Myers, chairman of the Joint Staff—one of thousands of notes that Pentagon wags labeled "snowflakes" that the secretary showered upon his subordinates. "The only USG [US government] entity currently capable of dealing with many of the key elements of a truly 'catastrophic event' is DOD," Rumsfeld mused, citing "planning, crisis management, prompt deployment of large numbers and appropriate disaster equipment, as opposed to post-crisis domestic reconstruction,"[5] practically plagiarizing Senator Warner while parroting the commander in chief. With FEMA on the ropes and the nation clearly looking to the military, Rumsfeld was a sheer opportunist and contrarian. Plus if there was a budget battle to be won in a power shift, the secretary couldn't resist.

Between the lines, the true authors of Warner's amendment[6]—the very same executive agents who called the people of New Orleans insurgents—had their own parallel plan for unity of command just in case some girl again stood in the way, upending the existing decades-old system of response, built on the precepts of federalism. The White House "lessons learned" report for Hurricane Katrina finally said federalism "has been based on a model whereby local and State governments wait to reach their limits and exhaust their resources before requesting Federal assistance....In other words, the system was biased toward requests and the concept of 'pull' rather than toward anticipatory actions and the proactive 'push' of Federal resources."[7]

The White House report, which its authors proudly said was written based upon "the facts" and without any tampering or watering-down reviews by any outsiders,[8] asserted that catastrophic events and the likelihood of "mass casualty terrorism" demanded that the federal government "actively prepare," that homeland security more emulate the six-decade-old national security system, that it recognize the demand for a chain of command and unity from the president down to the commander in the field.[9] "While we remain faithful to basic constitutional doctrine and time tested principles," it said, "we must likewise accept that events such as Hurricane Katrina and the terrorist attacks of September 11, 2001, require us to tailor the application of these principles to the threats we confront in the 21st Century."[10]

From the very beginning, Rumsfeld thought the Department of Homeland Security a nuisance and a bad idea.[11] Now he opined that it would be a waste of taxpayer money to create yet another new institution to deal with a catastrophe on a Katrina scale. So why not, he wondered, create some new class of problem—a "catastrophic event," be it natural or terrorist—and then designate the Defense Department as the lead agency for such an event? If such an event occurred, rather than waiting for civil government to "pull" items from the military by requesting them, the military would "push" capabilities as it saw needs emerge.[12]

Rumsfeld was following a snowball down the hill. Yet almost every detail that he cited in his memo to justify a change in policy and law was wrong: he conflated federal troops and the National Guard as being one when bragging about the size of the *Pentagon's* response to Katrina; then he complained about restrictions on use of "the military" after he had just talked about how historic the deployment was. Rumsfeld then repeated the official deceit that the Defense Department "does not organize, train, or equip" for the domestic mission; and most important, he ignored the toughest question of all: whether boots on the ground—not rescuers, engineers, or logisticians, but infantry as embodied in the 82nd Airborne Division, were even really ever needed during Katrina, the very kind of contrarian probe that the defense secretary was otherwise famous for.

At a routine Senate hearing on June 12, 2006, the Warner-Bush-Rumsfeld automatic-trigger avalanche gathered mass. Senator Saxby Chambliss of Georgia introduced Section 1076 to the upcoming defense authorization bill: "to clarify the role and use of the Armed Forces for domestic use during natural disasters or other events." Congress, he proposed, should "update" the Insurrection Act to make explicit the president's authority to use the armed forces to restore order and enforce federal law in cases where public order has broken down in situations like Katrina. Senator Warner spoke up in support: "The bill includes a provision that would update the provision in Title 10 known as the Insurrection Act to clarify the President's authority to use the Armed Forces to restore order and enforce Federal laws in cases where, as a result of a terrorist attack, epidemic, or natural disaster, public order has broken down beyond the ability of local law enforcement or State Guard, or a combination thereof, to effectively bring about law and order."[13]

Several governors questioned the need for a change that would have the effect, among several things, of taking the National Guard away from them.[14] Grumbling continued for months, but the amendment got tucked away in the $500-billion defense bill and passed on September 30, 2006.[15] Section 1076 amended the Insurrection Act of 1807 (renamed the Enforcement of the Laws to Restore Public Order statute)[16] to explicitly allow the president to use federal troops not just in the event of the four conditions contained in the act—"insurrection, domestic violence, unlawful combination, or conspiracy"—but now also to: "restore public order and enforce the laws of the United States when, as a result of a natural disaster, epidemic, or other serious public health emergency, terrorist attack or incident, or other condition in any State or possession of the United States, the President determines that…domestic violence has occurred to such an extent that the constituted authorities of the State or possession are incapable of maintaining public order…"

Senator Patrick Leahy of Vermont led the opposition, stating, "We certainly do not need to make it easier for Presidents to declare *martial law*. Invoking the Insurrection Act and using the military for law enforcement activities goes against some of the central tenets of our democracy. It creates needless tension among the various levels of government—one can easily envision governors and mayors in charge of an emergency having to constantly look over their shoulders while someone who has never visited their communities gives the orders."

The implications were enormous, he added, explaining that "using the military for law enforcement goes against one of the founding tenets of our democracy." He also complained that the amendment was slipped in with little chance of comment, and with no associated hearings.[17]

Dissent was not restricted to liberal senators. Lindsey Graham, Republican of South Carolina and also a lawyer in the Air Force Reserve, opined on Fox News that he was "not comfortable with suspending local laws and state laws and allowing American military people to come into any community, arrest people and seize property, unless there is a very good reason." The law of the land established prohibitions against the federal military "coming in and taking over a local community or a state and becoming law enforcement officers," he said. Graham acknowledged that it might be worthwhile to look more closely at existing laws to make sure the military "can provide assistance" when needed, "but we should not allow the federal government, willy-nilly, to take over state and local functions in terms of law enforcement."[18]

The National Governors Association—all fifty governors, Democrat and Republican alike—also expressed concerns about the expansion of federal authority, as did the Council of State Governments and the Adjutants General Association, representing the heads of the all the National Guards. They were joined by the National Guard Association of the United States, representing the rank and file; the National Sheriffs' Association; and the national Fraternal Order of Police, all demanding that Congress repeal the change in statute.[19]

Warner-Bush-Rumsfeld had argued in response that what happened in New Orleans hadn't qualified as an insurrection and that the language was therefore obsolete; they were doing nothing but updating and clarifying authorities the president already had.[20] But Section 1076 looked suspiciously like insurance for a future political fight when another governor declined federalization. The new wording gave the president authority to decide when an emergency was outside the capability of a state to maintain public order, and Congress was now implicitly encouraging him to federalize the National Guard at his sole discretion. The "other conditions" phrase in the new law even compelled the *New York Times* to argue in an editorial that presidential power was being dangerously expanded,[21] but except for that, the counterattack against Section 1076 was mostly an inside-Washington affair.

When the Democrats took control of the Senate after the 2006 election and Leahy became chair of the Judiciary Committee, he moved to muster the support needed to repeal the provision. Senator Warner weakly surrendered, saying that he was "receptive to the Senate reviewing this important matter."[22] The National Defense Authorization Act for Fiscal Year 2008, passed in January 2008, returned the Insurrection Act to its previous title and language. The episode was all but forgotten, the XYZ origins of the pull to push and the truth about Katrina never understood, though its stain propelled countless commissions and studies, working groups, "a 180-day plan," a "New FEMA," "One DHS,"[23] new laws relating to federal government military and civil authorities, new National Preparedness Guidelines and a new National Response Framework (eventually replacing the National Response Plan).[24]

After much debate, Congress passed the Post-Katrina Emergency Management Reform Act (PKEMRA), directing that most preparedness programs and functions that had been transferred to homeland security headquarters just four years earlier be put back into FEMA, and that the FEMA administrator, elevated in stature and mandated for the future to be a professional and not a political hack, would "integrate FEMA's emergency preparedness, protection, response, recovery, and mitigation responsibilities to confront effectively the challenges of a natural disaster, act of terrorism, or other man-made disaster." PKEMRA also expanded FEMA's mission to integrate preparedness with protec-

tion, response, recovery, and mitigation—Washington changes
that would precipitate a whole new round of directives and plans
and exercises but that were otherwise inexplicable to normal
humans. Regional offices would be given greater responsibility,
and each would have a Federal Preparedness Coordinator.[25]
FEMA also got new "push" authorities to enable the agency to do
things such as move personnel and equipment before a disaster
rather than having to wait for a state request or a federal proclamation.[26] And in April 2007, FEMA established a National Preparedness Directorate. By the fifth anniversary of the storm
FEMA had increased its permanent full-time employees from
1,700 to 4,457, an increase of approximately 75 percent.[27]

The National Response Framework issued in January 2008 officially turned one mission, now really three—terrorism, natural
disaster preparedness, and dealing with "other emergencies"—into
eight. "Man-made crisis" was added to emergency planning to
clarify matters; so was ensuring the overall "economic security"
of the nation—without defining what that meant—as well as
preserving civil rights and civil liberties and aiding in the fight
against illegal drug trafficking, that is, if doing so could be connected to terrorism.[28] The goal of unity of command that the
Bush administration fought for in Katrina was replaced by a
kinder, gentler unity of effort. "Even when a community is overwhelmed by an incident," the Framework stated, "there is still a
core, sovereign responsibility to be exercised at this local level,
with unique response obligations to coordinate with State, Federal, and private-sector support teams." Under the Framework,
federal, state, local, tribal, private-sector, and nongovernmental
organizations were encouraged to work together both prior to
and during a domestic emergency to create "a unified single
response."[29]

Not only did the new Framework rule the day, but the national lesson was that you couldn't expect a political leader, not at FEMA or at the Department of Homeland Security or even at the White House, to understand a Plan, to pull together all of what was really needed, to be in charge when being in charge was demanded. Nothing was actually resolved: the governors, now particularly alert to the aroma of federal takeover, insisted that they would take command of all military forces (state and federal) under some kind of dual command arrangement, but those who had spent decades with the confines of the national security community knew that such arrangements were contrary to the whole point. And by now, most of the public had accepted their logic.

CHAPTER FOURTEEN

Dual Command

*The United States shall guarantee to every state in this union a
republican form of government, and shall protect each of them
against invasion; and on application of the legislature, or of
the executive (when the legislature cannot be convened)
against domestic violence.*
ARTICLE IV, SECTION 4 OF THE CONSTITUTION

E verything about the first meeting of the Council of Governors on February 23, 2010, screamed American Coup:
a bipartisan council of ten governors—honorary executive
agents—gathering at the Pentagon, outnumbered ten to one by
just the lawyers, for a meeting that the Obama White House
described as organizing "synchronization and integration of State
and Federal military activities in the United States."[1]

Across the table from the ten was the national security management: Robert Gates; Janet Napolitano; General Gene Renuart, outgoing commander of NORTHCOM; General Craig R.
McKinley, chief of the National Guard Bureau; FEMA administrator Craig Fugate; and Admiral Thad Allen, commandant of
the Coast Guard and another man of Katrina fame who had taken
over from the hapless Michael Brown just two weeks after landfall. In the back seats, along the walls, were military aides and
assistants, more Defense Department and homeland security assistant and deputy assistant secretaries, and White House assistants

to the president and assistants to assistants. And also present was John Brennan, assistant to the president for homeland security and counterterrorism, later to be appointed head of the CIA, no doubt checking his BlackBerry for the latest on the kill list, his bifurcated job the epitome of an XYZ lurking within and a country that doesn't know what it already is.

The Council of Governors is Katrina's parting gift, conceived to iron out amicable joint custody of the National Guard.[2] Initially cochaired by Christine Gregoire of Washington and Jim Douglas of Vermont, the governors represented a broad spectrum, except perhaps that among the five Democrats and five Republicans, Louisiana was noticeably absent.[3] Present, though, were the military- and Washington-friendly governors of Maryland and Virginia, both trained and experienced go-betweens for any of the geographically challenged who didn't understand the extent of Washington's shadow.

"We now have a formal body to represent the view of the governors so that we have a negotiation partner," said Paul Stockton, Assistant Secretary of Defense for Homeland Defense and Americas' Security Affairs. "We have two chains of government; they both need to be respected," he added. "Any actions to improve unity of effort must acknowledge, respect, and take advantage of these constitutional dual sovereignties and dual chains of commands. We are going to fail if we have a unity of effort approach where one side is poaching on the other's turf." His ultimate vision, Stockton said, was a regional approach to disaster response.[4]

A regional approach: logical and sensible given how disasters really unfold. Yet the demand of the Constitution is that when the federal government comes in on a domestic matter, federalism has to be preserved and local wishes cannot just be shoved aside. What is more, civilian control of the military has to be maintained.

In comments at a 2006 breakfast hosted by the American Bar Association, Republican Paul McHale, the knowledgeable Katrina veteran who had been Stockton's predecessor, talked about civilian control. Reflecting on *The Federalist Papers* of Alexander Hamilton, McHale said that rather than fearing some kind of overt takeover, Hamilton was concerned about a dependency that could arise should civilian government look to the military to secure internal order. Hamilton feared that when government started deferring to the military, it would be embarking upon a path that would gradually lead to a total reliance at the price of civil liberties. It is for these reasons that the Founding Fathers created a system in which civilian authority is supreme and the military remains focused on its primary function: protecting the United States from external threat.[5]

"The Constitution of the United States was not written to support maximum effectiveness in military operations," McHale went on in congressional testimony about lessons learned from Katrina. "The Constitution was written to establish a federal system of government," he said, so that at the beginning of any domestic military mission, there will always be a separation between the governors, pursuant to their authorities and in control of their state National Guard forces, and the president, who commands federal forces. "We start any domestic mission with a breach in that principle of unity of command," proclaimed McHale. In a crisis, the breach can be addressed through federalization of the Guard or invocation by the president of the Insurrection Act. There can be unity of effort, McHale said, but "that means that instead of a command relationship over all those forces, you respect the normal Constitutional paradigm and insist upon close coordination among those forces." He added emphatically that stripping the Louisiana governor involuntarily of her command and control during Katrina was not the right course of action.[6]

As McHale hinted, and as the true history of Katrina shows, the whole reason for a Council of Governors arose from flawed premises: first, that a better external response to Katrina was actually possible; second, that somehow the mess created was caused by a flaw in the Constitution, the laws, or the chain of command; third, that the president's hands were tied in either being able to call up the Guard or in employing federal troops if that was what he wanted; and fourth, that governors needed new arrangements to secure outside help, specifically federal help.[7]

Yet there they were meeting, committing to a Joint Action Plan on Developing Unity of Effort, to a model Memorandum of Understanding, with the Secretary of Defense agreeing before a crisis to an arrangement of dual command; and to a Pentagon proposal to expand existing authorities to mobilize federal reserves—not the National Guard, but the *other* military reserves—for domestic emergencies. The states in return would obtain a pledge from Washington that it would never again agitate for a takeover. Together, the council and the administration would create the least provocative arrangement to achieve unity, as former Secretary Gates soothingly called it: "living up to our mutual obligation to protect American lives in the face of catastrophes."[8]

While the council deliberated, the army worked out a complex doctrine: in events short of an "extreme emergency," the secretary of the army would bring a designated dual-status commander onto active duty, or a federal officer would accept a commission from a governor into the state National Guard. The dual-status commander would "hold a federal hat in one hand and a nonfederal hat in the other hand but can wear only one hat at a time." There would still be two chains of command, with federal troops remaining under presidential control and, of course, never engaging in law enforcement.[9] Should any conflicts over authority arise, the federal commander, either in charge of a Joint Task Force or working under the governor's National Guard dual-status commander, would continue to execute his federal mission separate from the state mission.[10]

Those new Joint Task Forces in each of the fifty states, the Commonwealth of Puerto Rico, two US Territories, and the District of Columbia were actually step two in the transformation of the Guard's role. Defense Department–sanctioned, Joint Task Force–ready headquarters in each state would "provide command and control for domestic operations." Each JTF would predesignate "federally recognized" commanders and staff elements and work with NORTHCOM to facilitate unity.[11]

After 9/11, step one was when the Defense Department required that all fifty-four entities establish Joint Force Headquarters "to support the Federal missions," going out of its way to reassure state-level officials that the Pentagon couldn't order any governor to do anything as long as forces were under state control, except during exceptions.[12] Of course, all fifty-four National Guard establishments complied and miraculously decided they *needed* a single federal-compliant and connected headquarters, portraying the 2003 move as a way to save money by eliminating separate army and Air National Guard headquarters and disbanding State Area Commands that reported solely to the governors.[13]

Step three was the creation of rapid-reaction forces in each state National Guard to provide a trained and ready "combat arms force" capable of quickly delivering company- and battalion-sized units (300 to 1,800 soldiers), a beefed-up Garden Plot capability, one better trained for regular domestic law enforcement missions. The National Governors Association said these reaction forces would help local and state law enforcement agencies by protecting key sites such as power plants and transportation hubs, establishing roadblocks, and securing weapons of mass destruction incident sites.[14]

Step four, and the true severing of the local bond, was the creation of ten National Guard homeland response forces, one for each of ten FEMA regions, designed explicitly for regional response. Ever since the Clinton administration, Congress, the federal government, and the states aspired to create some kind of robust domestic chemical, biological, radiological, and nuclear consequence management enterprise—initially intended to be civilian but eventually foisted off on the National Guard—but the force failed to materialize as planned, a casualty mostly of the Defense Department's aversion to the domestic mission and a big, recalcitrant army that never wanted to commit active duty combat units for domestic cleanup. The National Guard had agitated for new WMD response capabilities before and after Katrina to boost its relevance portfolio,[15] and now its efforts began to pay off. Partly as a result of the Guard's enthusiasm during the Council of Governors, by 2009 it was decided that "homeland response forces" would largely supplant previously conceived-of formations, both for WMD and other missions, from disaster response to law enforcement.[16]

Regional response runs contrary to American doctrine and constitutional practice, though, precisely because National Guard officers are commissioned by the state, naturally and intentionally in a close relationship with the governor and with greater allegiance to local needs—as well as possessing the requisite local knowledge and aesthetic exemplified in the militia legacy. A concurrent system of dual command breaks that state bond. Each governor can appoint a Joint Task Force commander (certified to serve under federal guidelines), and on the surface, such a commander protects state prerogatives by being in total command of all of the individual domestic forces. In reality, though, the real need for greater state-federal cooperation and agreement is to fill interstate gaps, when National Guard, reserve, and active-duty troops are all operating across porous state borders.[17]

National Guard forces can cross state lines with gubernatorial approval (during Katrina, that is how they operated in 2005), but when Joint Task Forces operate outside their home state, they split off from being commanded by a governor and become one whole government adjunct, each state serving as subordinate units—their fifty-four separate post-9/11 command centers and homeland security departments and intelligence fusion centers melding into one domestic force more national than anything that previously existed. Multistate operations of the National Guard would be overseen and coordinated by the National Guard Bureau in Washington, improving Pentagon and NORTHCOM "access" to National Guard capabilities[18] and providing for more rapid and effective responses across state lines. Federal troops would "consult, coordinate with, and respond to State authorities," Washington said, but federal troops would remain operationally independent.[19] In other words, the National Guard would become in actuality a federal force operating outside the legal and political constraints of federal forces, under a misleading name.

The change had been a long time coming. A year before the Council of Governors meeting on January 28, 2008, the National Guard Empowerment Act was signed, "the most significant and sweeping reforms in the administration and organization of the National Guard" in a hundred years.[20] The head of the National Guard Bureau was elevated to being a "principal advisor" to the secretary of defense, the first step toward his joining the Joint Chiefs of Staff, an honor President Obama bestowed upon him in December 2011 and the first addition to the highest military decision-making body since the commandant of the marine corps was added in 1979.[21]

One might ask, first of all, what the National Guard Bureau *is*, let alone how it gained such status. (Most active-duty military officers asked that very question, including Chairman of the Joint Chiefs General Martin Dempsey.[22]) Not only was the bureau yet another Washington staff organization, but its director commanded nothing but his desk, as military people like to say.

"The Guard has grown to become a front-line, twenty-first-century force," Vermont Senator Patrick Leahy applauded when Congress mandated inclusion of the bureau head as a member of the Joint Chiefs. "This will help clear away those cobwebs and give the Guard a voice in the Pentagon that befits the scale of its missions."[23] In fact, it meant nothing of the sort: the Guard and its congressional supporters had merely won a Washington lobbying battle that turned the Guard into a better homeland first responder, but one more and more under Washington's direction and control.

In December 2011, all the governors further agreed to establish Contingency Dual-Status Command for emergency responses, the very dual command pushed (and rejected) by the Bush administration during Katrina.[24] One commander (chosen and approved by the relevant governor and the president) would command operations and serve the state and federal chains of command. NORTH-COM would train and certify these potential dual-status Joint Task Force commanders. (The first batch of thirty-one National Guards officers was ready to go by mid-2011.[25])

In the yearlong debate following the first Council of Governors meeting, a number of governors argued for guarantees that outside state and federal forces—National Guard, active-duty, and reserve—would indeed be commanded by the state under all circumstances. The best they could extract from Washington in the end was "tactical control" of federal troops and the provision of the two-hatted-never-at-the-same-time agreement.[26] The agreement was reached in an amicable setting, but the new design, in the words of one military study, just brought "complexity and bureaucracy to the coordination process rather than reducing it."[27] Another study concluded that "while the effect of the dual status command unifies efforts between DOD forces [federal troops and the National Guard]...it does not ensure unified effort between military and civilian agencies." That would require the Pentagon "to act as a lead federal agency"[28]—which, under the state of martial life, it does not and cannot, at least not overtly.

One might think that Governor Blanco—long since voted out of office—would be the hero and harbinger of what a model National Guard for the twenty-first century might look like, what with her resisting Washington's coup and declining to turn over state control to the dual command of subordinated unity. Far from it. Instead, governors and National Guard heads clamored so desperately to be consulted and to be a part of the decision-making, to preserve their role as the first of first responders, and fought so hard for prestigious Washington-conferred titles and authorities, they ultimately weakened the states. The institutions Washington demanded, the command relationships, the necessary technical and procedural commonality, combined with the complex paper trail of "assistance" and mutual support, left the National Guards and state homeland security and intelligence establishments so crisscrossed across state borders and so enmeshed in Washington's primacies that their very quality as local militia, citizen soldiers, and checks on federal domination was swallowed whole.

And then there are the exceptions, which the governors explicitly accepted as being just two: conditions of invasion or "attack"—homeland defense—and public unrest.[29] But two was actually just the beginning. The Pentagon also demanded that it be in charge in any matters that had to do with its bases or its "interests,"[30] and there were the additional exceptions of WMD and counterterrorism crisis management and government continuity, not to mention Title 10 missions themselves; Title 10 means "war," that is, the Guard service in any foreign wars waged by the United States, even when the activity takes place from American soil. The National Guard, in its own domestic operations manual, admits perhaps the biggest exception of all: state leadership, it says, would be overridden if "the [active] military [responded] to an emergency involving the use of a weapon of mass destruction, or a terrorist attack, or threatened terrorist attack that results, or could result, in a significant loss of life or property if the President determines that the requirements for emergency response exceed the capabilities of the local, state, and federal agencies."[31] In other words, for every condition that precipitated negotiations, the outcome was an exception.

The governors certainly mediated a more pleasing outcome than overt federal takeover, and emerged with a more powerful voice by uniting as one, now able to fight more effectively for Defense Department money in Washington battles, not an inconsequential short-term victory. But they did so oblivious to the fact that they are slowly losing control over their own hallowed independent military formations while presiding over the erosion of elected civilian control of America, in blissful ignorance of the dynamics and ambitions that exist between the lines.

CHAPTER FIFTEEN

Marching Orders

The right of the people to be secure in their persons, houses,
papers, and effects, against unreasonable searches and seizures,
shall not be violated. . . .
FOURTH AMENDMENT TO THE CONSTITUTION

S uperstorm Sandy formed just before Halloween 2012; the
Obama administration was at the ready. The "event" would
be greeted by the whole of government: federal agencies, the military, state and local partners, the public-private team, all in a
unity of effort, within the national response framework. The
response would consist of proactive support, lean-forward incident management and assistance, life-saving; it would be integrated, layered, resilient—scattered, smothered, covered, chunked,
topped, and diced, as they say at Waffle House. Government blogs,
emergency websites, Twitter feeds, Facebook pages sprang into
action; New Yorkers were encouraged to download the free hurricane app.

On October 26, the White House released an official photo of
President Obama, working man in shirtsleeves, talking on the
phone with FEMA administrator Craig Fugate and John Brennan, who was described in the caption as assistant to the president
for homeland security and counterterrorism. Obama directed
Fugate to ensure that all available resources were brought to bear

to support state and local responders. It wasn't disclosed what he directed Brennan to do; and maybe the incongruity of Brennan's counterterrorism presence struck others as odd, because he was soon ushered off the public stage and out of the photo ops, replaced by professionals with emergency management labels.

Obama had signed Presidential Policy Directive 8, National Preparedness, on March 30, 2011, reaffirming most post-Katrina Bush administration policies[1] but including an unmistakable anthem of cooperation and oneness, declaring, "Our national preparedness is the shared responsibility of all levels of government, the private and nonprofit sectors, and individual citizens."[2] This was in sync with Obama's National Security Strategy, which laid out a fundamental principle of the administration: "National security draws on the strength and resilience of our citizens, communities, and economy."[3]

By the time Sandy hit, Bush's National Response Framework had been joined by Obama's National Preparedness Goal, the National Preparedness System, and a series of five integrated National Planning Frameworks covering the new buzzwords "prevention, protection, mitigation, response, and recovery."[4] It had been Obama, of course, who'd chartered the Council of Governors, and his intensely political and cooperative secretaries of defense—Robert Gates and Leon Panetta—had seen that its substantial work was successfully completed. Talk of Insurrection Act and *Posse Comitatus* and federal takeover was expunged like a bad dream. There was no Cheney or Addington; no Karl Rove or Michael Brown, no open combat; even the sometime overzealous and uncertain NORTHCOM was moving from adolescence to adulthood.[5] With a respected hurricane professional at the helm, even FEMA had rehabilitated.

Thus for Sandy no one was on vacation and no one was caught unaware. With the exception of Mayor Michael Bloomberg's stumble in not canceling the New York City Marathon—and the firing of a New York State Emergency Management official who directed resources to clean up his driveway—no leadership mistakes were repeated. The National Response Coordination Center, the National Infrastructure Coordinating Center, the Homeland Infrastructure Threat and Risk Analysis Center, and the National Business Emergency Operations Center—all were ready, willing, and able. So, too, were private-sector entities important for national security, mobilized by newly created protective security advisors who are responsible for critical infrastructure: volunteers mustered in from nonprofits, church-based groups, and an unprecedented number of government-sponsored civilian adjuncts.[6] Without fanfare, the federal cavalry came: some 10,000 federal government civilians mobilized from outside the area, 7,700 FEMA personnel, reserves, and contractors at the peak; almost 1,000 from the Department of Homeland Security came, plus personnel from a half dozen other civil departments.[7] There was a National Power Restoration Taskforce; a Surge Capacity Force; and the newly created FEMA Corps, all working hand in hand with state and local authorities. This would be no Katrina.

Then there were the men and women in uniform—at least twice as many deployed as federal civilians: 12,000 National Guard from fourteen states; 4,000 specialists supporting NORTH-COM and its subordinate commands; three amphibious ships and over 4,000 personnel from the navy and marine corps; 3,000 from the Army Corps of Engineers, including 900 from outside the region.[8] For the first time in history, army reservists were activated for domestic response, implementing the Council of Governors' agreement.[9] Per the plan, Secretary Panetta quietly signed agreements with all of the region's governors to appoint dual status commanders.[10] NORTHCOM supplied active-duty deputies for each state.[11] Two dozen federal generals and admirals showed up for photo ops in the first week alone; hosted by their National Guard counterparts and state officials.[12] But there was no big federal military joint task force of note, no General Honoré to issue orders or steal the limelight from the politicians, in fact no overall commander at all except for the president. And of course all the men and women who were there in uniform were in their exact proper constitutional subordination to civil authorities.[13] "The military has had the honor of being one of the most trusted organizations by the American public the past few decades, so we know uniformed servicemen…help bring a sense of calm and confidence during a crisis," said Colonel Michael Miklos, defense coordinating officer for FEMA Region II.[14]

With a national election looming, a lot was riding on leadership and readiness and cooperation and subordination, and photos and videos of flooded tunnels and streets, ruined beachside towns and boardwalks, destroyed homes, underwater amusement park rides, and then extended blackouts and gas lines carried a certain political weight.

Sandy provoked heated arguments about the role of big government, the fate of the earth, and the perennial topic of the wisdom of using tax dollars to rebuild in storm-vulnerable areas. Across screens and pages, the coalescing message was that we are all vulnerable wherever we live. To most people, that meant the climate was changing for the worse, but for the executive agents it meant continuity, critical infrastructure, preparedness, and professionalism, and a whole nation in unison—and docilely subordinate.

The homeland security aesthetic to enforce unity has been to stress the practical matters. "Absolute confirmation of someone's identity," the department says, can mean the difference between life and death.[15] Identification challenges increase even more when the scale of an incident increases; particularly during terrorist incidents or civil disorder, the need for positive identification is made essential. Glitches and confusion at the World Trade Center on and after 9/11 convinced the executive agents of this need; and then in the aftermath of Katrina, when repair workers had difficulty gaining access to their equipment and facilities because police and National Guard refused to let them enter the disaster area,[16] everyone agreed that uniform credentialing—one card or at least one standard for one nation—made sense.

In August 2004, President Bush signed a directive mandating that all federal employees and contractors use a standard smart ID card for access to federal buildings and information systems.[17] The mandate was soon expanded to first responders as well, hopefully to include volunteers from state, local, tribal, and private-sector partners, as well as nongovernmental organizations with special statuses like the Red Cross and Salvation Army.[18] The law doesn't *require* nonfederal workers to submit to uniform biometric requirements and a national ID card, but as a 2011 homeland security report on first responders stated, the government "strongly encourages them to do so."[19] And those credentials should be even smarter, embedded with biometric data and tied to databases where skills are recorded so that the technical knowhow of emergency workers and health care professionals and even private-sector technicians can be known and tracked.

Register everyone before an emergency; collect verified information on the identity, licensure status, and professional credentials of volunteers. That philosophy meant that by the time of Superstorm Sandy, more than 9 million credentials had been issued to military personnel, federal civilians, and government contractors.[20] The Transportation Security Administration had made the greatest progress outside government, credentialing approximately 15 million individuals across the transportation sector.[21] Tens of millions of other types of government credentials had been issued to federal, state, and local workers and their contractors; and their dependents; and their official retirees; and to volunteers.

Homeland Security—the unified nation—is mightily counting on those volunteers. Just since 9/11—just over *one* decade—the federal government has established more than 100 different public-private partnerships to enlist citizen participation in martial life: Airport Watch, Amateur Radio Disaster Services, America's Waterway Watch, the Blue Campaign, Building Communities of Trust, the Business Emergency Operations Alliance, Citizen Corps, the College and University Security Effort, Communities Against Terrorism, Community Emergency Response Teams, the Counterintelligence Strategic Partnerships Program, Customs-Trade Partnership Against Terrorism, Deter Detect Defend, Disaster Mortuary Operational Response Teams, the Disaster Reserve Workforce, the Domestic Security Alliance Council, the Emergency System for Advance Registration of Volunteer Health Professionals, EPA Response Support Corps, FEMA Corps, Fire Corps, First Observer, GISCorps, the Hospital Preparedness Program, Know Your Customer, Medical Reserve Corps, the Multi-state Partnership for Security in Agriculture, the National Language Service Corps, Neighborhood Watch, Operation Community Shield, Partnership for Critical Infrastructure Security, Partnership for Public Warning, the Patriot Academy, PS-Prep, Radio Amateur Civil Emergency Services, Ready America, the Ready Campaign, Ready Communities Partnership, Ready Kids, See Something Say Something, the SECURE Program, Secure Communities, Securing the Cities, Stop Think Connect, Strategic Partnership Program Agroterrorism, Transit Watch, USA Freedom Corps, USA on Watch, Volunteers in Police Service, Voluntary Organizations Active in Disaster, and the Voluntary Private Sector Preparedness Accreditation and Certification Program.

USA Freedom Corps alone, announced by President Bush in his 2002 State of the Union address, has grown to a conglomeration of more than 1,100 Citizen Corps councils across America, with 175,000 full-time workers; its 2,100 separate Community Emergency Response Teams provide emergency response indoctrination to some 200,000 individuals each year. The Medical Reserve Corps numbers nearly 1,000 units across America in public and private hospitals, clinics, fire stations, and ambulance companies.

So how many people are actually a part of the national security effort, a part of homeland security, first responders, custodians of critical infrastructure, providers of emergency services, or the national reserves of disaster preparedness and response? The Department of Homeland Security refers to a community of some 23.5 million first responders in the nation, more than double the number that government officials referenced just a decade ago.[22] Just five million Americans wear the uniform of permanent war—the conventional arithmetic of federal troops, reserves, and National Guard—but counting military and pseudocivilian, federal and local, public and private, paid and volunteer, there are closer to 60 million Americans, about one-third of the adult population ages twenty to sixty-four, serving as a regimented conglomeration of troops and law enforcement officials, a gigantic all-hazards reserve trained in everything from storm spotting and first aid to animal rescue and crowd control, a combatant and noncombatant army, one fully enlisted in the world of *what-if.*

Today, if you are a pilot, ham radio operator, doctor, veterinarian, nurse, medic, emergency anything, ambulance driver, firefighter, police officer, sheriff, deputy, constable, park ranger, demolitions expert, aid worker, lifeguard, heavy equipment operator, utility lineman, trucker, bus driver, merchant mariner, port operator, stevedore, epidemiologist, biologist, agronomist, hydrologist, undertaker, community planner, civil engineer, mechanic, information technician, hacker, cybergeek, linguist, fish and wildlife specialist, dispatcher, security guard, technical climber, search and rescue expert, dog handler, dog lover, or dog, there is a place for you in "prevention, protection, mitigation, response, and recovery." And on virtually every inch of the political spectrum, we demand this, demand preparedness and security *today*. So government bureaucrats, homeland security officials, military commanders, and federal agents forge trigger-taut relationships with states, cities, counties, tribes, and local governments, all marching to the national security beat; utilities, telecommunications, the information technology industry, hospitals, the transportation sector are all deputized into government public-private partnerships; worst-case protocols are fed to corporations, universities, fraternal associations, nonprofits and faith-based organizations; tens of millions of volunteers are signed up, vetted, credentialed, and fitted out; networks of listeners, watchers, and sniffers are employed, all recording, saving, and panning for gold. Nary is a dispatch issued, nary a press release or a regulation goes out, nary an official speech is made without the new national lexicon: information sharing, unified command, unity of effort, whole of government, whole of community, whole of society.

So is anyone left who is just a civilian today?

The Program is not just about drawing millions into the XYZ web; others are in the process of a very particular withdrawal. The concept is called islanding: on the surface, it is turning military bases into "islands" with their own power and other utilities, to reduce their vulnerabilities should civilian assets be disrupted, either by system breakdown, natural disaster, cyberintrusion, or terrorist attack.[23] Islanding means that over 5,000 separate installations and outposts, including reserve centers and National Guard armories, can retreat to a few hundred self-sustaining and defensible fortresses during a national calamity. There the defenders will find independent energy,[24] radiation detection and WMD protection, disease surveillance, and even stockpiles of pharmaceuticals and food, all secured against an outsized vision of a looming Zombie America.[25] The ultimate goal is unplugging—what one briefing calls the "Preemptive Strike"—building an independent and self-sustaining island unaffected by power outages, cyberattack, fuel shortages, pandemics, or civil breakdown.[26]

Crucial to successful islanding is increasing the resilience and reserve of communications for military use. Real-world events from 9/11 to Katrina and Sandy repeatedly show a high probability not just that commercial wired and wireless communications will be saturated in an emergency, but that the public networks can and will be damaged and destroyed. As a result, bases all across America are building autonomous networks to survive massive failures in the commercial system, developing "deployable" cellular systems and rapidly erectable communications to supplement or supplant domestic commercial networks in a crisis, as well as autonomous satellite links that provide the full capabilities of Internet protocol communications.[27]

It isn't hyperbole, at least to those responsible for national security, to say that this is going on because there is no "over there" anymore. Military bases in the United States are no longer just preparing and shipping the operational forces to fight in places like Iraq and Afghanistan; they are also an integral part of that fight. This trend began in the 1990s, when the need to reduce the footprint of US forces stationed in Saudi Arabia to enforce Iraq no-fly zones (at the host nation's insistence), combined with greater bandwidth and more reliable communications, allowed the military to develop "reachback" whereby important functions—such as intelligence analysis—could be performed somewhere else. In the two decades since, capabilities resident in the United States have become the "virtual back end" for all operations overseas.[28] Drones flying over the Middle East and South Asia are piloted from a dozen bases in the United States; video is being scrutinized and intercepts are being translated and sorted at gigantic centers in Georgia, Hawaii, Maryland, and Texas. Major wars are being commanded from headquarters in Florida and Hawaii. The role of domestic military installations, Paul Stockton told Congress in 2011, involves "direct support of war fighting missions."[29]

Islanding is thus not just some survivalist plan in which military bases button up. Contingency plans are ready to protect civilian assets if remediation or mitigation is not possible, even in peacetime; that is, plans are in place for the military to move out and protect whatever needs protection if the civilian sector is to continue to operate, even doing so actively with troops moving into hostile territory beyond the "islands" if need be.[30] This naturally pits the needs of such islands against the needs of civil society.

Civilian communities and military bases have been strained for decades over "encroachment" issues, fighting about nuclear and chemical weapons, power, and waste; the need for access to training lands and airspace; noise levels for nearby civilians; and the impact of light pollution or communications interference on military operations and readiness.[31] Though in truth the Defense Department approaches conservation and environmental protection with the ferocity that it approaches everything else with, today it is as much focused on the islanding aspects of encroachment, acquiring adjacent lands or putting easements on private land to create more effective buffer zones around military fortresses to preserve both operations and security.[32] And the military is also eyeing civilian technologies that might interfere with its operations: wind farms in particular are being looked at because of their potential to alter radar performance; wind turbines and cell phone towers can also encroach on low-flying operations.[33]

The mission to protect all of this—called force protection or antiterrorism—also emerged in the early 1990s when service members deployed in places like Saudi Arabia became the targets of terrorists.[34] Protection against hostile actions was initially considered mostly an overseas requirement,[35] but after 9/11, that mission migrated to the United States itself.[36] Force protection inside the United States now even includes severe weather, accidents, domestic disturbances, and pandemic influenza, as well as unspecified "events" that might occur outside a military base and have an effect on off-base military families.[37] And in 2010 the Joint Chiefs of Staff went one step further with force protection, formally redefining it to mean "preventive measures to mitigate hostile actions."[38]

The islanding term of art that encompasses all of these tasks—force protection, antiterrorism, critical infrastructure protection—is "mission assurance."[39] A Pentagon Mission Assurance Asset Database (or MAAD) today includes about 1,400 so-called mission-critical assets, not just military facilities and defense industry but also civilian power plants, substations, natural gas compressor plants, wastewater treatment plants, airports, seaports, bridges, railroad yards, and communications nodes important to the Defense Department.[40] Everything from air traffic control to a banking system that is needed to pay the troops—off-base private-sector infrastructure "critical to the success of DOD national security mission"[41]—is eyed for greater resilience or emergency alternative. A 2009 Defense Department report elaborated that the island footprint had to include areas around installations "because supporting infrastructures and personnel transcend the installation's fence line."[42] For the first time, the phrase "outside the wire" is being applied domestically to refer to the danger zones beyond the barricades of domestic installations.[43]

Not since the Civil War, former NORTHCOM commander General Gene Renuart told an industry conference in 2009, have members of the American military feared for their families' lives and safety inside the United States.[44] That family is huge: almost 10 percent of the total US population, some 30 million people. That includes approximately 2.5 million servicepeople:[45] some 1.3 million men and women on active duty, another 1.1 million who serve in the National Guard and the reserves, and 680,000 direct-hire civilian employees. Then there are the immediate families of members of the military and even the family members of DOD civilian employees, all of whom are covered under the Pentagon protection umbrella.[46] There are also some 2 million military retirees, many people in their forties and fifties who are granted full access to the military establishment for health care, discounted food and gas, and the military way of life in exchange for the potential to be recalled to active duty.[47] Then there are the hundreds of thousands of contractors and industrial workers who are a part of the defense (and consulting) industry; some on military bases, some at government-owned factories and other private "critical" sites. Add to that the 28,000 wounded in ten-plus years of sustained combat and their families[48] and an additional 20 million veterans who are also loosely under the Department of Defense umbrella, an increasing number of whom require access to base hospitals and other facilities already retreating to the islands.[49]

Major General Jeff Mathis, head of force protection for the Joint Chiefs, has proclaimed that safety requires "much more than increased guards, guns, and bullets at the perimeter"; that insider threats are a growing problem.[50] Though Washington might focus on WikiLeaks-type insider threats—an extension of traditional counterintelligence efforts to protect government secrets—garrison commanders are more focused on "internal threats," particularly since army psychiatrist Major Nidal Malik Hasan opened fire on fellow soldiers at Fort Hood, Texas, on November 5, 2009, killing thirteen and injuring almost forty others.[51] The ABC response is enhanced emergency planning at bases, measures to improve active shooter protocols for military police, biometric scanners for identification, physical security to protect soldiers and their families, and, of course, government style, the *what-if* of preparedness for "multiple incidents" at the same time.[52]

As part of that ABC, the army chief sent a message to all army entities after Fort Hood requiring everyone to report any indicators of potential terrorist threats[53] and instituting new "business practices" to better vet certain people.[54] The implementing army regulation on "Threat Awareness and Reporting," updating a 1993 Cold War remnant that was still focused on communism, added "indicators of potential (international) terrorist-associated insider threats" as a tip-off for members of the family to consider. The specific signs, though—"hatred of American society," "expressing a duty to engage in violence against DOD or the United States in support of an international terrorist cause," and "evidence of terrorist training or attendance at terrorist training facilities"—are so exaggerated as to be useless.[55] The regulation also treats "espionage, international terrorism, sabotage, sub-version, theft or diversion of military technology, information systems intrusions, and unauthorized disclosure of classified information" as equivalent threats.

In the 101-page army regulation on personnel security—revised again in 2011 to account for the repeal of the "don't ask, don't tell" policy—religion is mentioned a total of three times and only then to stress that membership in any religious institution is not to be considered derogatory and that "religious beliefs and affiliations, beliefs and opinions regarding racial matters, political beliefs and affiliations of a non-subversive nature, opinions regarding the constitutionality of legislative policies, and affiliations with labor unions and fraternal organizations are not proper subjects for inquiry."[56] Even the questionnaire appended to the enlistment application for non-US citizen linguists asks them to divulge what "political" organizations they belong to and what books they read but never mentions al Qaeda or any terrorist organization. The counterintelligence briefing that foreign-born enlistees sign cautions them merely that agents of "communist" or hostile governments might seek government secrets.[57]

One reason for all this elliptical avoidance is that Nidal Hasan is a US citizen born in Virginia and an officer himself, sworn to uphold the Constitution. Even when the FBI discovered that Hasan was corresponding with an al Qaeda terror guru in Yemen—now known to be the assassinated American citizen Anwar al-Awlaki—the FBI concluded, in the absence of any additional derogatory information provided, that his communications were protected and consistent with research he was doing in his position as a psychiatrist at the Walter Reed Army Medical Center. "As with any criminal investigation, all suspects are presumed innocent unless and until they are proven guilty of a crime in a court of law," the FBI said in a statement less than a week after the shooting.[58]

Presupposition of guilt merely because of religious belief challenges one of the fundamental freedoms of the Constitution, the freedom of religion ("the free exercise of religion," to be precise) and the prohibition of a national religion. Thus investigations and implications associated with "religious beliefs and affiliations" can only exist between the lines. Force protection and antiterrorism officers at military garrisons inside the United States are advised to characterize the local geography—to spy—and to look for "radical extremist groups"[59] to protect the island, but the programs to do so are also highly compartmented, given their uncertain constitutional and legal status. And they are not characterized as intelligence programs, since they are performing basic protection missions for and about the military.

Suffice it to say that whatever the threats, they are ubiquitous and unrelenting. At home, the enemy is not just Muslim Americans or Arab Americans or Somalis or Palestinians or Middle Easterners or those of the Muslim faith. It is illegal Mexicans. It is drug lords and smugglers and gangs and organized crime and the sex trade. It is foreign visitors and students and overcurious tourists. It is sovereign citizens and white supremacists. It is disgruntled school kids with access to guns. There are the incarcerated, the lone wolves, and the mentally ill. There are libertarians, antiglobalizers, environmentalists, Occupy and Tea Party activists, constitutional oath-keepers and survivalists, hackers and copyright stealers, the antiwar and the antigovernment. There are those who are just evil and those who are macabre attention seekers. There are those who don't pay taxes, who want to keep their guns, who insist on living off the grid, who won't vaccinate their children, who don't want their library cards scrutinized or their Internet activity tracked, or who insist on drinking unpasteurized milk. Precisely because constitutionally no one group can be targeted as such, government attention has to be equally applied to everyone, everyone potentially and equally a threat,[60] a vast universe of potential dots, enemies of the state being not only those who take up arms or perform treasonous acts, but also those who insist on preserving ungoverned space in the ubiquitous martial landscape, where at home is already assumed to be over there, and over there, right here at home.

Martial Life

For when everything is classified, then nothing is classified,
and the system becomes one to be disregarded by the cynical or the
careless, and to be manipulated by those intent on
self-protection or self-promotion.
JUSTICE WILLIAM O. DOUGLAS, NEW YORK TIMES
CO. v. UNITED STATES, 403 US 713 (1971)
(PENTAGON PAPERS CASE)

B ombarded" is exactly the right word to describe America today: the country is bombarded with real-world events and *what-ifs*—terrorism, our wars, other people's wars, Iranian and North Korean nukes; loose nukes; biological and chemical weapons; instability in Afghanistan, in Pakistan, and throughout the Middle East and Africa; China emerging; Russia declining; crime syndicates and drug cartels and pirates; cyberwarfare, cyber-criminals; hurricanes, tsunamis, earthquakes, wildfires, drought; pandemics, genetically modified everything; global warming; water wars, resource wars, population explosions, financial melt-downs; rising sea levels. Audits and analysis indicate that 2012 was the second-costliest year in history in terms of natural disasters,[1] and everything—climate, resources, infrastructure, and human nature—conspires to make things worse in the future.

As a solution to these problems and threats, it's hard not to champion good government and better management, and even reorganization, to use the language of fraud, waste, and abuse; to want greater attention and internal coordination and leadership; to decry duplication and promote collaboration. Who doesn't want true priorities and the wise expenditure of tax dollars; who doesn't think there should be adequate staff if there's going to be staff at all? Suffice it to say: scratch the surface of any government program and you'll find that billions' worth go wrong—always—and that's not referring to the number of trees killed to draft and redraft and publish and revise, the rinse and repeat that has and will forever be the paper harvest of government. That is, after all, government's basic nature.

Yet even in the most seemingly urgent components of the Program—the highest-priority, the least bureaucratic, the freest and loosest to operate—there's no greater guarantee of economy. The BioWatch system of terrorism sniffers never lived up to its promise; it was poorly defined, slow to be executed, of questionable assurance, the next generation of automated equipment in question.[2] The Domestic Nuclear Detection Office is no different; technologies are constantly in need of better and more.[3] The FBI-led WMD crisis management and *in extremis* effort is also constantly in question.[4] And continuity is no better: rules for orderly evacuation and operations that ignore families and children; the assumptions about what 300,000 federal employees in Washington would do at the end of days, when even on a normal day the Beltway is pure gridlock. Post-9/11, the executive agents have introduced evacuation hoods and bunny suits in almost every national security office to facilitate movement in a chemical or biologically compromised environment. They've instituted "telework" and other virtual-office schemes and "social distancing operations" to take into consideration pandemics and other types of contamination. They've developed a variety of "family" support plans in hopes of increasing "employee availability."

They've pre-positioned vital records, handed out memory sticks with key documents and plans for evacuating personnel, invented an orderly "devolution" process to supplement the three-deep successor process and the delegations of authority to allow uninterrupted operations.[5] They are all fabulous (and expensive) ideas, but merely the duck and cover of our age; an entire apocalyptic drama of civil defense again being extended down to the states and cities, but one that has so many inherent flaws and such brittleness that it just confirms the need for something else, something higher.

The national argument that breaks out after any 9/11, any Katrina, or any Newtown is about what kind of nation we are and want to be, some saying that America should be ashamed because of what it is and what it has done, others grumbling that Americans are fat and lazy and selfish and too tolerant. Liberalism or religious fundamentalism or any fill-in-the-blank *ism* is said to be the true threat and the actual cause of our problems. There are those who argue that America is really controlled by an *x* or a *y*; that *they* are hell-bent on taking away the freedoms and rights that are the country's defining features. And one doesn't have to tap into some secret society of Freemasons or Trilateralists to get to a *they;* nor does one need some outside *other*—World Bank, World Health Organization, United Nations—to imagine an even more enormous and transposable threat.

For some, terrorists lurk everywhere within: if not personified by insider and homegrown threats, then in ecoterrorists and PETA activists, or in lawless government itself. Government detention camps wait to be filled up; trains are at the ready to take people there. *They*, the government bureaucrats, the liberals, Obama, are coming for the guns, ready to turn America over to international control, seeking to complete some socialist plot by erasing individual freedoms.[6] On the other side is an equally convinced group who think *they* are Bush or Cheney; the neo-cons, the evangelicals, the Tea Party, the radical right, K Street, Wall Street, the survivalists, the gun owners. For both sides, *they* are the Pentagon, homeland security, TSA, the CIA and FBI, for reasons wedded in a general sense to particular conspiracies. The two factions—already facetiously labeled Red and Blue—overlap more than they would like to admit; imagining secret programs with supposed real names—Chemtrail, Northwoods, Area 51, HAARP, Stellar Wind—all hiding clandestine plots under the rubric of the war on terror or emergency response, sweeping aside the Constitution and instilling government tyranny.

Somewhere in the middle is a vast and self-labeled reasonable center that decries extremism of any kind, that makes fun of the tinfoil-hat set, the rabid, and the overwrought. These people gawk at the estimated 5 million "preppers" readying individual and family survival plans; or shake their heads over as many as 25 million who worried about the Mayan apocalypse or the close to half of all Americans who think 9/11 was some kind of government conspiracy. This is American martial life at its very essence: the threats are so great, externally and internally, and the people are so divided, that it is the executive agents who have to act as furtive adjudicators of two warring realities, two motherlands in need of an ABC and XYZ to keep the peace. To be sure, some solutions might lurk in some legislative remedy of gun control or arms control, but these are small facets on a very big jewel. And bigger changes are blocked by those who need society to move forward under officiated parole with the illusion that security is well ordered and that no one's individual freedoms are invaded.

Government at almost all levels from local to federal has to pave the way for the XYZ through an increasingly thin facade of ABC, recognizing in so doing that one shouldn't make too many startling or threatening moves around a populace already so spooked and trigger happy. The product is the complete militari-zation of US civil, social, and political life in the defense of the nation, a deskbound takeover run by a powerful group of execu-tive agents sanctioned and even encouraged by our elected lead-ers, an invisible ruling class that works to save the nation from threats far and near. America floats on a comforting appearance of civilian purpose, where the pseudoenlistment of millions of erstwhile civilians confuses the distinctions between what is mili-tary and what is civilian. Though it is easy to fire back at "the" military-industrial complex, an Iron Triangle, Top Secret Amer-ica, inside the Beltway, the federal government, Congress, or even Washington itself, the Program flourishes because it is not any of these self-interested entities. These scapegoats *are* the problem, and that is precisely why the Program has to serve as captain of an exceptionally guileless ship of state, one that survives precisely because the dysfunction of the ABCs demands someone pursue the immutable between-the-lines needs of the XYZ.

"When a disaster strikes your state," former NORTHCOM commander Admiral Winnefeld told the 132nd General Confer-ence of the National Guard Association in 2010, "I don't want to be one second too early...nor do I want to be one second too late. I want to be limited only by physics, not by bureaucracy."[7] It is a rousing and sensitive call to arms. Winnefeld told the assembled guardians of the states that we are simply not as good as we need to be, that unity is achieved in not even having to define or fight about what *we* or *as we need to be* means.

"In the twenty-first century," Secretary of Defense Leon Panetta said in 2012, "we recognize that climate change can impact national security—ranging from rising sea levels, to severe droughts, to the melting of the polar caps, to more fre-quent and devastating natural disasters that raise demand for humanitarian assistance and disaster relief."[8] "We recognize," of course, means that the military recognizes. The *National Military Strategy*, a document written by the Joint Chiefs, pledges that the military will "provide the ways and means" to advance American "enduring national interests." It calls itself "facilitator, enabler, convener, and guarantor." Even the US national debt is labeled "a significant security risk."[9]

These days, any ranking officer worth his brass is both rousing and sensitive. These men (and women) pledge to "support and defend the Constitution of the United States against all enemies, foreign and domestic," the principles that embody America encapsulated in the Preamble:

> ...form a more perfect Union, establish Justice, insure domestic Tranquility, provide for the common defence [sic], promote the general Welfare, and secure the Blessings of Liberty to ourselves and our Posterity...

It is the Constitution that is to be defended; not the president, nor an administration nor the government, and not even just the physical security of the United States. Most Americans would be happy to turn over the country to these hallowed guardians, for who else would be trusted with the task? But they are still the military. Which is exactly why any notion of military dominance in domestic rule doesn't work. When Honoré declared Katrina the enemy and New Orleans a battlefield, when he took charge with Landreneau's guardsmen, he was hardly pulling off some coup. He was just thinking the way a military man thinks, doing what he was trained for.[10]

When the national PowerPoint slide utters "The Nation Is at War" in the first bullet point, it seems inevitable that the scenarios of national danger end up so broadly drawn that the terrorist threat is swallowed up in a great flood, every event equally menacing. The experts of *what-if* apply a universal template of internal danger, of overloaded networks, destroyed infrastructure, failed backups, scarce supplies, casualties, public panic, and political havoc. The Program emerged in this tangle as the fail-safe to ensure everyday life under this constant state of threat. Yet every Katrina and Newtown demonstrates that what has been created is incredibly complex and convoluted, that few even in government fully understand the laws and rules.

A weaker nation emerges with complex and unenforceable rules, with everyone and anyone having good reason to be wary of the authorities. That is the case with labyrinthine rules about civil life—whether it is the tax code or gun control—where any law-abiding citizen is potentially made into a criminal. The state is endowed with a set of powers to decide what is allowed, and those who are charged with enforcing the law are forced—since everyone is driving over the speed limit at some point—to make choices as to whom to go after. At the local level, the posse can be personal and racial and religious; at the federal level, it can be ludicrously fastidious and compassionless, not inconsequentially overseen by a set of administrative crusaders whose local community *is* national security—a combination of twenty- and thirty-something policy automatons condescending to locals of any stripe, and a military where more than 93 percent of everyone under arms joined up after 9/11,[11] an ahistoric group already infected by a peculiar opinion about threats and the nation.

The contingency becomes the contingency.

Once upon a time in America, a small standing army existed around which the people—a well-regulated militia, citizen soldiers—were mustered and discharged whenever an emergency presented itself. But when the emergencies never went away, the requirements of national survival demanded a permanent military establishment and then a professional one. In the era of terrorism and relentless vulnerability, that professional group is not just who is in uniform; it includes the forces of homeland security and law enforcement, first responders, and all the accompanying pseudosoldiers of the whole of the nation. Even inside the US government, what is military and what is civilian is increasingly obscured;[12] the state and local police forces are militarized and networked into one; states have their own intelligence establishments; the big cities make their own foreign policies.

In theory, the guardians of the state come first: state police, National Guard, local volunteers. Yet given the mobility of society and the erosion of the uniqueness of National Guardsmen, with combat units serving overseas and operating everywhere and anywhere in the United States, what even is local? Denied deep civic knowledge and established links with more distant officials when operating under the new regional arrangements, the Guard's answer is to just link everyone together in one nationwide "Joint Information Exchange Environment," a system it describes as "a web-based intelligence-driven picture of where they're operating, where others are, and where the threat is."[13] In other words, it is intelligence manufactured in Washington, perhaps more comprehensive but in terms of nuance and practical sensitivity about as remote as remote could be.

Many marveled during Katrina that General Honoré was local, but as he says, "Although I was born in Lakeland, Louisiana, in Pointe Coupee Parish little more than a hundred miles northwest of New Orleans, I had spent the last thirty-four years stationed everywhere but Louisiana."[14] Honoré admits to having had to start from scratch, just as the National Guard does today in pursuit of its "homeland" mission. So that's the way it is.

Our constitutional design of a community-supplied common defense — of a community of shared interests — is not only gone; the executive agents and the whole-of-society army firmly believe that it is obsolete and impractical and insufficient and even dangerous. And it is, for them. For the citizens, not only do pervasive threats and vulnerabilities sow fear and suspicion and strengthen the hand of the state, but mistrust and individual concern for one's survival and one's family feed apprehension—apprehension about speaking up, apprehension about assembling and crossing the government or the law enforcers. The American Coup complete, you are free to say what you want, believe what you want, assemble where you want, as long as you don't violate invisible limitations and barriers or interfere with the workings of the XYZ.

ACKNOWLEDGMENTS

They say that writing is a solitary business, but without my perfect love, Luciana Frigerio, and the always constant Chuck Gundersen, I might have forgotten to eat; and without Galen and Olivia, Jacques and Christine Guilloton, Kevin and Cory, and my new Norwich friends, I might have forgotten to live and laugh as well.

American Coup has its genesis in the *Top Secret America* project, and that project would not have been possible without those who indulged and supported me at the *Washington Post*, particularly Marcus and Raju, and without the incomparable Washington maneuverings of Dana Priest, who encouraged me to write my own book.

As for "sources," well, you know who you are. To help me think about the military and the society we live in, thanks to the always affable and wrongheaded Tom Powers, and thanks to my squadron of graybeards, including Phil, Steve, John, Mike, Tim, Dave, Dutch, Gary, Mace, Gene, Bob, and Dan, for years of inspiration. Thanks also to John Young, Steve Aftergood, Michael Ravnitzky, Hans Kristensen, the National Security Archive, and the people at the Public Intelligence and Government Attic websites, as well as the ACLU and EPIC for consistently and constantly pushing for the truth and then sharing what they find out with the public. I gained enormous knowledge from the works of authors whom I cite in the book.

Thanks to the many journalists who share information with me in spite of potential competition, trusting and knowing that what comes around goes around, particularly Greg, Sy, Eric, John, Bob, Tom, Justin, Graham, and Mark.

I live a lot more securely knowing that my attorney, Jeff Smith, can both be my attorney and work for the secret recesses of government when duty calls.

My editor at Little, Brown, Geoff Shandler, recognized what I was trying to say even before I did and conducted delicate and much-needed surgery on the manuscript. He has been a constant supporter. His former assistant Brandon Coward tended to the essential but boring, keeping me on the straight and narrow. Thanks also to my crew at Little, Brown and Company and Hachette: Barbara Perris, Ben Allen, Keith Hayes, Michelle Aielli, Heather Fain, Reagan Arthur, and Michael Pietsch.

Thanks also to Chip Fleischer for always giving me sound publishing advice.

I recognize, now going on forty years in this world of the military and government, that I love to collaborate but also tend to escape to my reading and the collection of facts. I'm a terrible friend, especially when I'm lost in a book project, but I couldn't sustain my soul without knowing that I have you in my corner: Julia and Reed, Philene and Darren, Peter and Eleanor, Steve and Hannah, Laura, Stan Norris, Bob Windrem, Marianne Manilov, Lena Ag, Andy Mack, Steve Shallhorn, David Chappell, Tom Cochran, Matthew McKinzie, John Robinson, and Marianne Szegedy-Maszak. Thanks also for the laughs and conversation and real world provided by my new friends Sara and Bob, Vicky, Watt and Roberta, Julia and T, Daniel and Cynthia, Linda and Rowlie, Colleen and Clif.

Thanks, Kimberly and Laurie. Thanks, Sondra and Ron, Danny and Jamie, and the Frigerio clan. To Rikki and Hannah, I love you.

NOTES

INTRODUCTION

1. In December 2001, when I wrote my first article about Cheney's underground bunker near Camp David, the White House urged my editors at the *Los Angeles Times* not to mention specific locations, which they agreed not to do. Weeks later, the locations were revealed anyhow in the news media; See William M. Arkin, "In 21st Century War, 2 Cavemen Stand Out; Strategy: From his underground center, Cheney directs cavern search for Bin Laden," *Los Angeles Times*, December 8, 2001.

2. Retired general Tommy Franks, in an interview in the December 2003 issue of *Cigar Aficionado* magazine (and released to the media on November 21, 2003), said that if the United States is hit with a WMD that inflicts large casualties, the Constitution will likely be discarded. Discussing the hypothetical dangers posed to the US in the wake of 9/11, Franks said that "the worst thing that could happen" is if terrorists acquire and then use a biological, chemical, or nuclear weapon that inflicts heavy casualties.

   If that happens, Franks said, "...the Western world, the free world, loses what it cherishes most, and that is freedom and liberty we've seen for a couple of hundred years in this grand experiment that we call democracy." Franks then offered "in a practical sense" what he thinks would happen in the aftermath of such an attack. "It means the potential of a weapon of mass destruction and a terrorist, massive, casualty-producing event somewhere in the Western world—it may be in the United States of America—that causes our population to question our own Constitution and to begin to militarize our country in order to avoid a repeat of another mass, casualty-producing event. Which in fact, then begins to unravel the fabric of our Constitution. Two steps, very, very important."

3. See, e.g., the chart created in NORTHCOM PowerPoint Briefing, James Terbush, CAPT, USN, MC, MFSCAPT, MFS; Keys to Preparedness: Communication and Relationships, n.d. (2006), obtained by the author.

4. This view is also reflected in Barton Gellman, *Angler: The Cheney Vice Presidency*, pp. 131–158.

5. Haters with historic amnesia suggest a third possibility: that the plotter was Barack Hussein Obama himself, setting up America for acquiescence to the new Islamic caliphate and socialist dictatorship under the thumb of the international community.

CHAPTER ONE: BETWEEN THE LINES

1. The Program Coordination Division and its responsibility for PEADs are mentioned in one unclassified document: FEMA, Mission and Functions Manual, FEMA Manual 1010.1, February 1, 2001, p. 59.

2. A declassified 1988 Defense Department document explains standby legal authorities: "Existing legal authorities for mobilization actions can be categorized as being available in peacetime, available when the security of the Nation is at grave risk, or available after a Presidential or congressional declaration of national emergency. Standby legal authorities should be prepared and maintained as on-the-shelf legislation, during peacetime, for enactment as needed during a period of rising tensions, national emergency, or war." See Department of Defense Master Mobilization Plan, DOD 3020.36-P, May 1988, p. 3.

3. Emergency Action Packages are defined in a declassified 1988 Defense Department document: "The Director for Emergency Planning (ODUSD(P)) is responsible for creating a variety of EAPs that come into play upon the declaration of a national emergency. A well-constructed EAP will include all documentation for requesting extraordinary powers in emergency circumstances. Agencies continually must monitor existing EAPs and suggest additions and deletions, as necessary.

"Each EAP contains specific instructions on how mobilization decisions are to be effected across these organizational lines. EAPs will ensure consistent mobilization planning across organizational lines. The EAPs will be updated periodically as determined by the proponent Agency, and will be tested for completeness and effectiveness in appropriate exercises." See Department of Defense Master Mobilization Plan, DOD 3020.36-P, May 1988, p. 2; Appendix B, B-2.

See also DOD Instruction (DODI) 3020.38, Promulgation and Administration of OSD Crisis Action Packages (CAPs), December 13, 1990. "Another product of the effort is the list of major emergency actions that require decisions by the National Command Authorities as part of mobilization, as well as the policy, planning, and preparedness activities"; DOD Annual Report, FY 1982, p. 287.

4. Executive Order 10346: Preparation by Federal Agencies of Civil Defense Emergency Plans, April 17, 1952. "In 1952, FCDA [Federal Civil Defense Administration] was given a key role in assisting federal agencies with

planning for service provision and continued functioning during emergencies (now referred to as "continuity of operations"). President Truman issued an executive order directing federal departments and agencies to consult with FCDA and to "prepare plans for providing [their] personnel, materials, facilities, and services…during…a civil defense emergency" and plans for maintaining continuity of government "during such a time." See CRS, Federal Emergency Management and Homeland Security Organization: Historical Developments and Legislative Options, June 1, 2006.

5. The Preamble states: "We the People of the United States, in Order to form a more perfect Union, establish Justice, insure domestic Tranquility, provide for the common defence, promote the general Welfare, and secure the Blessings of Liberty to ourselves and our Posterity, do ordain and establish this Constitution for the United States of America."

6. When President Truman asked Congress to establish what he called a "national defense council" in 1945, the name was changed to the National Security Council.

7. President Truman assigned civil defense planning responsibilities to the National Security Resources Board in 1949 on the grounds that it was the agency already responsible for civilian mobilization and support of military forces. A Federal Civil Defense Administration would formulate national policy and guide local efforts. Executive Order 10186, December 1, 1950, created the Federal Civil Defense Administration (FCDA) within the Office for Emergency Management, Executive Office of the President. When President Truman signed the Federal Civil Defense Act of 1950 (Public Law 920, 81st Congress) on January 12, 1951, FCDA became an independent agency in the executive branch of the government.

The 1950 act stated that "it is the policy and intent of Congress to provide a system of civil defense for the protection of lives and property in the United States from attack"; protecting lives and property was declared a mission independent of military affairs.

The years 1957 and 1958 represented a turning point in understanding of, and argument concerning, the national purpose of civil defense. The Gaither Report (1957), the RAND Corporation's Study of Non-Military Defense (1958), and the Rockefeller Brothers Fund study of International Security—The Military Aspect (1958) all saw civil defense as a critical need of the national military posture and strategy of deterrence.

Two reports published in 1958 became key to a battle between the Eisenhower administration and Congress over a proposed $32-billion program to support the building of fallout shelters: the Rockefeller Report, compiled by a board of experts and practitioners directed by Henry Kissinger, and the RAND Corporation report. Eisenhower never relented and even dissolved the FCDA, creating an Office of Civil and Defense Mobilization.

Executive Order 10952, signed by the new president on July 20, 1961, divided the Office of Civil Defense and Mobilization into two new organizations: the Office of Emergency Planning (OEP) and the Office of CivilDefense (OCD). OEP was part of the President's Executive Office and tasked with advising and assisting the President in determining policy for all nonmilitary emergency preparedness, including civil defense. OCD was assigned to the Defense Department.

8. A later history of postwar civil defense would say: "Three sets of policy problems have dominated the organizational history of modern civil defense: (1) the place of civil defense in national security policy and machinery; (2) the division of responsibility for civil defense between the Federal Government and State and local governments; and (3) the nature of the special governmental powers, particularly for emergency, that civil defense requires." See IDA, Federal Civil Defense Organization: The Rationale of Its Development, Study S-184, January 1965, p. 7.

9. IDA, Federal Civil Defense Organization: The Rationale of Its Development, Study S-184, January 1965, p. 40.

10. At the height of Cold War panic in the mid-1950s, when war with China over Formosa (now Taiwan) loomed, when fallout and radiation were made real, when intercontinental missiles were newly threatening American territory, Massachusetts governor Christian A. Herter asked the question on everyone's mind, complaining that the federal government was keeping the states in the dark on how to protect their populations: "We have no idea whether or not raincoats are preferable to cloth coats, whether hands or faces should be kept covered, whether or not riding in an automobile with all windows closed provides a degree of protection, and whether or not radioactive particles permeate windows or the walls of buildings, or seep into cellars," he said.

The federal government's response was hardly reassuring: Civil Defense Administrator Val Peterson told the Senate Armed Services Subcommittee in March 1955 that all citizens should build some sort of underground shelter "right now" to prepare for a hydrogen bomb attack. When that happens, he said, "we had all better dig and pray. In fact, we had better be praying right now." See Department of Transportation, Highway History, Civil Defense 1955.

11. IDA, Federal Civil Defense Organization: The Rationale of Its Development, Study S-184, January 1965, pp. ix, 1.

12. The Suspension Clause of the Constitution (Article I, Section 9, Clause 2) states: "The Privileges of the Writ of Habeas Corpus shall not be suspended unless when in Cases of Rebellion of Invasion the public Safety may require it." Although the Constitution does not specifically create the right to *habeas corpus* relief, federal statutes provide federal courts with the authority to grant *habeas* relief to state prisoners. Only Congress has

the power to suspend the writ of *habeas corpus*, either by its own affirmative actions or through an express delegation to the executive. The executive does not have the independent authority to suspend the writ.

Application for writ of *habeas corpus* cases generally involve not guilt or innocence per se, but rather the issue of whether a prisoner is restrained from personal liberty in violation of due process of law. Such due process is guaranteed under the Fourteenth Amendment. The function of the writ, if granted, is to release one from illegal imprisonment.

13. James C. Mercer, Federal Response to a Domestic Nuclear Attack, August 2009, p. 23.

14. The Treaty of Ghent, which ended the War of 1812, was signed on December 24, 1814.

15. National Park Service, Jean Lafitte National Historic Park and Preserve (Chalmette National Historical Park), Historical Handbook Number Twenty-Nine, 1958; U.S. Marshals Service, History—A Pirate, a Marshal, and the Battle of New Orleans, n.d.; http://www.usmarshals.gov/history/duplessis/index.html (accessed October 10, 2012).

16. Major Mynda G. Ohman, "Integrating Title 18 War Crimes into Title 10: A Proposal to Amend the Uniform Code of Military Justice," master's thesis, George Washington University School of Law, May 22, 2005, p. 16; Jim Bradshaw, "Andy Jackson, Opelousas solon differed on French patriotism," Acadiana Diary, *The Advertiser* (Lafayette, Louisiana), January 10, 2001.

17. President Roosevelt promulgated his Executive Order 5 days after the bombing of Pearl Harbor and under the authority of the Act of April 20, 1918, 40 Stat. 633 (now 18 U.S.C. 2155), the World War I antisabotage act. The president relied on this act to permit him to put guards on private property, during wartime, when civilians were unable to guard the property themselves. Two years later, the Supreme Court validated FDR's actions as constitutional; forty-four years later, President Reagan and Congress apologized and made reparations for the Japanese and others who were interned.

18. King Kamehameha V Judiciary History Center, "Hawaii Under Martial Law: 1941–1944," n.d. (2012); http://jhchawaii.net/martial-law (accessed October 15, 2012); *Personal Justice Denied*, Report of the Commission on Wartime Relocation and Internment of Civilians, Part I: Nisei and Issei, Chapter 11: Hawaii, December 1982; http://www.nps.gov/history/history/online_books/personal_justice_denied/index.htm (accessed October 17, 2012).

19. The Use of Military Tribunals D.C. Circuit Judicial Conference, Remarks of the Chief Justice, June 14, 2002; http://www.supremecourt.gov/publicinfo/speeches/viewspeeches.aspx?Filename=sp_06-14-02.html; Remarks of Chief Justice William H. Rehnquist, 100th Anniversary

Celebration of the Norfolk and Portsmouth Bar Association, Norfolk, Virginia, May 3, 2000.

20. Nagin signed the emergency order on August 27, 2005; see his story in C. Ray Nagin, *Katrina's Secrets: Storms after the Storms*, pp. 44–45.

21. "Martial law has been declared in New Orleans as conditions continued to deteriorate" (CBS News, August 30, 2005) and WWLTV (Louisiana), August 31, 2005; both quoted in Supplementary Report of the Findings of the Select Bipartisan Committee to Investigate the Preparation for and Response to Hurricane Katrina, Presented by the Select Committee on Behalf of Rep. Cynthia A. McKinney, Submitted February 6, 2006, p. 51.

22. A Failure of Initiative: The Final Report of the Select Bipartisan Committee to Investigate the Preparation for and Response to Hurricane Katrina, February 2006, p. 377.

23. The White House, Office of the Press Secretary, Press Briefing by Scott McClellan, James S. Brady Briefing Room, September 1, 2005; http://georgewbush-whitehouse.archives.gov/news/releases/2005/09/20050901-2.html (accessed October 12, 2012). It is important to note that the transcript misspells "martial law," spelling it "marshal law."

Blanco also never declared martial law, despite widespread reporting that she did. The State of Louisiana, in fact, had no statute for martial law; on August 26, the governor declared a "state of emergency," which is what state stature allowed for.

"However, each state has laws granting the governor exceptional executive powers. In Louisiana it is called a state of public health emergency, and when declared it permits the governor to suspend laws, order evacuations, and limit sale of items such as liquor and firearms....Governor Blanco declared this state of emergency on 26 August 2005, to expire on 25 September 2005"; James L. Clark, "Practical aspects of federalizing disaster response," *Critical Care*, 2006; 10(1): 107 [Published online December 14, 2005]; http://www.ncbi.nlm.nih.gov/pmc/articles/PMC1550837/.

24. Hurricane Katrina: The Defense Department's Role in the Response, S. Hrg. 109-813, p. 214; Allen G. Breed and David Espo, "Aid vs. Anarchy in New Orleans," *Philadelphia Inquirer*, September 2, 2005, p. A18; "Troops Told 'Shoot to Kill' in New Orleans," ABC News (Australian Broadcasting), September 2, 2005, quoted in Lisa Grow Sun, "Disaster Mythology and the Law," *Cornell Law Review*, Vol. 96:1131; J. Emery Midyette Jr., Military Analyst, "Resource and Structure of States' National Guard," Hurricane Katrina special edition, Joint Center for Operational Analysis (JCOA) Bulletin, June 2006, p. 28; A Failure of Initiative, p. 170.

25. Russel Honoré, *Survival: How a Culture of Preparedness Can Save You and Your Family from Disasters* (New York: Atria Books, 2009), pp. 126–127.

26. The NGB is responsible for "Coordinating, validating plans for, facilitating, overseeing and supporting multi-state National Guard execution of federally-requested/funded (Title 32) Homeland Security, Homeland Defense and Civil Support missions, as directed." See NGB Memorandum 10-5/38-101 (Provisional), July 1, 2003, p. 5.

27. DOD News Transcript, Lieutenant General H. Steven Blum, chief, National Guard Bureau, Defense Department Briefing on Ongoing National Guard Response to Hurricane Katrina, September 3, 2005; www.defense.gov/transcripts/transcript.aspx?transcriptid=2084.

28. Hurricane Katrina: The Defense Department's Role in the Response, S. Hrg. 109-813, p. 53.

29. Hurricane Katrina: The Defense Department's Role in the Response, S. Hrg. 109-813, p. 46.

30. Hurricane Katrina: The Defense Department's Role in the Response, S. Hrg. 109-813, p. 36. Clearly Blum was under enormous pressure from the White House as well. At 2 a.m. on the morning of Bush's announcement, according to one account, Blum called [aide to the governor] Ryder and urged him to get the governor to sign the White House Memorandum and letter. "He accused me of being political and he accused me personally of being responsible for the deaths in New Orleans by not telling the governor to sign," Ryder said; Christopher Cooper and Robert Block, *Disaster: Hurricane Katrina and the Failure of Homeland Security*, p. 215. See also A Failure of Initiative, p. 222.

31. The White House, President George W. Bush, Remarks at the US Department of Energy, September 26, 2005; http://www.whitehouse.gov/news/releases/2005/09/20050926.html; The White House, President Discusses Hurricane Effects on Energy Supply, Department of Energy, September 26, 2005.

32. The White House, President Holds Press Conference, October 4, 2005.
    The next day, asked to comment on *posse comitatus*, White House Press Secretary Scott McClellan said "when you're talking about the response that's needed for a storm of this magnitude and this scope, it's certainly something that came into play during all of the discussions...." The White House, Press Briefing by Scott McClellan; Claude Allen, Assistant to the President for Domestic Policy; and Al Hubbard, Assistant to the President for Economic Policy and Director, National Economic Council; September 16, 2005.

33. The White House, press briefing by Scott McClellan, September 26, 2006.

34. A Failure of Initiative, p. 15.

35. Ann Imse, "Proposal Would Use Military in Disasters," *Rocky Mountain News*, October 26, 2005, p. 16A.

36. The final National Response Plan, December 2004, superseded the Federal Response Plan, the U.S. Government Domestic Terrorism Concept Plan (CONPLAN), and the Federal Radiological Emergency Response Plan (FRERP).
37. DHS, National Response Plan, December 2004, p. 43.
38. DHS, Catastrophic Incident Supplement to the National Response Plan, Draft, April 2005, pp. 5–6.
39. President Bush declared Louisiana a major disaster on Saturday, August 27, the day before he declared the same for the states of Alabama and Mississippi. Governor Blanco followed Friday's state of emergency declaration with the first of many letters issued to President Bush and other federal officials. After the major disaster declaration, Governor Blanco wrote to President Bush, urging him to declare a federal state of emergency for the State of Louisiana under the Stafford Act, which then authorizes federal financial assistance to the state for the expenses it incurs. An emergency declaration is more limited in scope than a major disaster declaration; generally, federal assistance and funding for emergencies are provided to meet a specific need or to help prevent a major disaster from occurring. In 2004, a near-record disaster season, the president issued sixty-eight major disaster declarations and seven emergency declarations. See A Failure of Initiative, p. 63.
40. Hurricane Katrina: A Nation Still Unprepared, pp. 168, 483–484, 555–556; DHS IG, A Performance Review of FEMA's Disaster Management Activities in Response to Hurricane Katrina, p. 24.

    "With respect to Hurricane Katrina, when the Secretary of Homeland Security formally declared the event to be an INS on Tuesday, August 30, 2005, arguably an INS already existed, because two of the four HSPD-5 criteria noted above had already been satisfied"; The Federal Response to Hurricane Katrina: Lessons Learned, February 23, 2006, p. 14.

    "Given the well-known consequences of a major hurricane striking New Orleans, the Secretary should have designated an Incident of National Significance no later than Saturday, two days prior to landfall, when the National Weather Service predicted New Orleans would be struck by a Category 4 or 5 hurricane and President Bush declared a federal emergency"; A Failure of Initiative: The Final Report of the Select Bipartisan Committee to Investigate the Preparation for and Response to Hurricane Katrina, February 2006, p. 2.
41. Hurricane Katrina: A Nation Still Unprepared, p. 168, says that Chertoff never declared Katrina a "catastrophic incident," a more severe designation that would have made a difference, creating a "proactive national response to a catastrophic incident.

    "In a catastrophic situation, however, the traditional mode of operation under the Stafford Act may not serve the Act's purposes because state and local governments may become so overwhelmed that they can't effectively make specific requests for assistance. In such circumstances, the federal government may have to act without a request from a state. The NRP explicitly provides for a proactive federal response in the Catastrophic Incident Annex (NRP-CIA). The NRP defines a catastrophic event as 'any natural or manmade incident, including terrorism that results in extraordinary levels of mass casualties, damage, or disruption severely affecting the population, infrastructure, environment, economy, national morale, and/ or government functions.' According to the NRP, only the secretary of homeland security or the secretary's designee may initiate implementation of the NRP-CIA. The NRP-CIA recognizes that, in a catastrophe, "federal and/or national resources are required to augment overwhelmed state, local, and tribal response efforts" and therefore provides for the identification and rapid deployment of essential resources expected to be urgently needed to save lives and contain incidents. The NRP-CIA provides that standard procedures regarding requests for assistance 'may be expedited or, under extreme circumstances, temporarily suspended' in the aftermath of a catastrophe"; Hurricane Katrina: A Nation Still Unprepared, p. 212.

42. Chertoff himself did not understand the difference between the principal federal official as defined in the NRP and the federal coordinating officer as specified in the law; A Failure of Initiative, pp. 135–136.

Coast Guard Vice Admiral Thad Allen was appointed deputy PFO for Hurricane Katrina in New Orleans on September 5, essentially supplanting Brown; Michael Brown resigned as FEMA director on September 12. Almost two weeks after Chertoff selected Allen to replace Brown as PFO, the unprecedented decision was made to appoint Allen the FCO for Louisiana, Mississippi, and Alabama in addition to PFO. This step was necessary because DHS eventually recognized that Allen, as the PFO only, did not have the legal authority to commit the expenditure of federal funds or direct federal agencies under delegated authority from the president.

43. The Federal Response to Hurricane Katrina: Lessons Learned, February 23, 2006, p. 42. The JFO was established on September 12, 2005, and even then, it was not located with the State Emergency Operations Center in Baton Rouge.

44. "Over the past several months, we have become more than familiar with the disaster declaration process outlined in the Stafford Act. We understand the goals, structure and mechanisms of the National Response Plan. We've digested the alphabet soup of 'coordinating elements' established by the Plan"; A Failure of Initiative, p. x.

45. "The National Response Plan was used in response to Hurricane Katrina, but it fell far short of the seamless, coordinated effort that had been envisioned. Problems ranging from poor coordination of federal support to confusion about the roles and authorities of incident managers to

inadequate information sharing among responders plagued the response to this catastrophic disaster"; DHS IG, FEMA's Preparedness for the Next Catastrophic Disaster—An Update, p. 15.

46. The Federal Response to Hurricane Katrina: Lessons Learned, February 23, 2006, p. 94.

47. "That would have given more rapid opportunity for Federal forces to flow into the State to be able to assist us with the evacuation," General Landreneau later testified; Hurricane Katrina: The Defense Department's Role in the Response, S. Hrg. 109-813, p. 48; *Disaster: Hurricane Katrina and the Failure of Homeland Security*, p. 173.

48. "Only once has martial law existed in U.S. history: following the attack on Pearl Harbor on 7 Dec. 1941, martial law went into effect for the Territory of Hawaii and lasted nearly three years"; Paul J. Scheips, The Role of Federal Military Forces in Domestic Disorders 1945–1992, Army Historical Series, p. 143.

The fiction is repeated in Commanders Martha LaGuardia-Kotite and David L. Teska, US Coast Guard Reserve, "Team of Teams: All-Hazard Incident Response Operations Call for U.S. Military Emergency Preparedness Liaisons," in Center for Army Lessons Learned, Support to Civil Authorities: Protecting the Homeland Newsletter, July 2010, p. 97.

49. Department of the Army, Field Manual 3-28, Civil Support Operations, August 20, 2010, p. 5-4.

50. In June 1954 Albert Patterson, the nominee in question, was killed on a street in Phenix City. Alabama governor Gordon Persons declared martial law in Phenix City and dispatched the Alabama National Guard to take over the city. The commander of the National Guard appointed a military mayor, and the troops took control of the county courthouse and city hall. The troops physically removed certain officials from the courthouse and city hall, seized gambling equipment, and revoked liquor licenses.

Deploying federal troops under the Insurrection Act, as was done openly in Los Angeles in 1992 or other cases during the 1960s, is not synonymous with and does not require martial law; in fact, the law and government regulations implementing it are clear that the role of the military in such cases is to support, not supplant, civil authority.

51. DOJ PowerPoint Briefing, Military Assistance to Civilian Law Enforcement, November 15, 2003, obtained by the author. One law review article makes the claim that martial law has been declared nine times since World War II; E. W. Killam, "Martial Law in Times of Civil Disorder," *Law and Order*, vol. 37, issue 9 (September 1989), pp. 44–47.

52. "In the United States," says *West's Encyclopedia of American Law* (2005), "martial law has been instituted on the national level only once, during the Civil War, and on a regional level only once, during World War II."

53. One study states: "There is no statutory or explicit constitutional authority for the invocation of martial law or the use of the military for civil
governance, generally. The constitutional mandate of the President to
'take Care that the Laws be faithfully executed' and of the Congress to
'call forth the Militia to execute the Laws of the Union, suppress Insurrections and repel Invasions' have been cited as the authority for the use of
martial law, and judicial decisions have indicated that martial law, properly limited in scope and time, is an appropriate tool for exigent circumstances." SAIC (for DTRA), Preliminary Report on Literature Search for
Legal Weapons of Mass Destruction Seminars, March 26, 2002, p. 8.

54. By the time of Lincoln's inauguration (March 4, 1861), seven states
announced their secession from the Union; the Confederate provisional
government was established on February 4, 1861, and Jefferson Davis was
elected and installed as president of the Confederacy on February 18,
1861. An army was being mobilized by the secessionists. On April 19, Lincoln issued a proclamation establishing a blockade on the ports of the
secessionist states. By a proclamation of May 3, Lincoln ordered that the
regular army be enlarged by 22,714 men, that navy personnel be increased
by 18,000, and that 42,032 volunteers be sought for three-year terms of
service, a direct challenge to Congress because Article I, Section 8 of the
Constitution specifically endows Congress with the power "to raise and
support armies." Lincoln suspended the writ of *habeas corpus* in a special
message to Congress on July 4, 1861. On September 24, 1862, he issued a
proclamation declaring martial law and authorizing the use of military
tribunals to try civilians who were believed to be "guilty of disloyal practice" or who "afford[ed] aid and comfort to Rebels."

Congress subsequently legislatively authorized, and thereby approved,
the president's actions regarding increasing armed forces personnel and
other emergency actions; CRS, Harold C. Relyea, Specialist in American
National Government, Government and Finance Division, National
Emergency Powers, Updated August 30, 2007.

The martial law declared by Lincoln during the Civil War spawned
important legal challenges, one being Ex Parte Milligan, 71 U.S. (4 Wall.) 2,
18 L. Ed. 281 (1866). Lamdin Milligan, a civilian resident of Indiana,
was arrested on October 5, 1864, by federal military forces. He was
charged with five offenses: conspiring against the United States, affording
aid and comfort to rebels, inciting insurrection, engaging in disloyal practices, and violating the laws of war. Milligan was tried, found guilty, and
sentenced to prison by a military court. Although the *habeas corpus* petition
had been suspended, the Supreme Court accepted Milligan's petition for a
writ of *habeas corpus*. The Supreme Court held that neither the president
nor Congress could give federal military forces the power to try a civilian
who lived in a state that had federal courts. Milligan firmly established the

right of the US Supreme Court to review the propriety of martial law declarations.

55. Code of Federal Regulations (annual edition), July 1, 2002 Edition, Title 32—National Defense, Chapter V—Department of the Army, Subchapter A—Aid of Civil Authorities and Public Relations, Part 501—Employment of Troops in Aid of Civil Authorities, Sec. 501.4—Martial law, pp. 8–9; http://www.gpo.gov/fdsys/pkg/CFR-2002-title32-vol3/html/CFR-2002-title32-vol3-sec501-4.htm (accessed August 5, 2012).

56. JCS, "Basic Planning Directive for Land Defense of the Continental United States and Military Support of Civil Defense," February 15, 1983, pp. 20–21 (partially declassified and released under the Freedom of Information Act), says the following about martial law: "…An essential objective of martial law is to create conditions wherein civil government can be rapidly reconstituted. The justification for martial law is public necessity. Such necessity gives rise to the imposition justification, and limited duration of martial law. The extent of the military force used and the legal propriety of the measures taken, consequently, will depend upon the actual threat to order and public safety that exists at the time. In most instances, the decision to impose martial law is made by the President. Normally, the President announces the decision by a proclamation usually containing instructions concerning the exercise of martial law and any limitations thereon. However, the decision to impose martial law may be made by the local commander if circumstances demand immediate action and time and available communications facilities do not permit obtaining prior approval from higher authority.…In every case, control will be returned to civil authorities upon receipt of notification from a recognized civilian authority, at an authorized level, that civil authorities are prepared to exercise control."

57. SAIC (for DTRA), Preliminary Report on Literature Search for Legal Weapons of Mass Destruction Seminars, March 26, 2002, pp. 8–9.

58. Lieutenant Colonel Mark C. Weston, Review of the Posse Comitatus Act After Hurricane Katrina, March 15, 2006, p. 8.

59. Lieutenant Colonel Mark C. Weston, Review of the Posse Comitatus Act After Hurricane Katrina, March 15, 2006, p. 8.

60. JCS, Basic Planning Directive, February 15, 1983, pp. 20-21, obtained by the author.

61. A new term was also tried out: "domestic support operations," a sort of counterpart to peacekeeping operations overseas, but with similar doctrines; Department of the Army/US Marine Corps, Field Manual (FM) 100-19/Fleet Marine Force Manual (FMFM) 7-10, Domestic Support Operations, July 1993.

62. DOD Directive 3025.1, Military Support to Civil Authorities (MSCA), January 15, 1993; DOD Directive 3025.12, Military Assistance for Civil

Disturbances (MACDIS), February 4, 1994, Para 4.2.7; DOD Directive 3025.15, Military Assistance to Civil Authorities, February 18, 1997.

63. Richard Reeves, *President Kennedy: Profile of Power* (New York: Simon & Schuster, 1993), pp. 29–30.

64. The Operation Alert story is told primarily from Matthew L. Conaty, "The Atomic Midwife: The Eisenhower Administration's Continuity-of-Government Plans and the Legacy of 'Constitutional Dictatorship,'" *Rutgers Law Review*, vol. 62, no. 3, Spring 2010; Guy Oakes, *The Imaginary War: Civil Defense and American Cold War Culture* (New York: Oxford University Press, 1994); Federal Civil Defense Administration, Progress Report Fiscal Year 1955, Annual Statistic Report, June 30, 1955; National Archives, Office of Civil and Defense Mobilization, unscheduled records assigned to RG 304 and RG 396 at the Washington National Records Center.

65. Innis D. Harris, Deputy Assistant Director for Plans and Readiness, Office of Defense Mobilization, Presentation at the Industrial College of the Armed Forces, Lessons Learned from Operations Alert 1955–57, April 30, 1958.

66. Herbert Brownell with John P. Burke, *Advising Ike: The Memoir of Attorney General Herbert Brownell* (Lawrence, KS: University of Kansas Press, 1993), p. 274.

67. See JCS, Basic Planning Directive, February 15, 1983, p. 19, obtained by the author.

68. NCS, Briefing, Federal Emergency Plan D, n.d. (1981), AH 134-35, obtained by the author. The best description of the Eisenhower era and the path to PEADs is Matthew L. Conaty, "The Atomic Midwife: The Eisenhower Administration's Continuity-of-Government Plans and the Legacy of 'Constitutional Dictatorship,'" *Rutgers Law Review*, vol. 62, no. 3, Spring 2010.

69. Federal Emergency Plan C, first issued in 1957, dealt with full mobilization in anticipation of general war, and later became Federal Emergency Plan Other than Plan D (OTD). Federal Emergency Plan D dealt with continuity of government and national communications "in a Plan D situation," that is, "in a crippling nuclear attack on the United States." Federal Emergency Plan D-Minus was later prepared for "during and after a crippling [nonnuclear] attack on the United States, on overseas bases, and on allies." Other plans from the Eisenhower years included the National Plan for Civil Defense and Defense Mobilization, the Emergency Relocation Plan, the White House Emergency Plan, Mobilization Plan C, and Federal Emergency Plan D-Minus. See US Government Memorandum, Defense Plans—Presidential Emergency Action Documents, February 1, 1961 (partially declassified and released to government attic.org under the FOIA).

70. NCS, Briefing, Federal Emergency Plan D, n.d. (1981), AH 134-35, obtained by the author.

71. NCS, Briefing, Federal Emergency Plan D, n.d. (1981), AH 134-35, obtained by the author. See also US Congress, Intelligence Activities and the Rights of Americans; Book II; Final Report of the Select Committee to Study Governmental Operations with Respect to Intelligence Activities; United States Senate, Together with Additional, Supplemental, and Separate Views ("Church Committee"), April 26 (legislative day, April 14), 1976.

72. "Additional resources (1 attorney) are requested to enable the Office of Legal Counsel to conduct a legal review of 48 Presidential Emergency Action Documents (PEADs). PEADs are pre-coordinated legal documents designed to implement Presidential decision or transmit Presidential requests when an emergency situation does not allow for routine staffing and distribution. PEADs have applicability during a national emergency when the President requires immediate authority for, or direction of, emergency activities." Department of Justice, FY 2001 Budget Request, General Legal Activities, p. 54.

73. "SIES's National Security Emergency Preparedness (NSEP) program ensures that the U.S. industrial/technology base can respond effectively to the requirements of national emergencies. During FY 2001, SIES staff participated in interagency planning and execution of the joint civilian/military Positive Force 01 emergency mobilization exercise which took place in April 2001 to ensure appropriate civil agency and industrial base activities. Also, SIES staff reviewed three Presidential Emergency Action Documents (PEADs). The Commerce Department continues to lead federal agency response to industrial emergency preparedness planning and implementation of a variety of NSEP programs, and SIES remains a major contributor to ongoing interagency reviews and assessments of the industrial/technology base"; Department of Commerce, Annual Report 2001, Chapter 4: Strategic Industries and Economic Security, p. 4.

74. NRC, Interim pandemic Response Plan, June 29, 2006, p. 7.

75. "Initiated, designed and directed interagency and internal White House review and update of the Presidential Emergency Action Documents; pre-coordinated legal and policy documents designed to implement presidential decisions during an emergency"; Biography of Meghan O'Brien, Director of Continuity, Homeland Security Council, January 2008–January 2009; http://www.linkedin.com/pub/meghan-o-brien/1a/753/1b3.

76. "In order to ensure continuity of government, Defense Secretary Robert Gates has been designated by the outgoing administration, with the concurrence of the incoming administration, to serve as the designated successor during Inauguration Day," the White House announced. The White House, Office of the Press Secretary, press release, January 20, 2009.

77. In 1973, the secretary of the army was designated DOD executive agent in providing military support for peacetime civil emergencies with responsibility to be the lead organization for all Defense planning and/or response to the civil sector. A two-star general, designated the director of military support (DOMS), served as "action agent" for the secretary, with the authority to task and coordinate an appropriate commander in chief (CINC), based upon the geographical area of occurrence. The commander in chief, forces command (army FORSCOM), was the four-star commander for the continental US, serving as the principal operating agent under the secretary of the army for planning and response for peacetime disasters; he led "the most complex contingency planning effort within DOD."

78. One might ask why such procedures were developed after the assassination of President Kennedy. In some ways, the actual death of Kennedy was less messy for the Program, and Washington, though vigilant, wasn't gripped with fear of a Soviet nuclear attack. The Kennedy assassination did precipitate the Twenty-Fifth Amendment to the Constitution and strengthened the "national command authority," which dealt exclusively with the control of nuclear weapons, but it really wasn't until the uncertainties that arose with the Reagan assassination attempt that more extensive changes were pondered.

79. See Chapter 9, p. 151, for amplification of the *national mission force.*

CHAPTER TWO: HIGH WATER OR HELL

1. Hurricane Katrina made landfall at 0610 CDT (1110Z) as a CAT IV hurricane with 145 mph sustained winds near Buras, Louisiana. The basic facts about the hurricane and various government actions, unless otherwise noted, are taken from Louisiana National Guard Timeline of Significant Events Hurricane Katrina, Task Force Pelican, December 6, 2005; USNORTHCOM Hurricane Katrina Timeline (Unclassified/FOUO), n.d.; USCG, Katrina Timeline (Excel spreadsheet), April 20, 2005; NORTHCOM, Significant Events Timeline (2005); AF/A9, Katrina/Rita by the Numbers: Air Force Support to Hurricane Katrina/Rita Relief Operations (report prepared by Headquarters United States Air Force A9, 2006); DOD, Katrina Interim Timeline (Draft), Prepared by OASD HD 10/17/2005 (October 17, 2005); and A Failure of Initiative: The Final Report of the Select Bipartisan Committee to Investigate the Preparation for and Response to Hurricane Katrina, February 2006.

2. Again, there are many basic documents that summarize Katrina's impact, particularly A Failure of Initiative: The Final Report of the Select Bipartisan Committee to Investigate the Preparation for and Response to Hurricane Katrina, February 2006; Hurricane Katrina: A Nation Still Unprepared; The White House, Office of Homeland Security. Assistant

to the President for Homeland Security and Counterterrorism, The Federal Response to Hurricane Katrina: Lessons Learned, February 23, 2006; Rand Corporation, Hurricane Katrina: Lessons for Army Planning and Operations, 2007. Most of these documents declare 770,000 displaced, while *Disaster: Hurricane Katrina and the Failure of Homeland Security*, p. 122, more convincingly says 1.2 million fled the greater New Orleans area, leaving about 200,000 "poverty-stricken people and refuseniks behind."

3. "The National Guard of one state can assist other states responding to a disaster through formal agreements, such as the Emergency Management Assistance Compact (known as EMAC). Typically, this occurs in state active duty, and may transition to Title 32 status upon approval by the Secretary of Defense. When requested by the supported state's governor and authorized by the supporting state's governor under a separate memorandum of agreement, National Guard elements deploy to the supported state. The supporting National Guard operates under the operational control of the supported state's adjutant general. Typically, deployments under an assistance memorandum are limited to a specific period, such as 30 days. Often, military and civilian officials refer to all National Guard forces as 'Title 32 forces,' notwithstanding that some of them may be in a state active duty status—without federal funding"; Department of the Army, FM 3-28, Civil Support, 2010, pp. 1–8.

4. *Katrina's Secrets: Storms after the Storms*, pp. 115–116, 135. The particular guardsman was later found to have been shot in the foot in an accidental discharge of a military weapon, that of another soldier.

5. The story of the Ohio Guardsmen is told in Specialist Benjamin Cossel, "Evacuating the Superdome," *Buckeye Response* Special Edition 2005, pp. 16–17; Major Nicole Gabriel, "Ohio's 1–148th Infantry soldiers shine in New Orleans' muck," *Buckeye Guard*, Fall/Winter 2005, pp. 16–17; DVIDS, 196th Mobile Public Affairs Detachment (Story ID 3048), New Orleans Police Officers are also victims of Hurricane Katrina, September 18, 2005; James Janega, "Some storm survivors ride out the hardship," *Chicago Tribune*, September 4, 2005; "Kosovo a model for US in Iraq," *Washington Times*, November 15, 2004.

6. *Survival: How a Culture of Preparedness Can Save You and Your Family from Disasters*, pp. 12, 103–104. See also *Katrina's Secrets: Storms after the Storms*, p. 58.

7. *Survival: How a Culture of Preparedness Can Save You and Your Family from Disasters*, pp. 14, 19, 104. The Senate Congressional investigation agreed: "According to the Guard and police, the people in the Superdome were very unhappy and anxious, but they were never out of control"; A Failure of Initiative, p. 248.

8. *Survival: How a Culture of Preparedness Can Save You and Your Family from Disasters*, p. 100; Hurricane Katrina: The Defense Department's Role in the Response, S. Hrg. 109-813, p. 45.
9. *Katrina's Secrets: Storms after the Storms*, p. 121.
10. *Survival: How a Culture of Preparedness Can Save You and Your Family from Disasters*, pp. 4–5.
11. *Katrina's Secrets: Storms after the Storms*, pp. 103ff.
12. *The Washington Post* called Honoré "the Army officer in charge of the military task force set up to respond to Katrina"; Josh White and Peter Whoriskey, "Planning, Response Are Faulted," *Washington Post*, September 2, 2005, p. 1; "Commander of the joint task force coordinating military efforts in hurricane relief"; see Eric Schmitt and David S. Cloud, "Military Dealt with Combination of Obstacles Before Reaching Victims," *New York Times*, September 3, 2005, p. 1; "the cigar-chomping Louisiana native son who led National Guard units into the city center Friday morning," see Scott Gold, Alan Zarembo, and Stephen Braun, "Guardsmen Arrive in New Orleans; Pace of Evacuations Is Stepped Up," *Los Angeles Times*, September 3, 2005, p. 1; "The three-star Army general tapped to lead the National Guard's recovery operations along the battered Gulf Coast is a cigar-chomping 'John Wayne-type dude' with a Cajun accent"; Andy Geller, "Gen. Ragin' Cajun," *New York Post*, September 3, 2005.
13. *Survival: How a Culture of Preparedness Can Save You and Your Family from Disasters*, p. 89; Hurricane Katrina: The Defense Department's Role in the Response, S. Hrg. 109-813, p. 17; Hurricane Katrina: A Nation Still Unprepared, p. 478.

    On August 28, NORTHCOM headquarters in Colorado deployed an advance Joint Task Force—Forward to Camp Shelby, MS, to reconnoiter and command the entire area. JTF Katrina was formally established at 2200 CDT (10 p.m.) on the evening of August 30 and Honoré was appointed the task force commander. According to DOD, the Joint Task Force headquarters was fully operational on August 31, with 250 personnel in Atlanta providing rear support at JTF-Main.
14. Hurricane Katrina: A Nation Still Unprepared, p. 487. An e-mail to General Rowe J3 (Operations) of NORTHCOM from one of his planners shows that the marines' preparatory movements were not coordinated with NORTHCOM: "They do not have orders to move out yet but they are inside our [Joint Operating Area] w/out [Joint Task Force Katrina] or [NORTHCOM visibility]"; Hurricane Katrina: A Nation Still Unprepared, p. 494.

    The command and its role are comprehensively treated in *Top Secret America*, pp. 104–127; and Paul McHale, "Critical Mismatch: The

Dangerous Gap Between Rhetoric and Readiness in DOD's Civil Support Missions," Heritage Foundation SR-115, August 13, 2012.

15. *Survival: How a Culture of Preparedness Can Save You and Your Family from Disasters*, p. 165.

16. *Disaster: Hurricane Katrina and the Failure of Homeland Security*, pp. 192–193.

17. Governor Blanco pleaded with President Bush to send "everything you have got" and even General Landreneau used the same words in his first conversation with Honoré; *Survival: How a Culture of Preparedness Can Save You and Your Family from Disasters*, p. 101.

18. *Survival: How a Culture of Preparedness Can Save You and Your Family from Disasters*, p. 102.

19. Ray Nagin observes that when the three highest-ranking political leaders in the state of Louisiana first came to the Superdome, they "didn't even go over and talk to the suffering people, let alone go inside it"; *Katrina's Secrets: Storms after the Storms*, p. 79.

20. *Survival: How a Culture of Preparedness Can Save You and Your Family from Disasters*, p. 160.

21. A Failure of Initiative, pp. 2–3. "The choice of Brown as PFO—whether before landfall or after—was poor, even if for no other reason than his animosity toward the PFO concept, the NRP, and DHS, not to mention his lack of emergency-management training and experience"; Hurricane Katrina: A Nation Still Unprepared, p. 170.

22. *Disaster: Hurricane Katrina and the Failure of Homeland Security*, pp. 81, 188–189, 213. "Brown arrived in Baton Rouge on Sunday evening. He was accompanied by two FEMA press employees, a FEMA congressional-relations liaison, security detail, and his personal assistant, but no operations experts. They traveled on military aircraft; FEMA's operational personnel took commercial flights. Once in Baton Rouge, Brown went to dinner and to the hotel, but did not go to the state EOC"; Hurricane Katrina: A Nation Still Unprepared, pp. 176, 220.

There is a devastating portrait of Brown's red-carpet arrival in Baton Rouge in *Disaster: Hurricane Katrina and the Failure of Homeland Security*, p. 121. "He was...intensely concerned about his physical appearance on TV," Ray Nagin observed, among other things; *Katrina's Secrets: Storms after the Storms*, p. 104.

Honoré also tells the story of trying to get ahold of Brown at a crucial moment on Wednesday night, August 31, only to be told by his staff that he was unavailable because he was at a restaurant eating dinner; *Survival: How a Culture of Preparedness Can Save You and Your Family from Disasters*, pp. 109–110.

23. President Bush issued an executive directive in 2003, punctuating the law and designating the DHS secretary as "the principal Federal official for

coordinating the implementation of all-hazards preparedness in the United States"; Homeland Security Presidential Directive 8: National Preparedness, December 17, 2003, paragraphs 4 and 5. See also A Failure of Initiative, p. 131.

24. "Secretary Chertoff himself should have been more engaged in preparations over the weekend before landfall. Secretary Chertoff made only top-level inquiries into the state of preparations, and accepted uncritically the reassurances he received. He did not appear to reach out to the other Cabinet secretaries to make sure that they were readying their departments to provide whatever assistance DHS—and the people of the Gulf Coast—might need"; Hurricane Katrina: A Nation Still Unprepared, p. 6.

"In the critical days before landfall, DHS leadership mostly watched from the sidelines, allowed FEMA to take the lead, and missed critical opportunities to help prepare the entire federal government for the response.…In the days before Katrina made landfall, DHS Secretary Michael Chertoff's efforts in this regard fell short of what was reasonably expected of him.…During the weekend, as Katrina neared New Orleans, there was a need for initiative, for recognition of the unprecedented threat and the equally unprecedented response it required. Leadership—direction, encouragement, a sense of purpose and urgency—was needed. Secretary Chertoff did not provide it"; Hurricane Katrina: A Nation Still Unprepared, pp. 163–165. See also Michael D. Brown and Ted Schwarz, *Deadly Indifference: The Perfect (Political) Storm: Hurricane Katrina, the Bush White House and Beyond*, p. 92.

25. A Failure of Initiative, p. 131. In his own (very thin) book, Chertoff barely mentions Katrina, and even there, it is to blame "ill-maintained levees" and selfish individuals and the news media; *Homeland Security: Assessing the First Five Years*, pp. 90–91, 124–126.

Bush calls Chertoff "a brilliant lawyer and decent man who had resigned his lifetime appointment as a federal judge" to take the job of Secretary of DHS; George W. Bush, *Decision Points* (New York: Crown, 2010), p. 314. Cheney, in his autobiography, says Chertoff "did tremendous work"; Dick Cheney and Liz Cheney, *In My Time: A Personal and Political Memoir* (New York: Simon and Schuster, 2011), p. 432.

26. Hurricane Katrina: A Nation Still Unprepared, pp. 243–244; *Disaster: Hurricane Katrina and the Failure of Homeland Security*, pp. 101, 112, 123, 155; *Katrina's Secrets: Storms after the Storms*, pp. 105–108. Rumsfeld says in his autobiography that he left before noon after the ceremony to return to Washington; Donald Rumsfeld, *Known and Unknown: A Memoir*, p. 618.

27. A Failure of Initiative, p. 24; Nicole Gaouette, Alan C. Miller, Mark Mazzetti, Doyle McManus, Josh Meyer, and Kevin Sack, "Put to Katrina's Test: After 9/11, a master plan for disasters was drawn. It didn't weather the storm," *Los Angeles Times*, September 11, 2005, p. 1.

28. Article I, Section 8 of the Constitution recognizes these state militias, placing the responsibility of "organizing, arming, and disciplining the militia…" upon Congress, while reserving the training "according to the discipline prescribed by Congress…" to the states. These constitutionally based dual roles and missions result in each guardsman or -woman holding memberships in either the army or Air National Guard of his or her state and also in the army or Air National Guard of the United States.

    The army's manual on civil support states: "The Constitution also outlines the antipathy of the founding fathers towards the large militaries of the European powers. These men viewed a large standing army answering to the head of state as a continuous threat to civil liberty. Although the founders shared a fear of a large standing army, they also saw the necessity of a national army for the common defense. They balanced this requirement by providing the states with military capabilities. They had ample reasons for this balancing act"; Department of the Army, FM 3-28, Civil Support, 2010, pp. 1–4.

29. The US Code describes this unique dual status as "in federal service" (Title 10), and "when not in federal service" (state active duty or Title 32). Federal service is codified in Title 10 of the US Code, while nonfederal service is covered in Title 32 of the US Code and applicable state law. Hence, the National Guard of the several states may perform state roles and missions in either state active duty of Title 32 status, while only performing their federal training and ancillary federal missions in Title 32 status. Purely federal roles and missions performed as a reserve of the armed forces, i.e., in the Army or Air National Guard of the United States, are performed in a Title 10 status. Conducting National Guard activities under the appropriate state or federal statute is important for establishing presidential or gubernatorial commander-in-chief authority, operational command and control authority, and funding sources.

30. The National Guard operates under one of three statuses: state status (state funding and state control); Title 32 status (federal funding and state control); and Title 10 status (federal funding and federal control). State missions are authorized by executive order of the governor, who reimburses the federal government for utilization of federal equipment and facilities; How the Army Runs, p. 505.

31. Major General Landreneau later testified before Congress: "By Tuesday, the Louisiana National Guard had every resource committed. We had no reserves"; Hurricane Katrina: The Defense Department's Role in the Response, S. Hrg. 109-813, p. 45. See also *Survival: How a Culture of Preparedness Can Save You and Your Family from Disasters*, pp. 108–109.

    President Bush strangely states in his autobiography: "Contrary to later claims, there was never a shortage of Guardsmen available, either because of Iraq or any other reason"; *Decision Points*, p. 314. It is a statement that is an affirmation of a unique role for the Guard but one that also conflates the difference between the state's National Guard and the confederated National Guard as a whole.

32. NGB, "Hurricane Katrina: National Guard's Finest Hour" (from staff reports), August 28, 2006; Brock N. Meeks, "Guardsmen on a rescue and relief mission," MSNBC.com, August 30, 2005 (updated 8/30/2005 1:35:52 p.m. ET).

33. Under the constitutional guarantee in Article IV, Section 4, of "a Republican form of government" to the states, the president can act only upon receipt of a request from a state's legislature or from its governor if the legislature cannot be convened.

34. Congress established the Stafford Act to provide assistance "by the federal government to state and local governments in carrying out their responsibilities to alleviate the suffering and damage which result from...disasters."

35. The Federal Response to Hurricane Katrina: Lessons Learned, February 23, 2006, pp. 19, 24, 40; *Deadly Indifference: The Perfect (Political) Storm*, pp. 3, 56, 150; *Known and Unknown: A Memoir*, pp. 618, 621.

   Bush would write: "Katrina conjures impressions of disorder, incompetence, and the sense that government let down its citizens. Serious mistakes came at all levels..."; *Decision Points*, p. 310. Rumsfeld said: "Many perceived the response to Katrina as a slow train wreck. Most of the blame for the shortcomings was quickly placed on Washington....While some of the unfolding criticism was warranted, much of it was not"; *Known and Unknown: A Memoir*, p. 618.

36. *Survival: How a Culture of Preparedness Can Save You and Your Family from Disasters*, pp. 5, 57, 139, 163. In the most telling subdrama of the larger American tragedy, the army old guard took great exception to Honoré's blunt words and foul language, whispering that only a black officer could get away with speaking to the news media like that.

   An army study later observed: "Civilian leaders and concerned citizens should arguably remain vigilant so that an Army general does not create a false impression as to what is happening and who is in charge during an emergency. Lieutenant General Honoré's saturation of the media with news of JTF-Katrina may have ironically focused the public, including the critics, on the federal effort. Had the American public properly understood the role of the federal forces in accordance with tiered response doctrine, then perhaps the Bush Administration would not have endured the public outcry that prompted the change in the Insurrection Act. In any event, Lieutenant General Honoré's presence in New Orleans influenced nationwide public opinion and subsequent national policy. For a military officer to have such an impact on domestic policy is unusual." See Major Mark M. Beckler, US Army National Guard, Insurrection Act Restored:

States Likely to Maintain Authority Over National Guard in Domestic Emergencies, SAMS Monograph, 2008, p. 43.

37. *Survival: How a Culture of Preparedness Can Save You and Your Family from Disasters*, p. 92; *Deadly Indifference: The Perfect (Political) Storm*, p. 27; *Katrina's Secrets: Storms after the Storms*, pp. 47, 70, 77. At least according to Landreneau, Blanco issued "very clear command guidance...very clear, explicit direction"; Hurricane Katrina: The Defense Department's Role in the Response, S. Hrg. 109-813, p. 57.

This is not to say that Blanco was rock steady or didn't make terrible judgments, though refusing to relinquish control wasn't one of them. The governor's self-doubt was broadcast later when a conversation with her press secretary was caught on tape. "I really need to call for the military," she said as an aside during an interview. "Yes you do. Yes you do," the aide is heard responding. Blanco then admitted, "I should have started that in the first call," referring to her initial August 26 letter to President Bush. See Lisa Meyers, "How Much Blame Does Gov. Blanco Deserve?" NBC News, October 8, 2005, http://www.msnbc.msn.com/id/9613133/.

38. See Hurricane Katrina: A Nation Still Unprepared, p. 67.

Governor Blanco officially declared a state of emergency at 1800 CDT (6 p.m.), August 26, signing and issuing Proclamation No. 48 KBB 2005, Declaring a State of Emergency. She warned that "Hurricane Katrina poses an imminent threat to the state of Louisiana, carrying severe storms, high winds, and torrential rain that may cause flooding and damage to private property and public facilities, and threatens the safety and security of the citizens of Louisiana."

On Friday, September 2, Blanco further issued Executive Order KBB 2005-26, declaring a state of public health emergency and facilitating the acceptance of additional medical professional assistance, as well as allowing out-of-state medical professionals to treat those in need of urgent care.

"In Baton Rouge, Governor Kathleen Blanco looked at the latest forecasts on Saturday and took the unusual step of asking President Bush to preemptively issue a disaster declaration for Louisiana, which he did"; *Disaster: Hurricane Katrina and the Failure of Homeland Security*, p. 104.

39. According to Major General Landreneau, commander of the Louisiana National Guard, "When Governor Blanco declared a state of emergency, I recommended the activation of 2,000 National Guardsmen early on. This activation began a chain of events that initiated our emergency response plan and began the coordination with staff and units to implement preplanned support requirements for response operations. As we gathered more information on the strengthening storm, I recommended to Governor Blanco that we increase the activation to an additional 2,000 soldiers, for a total of 4,000, unprecedented pre-storm in Louisiana"; Hurricane Katrina: The Defense Department's Role in the Response, S. Hrg. 109-813, p. 44.

"Blanco canceled a trip she had planned for Saturday [to the Southern Governors Association Conference], even though the National Hurricane Center forecast no more than a 17 percent probability that the storm would hit anywhere within the state"; *Disaster: Hurricane Katrina and the Failure of Homeland Security*, p. 98; Hurricane Katrina: The Defense Department's Role in the Response, S. Hrg. 109-813, p. 204.

40. The Federal Response to Hurricane Katrina: Lessons Learned, February 23, 2006, p. 28.

41. *Decision Points*, p. 315.

42. *Disaster: Hurricane Katrina and the Failure of Homeland Security*, p. 168.

43. *Decision Points*, p. 321.

44. *Survival: How a Culture of Preparedness Can Save You and Your Family from Disasters*, pp. 18, 118, 128.

45. *Survival: How a Culture of Preparedness Can Save You and Your Family from Disasters*, p. 118.

46. *Survival: How a Culture of Preparedness Can Save You and Your Family from Disasters*, p. 119.

47. *Survival: How a Culture of Preparedness Can Save You and Your Family from Disasters*, pp. 107, 125–126.

48. "I was committed with dealing with the situation at the convention center and did not meet with him," Honoré says, matter-of-factly; *Survival: How a Culture of Preparedness Can Save You and Your Family from Disasters*, p. 127.

49. *Decision Points*, p. 308.

50. Evan Thomas, "How Bush Blew It: Bureaucratic Timidity; Bad Phone Lines; and a Failure of Imagination; Why the Government Was So Slow to Respond to Catastrophe," *Newsweek*, September 19, 2005.

51. Hurricane Katrina: The Defense Department's Role in the Response, S. Hrg. 109-813, p. 216; *Disaster: Hurricane Katrina and the Failure of Homeland Security*, p. 213; *Katrina's Secrets: Storms after the Storms*, pp. 169–172; *Deadly Indifference: The Perfect (Political) Storm*, p. 154.

52. *Decision Points*, p. 309.

53. *Decision Points*, p. 321.

54. The most extensive description of Addington and his role in the Bush administration is in Barton Gellman, *Angler: The Cheney Vice Presidency*. See also Stephen F. Hayes, *Cheney: The Untold Story of America's Most Powerful and Controversial Vice President*, pp. 313ff.

55. David S. Addington, e-mail to William J. Haynes, Aug. 28, 2005, 8:41 p.m.; provided to committee; filed as Bates no. 000007; quoted in Hurricane Katrina: A Nation Still Unprepared, p. 508. "Mr. Addington recommended that Mr. Haynes prepare a 'Proclamation to Disperse,' whereby the President would "immediately order the insurgents to disperse and retire peaceably within their abodes" (10 U.S.C. §334), and executive orders for 10 U.S.C. 332, "Use of militia and armed forces to enforce

Federal authority," and 10 U.S.C. §334, "Interference with State and Federal Law"; p. 542.

56. Paul J. Scheips, The Role of Federal Military Forces in Domestic Disorders 1945–1992, Army Historical Series, pp. 182–183.

57. "At that time, because of violent resistance in Western Pennsylvania to a federal tax on the production of whiskey, the President requisitioned 15,000 militiamen from Pennsylvania, Maryland, New Jersey, and Virginia, and placed Virginia Governor, General (Light Horse) Harry Lee, in command. According to Robert Coakley, Washington acted accordingly, 'issuing a cease and desist proclamation and citing that acts of treason had been committed against the United States,' which necessitated calling forth the militia"; Barrye La Troye Price, "The Use of Federal Troops in Quelling Civil Unrest in Washington DC, April 1968," master's thesis, 1994, p. 3. See also Combat Studies Institute (Matt Murphy), The Posse Comitatus Act and the United States Army: A Historical Perspective, Global War on Terrorism Occasional Paper 14, 2006, pp. 9ff.

58. *Decision Points*, p. 323; Hurricane Katrina: The Defense Department's Role in the Response, S. Hrg. 109-813, p. 36; *Disaster: Hurricane Katrina and the Failure of Homeland Security*, p. 215; Hurricane Katrina: A Nation Still Unprepared, p. 70.

59. *Disaster: Hurricane Katrina and the Failure of Homeland Security*, p. 213–215.

60. Hurricane Katrina: A Nation Still Unprepared, p. 522.

61. A brigade of the 1st Cavalry from Fort Hood, Texas, was included in this package and also deployed, but it was largely an aviation element. Boots on the ground followed and were used in door-to-door search and rescue missions, with a unit of the Texas National Guard embedded throughout the teams, just in case any law enforcement was needed; Hurricane Katrina: A Nation Still Unprepared, pp. 493–495.

62. Hurricane Katrina: A Nation Still Unprepared, p. 493. Donald Rumsfeld would also say that "their very presence had the effect of reducing crime and disorder"; *Known and Unknown: A Memoir*, p. 619.

63. Hurricane Katrina: The Defense Department's Role in the Response, S. Hrg. 109-813, pp. 20–22, 33-34, 162; *Survival: How a Culture of Preparedness Can Save You and Your Family from Disasters*, p. 142; *Katrina's Secrets: Storms after the Storms*, p. 90; A Failure of Initiative, p. 219; Armed Forces Information Service (AFIS), Gerry J. Gilmore, "82nd Airborne Division Becomes 'Waterborne' in New Orleans," September 21, 2005; Major Kevin L. Buddelmeyer, Military First Response: Lessons Learned from Hurricane Katrina, p. 11.

CHAPTER THREE: CRITICAL CONDITIONS

1. *Survival: How a Culture of Preparedness Can Save You and Your Family from Disasters*, pp. 171–172.

2. NGB, In Katrina's Wake: The National Guard on the Gulf Coast, 2005, pp. 29–30; Statement of Kenneth W. Kaiser, Special Agent in Charge, Boston Field Office Federal Bureau of Investigation, before the Senate Homeland Security and Governmental Affairs Committee, February 6, 2006.

3. FBI, Eye of the Storm; Our Response to Hurricane Katrina, November 2, 2005.

4. Hurricane Katrina: A Nation Still Unprepared, p. 176; A Failure of Initiative: The Final Report of the Select Bipartisan Committee to Investigate the Preparation for and Response to Hurricane Katrina, February 2006, p. 190.

5. Hurricane Katrina: A Nation Still Unprepared, p. 480.

    Conversely, when others were moving of their own initiative, the Joint Chiefs in Washington never moved from their focus on paperwork, even refusing to respond to any requests to render assistance until after the hurricane made landfall; Hurricane Katrina: A Nation Still Unprepared, p. 479. When the Second Fleet commander actually had the audacity to move a ship on exercise in the Gulf of Mexico closer to the coast to prepare it for posthurricane duty, the Office of the Secretary of Defense admonished him for moving without orders; Hurricane Katrina: A Nation Still Unprepared, pp. 194, 479; A Failure of Initiative, p. 224.

6. Louis A. Arana-Barradas, *Air Force Print News,* "People venture outside Keesler shelters," August 31, 2005.

7. Air National Guard, "Chronology of the Air National Guard in 2005 Hurricane Rescue and Relief Operations, 19 August–29 November 2005."

8. The incident is recorded in the documentary *Trouble the Water* (2008). Officers from the Naval Support Activity are seen saying "Get off our property," telling neighborhood residents seeking shelter that their responsibility was to "protect the interests of the government...and maintaining the base."

9. The Federal Protective Service—one of the smallest of the Department of Homeland Security's many law enforcement components—set up a clandestine team downtown not to take part in any rescue effort or assist the police, but to reconnoiter federal buildings and collect information on the situation on the ground, reporting back to Washington. See *Disaster: Hurricane Katrina and the Failure of Homeland Security*, pp. 174–175.

10. See Hurricane Katrina: A Nation Still Unprepared, p. 452; Statement of Kenneth W. Kaiser, Special Agent in Charge, Boston Field Office, Federal Bureau of Investigation, before the Senate Homeland Security and Governmental Affairs Committee, February 6, 2006.

11. *Disaster: Hurricane Katrina and the Failure of Homeland Security*, pp. 232–233.

12. Almost immediately after news of lawlessness emerged, the head of the Louisiana State Police faxed an urgent letter to Principal Associate Deputy Attorney General William Mercer requesting "any assistance" that the Department of Justice could provide; but since there was no formal request from Governor Blanco, Attorney General Gonzales hesitated to move people in. He ordered a surge of federal agents to a staging area in Baton Rouge. Hurricane Katrina: A Nation Still Unprepared, pp. 446, 450; *Disaster: Hurricane Katrina and the Failure of Homeland Security*, p. 168.

    By midnight on September 2, there were over 100 ICE agents in New Orleans; Border Patrol agents took up posts at the Louisiana State University; the federal air marshals of TSA staged at the New Orleans airport; A Failure of Initiative, p. 255.

    Governor Blanco issued a written request for law enforcement assistance on September 4 and Gonzales issued an order to Justice law enforcement officers authorizing them to assist the state in enforcing state and local laws; but even then, there was an additional holdup while the state issued deputization credentials; Hurricane Katrina: A Nation Still Unprepared, p. 452.

13. The New Orleans Police Department, at its full strength, was a force of about 1,688 officers. The Louisiana State Police was a force of only 1,050 troopers; Hurricane Katrina: A Nation Still Unprepared, pp. 446, 450.

14. The Louisiana State Police ultimately oversaw the deputization of more than 400 law enforcement officers from other states and more than 3,000 from the federal government; Hurricane Katrina: A Nation Still Unprepared, p. 448.

15. *Survival: How a Culture of Preparedness Can Save You and Your Family from Disasters*, p. 171.

16. The National Communications System (NCS) was established after the Cuban missile crisis in 1963, when communications problems were identified not only between the US and the Soviet Union, but also between NATO and foreign heads of state. President Kennedy ordered an investigation of national security communications, and an interdepartmental committee recommended the formation of a single unified communications system to serve the president, Department of Defense, diplomatic and intelligence activities, and civilian leaders. Consequently, in order to provide better communications support to critical government functions during emergencies, President Kennedy established the National Communications System by a Presidential Memorandum on August 21, 1963. The original NCS charter was to "link together, improve, and extend, on an evolutionary basis, the communications facilities and components of the various federal agencies...to provide necessary communications for the federal government under all conditions ranging from a normal situa-

tion to national emergencies and international crisis, including nuclear attack."

On April 3, 1984, President Ronald Reagan signed EO 12472, broadening the NCS's national security and emergency preparedness (NS/EP) capabilities, superseding President Kennedy's original 1963 memorandum. The NCS expanded from its original six members to an interagency group of twenty-three federal departments and agencies, and began coordinating and planning NS/EP telecommunications to support domestic crises and disasters.

17. Michael A. Ordonez, Critical Infrastructure Protection: How to Assess and Provide Remedy to Vulnerabilities in Telecom Hotels, Naval Postgraduate School, Master's thesis, September 2006, p. 4.

18. The Reagan National Security Division Directive 26 (NSDD-26) spelled out the objectives of promoting deterrence, improving natural disaster preparedness, and reducing the possibility of coercion by enemy forces. The unclassified version of NSDD-26 states: "It is a matter of national priority that the United States have a Civil Defense program which provides for the survival of the US population." However, NSDD-26 went further than PD 41 by stipulating a concrete deadline in 1989 for plans to protect the population, and it mandated that civil defense leaders investigate and enhance protection measures for critical industries in case of attack. NSDD-26 for the first time supported research into the development of strategies to ensure economic survival in the event of a nuclear attack; DHS, Civil Defense and Homeland Security: A Short History of National Preparedness Efforts, September 2006, p. 20.

19. The White House, National Security Decision Directive 207 (NSDD-207), The National Program for Combatting Terrorism, January 20, 1986, originally top secret but since declassified.

20. The White House, National Security Strategy for a New Century, May 1997, pp. 12–14.

21. The White House, Presidential Decision Directive/NSC 63, Critical Infrastructure Protection, May 22, 1998.

22. The White House, Office of the Press Secretary, Strengthening Cyber Security through Public-Private Partnership, February 15, 2000.

23. Other communications companies contacted the federal government seeking help with security, a mission foisted off on the Pentagon, which said it was more suited for the Louisiana National Guard, which of course was stretched beyond limits, so the companies hired private security guards; Hurricane Katrina: A Nation Still Unprepared, pp. 296, 322.

24. The Federal Response to Hurricane Katrina: Lessons Learned, February 23, 2006, p. 34.

25. The Federal Response to Hurricane Katrina: Lessons Learned, February 23, 2006, p. 61.

26. The Federal Response to Hurricane Katrina: Lessons Learned, February 23, 2006, p. 5.

27. The Federal Response to Hurricane Katrina: Lessons Learned, February 23, 2006, p. 5.

28. Hurricane Katrina: A Nation Still Unprepared, p. 484.

29. "The National Geospatial-Intelligence Agency (NGA) started collecting key infrastructure-related information (i.e., on airports, hospitals, police stations, emergency operations centers, highways, schools, etc.) well in advance of landfall....As the storm was tracked, NGA pre-deployed analysts and mobile systems to the affected areas that provided expertise and information on the ground and facilitated the delivery of additional information from NGA offices elsewhere. Because they had assets in place and focused on the region, NGA provided the first comprehensive overview of the damage resulting from the hurricane and flood. NGA merged imagery with other information, creating hundreds of intelligence products per day that could be used and applied by response professionals to aid in decision-making. NGA assessments were multi-dimensional, timely, relevant, and continuous. They addressed many issues, including but not limited to: recovery planning and operations, transportation infrastructure, critical and catastrophic damage, dike stability and breaches, industry damage, and hazard spills. The NGA World Wide Navigational Warning Service also provided navigation information to the US Navy, Merchant Marine, and Coast Guard, and relayed messages from the National Weather Service to people at sea. NGA also aided in the location and recovery of oil platforms. The imagery activities of NGA were essential to the restoration of critical infrastructure"; The Federal Response to Hurricane Katrina: Lessons Learned, February 23, 2006, p. 131.

30. Defense Program Office for Mission Assurance, Dangerous Materials Katrina Impact Zone, September 2, 2005; obtained by the author.

31. The Federal Response to Hurricane Katrina: Lessons Learned, February 23, 2006, p. 61.

32. NRO, The National Reconnaissance Office at 50 Years: A Brief History, September 2011, p. 29.

33. Eagle Vision resources from the HQ USAF Combat Support Office (AFCSO), Ramstein Air Base, Germany; Nevada ANG; and South Carolina ANG provided federal, state, and municipal decision makers with 690,000 square kilometers of unclassified commercial space imagery; Air Force Support to Hurricane Katrina/Rita Relief Operations, August–September 2005, p. 11.

34. On August 30, ANG RC-26B from Ellington, Texas, flew the first support and reconnaissance missions. The Air Guard deployed seven RC-26B ISR aircraft and nine crews from eight states to assist in Hurricane

Katrina relief operations. During seventeen days of operations, they flew 297.9 hours in support.

35. On August 31, NORTHCOM tasked U-2 flights over Katrina JOA [joint operating area] for September 1, 2, and 6. The 27th Intelligence Support Squadron at Beale AFB, California, processed much of the U-2 imagery and uploaded hundreds of images daily. In the end, over 2,300 imagery and mapping products were produced. See Major Kevin L. Buddelmeyer, Military First Response: Lessons Learned from Hurricane Katrina, pp. 20–21.

36. The Civil Air Patrol (CAP) flew C-172, C-182, and GA-8 planes. CAP crews conducted aerial photography using the Airborne Real-time Cueing Hyperspectral Enhanced Reconnaissance (ARCHER) system. They linked ARCHER with a satellite-transmitted digital imaging system and transmitted photos via satellite; Air Force Support to Hurricane Katrina/Rita Relief Operations, August–September 2005, p. 11.

37. The OC-135 is equipped with a KS-87 framing camera used for low-altitude photography and a KA-91 pan camera to provide a wide sweep at high altitude. Like the U-2, the OC-135 uses wet optical film and may take up to three days to process, exploit, and digitize. However, unlike the Dragon Lady, processing for OC-135 IMINT was conducted at the National Air and Space Intelligence Center (NASIC) at Wright-Patterson AFB, Ohio; Lieutenant Colonel Christina M. Stone, Air Force Intelligence Role in Combating Weapons of Mass Destruction, Air War College, Maxwell Paper No. 39, November 2006, p. 20; Major Kevin L. Buddelmeyer, Military First Response: Lessons Learned from Hurricane Katrina, p. 22.

38. On September 3, one C-130 Scathe View of the Nevada National Guard deployed to Maxwell AFB, Alabama, from Reno, Nevada, and imaged on the same day.

39. DIA DC-3 overflights commenced on September 7, providing environment and infrastructure survey; Air Force Support to Hurricane Katrina/Rita Relief Operations, August–September 2005, pp. 26–27.

40. Air Forces Northern Command (AFNORTH) PowerPoint Briefing, "ISRD Support to DSCA," AFNORTH, Tyndall AFB, Florida, April 26, 2006, obtained by the author; Air Force Print News (Captain Ken Hall), "ROVERs aid in search and rescue," September 24, 2005. The jets included A-10s, F-14s, and F-16s.

41. This despite news reports that those spoilsports at the Federal Aviation Administration declined to issue the necessary permits for unmanned vehicles to overfly New Orleans—and despite government denials; see US Congress, House of Representatives, Hearing on Unmanned Aerial Vehicles and the National Airspace System, 109th Cong., 2nd sess., 2006,

p. 11; Air Force Support to Hurricane Katrina/Rita Relief Operations, August–September 2005, p. 12.

See also Testimony of Dyke D. Weatherington, Deputy, Unmanned Aircraft Systems Planning Task Force, Office of the Under Secretary of Defense (Acquisition, Technology and Logistics), before House Committee on Transportation and Infrastructure, Subcommittee on Aviation, March 29, 2006: "DOD UA [unmanned aerial] support for disaster relief in the wake of Hurricane Katrina was available, but not authorized. Instead small UA were attached to helicopter skids to provide some *limited* electronic collection capability" (emphasis added).

42. The drones included an experimental Evolution UAV, Puma AE (All Environment), Shadow 200, Silver Fox, and the T-Rex unmanned helicopter. "NORTHCOM is already collecting with Predator and Open Skies aircraft"; NORTHCOM NC J3 Teleconference Notes, 1000 MDT 01 Sep 2005 [September 1, 2005], obtained by the author.

Five Silver Fox UAVs were used for search and rescue operations; University of Minnesota PowerPoint briefing, Demoz Gebre-Egziabher, Department of Aerospace Engineering & Mechanics, University of Minnesota, Twin Cities, Minneapolis,"Miniature Aerial Vehicles for Traffic Management and Transportation Infrastructure Security," Presentation at "Heartland Security" Conference, Minneapolis, July 11, 2007. See also "USF Deploys Unmanned Aerial Vehicles to Katrina Rescue Operations," *Science Daily*, September 7, 2005; http://www.sciencedaily.com/releases/2005/09/050908081119.htm (accessed August 28, 2012); Major Kevin L. Buddelmeyer, Military First Response: Lessons Learned from Hurricane Katrina, pp. 23–24.

43. See statement of General Ronald E Keys, "Striking the Balance: Today's War, Tomorrow's Threat" (paper presented at the Air Force Association Air Warfare Symposium, Orlando, Florida, February 8, 2007); "Initial attempts to use the Evolution Tactical UAV and MQ-1 Predator were restricted due to a flight restriction on UAV access to Federal Aviation Administration (FAA) airspace. Yet, even with these imposed restrictions, the JTACs persisted and provided a 'work-around' by duct-taping the small Evolution UAV to the bottom of an UH-60 helicopter to provide streaming video to the ground"; Major Kevin L. Buddelmeyer, Military First Response: Lessons Learned from Hurricane Katrina, p. 23.

Within twenty-four hours of storm landfall, the Pentagon and NORTHCOM had direct feeds from full-motion video being passed via the Remotely Operated Video Enhanced Receiver (ROVER) systems from a variety of platforms; Major Kevin L. Buddelmeyer, Military First Response: Lessons Learned from Hurricane Katrina, pp. 23–24. See also *Air Force Print News* (Captain Ken Hall), "ROVERs aid in search and rescue," September 24, 2005.

44. NORTHCOM, (U//FOUO) United States: Hurricane Katrina Damage Assessments Derived from U-2 Imagery, n.d., obtained by the author.

45. HHT 170 LAKE PONTCHARTRAIN, LA I-10 CAUSEWAY DAMAGE; Tasking Requirement(s): 01; Date/Time of Report: 1116L 19-SEP-05 [September 19, 2005], obtained by the author.

46. Technical Image Analysis of Chalmette Petrol Storage Facility, New Orleans, LA 7-SEP-05 [September 7, 2005], obtained by the author.

47. The Federal Response to Hurricane Katrina: Lessons Learned, February 23, 2006, p. 131.

48. Master Sergeant Mark Haviland, Air Combat Command Public Affairs, "After Katrina: ACC's intel[ligence] team applies lessons learned," August 31, 2006.

49. The graphic appears in the photographs in the centerfold; see insert p. 3.

50. *Survival: How a Culture of Preparedness Can Save You and Your Family from Disasters*, p. 11.

51. Hurricane Katrina: A Nation Still Unprepared, p. 8; *Disaster: Hurricane Katrina and the Failure of Homeland Security*, pp. 123, 205.

52. *Disaster: Hurricane Katrina and the Failure of Homeland Security*, p. 123.

53. Minnesota senator Mark Dayton would later scold the homeland security watch-stander: "You know you don't need to send satellites over; turn on CNN." *Disaster: Hurricane Katrina and the Failure of Homeland Security*, pp. 198, 242.

54. Hurricane Katrina: A Nation Still Unprepared, p. 483.

55. Hurricane Katrina: A Nation Still Unprepared, p. 484.

56. *Disaster: Hurricane Katrina and the Failure of Homeland Security*, p. 207.

57. For details on the intelligence problems, see the excellent summary by Major Jennifer P. Sovada, "Intelligence, Surveillance, and Reconnaissance Support to Humanitarian Relief Operations within the United States: Where Everyone Is in Charge," Naval War College, Newport, RI, April 23, 2008. See also GAO, Hurricane Katrina: Better Plans and Exercises Needed to Guide the Military's Response to Catastrophic Natural Disasters, in *GAO-06-808T* (2006), p. 7; AFNORTH Air Support Handbook, January 1, 2009, pp. 96–97; Air Force Support to Hurricane Katrina/Rita Relief Operations, August–September 2005, p. 3. Referring to the U-2 imagery, one air force observer later wrote: "Unfortunately, much of this intelligence did not make its way to first responders in a timely manner." Major Kevin L. Buddelmeyer, Military First Response: Lessons Learned from Hurricane Katrina, p. 21. The vast majority of the imagery and information was fed directly to the NORTHCOM Joint Forces Air Component Commander (JFACC) for command situational awareness, not on-scene providers, Buddelmeyer says; Military First Response: Lessons Learned from Hurricane Katrina, p. 4.

58. A Failure of Initiative, p. 223.

59. *Survival: How a Culture of Preparedness Can Save You and Your Family from Disasters*, p. 166.

60. HQ USNORTHCOM FORCE PROTECTION (FP) ADVISORY MESSAGE 05-245, 020840ZSEP05 [September 2, 2005], obtained by the author; and HQ US NORTHCOM FP ADVISORY MESSAGE 05-243 HURRICANE KATRINA, 310754ZAUG05 [August 31, 2005], obtained by the author.

61. FBI/DHS Intelligence Bulletin 176, *Period of Uncertainty Merits Increased Awareness*, September 7, 2005, obtained by the author; NORTHCOM FP [Force Protection] Advisory Message 05-243, *September 11 Anniversary*, September 7, 2005, obtained by the author.

62. JFHQ-NCR J2 Daily Intelligence "Guardian," 080900 Sep 05 [September 8, 2005] (Secret/NOFORN); JFHQ-NCR, Force Protection Advisory, Increased Vigilance During the 9-11 Memorial Period, September 8, 2005.

CHAPTER FOUR: *POSSE COMITATUS*

1. *Decision Points*, p. 321. "All my instincts told me we needed to get federal troops into New Orleans to stop the violence and speed the recovery. But I was stuck with a resistant governor, a reluctant Pentagon, and an antiquated law. I wanted to overrule them all. But at the time, I worried that the consequence could be a constitutional crisis, and possibly a political insurrection as well."

2. The *Oxford English Dictionary* defines *Posse Comitatus* as the force of the county; the body of men above the age of fifteen in a county (exclusive of peers, clergymen, and infirm persons), whom the sheriff may summon or "raise" to repress a riot or for other purposes; also, a body of men actually so raised and commanded by the sheriff.

3. Combat Studies Institute (Matt Murphy), The Posse Comitatus Act and the United States Army: A Historical Perspective, Global War on Terrorism Occasional Paper 14, 2006, p. 5. See also the discussion by Commander James S. Campbell, "Current Obstacles to Fully Preparing Title 10 Forces for Homeland Defense and Civil Support," May 2008, pp. 70–71.

"Concerned about the repeated routine use of federal military to enforce civil laws in contravention of the Founding Fathers' concern for restrains on a standing army, Congress restricted the routine use of federal military troops in the PCA"; Lieutenant Colonel Mary J. Bradley, Lieutenant Colonel Stephanie Stephens, Mr. Michael Shaw (Joint Task Force Civil Support Fort Monroe, Virginia), "Notes from the Field: The Posse Comitatus Act: Does It Impact the Department of Defense during Consequence Management Operations?," *Army Lawyer*, DA PAM 27-50-413, October 2007, p. 70.

4. Barrye La Troye Price, "The Use of Federal Troops in Quelling Civil Unrest in Washington DC," April 1968, master's thesis, 1994, p. 5.

5. On December 1, 1865, the Union Army was demobilized. From a force of one million in arms on May 1, only some 152,000 Union soldiers remained in the South by the end of 1865. On October 1, 1866, more were demobilized, with only about 38,000 remaining in the South by the end of the year. In 1867, Congress additionally suspended the Southern states' right to organize their militias until those states were firmly under the control of acceptable post-Confederate governments.

6. Combat Studies Institute (Matt Murphy), The Posse Comitatus Act and the United States Army: A Historical Perspective, Global War on Terrorism Occasional Paper 14, 2006, p. 25.

7. Combat Studies Institute (Matt Murphy), The Posse Comitatus Act and the United States Army: A Historical Perspective, Global War on Terrorism Occasional Paper 14, 2006, p. 26.

8. Combat Studies Institute (Matt Murphy), The Posse Comitatus Act and the United States Army: A Historical Perspective, Global War on Terrorism Occasional Paper 14, 2006, p. 26.

9. Combat Studies Institute (Matt Murphy), The Posse Comitatus Act and the United States Army: A Historical Perspective, Global War on Terrorism Occasional Paper 14, 2006, p. 29.

10. Combat Studies Institute (Matt Murphy), The Posse Comitatus Act and the United States Army: A Historical Perspective, Global War on Terrorism Occasional Paper 14, 2006, p. 30.

11. Combat Studies Institute (Matt Murphy), The Posse Comitatus Act and the United States Army: A Historical Perspective, Global War on Terrorism Occasional Paper 14, 2006, pp. 30–31.

12. Lieutenant Colonel Mark C. Weston, Review of the Posse Comitatus Act After Hurricane Katrina, March 15, 2006, p. 3.

The *Posse Comitatus* Act, 18 USC, Section 1385, today states, "Whoever, except in the cases and under circumstances expressly authorized by the Constitution or Act of Congress, willfully uses any part of the Army or the Air Force as a *posse comitatus* or otherwise to execute the laws shall be fined not more than $10,000 or imprisoned not more than two years, or both." Although the *Posse Comitatus* Act, by its own terms, applies to only the army and the air force, the *Posse Comitatus* Act's restrictions have been extended to the navy and marine corps as a matter of DOD policy. Federal court rulings have stipulated that it only governs the federal military and the National Guard when serving in its federal capacity.

Concern over the domestic role also led the states to reexamine their need for a well-equipped and trained militia, and between 1881 and 1892, every state revised its military code to provide for an organized force.

Most called their state militias the National Guard, following an example set by the state of New York.

13. Combat Studies Institute (Matt Murphy), The Posse Comitatus Act and the United States Army: A Historical Perspective, Global War on Terrorism Occasional Paper 14, 2006, p. 33.

14. Combat Studies Institute (Matt Murphy), The Posse Comitatus Act and the United States Army: A Historical Perspective, Global War on Terrorism Occasional Paper 14, 2006, p. iii.

15. Donald J. Currier, "The Posse Comitatus Act: A Harmless Relic from the Post-Reconstruction Era or a Legal Impediment to Transformation?," Carlisle Papers in Security Strategy, September 2003, pp. 5–6.

16. Commander James S. Campbell, "Current Obstacles to Fully Preparing Title 10 Forces for Homeland Defense and Civil Support," May 2008, p. 71.

17. The Robert T. Stafford Disaster Relief and Emergency Assistance Act, 42 USC 5121-5206, Disaster Relief and Emergency Assistance Act of 1988 (Stafford Act), consolidated federal statutory authorities and continues to guide many of FEMA's and DHS's actions. The act gives the president the authority to direct federal capabilities from various federal agencies to provide assistance to states in the wake of an emergency or major disaster. The Stafford Act defines an emergency as "any occasion or instance for which, in the determination of the President, federal assistance is needed to supplement state and local efforts and capabilities to save lives and to protect property and public health and safety, or to lessen or avert the threat of a catastrophe in any part of the United States."

18. These statutory exceptions include the Protection of Nuclear Materials Act (18 USC 831), Chemical-Biological Terrorism (10 USC 382), and Secret Service Assistance (10 USC 3056):

- Under the Prohibited Transaction Involving Nuclear Materials statute (Section 831, Title 18, USC), if the attorney general and the secretary of defense jointly determine that the nation faces an emergency, the secretary of defense may authorize federal military forces to provide direct support to civilian authorities to protect nuclear materials.
- Under the Emergency Situations Involving Chemical or Biological Weapons of Mass Destruction statute, (Section 382, Title 10, USC), if the attorney general and the secretary of defense jointly determine that the nation faces an emergency involving an attack using chemical, biological, radiological, or high-yield explosives, the secretary of defense may provide resources and personnel to assist civil authorities to enforce this statute.

See NGB, Domestic JTF Commander Handbook, 2011, pp. 105–106.

19. Lieutenant Colonel Mark C. Weston, Review of the Posse Comitatus Act After Hurricane Katrina, March 15, 2006, p. 5.

20. NGB, Domestic JTF Commander Handbook, 2011, p. 105. The handbook states explicitly that the *Posse Comitatus* Act does not apply in these circumstances. See also Department of the Army, AR 500-1, Aircraft Piracy Emergencies, October 6, 1972, p. 1.

Pursuant to DOD Instruction (DODI) 5525.5 [DOD Directive (DODD) 5525.5, DOD Cooperation with Civilian Law Enforcement Officials, January 15, 1986], "the military may provide direct assistance to civilian law enforcement authorities if the actions are taken for the primary purpose of furthering a military or foreign affairs function of the United States, regardless of incidental benefits to civilian authorities."

NORTHCOM says: "the protection of DOD personnel, DOD equipment, classified military information or equipment, and official guests of the DOD, and such other actions that are undertaken primarily for a military or foreign affair's purpose are not prohibited"; NORTHCOM Operations Order (OPORD) 05-01, Antiterrorism, May 6, 2005, p. 6.

The Military Purpose Doctrine provides the authority for military personnel acting as undercover agents in off-post drug investigations where civilians are either the source of drugs being introduced to the post or are suspected of being involved in drug transactions with service members.

21. "Under imminently serious conditions, when time does not permit approval from higher headquarters, any local military commander, or responsible officials of DOD Components may, subject to any supplemental direction that may be provided by their higher headquarters, and in response to a request from civil authorities, provide immediate response to save lives, prevent human suffering, or mitigate great property damage." See DOD Directive 3025dd (predecisional draft), Defense Support of Civilian Authority, 2006, p. 9.

"The immediate response authority is not provided for in any statute, but is said to have deep historical roots. Although there is no statutory authority to do so, DODD 3025.15 and 3025.1 establish a CDR's 'immediate response' authority. Immediate response authority is very limited and should be invoked only for bona fide emergencies. When imminently serious conditions exist and time does not permit prior approval from higher headquarters, immediate response authority permits local military CDRs and responsible officials of other DOD components to act immediately 'to save lives, prevent human suffering, and mitigate great property damage' in imminently serious conditions when time does not permit approval from higher headquarters. Types of support authorized include rescue, evacuation, emergency treatment of casualties, and maintenance or restoration of emergency medical capabilities; emergency restoration of essential public services (including fire-fighting, water, communications, transportation, power, and fuel); emergency removal of debris and explosive ordnance; and recovery, identification, registration, and disposal of the dead; monitoring and decontaminating radiological, chemical, and biological effects; controlling contaminated areas; and reporting through national warning and hazard control systems; roadway movement control and planning; safeguarding, collecting, and distributing food, essential supplies, and materiel on the basis of critical priorities; damage assessment; interim emergency communications; and, facilitating the reestablishment of civil government functions. DOD support under immediate response authority is limited to the time that local or state authorities can resume control (generally 72 hours or less)." See NGB, *Domestic JTF Commander Handbook*, 2011, p. 103.

Joint Publication 3-28, Civil Support, sanctions immediate-response authority, though the policy "is limited, restrictive, and conditional"; Center for Army Lessons Learned, *Disaster Response Staff Officer's Handbook*, 2010.

Defense Department policy, Honoré writes, "allows commanders to help local communities save lives without having to wait for an order from the Pentagon"; *Survival: How a Culture of Preparedness Can Save You and Your Family from Disasters*, p. 89.

22. In cases such as a CBRNE incident, local law enforcement agencies may request immediate assistance from local military forces. DOD Directive 5535.05, *DOD Cooperation with Civilian Law Enforcement*, Section E4.1.2.3.1, states that the emergency authority authorizes federal action including the deployment of military forces to prevent loss of life or destruction and to restore public order only if local authorities are unable to do so. See The Department of Defense Chemical, Biological, Nuclear and High Yield Explosive Response Enterprise: Have We Learned the Lessons to Ensure an Effective Response?, p. 14.

23. DOD Directive 3025.12, Military Assistance for Civil Disturbances (MACDIS), Section 4.2.2 and 4.2.2.1, states that military forces shall not be used for MACDIS unless authorized by the president under emergency circumstances, and the acting commander must have exhausted all resources to obtain prior authorization from the president. These exceptions to *Posse Comitatus* allow local commanders to act on their own authority to provide assistance to local law enforcement during incident management. The Department of Defense Chemical, Biological, Nuclear and High Yield Explosive Response Enterprise: Have We Learned the Lessons to Ensure an Effective Response?, p. 14.

24. How the Army Runs, 2011–2012, p. 515.

    Posse Comitatus had become more of a "procedural formality than an actual impediment to the use of military forces in homeland defense"; Major Craig T. Trebilcock, USA, *The Myth of Posse Comitatus*, October 2000.

    "Bottom line, the President has the legal authority to quell insurrection with State request, without State request, and even over State opposition"; DOD, Reserve Components of the United States Military, December 2008, p. 34.

25. Major Mark M. Beckler, US Army National Guard, Insurrection Act Restored: States Likely to Maintain Authority Over National Guard in Domestic Emergencies, SAMS Monograph, 2008, p. 7.

26. The Insurrection Act (10 USC 331-335 and 12301, et seq., as amended). See Major Mark M. Beckler, US Army National Guard, Insurrection Act Restored: States Likely to Maintain Authority Over National Guard in Domestic Emergencies, SAMS Monograph, 2008; Lieutenant Colonel Mary J. Bradley, Lieutenant Colonel Stephanie Stephens, Mr. Michael Shaw (Joint Task Force Civil Support Fort Monroe, Virginia), "Notes from the Field: The Posse Comitatus Act: Does It Impact the Department of Defense during Consequence Management Operations?" *Army Lawyer*, DA PAM 27-50-413, October 2007, p. 71.

27. Paul J. Scheips, The Role of Federal Military Forces in Domestic Disorders 1945–1992, Army Historical Series, p. 143.

28. After issuing a cease and desist order, the president issues an executive order that directs the attorney general and the secretary of defense to take appropriate steps to disperse insurgents and restore law and order. The attorney general is then responsible for coordinating the federal response to domestic civil disturbances. "The restrictions of the Posse Comitatus Act no longer apply to federal troops executing the orders of the President to quell the disturbance in accordance with Rules of the Use of Force (RUF) approved by the DOD General Counsel and the Attorney General." See How the Army Runs, p. 515.

    Section 335 simply recognizes the territories of Guam and the Virgin Islands as states for the purposes of the Insurrection Act.

29. See discussion also of the president's responsibility in Major Mark M. Beckler, US Army National Guard, Insurrection Act Restored: States Likely to Maintain Authority Over National Guard in Domestic Emergencies, SAMS Monograph, 2008, pp. 19–20.

30. DHS IG, A Performance Review of FEMA's Disaster Management Activities in Response to Hurricane Katrina, p. 4; A Failure of Initiative: The Final Report of the Select Bipartisan Committee to Investigate the Preparation for and Response to Hurricane Katrina, February 2006, p. 7. Honoré writes that more than 1,800 people died, about 1,600 of them in

Louisiana; *Survival: How a Culture of Preparedness Can Save You and Your Family from Disasters*, p. 3; The Federal Response to Hurricane Katrina: Lessons Learned, February 23, 2006, p. 8.

The actual death toll for Louisianans was closer to 1,375 when those who died out of state were added. Michelle Hunter, "Deaths of evacuees push toll to 1,577," *Times-Picayune*, May 19, 2006, p. 1, reported that the Louisiana Department of Health and Hospitals added 281 victims to earlier counts on May 18, 2006, after officials concluded from a review of evacuees' out-of-state death certificates that many were Katrina-related, such as from stress or loss of access to essential medications. See also Hurricane Katrina: A Nation Still Unprepared, p. 38; *Survival: How a Culture of Preparedness Can Save You and Your Family from Disasters*, p. 120.

31. Tony S. Lombardo, Collaboration or Control?: The Struggle for Power in Catastrophic Disaster Response, December 2007, pp. 29–30.

32. The Federal Response to Hurricane Katrina: Lessons Learned, February 23, 2006, p. 8.

33. Hurricane Katrina: The Defense Department's Role in the Response, S. Hrg. 109-813, p. 18.

34. McHale also said after Katrina that he was grateful that the Insurrection Act wasn't invoked. Hurricane Katrina: The Defense Department's Role in the Response, S. Hrg. 109-813, p. 15.

35. National Guard forces reached peak deployment numbers for Katrina relief on September 8. With 51,039 guard personnel mobilized on that day, the guard exceeded by three times its previous largest deployment ever for a natural disaster (16,599 in 1989–1990 following the San Francisco Loma Prieta earthquake).

36. Hurricane Katrina: A Nation Still Unprepared, p. 333.

37. Hurricane Katrina: A Nation Still Unprepared, p. 333; The Federal Response to Hurricane Katrina: Lessons Learned, February 23, 2006, p. 38.

38. "Meanwhile, having been stationed in the Gulf of Mexico at the conclusion of a previously scheduled exercise held prior to Katrina, the USS Bataan followed Katrina, and by Tuesday morning was within 150 to 200 miles of New Orleans. Watching the news, the vessel's commanders began identifying ways to help. At 3 p.m. CT, the Bataan received orders from Second Fleet to send helicopters into New Orleans to conduct search and rescue missions in coordination with Coast Guard District Eight. The Navy and Marine Corps helicopters were in the air by 5 p.m., and reported to the Coast Guard Air Station commander, that, as the designated On-Scene Commander, he held responsibility for coordinating all air search-and-rescue assets. They were joined by two Navy SH-3 helicopters from Pensacola that arrived unannounced at the Coast Guard station, offering their services. In all, USS Bataan's aircraft rescued, evacuated, or transported over 2,000 persons"; Hurricane Katrina: A Nation Still Unprepared, p. 343, 489.

39. Hurricane Katrina: The Defense Department's Role in the Response, S. Hrg. 109-813, p. 37.

40. *Disaster: Hurricane Katrina and the Failure of Homeland Security*, p. 122.

41. Hurricane Katrina: A Nation Still Unprepared, p. 439–441; *Katrina's Secrets: Storms after the Storms*, pp. 7, 136. NOPD had a force of 1,668 sworn officers. By the time the storm had passed, only about 147 failed to report for duty.

42. Hurricane Katrina: A Nation Still Unprepared, p. 439. National Guard officials said there were only 50 weapons found among the 30,000 people searched as they entered; A Failure of Initiative, p. 248.

43. *Survival: How a Culture of Preparedness Can Save You and Your Family from Disasters*, p. 120.

44. *Disaster: Hurricane Katrina and the Failure of Homeland Security*, p. 223. See also *Survival: How a Culture of Preparedness Can Save You and Your Family from Disasters*, p. 120.

45. Michael Greenberger and Arianne Spaccarelli, "The Posse Comitatus Act and Disaster Response," in *From Homeland Security and Emergency Management: A Legal Guide for State and Local Governments* (Ernest B. Abbott and Otto J. Hetzel, eds., American Bar Association, 2d ed. 2010), pp. 46–47.

46. The narrative of the killing is based upon Alabama Department of Public Safety news releases and AP reporting (as compiled by al.com, the Alabama Media Group of newspapers), as well as Corky Siemaszko, "Michael McLendon, gunman who killed 10, self, in Samson, Alabama shooting spree, had revenge list," *New York Daily News*, March 11, 2009.

47. NGB, Domestic JTF Commander Handbook, 2011, p. 105.

48. *Decision Points*, p. 320.

49. "During the eleven-year period between 1885 and 1895 military forces were mobilized 328 times for riot duty; 118 involved labor conflicts....During the twentieth century the Army's role in quelling civil disturbances was both more frequent and more diverse. The Regular Army suppressed civil unrest at the Nevada gold mines in 1907; at the Colorado coal mines in 1913 and 1914; at the Winston-Salem, North Carolina, riots in 1918; at the Washington, DC, riots in 1919; at the Omaha, Nebraska, riots in 1919; at the West Virginia mines in 1921; and thwarted the activities of Army veterans during the Bonus March in Washington, in 1932." See Barrye La Troye Price, "The Use of Federal Troops in Quelling Civil Unrest in Washington DC," April 1968, master's thesis, 1994, p. 10.

Though law enforcement was not the primary purpose, federal troops have also been used during Hurricane Andrew and Typhoon Iniki in 1992, during Hurricane Marilyn in 1995, and during Hurricane Floyd in 1999, and to fight forest fires in the western states starting in 2000; Rand, Army Forces for Homeland Security, 2004, pp. 4–5.

50. See, for example, the extensive discussion in Tony S. Lombardo, Collaboration or Control?: The Struggle for Power in Catastrophic Disaster Response, December 2007.

51. Donald J. Currier, The Posse Comitatus Act: A Harmless Relic from the Post-Reconstruction Era or a Legal Impediment to Transformation?, 2003, pp. 8–10.

52. Covault's decision also removed 10,000 California National Guard troops, now federalized, from assisting the Los Angeles police and sheriff, ultimately prolonging the criminal violence in the city. The guard could have been placed back in state active duty status, but it would have required a different command relationship with the federal troops.

   The story of the 1992 riots is ably told in Combat Studies Institute (Matt Murphy), The Posse Comitatus Act and the United States Army: A Historical Perspective, Global War on Terrorism Occasional Paper 14, 2006, pp. 47–59. See also Donald J. Currier, The Posse Comitatus Act: A Harmless Relic from the Post-Reconstruction Era or a Legal Impediment to Transformation?, September 2003.

53. AP, Army launches review into use of soldiers at Samson following south Alabama shootings, Wednesday, March 18, 2009, 10:13 a.m.; Lance Griffin, "Army report: Fort Rucker MPs in Samson after shooting a violation," Dothan Eagle, October 19, 2009; AP, Army says dispatch of MPs to Samson murders in March violated federal law, Monday, October 19, 2009, 6:02 p.m.

54. Mark Ames, "After the Billionaires Plundered Alabama Town, Troops Were Called In…Illegally," Alternet, October 23, 2009; http://www.alternet.org/story/143485/after_the_billionaires_plundered_alabama_town,_troops_were_called_in_…_illegally.

55. "US Army Soldiers Deployed on the Streets of Samson, Alabama," March 12, 2009; CNS.com story at http://cryptogon.com/?p=7433.

56. "THIS IS A DRILL! THIS IS A DRILL! Samson Alabama, 10 March 2009;" http://jaghunters.blogspot.com/search?q=Sampson.

57. Jim Kouri, "Obama stealth executive order creating firestorm," Examiner.com, January 20, 2010; http://www.examiner.com/article/obama-stealth-executive-order-creating-firestorm. See also Kouri's biography at Renew America; http://www.renewamerica.com/columns/kouri (accessed August 9, 2012).

58. Lance Griffin, "Samson police chief: Town supports Rucker MPs," Dothan Eagle, October 20, 2009.

59. Known and Unknown: A Memoir, p. 619.

CHAPTER FIVE: THE GARDEN PLOT

1. Army Strategic Studies Institute, Nathan Freier, *Known Unknowns: Unconventional "Strategic Shocks" in Defense Strategy Development*, November 2008, p. 32.

2. *Survival: How a Culture of Preparedness Can Save You and Your Family from Disasters*, p. 89. See also Hurricane Katrina: A Nation Still Unprepared, p. 491.

3. Department of the Army Historical Summary: FYs 1990 & 1991, p. 17; Army Forces Command Domestic Plans Branch, DOD Emergency Preparedness Course, Domestic Emergencies Handbook, Second Edition, March 15, 1999, p. 48; NORTHCOM, Civil Support Concept of Employment, August 20, 2004, pp. 4–77; Jay Price, "Stretched Thin, 82nd Airborne Giving Up Rapid-Reaction Unit; Division will no longer maintain brigade that can move on short notice," *Raleigh News and Observer*, March 22, 2007, p. 1.

4. "The Commander of the Joint Civil Disturbance Task Force is the Commander for all federal forces, including National Guard forces in Title 10 status, in a civil disturbance area of operations. He is the DOD representative in the civil disturbance area and performs civil disturbance missions assigned by the SCRAG. Civilian officials remain in charge of civil disturbance operations"; Army, *Domestic Operational Law Handbook, 2011 Handbook for Judge Advocates*, pp. 75–76. The SCRAG is the senior civilian representative of the attorney general.

5. USCINCACOM FUNCPLAN 2502-97 (U), Garden Plot, Final Draft, 1998, p. v, obtained by the author.

6. USPACOM also provides an Alaska-based QRF/RRF for employment by USNORTHCOM for HD operations in the Alaska joint operating area (JOA); JCS, Homeland Defense, Joint Publication 36.1 First Draft, October 28, 2005, p. III-5.

7. USCINCACOM FUNCPLAN 2502-97 (U), Garden Plot, Final Draft, 1998, pp. vi, vii.

8. Mobilized Marine Corps Reserve infantry battalions have also served as ready reaction forces, "on call" to support FEMA (including supporting Joint Task Force Katrina); NGB, National Guard and Reserve Equipment Report for Fiscal Year 2007 (NGRER FY 2007), February 2006, pp. 3–7.

9. After 9/11 JFCOM "sourced" five battalions to support a light infantry Rapid Reaction Force (RRF), by FEMA region: the XVIII Airborne Corps was responsible for Regions I, II, IV, and V; the III Corps was responsible for Regions VI, VII, and VIII; Marine Corps Forces Atlantic (MARFORLANT) was responsible for Region III and IX; and PACOM (through I Corps) was responsible for Region X; JFCOM PowerPoint Briefing, Joint Force Headquarters Homeland Security Command Brief, n.d. (July 13, 2002); obtained by the author.

"These forces are designed to provide responsive, mission-tailored, lightly armed ground units that can deploy on short notice, with minimal lift assets, and capable of providing immediate or emergency response for DSCA missions consistent with the law and DOD policy"; USNORTH-COM CONPLAN 2501-05, Defense Support of Civil Authorities, May 8, 2006, pp. C-24-2, C-24-3; obtained by the author. See also Major Jay L. Lunkins, How Airlift Meets U.S. NORTHERN Command's Requirements, AFIT, June 2003, pp. 39–40.

10. USCINCACOM FUNCPLAN 2502-97 (U), Garden Plot, Final Draft, 1998, p. vii, obtained by the author. In 2009, a Fort Hood regulation on the III Corps assignment for domestic duties stated:

III Corps provides forces to respond to civil disturbances according to the DOD Civil Disturbance Plan (Garden Plot). The force package is a quick-reaction force (QRF) composed of a brigade head-quarters, a minimum of two battalions, and a support element with an alert response time of 24 hours by air or convoy.

b. Requirements.
(1) The following training is required for individuals assigned to or alerted for civil disturbance response:
(a) Qualification with individual weapon in the last 12 months.
(b) CBRN [chemical, biological, radiological and nuclear] mask confidence exercise/training in the last 12 months.
(2) The following training is recommended:
(a) Classes in the use of force, application of minimum force, riot control agents and munitions, search and seizure policies and procedures, and apprehension and detention procedures.
(b) The legal considerations for civil disturbance response.
(c) Units authorized to train with CS [tear gas] or large amounts of OC/spray are required to have approval of the senior commander (through coordination with III Corps G-3) prior to conducting training exercises.

See III Corps, Training and Leader Development, III Corps and Fort Hood Regulation 350-1, March 30, 2009, p. 79.

11. Message, Subject: FRAGO 3 TO JTF-KATRINA EXORD, 050458ZSEP05 [September 5, 2005], obtained by the author.

12. Quoted in Major Daniel J. Sennott, "Interpreting Recent Changes to the Standing Rules for the Use of Force," *Army Lawyer*, November 2007, p. 73.

13. NORTHCOM Special Instructions (SPINS), September 3, 2005, paragraph D, point 4, point 5, obtained by the author.

14. Message, Subject: FRAGO 3 TO JTF-KATRINA EXORD, 050458ZSEP05 [September 5, 2005], obtained by the author.

15. DOD Directive 3025.1, Responsibilities for Employment of Military Resources in Domestic Emergencies Other than Civil Defense, July 14, 1956 (and retained in changes through April 23, 1963), assigned "primary responsibility" in CONUS to the Department of the Army, while the JCS were excluded (except for specified overseas areas). This role was codified in the highest war plan, the Joint Strategic Capabilities Plan (JSCP), and with respect to civil disturbances, the JCS, by formal directive, SM-685-63, named the chief of staff of the army (CSA) executive agent for the Joint Chiefs of Staff and gave him wide prerogatives for autonomous action. See Office of the Director of Defense Research and Engineering, Weapons Systems Evaluation Group, Joint Staff Command and Control Problems Attending Support Operations in Domestic Emergencies: Steep Hill-14 and Tempest Rapid "Betsy," 1965, June 8, 1966, partially declassified and released under the FOIA.

16. Army Chief of Military History, Walter G. Hermes, Global Pressures and the Flexible Response, in American Military History, Army Historical Series, 1989, p. 604.

17. Paul J. Scheips, The Role of Federal Military Forces in Domestic Disorders 1945–1992, Army Historical Series, p. 143.

18. Although the Los Angeles "Watts" riots of 1965 were a pivotal point for the army as a whole, only California National Guard troops were utilized in quelling the unrest; federal troops only provided a supporting role. See Barrye La Troye Price, "The Use of Federal Troops in Quelling Civil Unrest in Washington DC," April 1968, master's thesis, 1994, p. 11.

19. Barrye La Troye Price, "The Use of Federal Troops in Quelling Civil Unrest in Washington DC," April 1968, master's thesis, 1994, p. 32.

20. The most thorough military study of Detroit is Paul J. Scheips, The Role of Federal Military Forces in Domestic Disorders 1945–1992, Army Historical Series, pp. 177–205.

21. Barrye La Troye Price, "The Use of Federal Troops in Quelling Civil Unrest in Washington DC," April 1968, master's thesis," 1994, pp. 30–31.

22. Barrye La Troye Price, "The Use of Federal Troops in Quelling Civil Unrest in Washington DC," April 1968, master's thesis, 1994, p. 37.

23. Quoted in Paul J. Scheips, The Role of Federal Military Forces in Domestic Disorders 1945–1992, Army Historical Series, p. 185.

24. David S. McLellan, Cyrus Vance (Totowa, NJ: Rowman & Allanheld, 1985), pp. 8–9.

25. Paul J. Scheips, The Role of Federal Military Forces in Domestic Disorders 1945–1992, Army Historical Series, p. 198.

26. Paul J. Scheips, The Role of Federal Military Forces in Domestic Disorders 1945–1992, Army Historical Series, p. 202.

27. For the Washington, DC, riots following the assassination of Martin Luther King, Jr., the executive agent again was Cyrus Vance, private citizen, with as his subordinates the district's director of public safety, Patrick Murphy; Under Secretary of the Army David McGiffert; and Deputy United States Attorney General Warren Christopher. Army General Ralph Haines, Jr., the army vice chief of staff, was directly involved; Barrye La Troye Price, "The Use of Federal Troops in Quelling Civil Unrest in Washington DC," April 1968, master's thesis, 1994, pp. 61–64, 79.

28. Barrye La Troye Price, "The Use of Federal Troops in Quelling Civil Unrest in Washington DC," April 1968, master's thesis, 1994, p. 15.

29. The National Defense Authorization Act of 1989 also gave the Department of Defense responsibility for certain aspects of drug enforcement, including detection and monitoring and command, control, communications, and intelligence (C3I).

30. Major Craig T. Trebilcock, USAR, "The Myth of Posse Comitatus," *Journal of Homeland Defense*, October 27, 2000.

   It is interesting to note that in his autobiography, Weinberger does not address domestic use of the military at all; Caspar Weinberger, *Fighting for Peace: Seven Critical Years in the Pentagon* (New York: Warner Books).

31. Paul McHale, "Critical Mismatch: The Dangerous Gap Between Rhetoric and Readiness in DOD's Civil Support Missions," Heritage Foundation SR-115, August 13, 2012.

32. The army always favored a joint command under, of course, an army general to command those standing military forces not assigned overseas and not a part of the strategic nuclear forces. The navy loudly opposed such a command in the early 1960s, vowing that its fleets wouldn't be further subordinated or constrained. A compromise joint Strike Command (STRICOM) was created in 1962, responsible for army and air force training and doctrine, and for planning overseas contingency operations, including, at least on paper, mustering the forces for reinforcement, even if initially it was without naval forces. Part of STRICOM's mission was also allocating forces for domestic duty, brokering what was available, because as a joint command it was the best equipped to take into consideration war plans, ongoing missions, and upcoming combat deployments. But the other army—led by DOMS—never relinquished true control.

   In 1972, STRICOM was axed as a supposed belt-tightening measure by a supposedly war-weary Nixon administration. The real reason was that the JCS and other regional commands feared that STRICOM would become too powerful and turn into an overall global command—one command, one military—especially since it had responsibility not just for rapid deployment but also for the unassigned areas of the world (then including the Middle East, Africa, and South Asia, referred to as MEAFSA). STRICOM was replaced by Readiness Command (RED-

COM), with STRICOM divested of rest-of-the-world (ROW) responsibility. REDCOM lasted less than a decade, the domestic mission being directly assigned to Army Forces Command (FORSCOM), which was designated a JCS "specified command" under FORSCOM and was supplanted by another joint command, US Atlantic Command (ACOM), which was itself supplanted by Joint Forces Command (JFCOM), which gave up its domestic mission to the new homeland defense Northern Command in 2002 (and then was eliminated). See Department of the Army Historical Summary: FY 1987, pp. 73–74; DOD, Review of Unified and Specified Command Headquarters, February 1988, Appendix J, p. 8; JCS Joint History Office, The History of the Unified Command Plan: 1946–1993, pp. 4, 33–34.

33. NORTHCOM PowerPoint Briefing, MACDIS Strategic Mission Analysis, Major Dotson, NC-J531 Civil Support Planner, n.d. (September 14, 2004); obtained by the author.

34. Department of the Army, AR 500-60, Disaster Relief, August 1981.

35. Department of the Army, AR 500-4, Military Assistance to Safety and Traffic, January 1982.

36. Department of the Army, AR 500-70, Military Support of Civil Defense, October 1982.

37. DOD Directive (DODD) 5525.5, Department of Defense Cooperation with Civilian Law Enforcement Officials, January 15, 1986; Secretary of the Navy Instruction (SECNAVINST) 5820.7B, Cooperation with Civilian Law Enforcement Officials, March 28, 1988.

38. Chief of Naval Operations, OPNAVINST 3440.16B, Department of the Navy Civil Emergency Assistance Program, September 4, 1991.

39. Department of the Air Force, AFR 355-1, Disaster Preparedness Planning and Operation, December 1989; Department of the Air Force, AFI 10-803, Air Force Support During Disasters, January 1994.

40. Chief of Naval Operations, OPNAVINST 3440.16C, Navy Civil Emergency Management Program, March 10, 1995.

41. Marine Corps Warfighting Publication (MCWP) 3-33.4, Domestic Support Operations, July 1993.

42. DOD Directive (DODD) 3020.36, Assignment of National Security Emergency Preparedness (NSEP), Responsibilities to Department of Defense Components, November 2, 1988.

43. DOD Directive (DODD) 3025.1, Military Support to Civil Authorities (MSCA), January 15, 1993; National Guard Regulation 500-1, Military Support to Civil Authorities, October 1991.

44. DOD Directive (DODD) 3025.15, Military Assistance to Civil Authorities, February 18, 1997.

45. Chairman of the Joint Chiefs of Staff, CJCSI 3125.01, Military Assistance to Domestic Consequence Management Operations in Response to a

Chemical, Biological, Radiological, Nuclear, or High-Yield Explosive Situation, August 3, 2001.

46. Marine Corps Doctrinal Publication (MCDP) 1-0 10-7, Military Support to Civilian Operations, September 2001.

47. Department of the Army, AR 500-50, Civil Disturbances, April 1972; Marine Corps Warfighting Publication (MCWP) 3-33.2, Civil Disturbances, November 1985.

48. DOD Directive (DODD) 3025.12, Employment of Military Resources in the Event of Civil Disturbances (MACDIS), February 4, 1994.

49. Department of the Army, FM 19-15, Civil Disturbances, November 1985.

50. DOD Directive (DODD) 3025.15, Military Assistance to Civil Authorities (MACA), February 18, 1997, defines Military Assistance to Civil Authorities as: "Those DOD activities and measures covered under MSCA (natural and manmade disasters) *plus* DOD assistance for civil disturbances, counter drug, *sensitive support*, counterterrorism, and law enforcement" (emphasis added).

51. Shortly after 9/11, Secretary of Defense Rumsfeld reiterated DOD homeland security arrangements: the US Joint Forces Command (JFCOM) was responsible for the land and maritime defense of the continental United States; the secretary of the army was appointed the DOD Executive Agent for Homeland Security, including homeland security and military support to civilian authority; and the North American Aerospace Defense Command (NORAD) was responsible for defense against aerospace weapons.

The prevailing Unified Command Plan (UCP) on 9/11, the presidentially approved document that establishes the missions, responsibilities, and force structure for commanders of the unified combatant commands, tasked JFCOM with providing military assistance to civil authorities in the event of a terrorist incident within the United States. JFCOM was also required to provide military support to civil authorities (MSCA) and military assistance for civil disturbances (MACDIS), subject to SECDEF approval. See Joint Staff, Extracts from Unified Command Plan, ed. Gerry Dillon (Naval War College: September 1999), p. 12.

52. Quoted in Antulio J. Echevarria II, The Army and Homeland Security: A Strategic Prospective, Army War College Strategic Studies Institute, 2001, p. 7.

53. The term "homeland defense" was reportedly first used in the 1997 Report of the National Defense Panel, and thereafter was loosely seen as a subset of the term "homeland security"; see Lieutenant Colonel Gus Sankey, The Role of the Army National Guard in Homeland Defense, USAWC Fellowship Research Paper, April 9, 2002, p. 3.

54. "Homeland Defense operations are conducted in the air, land, maritime, and space domains and in the information environment. DOD is the pri-

mary federal agency for Homeland Defense, supported by other agencies. On order of the President or Secretary of Defense, National Guard units may be called to defend the Homeland against external threats. Certain National Guard units have been assigned roles in support of Homeland Defense missions, including the Air Defense of the Homeland and the Anti-Missile Defense of the Homeland. The general focus of National Guard Homeland Defense missions is on deterring and detecting external threats to the Homeland"; NGR 500-1/ANGI 10-8101, June 13, 2008, National Guard Domestic Operations, p. 5.

55. The DOD Strategy issued in 2005 made clear that unless otherwise directed by the secretary of defense, homeland defense missions and ongoing traditional military activities take priority over civil support. See DOD, *Strategy for Homeland Defense and Civil Support*, 2005.

56. The last formal Garden Plot plan was: Headquarters, Department of the Army, Department of Defense Civil Disturbance Plan, February 15, 1991. There was also a 2001 plan prepared by US Joint Forces Command, the force provider prior to the existence of NORTHCOM; USCINCJFCOM FUNCPLAN 2502-98 Civil Disturbance Plan (FOUO), June 25, 2001, obtained by the author. The 1991 plan replaced Department of the Army Civil Disturbance Plan, March 1, 1984, making it a Department of Defense plan and not just a Department of the Army plan. The 1984 plan was preceded by OPLAN 55-2, "Garden Plot," 1968, which was employed during the riots of 1967–1971.

The 2002 Unified Command Plan signed by President Bush moved the responsibility for general civil support planning from the army to the regional combatant commands, but there was no regional command for the United States at the time. Responsibility thus fell to JFCOM as the force provider, but for the continental US only; Pacific Command (PACOM) was designated the civil support planning authority for Alaska and Hawaii. See NGB, Domestic JTF Commander Handbook, 2011, p. 121.

57. DOD Directive 3025.15, Military Assistance to Civil Authorities (MACA), February 18, 1997; DOD Directive 3025.12, Military Assistance for Civil Disturbances (MACDIS), February 4, 1994; DOD Directive 3025.1, Military Support to Civil Authorities (MSCA), January 15, 1993.

58. Deputy Secretary of Defense Memorandum, Implementation Guidance Regarding the Office of the Assistant Secretary of Defense for Homeland Defense, March 25, 2003, obtained by the author; JCS Message, Subject: Transfer of the Army Director of Military Support to the Joint Staff, 141916Z May 03 [May 14, 2003], obtained by the author.

59. NORTHCOM PowerPoint Briefing, USNORTHCOM J53 MACDIS Planners' Workshop, Legal Perspective, Lieutenant Colonel Oliver Johnson, USNORTHCOM JA, September 14, 2004, obtained by the author; NORTHCOM PowerPoint Briefing, MACDIS Strategic Mission

Analysis, Major Dotson, NC-J531 Civil Support Planner, n.d. (September 14, 2004); obtained by the author.

60. The workshop is described in: NORTHCOM PowerPoint Briefing, DOD Civilian Disturbance Plan and Policy Review, Mr. Vernon Lindgren USNORTHCOM J531, September 14, 2004, obtained by the author; NORTHCOM PowerPoint Briefing, USNORTHCOM MACDIS Planners' Workshop, Draft MACDIS PLANORD Review, Mr. Vernon Lindgren, NC-J531, September 15, 2004, obtained by the author; NORTHCOM PowerPoint Briefing, USNORTHCOM MACDIS Planners' Workshop, J5 Closing Remarks, Colonel Guy Dahlbeck, USAF, NCJ5, September 15, 2004, obtained by the author; NORTHCOM PowerPoint Briefing, USNORTHCOM MACDIS Workshop, Overall Issues & Take-aways, Mr. Vernon Lindgren, NC-J531, September 15, 2004, obtained by the author.

NORTHCOM CONPLAN 2501, Defense Support of Civil Authorities (DSCA), 2006, stated under Para 1(d), Enemy: "Enemy forces are not expected during the conduct of DSCA operations. If a situation with enemy forces should arise, it would trigger CONPLAN 2002, Homeland Defense, or other plans in the USNORTHCOM family of plans"; US Northern Command (NORTHCOM), CONPLAN 2501-05, Defense Support of Civil Authorities (DSCA), April 2006, p. 14, obtained by the author.

61. NORTHCOM J5 Message, Military Assistance for Civil Disturbances (MACDIS) Planning Order (PLANORD), November 4, 2004, obtained by the author.

62. The SRUF supersede Chairman of the Joint Chiefs of Staff Instruction (CJCSI) 3121.02, Rules for the Use of Force (RUF) for DOD Personnel Providing Support to Law Enforcement Agencies Conducting Counterdrug Operations in the United States, RUF in Enclosure 2 to DOD Directive (DODD) 5210.56, Use of Deadly Force by DOD and Contract Law Enforcement Personnel on DOD Installations, and the rules for the use of force in the DOD Civil Disturbance Plan (Garden Plot).

63. USNORTHCOM Concept Plan (CONPLAN) 3502, Civil Disturbance Operations, replaced Garden Plot and CONPLAN 2502.

64. CJCSI 3121.01B, Standing Rules of Engagement/Standing Rules for the Use of Force for US Forces, June 13, 2005.

"The SRUF (Enclosures L through Q) establish fundamental policies and procedures governing the actions to be taken by US commanders and their forces during all DOD civil support (e.g., military assistance to civil authorities) and routine Military Department functions (including AT/FP duties) occurring within US territory or US territorial seas. SRUF also apply to land homeland defense missions occurring within US territory and to DOD forces, civilians and contractors performing law enforcement and security duties at all DOD installations (and off installation while conducting official DOD security functions), within or outside US territory, unless otherwise directed by the SecDef."

See also Joint Publication 3-26.1, Homeland Defense, First Draft, October 28, 2005, p. I-25.

65. CJCSI 3121.01B, Standing Rules of Engagement/Standing Rules for the Use of Force for US Forces, June 13, 2005, p. 3.

66. "These include the concept of use of 'minimum force,' the general prohibition on the use of warning shots by land forces, the use of warnings to include verbal warnings, and the introduction of restrictions that go beyond that required by the SRUF that may have the inadvertent effect of depriving a Soldier of otherwise valid defenses available to federal officers acting in their official capacities. Such restrictions could come from the imposition of additional preconditions to the use of force beyond that of 'reasonable belief,' imposing a duty to retreat by inappropriately relying on state law as it relates to the use of force by private citizens, or by attempting to further restrict the right of self-defense." See Domestic Operational Law Handbook 2011, p. 190.

"In RUF, the authority to use deadly force exists for limited purposes. Most RUF plans and policy reflect or incorporate the policy set forth in DOD Directive 5210.56. DOD Directive 5210.56 authorizes the use of deadly force only after a service member has determined: lesser means have been exhausted, are unavailable, or cannot be reasonably employed; the risk to innocent persons is not significantly increased by its use; and one or more of the following seven purposes apply. The draft Standing Rules for Use of Force will, when effective, assist in unifying the guidance on domestic use of force. It will also provide a consistent training template to avoid the ad hoc approach currently seen in domestic operations RUF practice." See Center for Law and Military Operations, Domestic Operational Law (DOPLAW) Handbook for Judge Advocates, vol. I, 2005, p. 236.

67. "Do not confuse the two" — ROEs and rules for the use of force — a manual intended for tactical commanders warned. DSCA Handbook Tactical Level Commander and Staff Toolkit, p. B-1.

A draft army doctrine later referred to the SRUF mistakenly as applying "in domestic, noncombat situations"; only later was this corrected to recognize that they applied to "federal military forces performing a homeland defense mission," which could include combat. See Department of the Army, FM 3-28 (Signature Draft—Not for Implementation), Civil Support Operations (Draft), June 4, 2010, p. 1-15; and Department of the Army, FM 3-28, Civil Support Operations, August 20, 2010, p. 3-24.

There were also warnings that separate rules for the use of force existed in each of the 54 National Guards of the states and territories, at least under state active duty and not federal mobilization. "SRUF also apply to land homeland defense missions occurring within US territory and to DOD forces, civilians, and contractors performing law enforcement and security duties at all DOD installations (and off-installation while conducting official DOD security functions), within or outside US territory, unless otherwise directed by the SecDef"; See CJCSI 3121.01B, Standing Rules of Engagement/Standing Rules for the Use of Force for US Forces, June 13, 2005, para. 3b.

68. DSCA Handbook Tactical Level Commander and Staff Toolkit, p. B-1. The Fourth Amendment states, "The right of the people to be secure in their persons, houses, papers, and effects, against unreasonable searches and seizures, shall not be violated, and no Warrants shall issue, but upon probable cause, supported by Oath or affirmation, and particularly describing the place to be searched, and the persons or things to be seized."

69. Diana L. Johnson, Major, USAF, Capability Does Not Equal Authority: A Primer for Judge Advocates on Defense Support of Civil Authorities in a Natural Disaster Scenario, April 2008, p. 24.

70. Major Daniel J. Sennott, "Interpreting Recent Changes to the Standing Rules for the Use of Force," *Army Lawyer*, November 2007, p. 57.

CHAPTER SIX: ALL HELL BREAKS DOWN

1. Quoted in Jiri Nehnevajsa, *Civil Defense and Society* (Pittsburgh: University of Pittsburgh, 1964).

2. Cheney, *In My Time: A Personal and Political Memoir*, pp. 341ff.

3. "New location for LLNL's NCR BioWatch Lab," *Lab News* (published for the employees of Lawrence Livermore National Laboratory), February 15, 2008.

4. Condoleezza Rice, *No Higher Honor: A Memoir of My Years in Washington* (New York: Crown, 2011), p. 101.

5. Bush and Rice made the same odd comment about Powell's demeanor and calculations; see *Decision Points*, p. 153; *No Higher Honor: A Memoir of My Years in Washington*, p. 101.

6. *No Higher Honor: A Memoir of My Years in Washington*, p. 102.

7. The primary overall source for this narrative is Coast Guard Captain VanHaverbeke, PowerPoint briefing and report, M/V Palermo Senator, n.d. (2002); obtained by the author. See also DOJ IG, The Federal Bureau of Investigation's Efforts to Protect the Nation's Seaports (Redacted and Unclassified), Audit Report 06-26, March 2006; Statement of JayEtta Z. Hecker, Director, Physical Infrastructure Issues, GAO before the Subcommittee on National Security, Veterans Affairs, and International Relations, House Committee on Government Reform, "Current Efforts to Detect Nuclear Materials, New Initiatives, and Challenges," Novem-

ber 18, 2002; Transcript, Admiral Thomas H. Collins, USCG, World Shipping Council, September 17, 2002.

8. DHS, Chronology of Changes to the Homeland Security Advisory System, May 5, 2011.

9. The White House, Presidential Decision Directive 39 (PDD-39), US Policy on Counterterrorism, June 21, 1995; originally secret.

10. "The FBI scientific portion... is the Hazardous Material Response Unit, which is based out of Quantico, Virginia"; Proceedings, *DTRA First Biennial Threat Reduction Conference*, Waterside Marriott Hotel, Norfolk, Virginia, September 4–7, 2001, p. 102. "FBI Evidence Recovery Teams and the FBI Hazardous Material Response Unit (HMRU) handle the collection of forensic evidence from a contaminated crime scene"; CNI 3400.17, Navy Installation Emergency Management Program Manual, October 27, 2005.

"In 1996, the FBI responded to the growing threat posed by WMD by creating the Hazardous Material Response Unit (HMRU) to gather and process evidence at scenes involving chemical, biological and/or radiological materials. Responsibility for analysis of the material was moved to the FBI's newly created Chemical Biological Sciences Unit (CBSU) in April of 2002"; LLNL (Donald Prosnitz), Department of Justice Role in Countering WMD, January 13, 2004, p. 3.

11. Ronald Smothers, "Ship's Radiation Is Traced to Harmless Tiles," *New York Times*, September 14, 2002; Ronald Smothers, "Vigilance and Memory: New Jersey; Container Ship Is Held Offshore After Search Discovers Radiation," *New York Times*, September 12, 2002; ABC News, Pierre Thomas, "Detained Ship Searched for Radioactive Material," September 12, 2002; http://abcnews.go.com/WNT/story?id=130115&page=1#.T66 Tw8XwDKc (accessed May 12, 2012); FoxNews.com, "Navy SEALs Inspecting Radioactive Ship off New Jersey," September 12, 2002; http://www.foxnews.com/story/0,2933,62897,00.html#ixzz1ufTrrsb1 (accessed May 12, 2012).

12. DHS, T4 FSE Private Sector Player Handbook, FINAL, October 9, 2007, p. 3, obtained by the author; FEMA, National Exercise Division, Homeland Security Exercise and Evaluation Program, Quarterly Newsletter, Summer 2008.

13. State of Oregon, The TOPOFF 4 Exercise, Fact Sheet, 2007; http://www .oregon.gov/osp/docs/oregon_t4_fact_sheet.pdf (accessed October 29, 2012); FBI press release, The Topoff Terror Drill; Why It Matters to Us and You, October 19, 2007.

14. JFHQ-NCR Exercise Order 06-0 (TOPOFF 4 CPX 06), June 6, 2006, obtained by the author.

Chapter Seven: Enough to Make You Sick

1. Arizona Department of Health Services (Developed and Maintained by the Bureau of Emergency Preparedness and Response), Pandemic Influenza Mass Fatality Response Plan, June 22, 2007 (Version 4.0), p. 11; obtained by the author.

2. Department of Energy Performance and Accountability Report: FY 2001, p. A60; "BASIS Counters Airborne Bioterrorism," Science and Technology Review (LLNL), October 2003; Lauren de Vore, "New location for LLNL's NCR BioWatch Lab," Livermore Lab Newsline, February 15, 2008.

3. Dugway Proving Ground FAQs, What biological agents were tested at Dugway Proving Ground?, September 8, 2008. "The following are the principal biological agents that were used in testing:

   a. Bacillus anthracis
   b. Brucella melitensis
   c. Brucella suis
   d. Clostridium botulinum toxin
   e. Coccidioides
   f. Coccidioides uranine
   g. Coxiella burnettii
   h. Pasteurella pestis (Versinia pestis)
   i. Pasteurella tularensis (Francisella tularensis)
   j. Psittacosis virus."

4. Department of Defense Fiscal Year (FY) 2011 President's Budget, Chemical and Biological Defense Program Justification Book, Research, Development, Test & Evaluation, Defense-Wide, February 2010, pp. 515–516.

5. In August 2001, Livermore and Los Alamos scientists successfully characterized types of pathogens with detectors in a program called Biological Aerosol Sentry and Information System (BASIS); Department of Energy Performance and Accountability Report: FY 2001, p. A60.

6. "BASIS Counters Airborne Bioterrorism," Science and Technology Review (LLNL), October 2003.

7. Nancy S. Bush, "BioWatch: Case for Change of Traditional Leadership to Improve Performance," master's thesis, Naval Postgraduate School, September 2009, p. 34; "BASIS Counters Airborne Bioterrorism," Science and Technology Review (LLNL), October 2003; North American Technology and Industrial Base Organization (NATIBO), Biological Detection System Technologies: Technology and Industrial Base Study; A Primer on Biological Detection Technologies; Final Report, February 2001, p. 7.29.

8. Angler: The Cheney Vice Presidency, pp. 185, 226–234, 343.

9. No Higher Honor: A Memoir of My Years in Washington, pp. 99–100.

10. In February 2001, President Bush asked Vice President Cheney to undertake a review of issues related to how well prepared the United States was domestically to deal with incidents of weapons of mass destruction; Responding to Terror: A Report of the US Army War College Consequence Management Symposium, August 21–23, 2001, p. 81.

11. Nancy S. Bush, "BioWatch: Case for Change of Traditional Leadership to Improve Performance," master's thesis, Naval Postgraduate School, September 2009, p. 34. See *Cheney: The Untold Story of America's Most Powerful and Controversial Vice President*, pp. 319ff, for a description of the WMD assignment to Cheney's office.

12. DHS, FY 2013 Budget Request and Supporting Information: Office of Health Affairs, p. 2255.3

13. DHS, National Capital Region Coordination: First Annual Report to Congress, 2005, p. F-4; Integrated Chemical and Biological Defense Research, Development and Acquisition Plan: Chem-Bio Point Detection, Decontamination and Information Systems Technology Areas, April 2003, p. 28; Defense Science Board 2003 Summer Study on DOD Roles and Missions in Homeland Security, p. 40.

14. An excellent summary of the group and the incident is contained in Army Training and Doctrine Command TRADOC G2 Handbook No. 1.01, Terror Operations: Case Studies in Terrorism, July 25, 2007. See also Senate, Committee on Government Affairs, Subcommittee on Investigations, Hearings, Global Proliferation of Weapons of Mass Destruction, 31 October–1 November 1995, Part 1, pp. 68–80. See also Judith Miller, William J. Broad, and Stephen Engelberg, *Germs: Biological Weapons and America's Secret War*, pp. 151–163.

15. Other events occurred during the same period to convince the president and the Clinton administration of the growing WMD threat; in August 1995, Saddam's minister of industry, his son-in-law, and a gaggle of family members showed up at the Jordanian border, ready to spill the beans on how Iraq continued to hold back and how Saddam successfully hid his biological weapons program from UN inspectors. The defectors presented chapter and verse on Saddam's various foreign partners in the acquisition of forbidden material, including Sudan, where the radical Osama bin Laden was living and already the subject of WMD intelligence reports. Intelligence also showed Iraq-Serbian cooperation in the development of chemical weapons, and what seemed like an increasingly vibrant trade in both nuclear technology and missiles being perpetrated by North Korea, Pakistan, China, Russia, and various brokers from the former Soviet Union. When the FBI got its hands on an al Qaeda defector in 1996, the WMD scare went viral. Jamal Ahmad al-Fadl spoke of bin Laden's attempts to obtain chemical weapons and to buy highly enriched uranium from South Africa, as well as details of al Qaeda contacts with Iranian,

Pakistani, former Soviet, and North Korean chemical and nuclear experts and brokers, this information being fed directly to the president. Tenet later wrote: "We learned [from al-Fadl] that al Qaeda had attempted to acquire material that could be used to develop chemical, biological, radiological, or nuclear weapons capability. He had gone so far as to hire an Egyptian physicist to work on nuclear and chemical projects in Sudan"; George Tenet, *At the Center of the Storm: My Years at the CIA*, p. 102.

16. George Tenet, then a national security staffer at the White House, drafted the directive; Richard A. Clarke, *Against All Enemies: Inside America's War on Terror*, p. 387. Richard Clarke, also then a national security staffer and one of the drafters, says he inserted the language about WMD, an inclusion, he later writes, that other departments found "odd."

   "No one in the departments objected to my including a policy on counterterrorism and weapons of mass destruction; they just thought it was odd"; *Against All Enemies: Inside America's War on Terror*, p. 92.

17. The White House, Presidential Decision Directive 39 (PDD-39), US Policy on Counterterrorism, June 21, 1995; originally secret.

18. In 1979 the FBI director and the Coast Guard commandant additionally signed an MOU agreeing to a policy of mutual assistance in support of FBI and coast guard operations to counteract terrorist activities in the maritime environment. According to the MOU, the FBI: maintains a large number of strategically located Special Weapons and Tactics (SWAT) teams; has personnel trained to act as negotiators in dealing with terrorists' demands; and can use SWAT teams to suppress terrorists' actions during direct confrontation scenarios. See DOJ OIG, The Federal Bureau of Investigation's Efforts to Protect the Nation's Seaports (Redacted and Unclassified), Audit Report 06-26, March 2006.

   As former FBI Director Louis Freeh stated before 9/11, PDD-39 states: "Unless otherwise specified by the Attorney General, the FBI shall have lead responsibility for operational response to terrorist incidents that take place within U.S. territory or that occur in international waters and do not involve the flag vessel of a foreign country. Within this role, the FBI functions as the on-scene manager for the US Government." Moreover, "the FBI shall have lead responsibility for investigating terrorist acts planned or carried out by foreign or domestic terrorist groups in the US or which are directed at US citizens or institutions abroad." See Testimony of Louis J. Freeh, Director, FBI, before the House Appropriations Subcommittee, May 16, 2001.

   See also The White House, Presidential Decision Directive 39 (PDD-39), U.S. Policy on Counterterrorism, June 21, 1995 originally secret.

19. PL 104-201, September 23, 1996, also known as Nunn-Lugar-Domenici Act.

20. Richard Preston, *The Cobra Event* (New York: Random House, 1st edition, 1997).

21. In April 1998, President Clinton hosted a roundtable at the White House with Dr. J. Craig Venter, head of the Institute for Genomic Research; Joshua Lederberg; and Jerry Hauer, director of emergency services in New York, to discuss biological weapons. The three urged the president to start a crash program to improve US public health capabilities and build a national vaccine stockpile. See Daniel Benjamin and Steven Simon, *The Age of Sacred Terror: Radical Islam's War Against America*, p. 254.

22. "A lone madman or fanatics with a bottle of chemicals, a batch of plague inducing bacteria or a crude nuclear bomb can threaten or kill tens of thousands of people in a single act of malevolence," Cohen repeated. "These are not far off or far-fetched scenarios. They are real; they are here; and they are now"; Bill Gertz, "Cohen Details Threats Posed by Baghdad," *Washington Times*, November 26, 1997.

    In his last press conference as secretary of defense, William Cohen released the study *Proliferation: Threat and Response* (January 2001), which stated:

    > At the dawn of the 21st Century, the United States now faces what could be called a Superpower Paradox. Our unrivaled supremacy in the conventional military arena is prompting adversaries to seek unconventional, asymmetric means to strike what they perceive as our Achilles heel....Looming on the horizon is the prospect that these terror weapons will increasingly find their way into the hands of individuals and groups of fanatical terrorists or self-proclaimed apocalyptic prophets. The followers of Usama bin Laden have, in fact, already trained with toxic chemicals....The race is on between our preparations and those of our adversaries. There is not a moment to lose.

23. Tom Ridge and Larry Bloom, *The Test of Our Times: America Under Siege...And How We Can Be Safe Again*, p. 48.

24. The conference call took place on January 9, 2003, hosted by the Environmental Council of the States. The state EPA departments were instructed to coordinate with state homeland security advisors and health departments after the call; however, those entities were not invited to the initial planning calls or meeting regarding the program and were never given a chance to contribute to the planning and rolling out of the program; Nancy S. Bush, "BioWatch: Case for Change of Traditional Leadership to Improve Performance," master's thesis, Naval Postgraduate School, September 2009, pp. 5–6, 33–34.

25. The White House, Executive Office of the President, State of the Union Address, January 28, 2003.

26. Commencing January 10, 2003, the White House Office of Homeland Security (later to become the Department of Homeland Security)

embarked on the effort, with support from the Environmental Protection Agency (EPA), the Centers for Disease Control and Prevention (CDC), the Department of Health and Human Services (DHHS), the Department of Energy (DOE), the DOD, the FBI, and the National Laboratories. See DHS IG, DHS' Management of BioWatch Program, OIG-07-22, January 2007, p. 4; EPA OIG, Evaluation Report, EPA's BioWatch Role Reduced, Report No. 10-P-0106, April 20, 2010.

27. "In the event of a bioattack, thousands of samples, collected both from BioWatch sensors and from the environment, would require lab analysis. DHS S&T is part of the Integrated Consortium of Laboratory Networks (ICLN), formed in 2005 to harmonize analytical protocols and to ensure that results from the wide array of federal, state and private laboratories involved in evaluating BioWatch samples are comparable. ICLN is addressing such questions as how labs would work together to confirm the nature and extent of contamination following a biological (or chemical or radiological) release." Testimony of Tara O'Toole before the House Subcommittee on Homeland Security Appropriations, on Biosurveillance, April 16, 2010.

28. "In March 2003, emplacement of outdoor and indoor air sample collectors and implementation of filter retrieval and sample analysis on a once per day cycle was achieved. With the elevation of the Homeland Security Advisory System from Yellow to Orange on December 22, 2003, increased BioWatch Urban Monitoring for the NCR was implemented by increasing the sample collection and analysis cycle to twice per day. This operational tempo was maintained until April 2005 when sample collection and analysis was reduced to once per day. In FY 2004, BioWatch expanded coverage in the NCR by deploying additional collectors in Northern Virginia and Maryland. Additional underground Metro stations had collectors installed to enhance coverage of the system. BioWatch also added multiplexed bio-toxin detection to the system capability to the NCR in conjunction with CDC/DHHS and LLNL during this time frame." See DHS, National Capital Region Coordination: First Annual Report to Congress, p. F-4.

29. Nancy S. Bush, "BioWatch: Case for Change of Traditional Leadership to Improve Performance," master's thesis, Naval Postgraduate School, September 2009, p. 27.

30. DHS, National Planning Scenarios: Created for Use in National, Federal, State, and Local Homeland Security Preparedness Activities, April 2005; Scenario 1: Nuclear Detonation—10-kiloton Improvised Nuclear Device, obtained by the author.

31. National Security Presidential Directive 43/Homeland Security Presidential Directive 14, Domestic Nuclear Detection, April 15, 2005. DNDO was established as a statutory entity via Section 501 of the SAFE Port Act

of 2006. See Security and Accountability for Every Port Act of 2006, HR 4954, §§ 501-502 (2006) ("SAFE Port Act").

32. DHS, Exploratory Research in Nuclear Detection Technology, Broad Agency Announcement No. BAA09-101 for Domestic Nuclear Detection Office (DNDO) and Transformational and Applied Research Directorate (TARD), p. 4.

    DNDO also would coordinate nuclear forensics efforts across the US government with the Federal Bureau of Investigation, the Departments of Defense, Energy, and State, and the Office of the Director of National Intelligence. "Nuclear forensics helps trace the origin of seized nuclear and other radioactive materials or devices, supports the identification of smuggling networks, aids prosecution efforts of such illicit trafficking, and assists in uncovering vulnerabilities in security measures to ensure nuclear and other radioactive materials remain under regulatory control"; DHS, 2012 Nuclear Security Summit, as of April 5, 2012.

33. DHS, Job Description DHSHQ 09-2007, Nuclear Assessment Specialist, 2007.

34. GAO, Combating Nuclear Terrorism: DHS's Program to Procure and Deploy Advanced Radiation Detection Portal Monitors Is Likely to Exceed the Department's Previous Cost Estimates (Letter Report to Congressional Requesters), September 22, 2008; GAO-07-133R DNDO's Cost-Benefit Analysis, October 17, 2006, p. 4.

35. The Southeast Transportation Corridor Pilot (SETCP), launched in 2008, was designed to "red team" a sensor web. The idea was to take radioactive material that represented a threat and see if operators at truck weighing stations could detect it; DHS, The DHS Domestic Nuclear Detection Office Goes NIEM, from a Portfolio of NIEM Success Stories, 2010.

36. Statement of Warren M. Stern, Director, Domestic Nuclear Detection Office, Department of Homeland Security, Before the House Committee on Science, Space, and Technology Subcommittee on Technology and Innovation Research and Development Priorities and Strategic Direction, March 15, 2011.

37. In June 2002, Congress passed the Public Health Security and Bioterrorism Preparedness and Response Act of 2002 (the Bioterrorism Act).

38. The White House, *National Strategy for Homeland Security*, July 2002. The *National Strategy* also identifies as crucial the need for sharing vulnerability assessment information between federal and nonfederal agencies, and particularly with the private sector. To do this effectively, the "law" section of the *National Strategy* recommends that an attorney general–led panel propose the legal changes needed to enable the sharing of essential security information. The legal changes would give the private sector reasonable assurance that good faith

disclosures about vulnerabilities and preparedness would not expose firms to liability, a drop on share value, loss of competitive advantage, or anti-trust action.

39. DHS, National Planning Scenarios: Created for Use in National, Federal, State, and Local Homeland Security Preparedness Activities, April 2005; Scenario 13: Biological Attack—Food Contamination. See also Association of State and Territorial Health Officials, "Issue Brief: State Activities in Food Security," April 2004.

The three incidents are:

- In 1984, members of the Bhagwan Rajneesh cult poisoned ten Oregon salad bars with salmonella, resulting in 751 individual cases of illness.
- In 1996, a disgruntled employee of a Texas hospital tainted snacks in a staff break room, causing 12 illnesses.
- In 2003, a Michigan supermarket employee infected 200 pounds of beef with an insecticide, causing 92 illnesses.

40. FDA, Risk Assessment for Food Terrorism and Other Food Safety Concerns, October 13, 2003.

41. President's Council of Advisors on Science and Technology, *The Science and Technology of Combating Terrorism*, July 2003, p. 5.

42. Homeland Security Presidential Directive (HSPD) 9, Defense of United States Agriculture and Food, January 30, 2004.

HSPD 9 set out numerous related requirements for DHS, USDA, and FDA, among other federal agencies, and appointed DHS "responsible for coordinating the overall national effort" to protect the food and agriculture sectors, and designated the DHS secretary as "the principal [f]ederal official to lead, integrate, and coordinate implementation of efforts" among federal, state, local, and private sector elements (paragraph 6).

43. William Branigin, Mike Allen, and John Mintz, "Tommy Thompson Resigns from HHS," *Washington Post*, December 3, 2004.

44. Lawrence M. Wein and Yifan Liu, "Analyzing a bioterror attack on the food supply: The case of botulinum toxin in milk," *Proceedings of the National Academy of Sciences*, July 12, 2005, pp. 9984–9989.

45. FDA, "Risk Assessment for Food Terrorism and Other Food Safety Concerns," October 13, 2003.

46. DHS, National Infrastructure Protection Plan, June 30, 2006, p. 1. The plan stated that the impact of an attack on food would undermine "the public's psychological well-being, and the effectiveness of government."

47. DHS IG, DHS' Role in Food Defense and Critical Infrastructure Protection, p. 2.

48. DHS IG, DHS' Role in Food Defense and Critical Infrastructure Protection, p. 15.

49. Vice Admiral Richard H. Carmona, MD, MPH, FACS, United States Surgeon General, "Prevention and Preparedness: Medical Reserve Corps Serving America," Nashville Surgical Society, remarks as prepared; not a transcript; Tuesday, October 7, 2003.

50. Duncan Hunter National Defense Authorization Act for Fiscal Year 2009, Report of the Committee on Armed Services, House of Representatives, Report 110-652, 2008, p. 652.

51. Department of Homeland Security Appropriations Bill, 2013, Senate Report 112-169, p. 103.

52. If automated and more ubiquitous Generation 3 BioWatch detectors are installed, the cost will be four times that. DNDO's ten-year plan to equip ports of entry with new radiation detection equipment could run as much as $3.8 billion through 2017. See GAO, Combating Nuclear Terrorism: DHS's Program to Procure and Deploy Advanced Radiation Detection Portal Monitors Is Likely to Exceed the Department's Previous Cost Estimates (Letter Report to Congressional Requesters), September 22, 2008.

53. US HLS-HLD Markets—2011–2014, p. 68.

54. Al Mauroni, "Progress of 'Biodefense Strategy for the 21st Century': A Five-Year Evaluation," in Army War College, Strategic Studies Institute Book Project on National Security Reform, Case Studies Working Group Report, vol. II, March 2012, p. 161.

55. Statement of Warren M. Stern, Director, Domestic Nuclear Detection Office, Department of Homeland Security, Before the House Committee on Science, Space, and Technology Subcommittee on Technology and Innovation Research and Development Priorities and Strategic Direction, March 15, 2011.

56. DHS, Exploratory Research in Nuclear Detection Technology, Broad Agency Announcement No. BAA09-101 for Domestic Nuclear Detection Office (DNDO) and Transformational and Applied Research Directorate (TARD), p. 4.

57. DHS, The DHS Domestic Nuclear Detection Office Goes NIEM, from a Portfolio of NIEM Success Stories, 2010.

58. Nominations before the Senate Armed Services Committee, Second Session, 111th Congress, S. Hrg. 111-896, 2010, p. 181.

CHAPTER EIGHT: PATHWAYS

1. FBI News Stories, "'Play How You Practice': FBI's WMD Training Workshop Tests Massive Response," July 24, 2012; http://www.fbi.gov/news/stories/2012/july/wmd-training-workshop-tests-massive-response (accessed November 8, 2012).

2. The White House, Presidential Decision Directive 39 (PDD-39), US Policy on Counterterrorism, June 21, 1995; originally secret. The attorney general and the FBI "shall ensure the development and implementation of policies directed at preventing terrorist attacks...." The FBI was given authority to "direct the efforts of other member of the law enforcement community and coordinate with other federal agencies, to prevent or preempt terrorist acts, and to ensure efficient direction of investigations related to terrorism.

   "Crisis management activities include active measures for prevention, immediate incident response, and post-incident response. Activities include command of the operational response as the on-scene manager for an incident in coordination with other Federal agencies and State and local authorities": Department of Defense Plan for Integrating National Guard and Reserve Component Support for Response to Attacks Using Weapons of Mass Destruction, Prepared by the DOD Tiger Team, January 1998.

   Even as crisis management gave way to critical incident management in the January 2008 National Response Framework, WMD action and prevention remained the charge of the FBI, and the use of the term "crisis management" persists.

3. FBI, WMD Directorate PowerPoint Briefing, National User Facility Organization: Assessing the Chemical Threat, Mitigating Potential Risks and Building a Culture of Responsibility, Trust, and Cooperation, June 19, 2012; obtained by the author.

   The FBI manages any aspect of the response that involves:

   - specialized weapons and tactics to prevent or break up terrorist activity;
   - specialized HAZMAT/NBC operations to identify, assess, dismantle, transfer, or dispose of an agent or weapon;
   - access to the crime scene;
   - evidence collection and preservation; and
   - investigation of the crime.

   See also FEMA PowerPoint Briefing, Federal Response to Terrorism, 1999.

4. The White House, National Security Decision Directive 30 (NSDD-30), Managing Terrorist Incidents, April 10, 1982; originally secret but since declassified; General Accounting Office, Combating Terrorism: Federal Agencies' Efforts to Implement National Policy and Strategy, GAO/NSIAD-97-254, September 1997, p. 39. It is unknown which, if any, federal agency had the lead prior to 1982.

5. CJCSI 3125.01B, Defense Support of Civil Authorities (DSCA) for Domestic Consequence Management (CM) Operations in Response to a

Chemical, Biological, Radiological, Nuclear, or High-Yield Explosive (CBRNE) Incident, August 19, 2009, pp. D-3, D-4.

6. Paul Murphy, "FBI, local first responders stage mock emergency on riverfront," WWLTV Eyewitness News [WWLTV.com], May 23, 2012.

7. Paul Murphy, "FBI, local first responders stage mock emergency on riverfront," WWLTV Eyewitness News [WWLTV.com], May 23, 2012.

8. Mark Rockwell, "FBI's WMD directorate sets workshop on agriculture and water infrastructure security," *Government Security News*, July 23, 2012.

9. During 2005, FBI director Mueller requested that the newly formed National Security Branch design an organizational element to deal with WMD; by July 2006, the FBI established the Weapons of Mass Destruction Directorate (WMDD). The directorate incorporated preexisting units from the Domestic Terrorism Section of Counterterrorism Division, in addition to new ones. See DOJ IG, The Federal Bureau of Investigation's Weapons of Mass Destruction Coordinator Program, p. i.

10. FBI Weapons of Mass Destruction Frequently Asked Questions, n.d. (2009); http://www.fbi.gov/about-us/investigate/terrorism/wmd/wmd_faqs (accessed November 10, 2012). See also Statement of Vahid Majidi, Assistant Director, Weapons of Mass Destruction Directorate, Federal Bureau of Investigation, Before the Senate Committee on Homeland Security and Governmental Affairs, October 18, 2011. He called the directorate a "unique combination of law enforcement authorities, intelligence analysis capabilities, and technical subject matter expertise focused on chemical, biological, radiological, nuclear, and explosive matters."

11. In April 2008, the FBI WMD Operations Unit asked field divisions to designate WMD coordinators as a full-time duty. To encourage field divisions to designate a full-time WMD coordinator, the WMD Directorate offered many field divisions a headquarters-funded position to replace the one filled by the full-time WMD coordinator.

    See FBI PowerPoint Briefing, Investigative Response: FBI Hazardous Materials Response Unit, Federal Bureau of Investigation, Laboratory Division, Hazardous Materials Response Unit, n.d. (2007), obtained by the author.

12. According to an FBI briefing, the WMDOU mission is: "to prevent, interdict plans to use a WMD; coordinate response to WMD incident; provide oversight to WMD criminal investigation; conduct threat assessment; and provide information to interagency and federal government partners." See FBI PowerPoint Briefing, FBI Counterterrorism Program Overview, Special Agent Keith Howland, PhD, WMD Coordinator, Colorado Springs RA, Denver Division; presented at the US Northern Command Emergency Preparedness Course, July 28, 2005, obtained by the author.

13. FBI Stories, "WMD Threats; How We Respond," May 3, 2007.

14. See USDOJ/FBI and CDC, Criminal and Epidemiological Investigation Handbook, 2011 Edition, pp. 11–12, 29–30; National Response Framework, Biological Incident Annex, August 2008, p. BIO-3; LLNL (Donald Prosnitz), Department of Justice Role in Countering WMD, January 13, 2004 p. 6; DOJ IG, The Federal Bureau of Investigation's Efforts to Protect the Nation's Seaports (redacted and unclassified), Audit Report 06-26, March 2006.

15. Right up there with the radiation detectors and DNA specialists are the WMD psychologists of Behavioral Assessment Unit 1 (part of the Behavioral Science Unit), specialists who evaluate threatening communications and stalking and arson cases, and then act as part of negotiation and decision-making teams during active "crisis situations."

16. LLNL (Donald Prosnitz), Department of Justice Role in Countering WMD, January 13, 2004, p. 7.

17. "In accordance with PKEMRA, the FEMA Administrator has the responsibility for directing the DEST. NSPD-46/HSPD-15 further identifies the DEST as a specialized interagency team designed to expeditiously provide expert advice, guidance, and support to the FBI On-Scene Coordinator (OSC) during a weapons of mass destruction (WMD) incident or credible threat. FEMA is statutorily responsible for directing the operations of the DEST; coordinating the interagency team for mission planning purposes; and deploying as part of the team"; FY 2012 Department of Homeland Security Congressional Budget Justification, FEMA Management and Administration, p. 39.

18. A small Crisis Management Unit (CMU) within CIRG has worldwide responsibilities for standing up and training task forces. "CMU also conducts a broad spectrum of crisis management training for the FBI and other federal, state, and local agencies and has programmatic oversight of the crisis management coordinators located in each of the 56 field divisions. CMU also conducts research into new crisis management procedures and information techniques"; FBI, Investigations & Operations Support; http://www.fbi.gov/about-us/cirg/investigations-and-operations-support (accessed May 11, 2012); FBI, "Protecting Against Terrorist Attack; It's the Middle Name of the FBI's Crisis Management Unit," September 27, 2004; http://www.fbi.gov/news/stories/2004/september/cirg 092704 (accessed May 11, 2012).

19. Multiservice Tactics, Techniques, and Procedures for Nuclear, Biological, and Chemical Aspects of Consequence Management, FM 3-11.21, MCRP 3-37.2C, NTTP 3-11.24, AFTTP (I) 3-2.37, December 2001, p. D-19.

20. CIRG also includes a Technical Operations section that "provides training, equipment, and advanced technical support to federal, state, local, and law enforcement partners in order to coordinate and integrate the

operational response to resolve the full-threat spectrum of hazardous devices within the United States."

21. The HRT, almost 250 strong, is the "tactical unit" of the FBI, "the only full-time civilian asset of the US Government with the enhanced manpower, training, resources and authority to confront the most complex of tactical threats within the United States," a unit described in an uncharacteristically garrulous FBI budget document as "available for situations where the only other available option would be the domestic use of the Department of Defense's Special Mission Units to enforce civilian law." See DOJ, FY 2009 FBI Budget Justification Material, n.d. (2009), pp. 6-3, 6-4, obtained by the author; DOJ IG, The Federal Bureau of Investigation's Efforts to Protect the Nation's Seaports, Audit Report 06-26, March 2006, partially declassified and released by the DOJ, p. 92.

22. The GAO stated in a 1999 report: "There are over 600 local and state hazardous materials (HAZMAT) teams in the United States that assess and take appropriate actions in incidents almost daily involving highly toxic industrial chemicals and other hazardous materials...the Domestic Preparedness Program is providing teams from the largest 120 cities in the United States with the opportunity to expand their capabilities to counter WMD incidents. In addition, there are numerous military and federal civilian organizations that can help local incident commanders deal with WMD incidents by providing advice, technical experts, and equipment"; GAO Testimony, Combating Terrorism: Use of National Guard Response Teams Is Unclear, GAO/T-NSIAD-99-184, June 23, 1999.

A 2006 FBI briefing stated that 441 state/local squads had been trained in terms of WMD tiered response; FBI PowerPoint Briefing, Transformation and Evolution of the FBI Since 9/11, Presentation at Naval Postgraduate School Center for Homeland Security, "Comparative Government for Homeland Security," J. Stephen Tidwell, Assistant Director in Charge, Los Angeles Field Office, 2006, obtained by the author.

23. This includes the ATF, the CDC, the EPA, the Department of Health and Human Services, FEMA, the military, and of course the Department of Homeland Security.

See DHS PowerPoint Briefing, S&T Stakeholders Conference; Peter T. Pesenti, PhD, Program Manager, Bioforensics Threat Characterization and Attribution Office, Chemical-Biological Division, Science and Technology Directorate, Draft, May 19, 2008, obtained by the author.

24. "The FBI may also use other Federal, state and local resources to investigate WMD incidents, to include the National Guard CSTs [civil support teams], when and where appropriate, and in full recognition of their status as State-level assets. States should work with the respective FBI WMD Coordinator to coordinate the employment of their resources"; NGR

500-3/ANGI 10-2503, May 9, 2011, Emergency Employment of Army and Other Resources, Weapons of Mass Destruction Civil Support Team Management, p. 16.

25. DOJ IG, Review of the Department's Preparation to Respond to a WMD Incident, May 2010.

26. DOJ IG, The Federal Bureau of Investigation's Weapons of Mass Destruction Coordinator Program, p. 47.

27. "Each FBI field office has a WMD Incident Contingency Plan (WMDICP) which is prepared by the WMD coordinator. These plans were designed to quickly identify field office, as well as state, local and regional Federal assets that can be called upon by the field office to assist in the response to any type of WMD event. In formulation of these plans, field offices have been instructed to identify critical facilities as well as appropriate security contacts at these facilities"; Statement of Ronald L. Dick, Deputy Assistant Director, Counterterrorism Division, and Director, National Infrastructure Protection Center, FBI; before the House Committee on Transportation and Infrastructure, Subcommittee on Water Resources and Environment, October 10, 2001.

28. DOJ IG, The Federal Bureau of Investigation's Weapons of Mass Destruction Coordinator Program, p. i.

29. LLNL (Donald Prosnitz), Department of Justice Role in Countering WMD, January 13, 2004, p. 4.

30. DOJ IG, The Federal Bureau of Investigation's Weapons of Mass Destruction Coordinator Program, pp. iv, vi.

31. DOJ IG, The Federal Bureau of Investigation's Weapons of Mass Destruction Coordinator Program, p. 13.

32. Weapons of Mass Destruction (WMDs) are defined as "Weapons that are capable of killing a lot of people and/or causing a high-order magnitude of destruction, or weapons that are capable of being used in such a way as to cause mass casualties or create large-scale destruction. WMDs are generally considered to be nuclear, biological, chemical, and radiological devices, but WMDs can also be high-explosive devices." See DHS, Federal Continuity Directive (FCD), November 1, 2007, p. P-10.

"WMDs include any explosives and incendiary devices designed to cause death or serious bodily injury through the release, dissemination, or impact of toxic or poisonous chemicals, disease organisms, or radiation at a level dangerous to human life," the Department of Justice simply says. Yet the Weapons of Mass Destruction Statute makes clear that the term WMD doesn't only include explosives, but includes "any weapons involving a disease organism" capable of causing biological "malfunction, disease, or death in a living organism" (Title 18 U.S.C. Section 178).

As defined in Title 18, U.S.C. § 2332a, a WMD is "(1) any explosive, incendiary, or poison gas, bomb, grenade, rocket having a propellant charge of more than 4 ounces, or missile having an explosive or incendiary charge of more than one-quarter ounce, or mine or similar device; (2) any weapon that is designed or intended to cause death or serious bodily injury through the release, dissemination, or impact of toxic or poisonous chemicals or their precursors; (3) any weapon involving a disease organism; or (4) any weapon that is designed to release radiation or radioactivity at a level dangerous to human life." See also Coast Guard, Incident Manager's Handbook, 2006, Glossary 25-26; DHS, National Infrastructure Protection Plan (NIPP), 2006, p. 105.

33. The White House, National Security Presidential Directive-17/Homeland Security Presidential Directive-4 (NSPD-17/HSPD-4), Combating Weapons of Mass Destruction, Annex 5, February 26, 2008.

34. State of Minnesota, PowerPoint Briefing, Emergency Preparedness: Surge capacity, all-hazards, and the Republican National Convention, Moe Sullivan, Minnesota Department of Health Public Health Laboratory, n.d. (2009), obtained by the author. The pertinent slide states:
    "Federal Assets: FBI

    - 400 additional agents, scientists, technical support
    - Including the Hazardous Materials Response Unit (HMRU) from Quantico, Virginia
    - Full HMRU capabilities (bio, chem, rad)
    - 800 cameras watching the area
    - 11 Federal/State arrests with respect to WMD (all Molotov cocktails)."

    See also Report of the Republican National Convention Public Safety Planning and Implementation Review Commission, January 14, 2009, pp. 35–36.

35. JCS, National Military Strategy of the United States of America 2004, p. 1.

36. FBI PowerPoint Briefing, FBI Counterterrorism Program Overview, Special Agent Keith Howland, PhD, WMD Coordinator, Colorado Springs RA, Denver Division; presented at the US Northern Command Emergency Preparedness Course, July 28, 2005, obtained by the author.

37. FBI WMD Directorate PowerPoint Briefing, Mitigating the Chemical Threat at Your Facility, Bill DelBagno, Supervisory Special Agent, Mitigating the Potential Risks and Building a Culture of Awareness, Communication, and Prevention, n.d. (2012); FBI WMD Directorate PowerPoint Briefing, National User Facility Organization: Assessing the Chemical Threat, Mitigating Potential Risks, and Building a Culture of Responsibility, Trust, and Cooperation, June 19, 2012.

38. LLNL (Donald Prosnitz), Department of Justice Role in Countering WMD, January 13, 2004, p. 4.

39. FBI PowerPoint Briefing, Agroterrorism Threat Briefing, Peter M. de la Cuesta, Supervisory Special Agent WMD Countermeasures Unit, Infrastructure Counterterrorism Team, n.d. (2012), obtained by the author; FBI PowerPoint Briefing, Nathan E. Head, PhD, Supervisory Special Agent, WMD Directorate, Federal Bureau of Investigation, The FBI's Efforts to Address the Biological Threat, September 18, 2012, obtained by the author; FBI PowerPoint Briefing, FBI Perspective: Addressing Synthetic Biology and Biosecurity, Edward H. You, Supervisory Special Agent, Bioterrorism Program, Countermeasures Unit I, FBI Weapons of Mass Destruction Directorate, July 9, 2010, obtained by the author.

40. FBI WMD Directorate PowerPoint Briefing, National User Facility Organization: Assessing the Chemical Threat, Mitigating Potential Risks, and Building a Culture of Responsibility, Trust, and Cooperation, June 19, 2012, obtained by the author.

41. FBI PowerPoint Briefing, Nathan E. Head, PhD, Supervisory Special Agent, WMD Directorate, Federal Bureau of Investigation, The FBI's Efforts to Address the Biological Threat, September 18, 2012, obtained by the author.

42. Statement of Vahid Majidi, Assistant Director, Weapons of Mass Destruction Directorate, Federal Bureau of Investigation, Before the Senate Committee on Homeland Security and Governmental Affairs, October 18, 2011.

43. Statement of Vahid Majidi, Assistant Director, Weapons of Mass Destruction Directorate, Federal Bureau of Investigation, Before the Senate Committee on Homeland Security and Governmental Affairs, October 18, 2011.

44. "The Terrorist Threat Confronting the United States," Testimony of Dale L. Watson, Executive Assistant Director, Counterterrorism/Counterintelligence Division, FBI, Before the Senate Select Committee on Intelligence, February 6, 2002.

45. Shay Sokol, "Attack Response, Dinner Coordinated at Weapons of Mass Destruction ConFab, *NOLA Defender*, May 23, 2012; http://noladefender .com/content/attack-response-dinner-c45oordinated-weapons-ma7ss -destruction-confab (accessed November 12, 2012).

CHAPTER NINE: *IN EXTREMIS*

1. Testimony by Secretary of Defense Donald H. Rumsfeld on Homeland Security before Senate Appropriations Committee, May 7, 2002. Rumsfeld said:

"First, under extraordinary circumstances that require the department to execute its traditional military missions. In these circumstances, DOD would take the lead. Combat air patrols and maritime defense operations are examples of such missions....

"...Second, in emergency circumstances of a catastrophic nature — for example, responding to an attack or assisting in response to forest fires or floods, hurricanes, tornadoes and so forth. In these instances, the Department of Defense may be asked to act quickly to provide or to supply capabilities that other agencies simply do not have....

"...Third, missions or assignments that are limited in scope, where other agencies have the lead from the outset. An example of this would be security at a special event, like the Olympics....

"...The first of those three categories, extraordinary circumstances, when DOD conducts military missions to defend the people or territory of the United States at the direction of the president, falls under the heading of homeland defense.... The second and third categories, which are really emergency or temporary circumstances, in which other federal agencies take the lead, and DOD lends support, are appropriately described as homeland security."

2. Testimony of Secretary of Defense Donald Rumsfeld to the House Select Committee on Homeland Security, July 11, 2002; http://www.defenselink.mil/speeches/2002/s20020711-secdef.html (accessed August 9, 2012). Rumsfeld said: "First, under *extraordinary circumstances* that require the department to execute traditional military missions, such as combat air patrols and maritime defense operations. In these circumstances, the Department of Defense would take the lead in defending people in the territory of our country supported by other agencies. And plans for such contingencies would be coordinated, as appropriate, with the National Security Council and with the Department of Homeland Security...."

See also Statement by Mr. Paul McHale, Assistant Secretary of Defense for Homeland Defense, Senate Armed Services Committee, April 8, 2003.

3. Prepared Statement on Homeland Security by Deputy Secretary of Defense Paul Wolfowitz, Thursday, July 11, 2002; http://www.defense.gov/Speeches/Speech.aspx?SpeechID=265 (accessed August 21, 2012). Wolfowitz described extraordinary circumstances as those "that require the department to execute its traditional military missions to deter, dissuade or defeat an attack from external entities....

- DOD and the Secretary of Defense would take the lead,
- Plans for such contingencies would be coordinated as appropriate and, to the extent possible, would be coordinated, with the National Security Council, the Homeland Security Council, the Department of Homeland Security and other affected Departments and agencies.

"As an example, in the case of combat air patrols, the FAA, a civilian agency, would provide data to assist the efforts of Air Force fighter pilots in the Guard and Reserve in identifying and, if necessary, intercepting suspicious or hostile aircraft.

"Also included in the category of extraordinary circumstances are cases in which the President, exercising his Constitutional authority as

Commander-in-Chief and Chief Executive, authorizes military action. This inherent Constitutional authority may be used in cases, such as a terrorist attack, where normal measures are insufficient to carry out federal functions."

4. US Code, Title 10, Section 382: Emergency situations involving chemical or biological weapons of mass destruction "Pursuant to 10 U.S.C. 382, in response to an emergency involving biological or chemical WMD that is beyond the capabilities of civilian authorities to handle, the Attorney General may request DOD assistance directly. Assistance to be provided includes monitoring, containing, disabling, and disposing of the weapon, as well as direct law enforcement assistance that would otherwise violate the Posse Comitatus Act. Among other factors, such assistance must be considered necessary for the immediate protection of human life."

18 U.S.C. 831(e) authorizes the attorney general to request DOD law enforcement assistance—including the authority to arrest and conduct searches—notwithstanding the prohibitions of the *Posse Comitatus* Act—when both the attorney general and the secretary of defense agree that an "emergency situation" exists and the secretary of defense determines that the requested assistance will not impede military readiness. An emergency situation involving nuclear material is defined as a circumstance that poses a serious threat to the United States in which (1) enforcement of the law would be seriously impaired if the assistance were not provided and (2) civilian law enforcement personnel are not capable of enforcing the law. In addition, the statute authorizes DOD personnel to engage in "such other activity as is incident to the enforcement of this section, or to the protection of persons or property from conduct that violates this section." See National Response Plan (Draft #1), February 25, 2004, pp. 70–71.

5. JCS, Defense Support of Civil Authorities (DSCA) for Domestic Consequence Management (CM) Operations in Response to a Chemical, Biological, Radiological, Nuclear, or High-Yield Explosive (CBRNE) Incident, CJCSI 3125.01B, August 19, 2009, p. A-8.

6. Hearing, Nominations Before the Senate Armed Services Committee, Second Session, 111th Congress, S. Hrg. 111-896, 2010, p. 191. Winnefeld wrote: "In most cases, the incident will be managed at the State level with DOD in support. For all incidents, Federal forces would 'lean forward,' as permitted under the National Response Framework, in order to monitor and assess CBRNE capabilities and provide additional support if requested. If title 10 forces do respond, I believe the Commander of NORTHCOM should maintain command and control of these forces in a 'direct support' relationship aligned closely with the primary Federal agency and the affected State Governor(s) under the principle of unity of

effort. In certain rare circumstances, the NORTHCOM Commander may be asked to assume overall command and control due to the nature or scope of an incident. If confirmed, I will ensure that Federal forces under my command are responsive under either command and control framework."

7. The National Response Framework (NRF) of January 2008 includes annexes called Emergency Support Functions (ESF) that assign specific responsibilities to federal agencies in the event of a disaster. In ESF-13, the DOJ is assigned responsibility for coordinating federal law enforcement activities in response to a critical incident, such as a WMD attack, and for ensuring public safety and security in the event an incident overwhelms state and local law enforcement. The department designated the Bureau of Alcohol, Tobacco, Firearms and Explosives (ATF) as the lead agency to implement this requirement in the aftermath of a WMD incident. See DOD IG, Review of the Department's Preparation to Respond to a WMD Incident, May 2010, p. ii.

8. The White House, National Security Decision Directive 30 (NSDD-30), Managing Terrorist Incidents, April 10, 1982; originally secret.

9. The White House, National Security Decision Directive 138 (NSDD-138), Combating Terrorism, April 3, 1984; originally top secret/sensitive.

10. Lieutenant Commander Dennis E. Granger, USN, The Marine Expeditionary Unit: A Limited Conventional Response Force—Not a SOF Substitute, Naval War College, June 23, 1994, p. 15.

11. Official DOD Definition; http://www.dtic.mil/doctrine/jel/DODdict/data/i/428.html (accessed August 9, 2012).

12. Lieutenant Colonel Mastin M. Robeson, USMC, The Operational Implications of the Forward-Deployed MAGTF in a Joint Environment: A Monograph, School of Advanced Military Studies, AY 96-97 [1997].

The CIF is sometimes also referred to as the Combatant Commander In Extremis Force (CIF), to distinguish it from other *in extremis* forces that could exist at lower echelons.

13. Major Lawrence D. Nicholson, An Analysis of the Twenty-One Missions of the Marine Corps Expeditionary Unit (Special Operations Capable), A thesis presented to the Faculty of the US Army Command and General Staff College in partial fulfillment of the requirements for the degree Master of Military Art and Science, 1994, pp. 15–16, 104.

14. "Should National assets not arrive, the MEU (SOC) [today Marine Special Operations Command] will be prepared to conduct an emergency assault to resolve the situation and remove the hostages/sensitive items to a safehaven. The intent is not to duplicate National capability (mission of the national counter-terrorist agencies assigned this mission), but, as a forward deployed MAGTF, be prepared to provide the CINC with an adequate force, capable to respond to an emergency situation; Major Lawrence D. Nicholson, An Analysis of the Twenty-One Missions of the

Marine Corps Expeditionary Unit (Special Operations Capable), A thesis presented to the Faculty of the US Army Command and General Staff College in partial fulfillment of the requirements for the degree Master of Military Art and Science, 1994, pp. 15–16, 104.

15. GAO-01-822 Combating Terrorism, pp. 61–62.

16. Even in a 2009 report on special operations forces, a knowledgeable insider testifying before Congress only referred to the overseas possibility of involvement of national mission forces, and even then, portrayed the possibility as extraordinary: "In rare circumstances, they might be called upon to undertake counter-proliferation operations against critical WMD-related infrastructure that cannot be reliably and safely targeted by other means, including sites in denied, deep inland areas. SOF would likely also play a role in retaliatory attacks against state or non-state actors who employ WMD. Its primary contribution to the US Government's response to this challenge, however, will likely be in tracking down and rendering safe 'loose' WMD material or devices"; Robert Martinage, Senior Fellow, Center for Strategic and Budgetary Assessments, "Special Operations Forces: Challenges and Opportunities," Testimony Before the US House of Representatives, House Committee on Armed Services Subcommittee on Terrorism, Unconventional Threats and Capabilities, March 3, 2009, p. 10.

17. National Security Decision Memorandum 312, Nuclear Weapons Recovery Policy, 1975, signed in the Ford administration, established most of the modern-day demands of the involvement of special operations forces in both assessing US nuclear safety and preparing for the recovery of a lost or stolen US nuclear weapon. It and two other presidential directives (National Security Decision Directive 281 (NSDD-281), Nuclear Weapons Command and Control (1987); and National Security Decision Directive 309 (NSDD-309), Nuclear Weapons Safety, Security, and Control (1988), were superseded by National Security Presidential Directive 28 (NSPD-28), US Nuclear Weapons Command and Control, Safety, and Security, signed by President Bush on June 20, 2003. All of the documents remain classified.

18. The 1999 Terrorism Incident Annex to the Federal Response Plan stated: "As directed in PDD-39, the Department of Defense will activate technical operations capabilities [i.e., render safe procedures] to support the federal response to threats or acts of WMD terrorism. DOD will coordinate military operations within the United States with the appropriate civilian lead agency(ies) for technical operations"; FEMA, Federal Response Plan, Terrorism Incident Annex, April 1999, p. TI-11.

A series of memoranda of understanding and interagency agreements made DOD's lead role in support of the mission abundantly clear: Memorandum of Understanding Between the Energy Research and Development Administration [ERDA, later the Department of Energy] and the Federal Bureau of Investigation for Responding to Nuclear Threat Incidents, June 11, 1976. This memorandum was modified in June 1982 to include DOE (which replaced ERDA) support of the FBI response to non-nuclear sophisticated improvised explosive devices (SIEDs). The FBI, however, retained responsibility for requesting DOD explosive ordnance disposal (EOD) support as appropriate. See Modification to Memorandum of Understanding between the Department of Energy and the Federal Bureau of Investigation for Responding to Nuclear Incidents, June 1982.

See also Joint Federal Bureau of Investigation, Department of Energy, and Department of Defense Agreement for Response to Improvised Nuclear Device Incidents, February 27, 1980; Memorandum of Understanding Between the Department of Justice, the Department of Defense, and the Department of Energy for Response to Domestic Malevolent Nuclear Weapon Emergencies, 1991; quoted in Chris Quillen, "Posse Comitatus and Nuclear Terrorism," *Parameters*, Spring 2002, pp. 60–74.

19. The White House, Fact Sheet on National Security Presidential Directive No. 46/Homeland Security Presidential Directive No. 15 (NSPD-46/HSPD-15), United States Policy and Strategy in the War on Terror, March 6, 2006, rescinding Presidential Decision Directives 39 and 62. The National Implementation Plan for the War on Terror (NIP-WOT), September 2008, integrates US government counterterrorism activities and provides a common strategic direction to implement NSPD-46/HSPD-15.

The compartmented Domestic Deployment Guidelines of PDD-39 (NSPD-46/HSPD-15, "US Policy and Strategy in the War on Terror," Annex II [Consolidation and Updating of Outdated Presidential Counterterrorism Documents], January 10, 2007), mandated that the FBI be the lead agency for all "operational response" issues related to domestic terrorist events. Where terrorism and weapons of mass destruction were mixed, the use of specialized military assets, including the Joint Special Operations Task Force, would fall under FBI jurisdiction, except even when the FBI was overwhelmed or the circumstances demanded a different presidential decision. On October 1, 2009, WMDD achieved FBI National Program status. Achieving program status gave the directorate full oversight over initiatives and program activities (prevention, preparedness, countermeasures, investigations, and operational response), as well as the ability to lead field personnel.

For a description of the annex, see FBI/US Attorney/Department of Justice, Hazardous Materials/WMD Incident Support Plan, August 13, 2008; FBI PowerPoint Briefing, Nuclear/Radiological Outreach, Bernadette R. Bland, Supervisory Special Agent Countermeasures; Oscar R.

Hernandez, SNL IPA Intelligence Analysis; September 23, 2010, obtained by the author.

Annex II gives the FBI "the primary responsibility for finding and neutralizing weapons of mass destruction within the United States in response to information received from law enforcement, intelligence, or other channels." DOD provides support in the US: it provides personnel, survey and search assets, and logistical support to the FBI; in coordination with FBI, DHS, and DOE, it conducts training and exercises to personnel who would conduct search and survey operations; and it provides transportation assistance for the deployment and redeployment of response personnel and equipment. See Thomas P. D'Agostino, Administrator, National Nuclear Security Administration, before the Advisory Panel on Department of Defense Capabilities for Support of Civil Authorities after Certain Incidents; in Before Disaster Strikes: Imperatives for Enhancing Defense Support of Civil Authorities, The Report of the Advisory Panel on Department of Defense Capabilities for Support of Civil Authorities After Certain Incidents to the Secretary of Defense and the Chairmen and Ranking Minority Members, Committees on Armed Services, US Senate and US House of Representatives, September 15, 2010, p. 140.

20. Nominations before the Senate Armed Services Committee, Second Session, 111th Congress, S. Hrg. 111-896, 2010, p. 182.

The Top Secret NSDD 207, The National Program for Combating Terrorism, modifying NSDDs 30 and 138, and signed on January 20, 1986, now also declassified, acknowledged for the first time a "national program" to include "measures to deter, resolve and, when necessary, respond proportionately to terrorist attacks." Within US territory, the attorney general, through the FBI, was designated the "lead agency" responsible for all aspects of a terrorist incident, but again there was no mention of the Defense Department or any extraordinary rules. Nevertheless, the secretary of defense was directed to "consider…public acknowledgment of the existence of US CT [counterterrorism] forces." Even in a top secret directive, those forces were too sensitive to further discuss.

Robert A. Blecksmith, the director of the FBI's Critical Incident Response Group, said during the 2009 inaugural that there might be potential shortages of FBI assets in a multiple 9/11-like event. FBI News, Radio Interview on Inauguration Security, January 23, 2009; http://www.fbi.gov/inside/archive/inside012309.htm (accessed February 6, 2009).

See also Lieutenant Colonel Daniel M. Klippstein, USA, "Homeland Security: The Department of Defense, the Department of Homeland Security and Critical Vulnerabilities," USAWC Strategy Research Project, March 7, 2003, pp. 20–21. Klippstein suggests that in the case of a domestic weapon of mass destruction, the president might direct the Defense Department to "stabilize" a crisis.

21. *The Test of Our Times*, pp. 44–45.

22. *Against all Enemies*, p. 155.

23. JCSI 5113.01C, "Charter of the Counterterrorist Joint Task Force," November 16, 2006, defines National Mission Forces. This directive replaced CJCS Instruction 5113.01B, Charter of the Counterterrorist Joint Task Force, May 31, 2000, which replaced CJCSI 5113.01, Charter of the Counterterrorist Joint Task Force, October 1, 1996, which superseded CJCSI 5113.01, September 30, 1993.

   The normal description of special operations forces include counterinsurgency, counterterrorism, unconventional warfare (in which indigenous fighting forces are used to topple adversaries), and foreign internal defense (improving a country's security, governance, and economic institutions to address the threats it faces). A "national mission force" is often alluded to, operating under a separate chain of command and control, but even there its mission is described exclusively as counterterrorism, albeit in "direct action raids" going after the highest-value targets, like Saddam Hussein and Osama bin Laden. See Testimony on Special Operations Forces, Linda Robinson, Adjunct Senior Fellow for US National Security and Foreign Policy, Council on Foreign Relations, Before the House Committee on Armed Services Subcommittee on Emerging Threats and Capabilities, July 11, 2012; Sean D. Naylor, "Chinook crash highlights rise in spec ops raids," *Army Times*, Aug 21, 2011; Sean D. Naylor, "JSOC task force battles Haqqani militants," *Army Times*, September 13, 2010; Linda Robinson, "Inside the 'New' Special Operations Force," *USNI Proceedings*, July 2009.

24. FBI PowerPoint Briefing, Transformation and Evolution of the FBI Since 9/11, Presentation at Naval Postgraduate School Center for Homeland Security, "Comparative Government for Homeland Security," J. Stephen Tidwell, Assistant Director in Charge, Los Angeles Field Office, 2006, obtained by the author.

25. "The FBI provides guidance on the crisis-management response in the FBI Nuclear/Incident Contingency Plan [classified] and the FBI Chemical-Biological Incident Contingency Plan [classified]"; Multiservice Tactics, Techniques, and Procedures for Nuclear, Biological, and Chemical Aspects of Consequence Management, FM 3-11.21, MCRP 3-37.2C, NTTP 3-11.24, AFTTP (I) 3-2.37, December 2001, p. H-5. See also Department of Defense Plan for Integrating National Guard and Reserve Component Support for Response to Attacks Using Weapons of Mass Destruction, Prepared by the DOD Tiger Team, January 1998.

26. JSOC, of course, is merely a command headquarters located in North Carolina, and it merely oversees the "black" special operations force units

that feed various ad hoc task forces, whether they be in Iraq or Afghanistan or Yemen or beyond; each task force is tailor-made for a specific mission. In the war on terror, that mission can colloquially be referred to as man-hunting, the pursuit of high-value targets, and indeed can be *in extremis*, from a battlefield setting in the deserts of Arabia or the mountains of Afghanistan, all the way up to a mission deep inside Pakistan to kill Osama bin Laden, one that literally took years of preparation and one that even the president was watching in real time.

27. An August 10, 2000, DOD memorandum answers some of the questions regarding the distinction between black and white forces. It states that some chemical, biological, radiological, nuclear, and high-yield explosive incidents may have qualitative and quantitative differences from routine incidents. Thus, all official requests for DOD support for chemical, biological, radiological, nuclear, and high-yield explosive incidents are to be routed through the executive secretary of the Department of Defense, who determines whether the incident warrants "special operational management." For incidents not requiring special operations, the secretary of the army will serve as the executive agent through the director of military support channels, since changed to the JCS through JDOMS; See SecDef Memorandum, Management of DOD Operational Response to Consequences of Certain Incidents Involving Chemical, Biological, Radiological, Nuclear, and High Yield Explosives, August 10, 2000; obtained by the author.

28. The 160th SOAR, for example, is responsible for maintaining a national mission alert force. See 160th Special Operations Aviation Regiment (Airborne) "Night Stalkers"; http://www.campbell.army.mil/units/160thSOAR/Pages/160thSOAR.aspx (accessed November 6, 2012).

29. "DHS has established a DHS Situational Awareness Team (DSAT) to provide timely and accurate information to the Secretary and Departmental Leadership for potential or actual Incidents of National Significance. The DSAT capability is comprised of a Tier One national team consisting of six DHS/ICE special agents with high-capability communications equipment such as satellite and streaming video. These agents are supported by an additional 26 special agents, designated as Incident Response Coordinators, located in DHS/ICE field offices across the Nation. A public affairs contingent is incorporated within the DSAT and will deploy and operate with the agents. Upon deployment, team personnel come under the tasking authority of DHS Office of Operations and administrative control remains under the authority of DHS/ICE. The DSAT is an early entry capability and will report simultaneously to the NOC and PFO to ensure that the Secretary and PFO have early situational awareness." See DHS, Notice of Change to the National Response Plan, Version 5.0, May 25, 2006, p. 21.

30. *Germs: Biological Weapons and America's Secret War*, pp. 152–153. The three reporters from the *New York Times* said that the army technical escort unit from Aberdeen Proving Ground, Maryland, deployed to New York. "The army's unit was not much help. Its best detection equipment, designed for the battlefield and mounted on a large truck, was useless in a covert search of an apartment building on a busy midtown Manhattan street."

31. *Eyes on the Horizon: Serving on the Front Lines of National Security*, p. 10. General Myers writes: "...the FBI had been designated the lead civilian agency in the crisis, with the military standing by as needed if the terrorist attacks involved weapons of mass destruction."

32. JFHQ-NCR PowerPoint Briefing, Concept of Operations World War II Dedication Celebration, 27–30 May 2004, April 7, 2004, obtained by the author; JTF-NCR Message, WW II Dedication SITREP/JTF-NCR 30 May 04, 302200Z May 04 (May 30, 2004), obtained by the author.

33. FBI PowerPoint Briefing, Transformation and Evolution of the FBI Since 9/11, Presentation at Naval Postgraduate School Center for Homeland Security, "Comparative Government for Homeland Security," J. Stephen Tidwell, Assistant Director in Charge, Los Angeles Field Office, 2006, obtained by the author.

34. Department of the Army, Field Manual 3-28, Civil Support Operations, August 20, 2010, p. X.

    The air force also has a definition, and it says the term means "the temporary military government of a civilian population," using the same benevolent language to elaborate, saying that martial law "provides relief and rehabilitation of the people" in order to restore the country to normal. "Declaring US federal martial law might require the US to exercise jurisdiction over the civilian population. In time of an emergency, military jurisdiction over the civilian population extends beyond the restoration of law and order. It provides relief and rehabilitation of the people, the resumption of industrial production, the re-establishment of the economy, and the protection of life and property"; see Department of the Air Force AFI 31-201, March 30, 2009; Air National Guard Supplement, March 24, 2011; Security Forces Standards and Procedures, March 24, 2011, p. 20.

35. Field Manual 3-28, Civil Support Operations, August 20, 2010, p. X.

36. DOD Directive 3025.18, Defense Support of Civil Authorities (DSCA), December 29, 2010; Incorporating Change 1, September 21, 2012.

CHAPTER TEN: THE PROGRAM

1. DHS, Securing Our Homeland: US Department of Homeland Security Strategic Plan 2004, February 24, 2004, p. 5.

2. Dan Emmett, *Within Arm's Length: The Extraordinary Life and Career of a Special Agent in the United States Secret Service* (Bloomington, IN: iUniverse, 2012), p. 98.

3. The White House, Memorandum for the White House Deputy Chief of Staff, Subject: Internal Review Concerning April 27, 2009 Air Force One Flight, May 5, 2009.

4. "The White House Communications Agency (WHCA) is a joint service military agency under the operational control of the White House Military Office (WHMO) and administrative control of the Defense Information System Agency (DISA). The mission of WHCA is to provide telecommunications and other related support to the President of the United States (POTUS) in his role as Commander in Chief (CINC), Chief Executive Officer of the United States, and Head of State; and other elements related to the President. Elements related to the President include the Vice President, the First Lady, the first family, the United States Secret Service (USSS), the White House Staff, the White House Press Office, the National Security Council, WHMO and others as directed." See Fiscal Year (FY) 2013 IT President's Budget Request, Section 351 Report, DOD IT_1 Report, PB 2013, n.d. (2012) (Excel file), obtained by the author.

5. General Hugh Shelton, chairman of the Joint Chiefs on 9/11, describes the enormity: "Even in our post–Cold War environment, the safeguards that go into ensuring the integrity of our nuclear command-and-control systems are mindboggling...they are all dependent on one vital element without which there can be no launch; and that's the Presidential authorization codes...which are to remain within very close proximity to the President at all times...movies may show the President wearing these codes around his neck, it's pretty standard that they are safeguarded by one of his aides, but that aide sticks with him like glue." See Hugh Shelton, *Without Hesitation: The Odyssey of an American Warrior,* pp. 391–392.

6. In January 2002, Secretary of Defense Rumsfeld directed that the use of the term "National Command Authority" be discontinued. Instead, he stated that "President," "SecDef," or both, should be used if applicable. Memorandum, Director, Joint Staff, Joint Chiefs of Staff Memorandum (Lieutenant General John P. Abizaid), to Joint Staff Directors, Joint Chiefs of Staff, Subject: Use of the Term "National Command Authority," January 11, 2002.

   For a continuation of the use of the term, despite Rumsfeld's order, see JCS, Doctrine for the Armed Forces of the United States, JP-1, May 14, 2007, p. II-5.

7. *Deadly Indifference: The Perfect (Political) Storm,* p. 10.

8. "We exist in a political context," former NSA and CIA director Michael Hayden is quoted as saying in *Angler: The Cheney Vice Presidency.* "We cannot have...an approach to terrorism...that has an on/off switch every other November. It has to have stability." See *Angler: The Cheney Vice Presidency,* p. 181.

9. CBS News, "Napolitano Avoids Terror Terminology," March 12, 2009; http://www.cbsnews.com/2100-201_162-4826437.html (accessed April 27, 2012).

10. Jeff Bliss and Nadine Elsibai, "Napolitano Says Fixing Immigration System a Priority," Bloomberg News, January 15, 2009.

11. DHS Press Release, Secretary Napolitano Issues First in a Series of Action Directives, January 21, 2009.

12. The White House, press briefing by Secretary of Homeland Security Janet Napolitano, Deputy Secretary of State Jim Steinberg, and Deputy Attorney General David Ogden on US-Mexico Border Security Policy, March 25, 2009.

13. Obama's initial *National Security Strategy* declared that the traditional distinction between national and homeland security was disappearing. The White House, *The US National Security Strategy*, May 2010. The 2009 *US National Security Strategy* identified Homeland Security as a critical dimension of US national security, noting: "We are now moving beyond traditional distinctions between homeland and national security. National security draws on the strength and resilience of our citizens, communities, and economy. This includes a determination to prevent terrorist attacks against the American people by fully coordinating the actions that we take abroad with the actions and precautions that we take at home."

14. The White House, Presidential Policy Directive 8 (PPD-8), National Preparedness, March 30, 2011.

15. Bob Woodward, *Obama's Wars* (New York: Simon & Schuster, 2011), p. 363.

16. The Clock Is Ticking, A Progress Report on America's Preparedness to Prevent Weapons of Mass Destruction Proliferation and Terrorism, October 21, 2009.

17. Testimony of Assistant Secretary Dr. Alexander Garza Before the House Appropriations Committee, Subcommittee on Homeland Security, "Office of Health Affairs Current Biosurveillance Capabilities," February 26, 2010.

    The new administration was committed to supporting the entire network "to detect, characterize, respond to and recover from covert terror attacks using biological weapons," assured Dr. Tara O'Toole, under secretary for science and technology at the Department of Homeland Security; Testimony of Tara O'Toole before the House Subcommittee on Homeland Security Appropriations, on Biosurveillance, April 16, 2010.

18. The White House, *The US National Security Strategy*, May 2010.

19. A. G. Sulzberger and Matthew L. Wald, "White House Apologizes for Air Force Flyover," *New York Times*, City Room Blogs, April 27, 2009, 10:36 am, http://cityroom.blogs.nytimes.com/2009/04/27/air-force-one-backup-rattles-new-york-nerve/ (accessed October 21, 2012); American Forces Press Service (Jim Garamone), "Military Office Director Resigns in Wake of New York Fly-by," May 8, 2009; ABC News (Lindsey Ellerson), "Deputy

in White House Military Office Promoted, Replacing Boss Who Resigned Over 'Scare Force One' Incident," Oct 16, 2009 5:37 p.m.; http://abcnews.go .com/blogs/politics/2009/10/deputy-in-white-house-military-office -promoted-replacing-boss-who-resigned-over-scare-force-one-inci/ (accessed October 21, 2012).

20. The White House, Office of the Press Secretary, President Obama Names Director of the White House Military Office, October 16, 2009; DOD News Release, No. 205-10, Senior Executive Service Appointments and Reassignments (corrected), March 16, 2010.

CHAPTER ELEVEN: FIRST FAMILY

1. *Cheney: The Untold Story of America's Most Powerful and Controversial Vice President*, p. 334.
2. Interview with *People Magazine* online, originally located at http://people .aol.com/people/articles/0,19736,1191271_2,00.html.
3. The vice president's daughter was the deputy assistant secretary of state for Near Eastern affairs.
4. *Cheney: The Untold Story of America's Most Powerful and Controversial Vice President*, p. 332.
5. *In My Time: A Personal and Political Memoir*, p. 4.
6. When the chairman of the Joint Chiefs of Staff went to his first post-9/11 National Security Council meeting, he entered a place, the bunker of the Presidential Emergency Operations Center, that *he* had never been to before, despite his rank and thirty-five years in the military. Secret Service agents escorted the general down from the West Wing "past thick blast doors and through a long underground tunnel that terminated under the East Wing," he says. See *Without Hesitation*, pp. 436–437.
7. Lieutenant Colonel Robert J. Darling, USMC (Ret.), *24 Hours Inside the President's Bunker: 9-11-01 The White House*, pp. 49–50.
8. *No Higher Honor: A Memoir of My Years in Washington*, p. 70.
9. *Angler: The Cheney Vice Presidency*, pp. 116–118; *In My Time: A Personal and Political Memoir*, pp. 1–10.
10. *Angler: The Cheney Vice Presidency*, p. 129; *Cheney: The Untold Story of America's Most Powerful and Controversial Vice President*, pp. 333–334.
11. Robert Draper, *Dead Certain: The Presidency of George W. Bush*, p. 142.
12. See in particular the account of one WHMO Marine Corps officer: Lieutenant Colonel Robert J. Darling, USMC (Ret.), *24 Hours Inside the President's Bunker: 9-11-01 The White House*.
13. *Cheney: The Untold Story of America's Most Powerful and Controversial Vice President*, p. 343; *No Higher Honor: A Memoir of My Years in Washington*, p. 75.
14. Laura Bush, *Spoken from the Heart*, pp. 197–203.
    Some of the others with Laura Bush were Andi Ball, the First Lady's chief of staff; White House domestic policy advisor Margaret Spellings;

Noelia Rodriguez, press secretary to Laura Bush; Ashleigh Adams, deputy press secretary to Laura Bush; John Meyer, advance man; and Sarah Moss, the First Lady's personal aide.

Noelia Rodriguez, press secretary to First Lady Laura Bush, recalls: "We then went to Senator Gregg's office. My worry was the pool reporters. It's funny what you think about in an emergency. We put them all in a room, and the agents said to me, 'We have to leave here—and we can't take them with us.' Larry [a reporter from *USA Today*] said, 'Don't worry about us.' We left the Capitol at 10:10. Mrs. Bush had a lot of staffers there and some of us were in the limo, which was parked in the portico at the Capitol, and we were talking excitedly: 'What could this be? Where are we going? What's next?'—just chatter, you know. Then the driver said something like, 'Ladies, this is a time to pay attention.' He meant it was a time to be quiet. I think he wanted to hear the instructions he was getting in his earpiece. Just then, what seemed like two dozen of these ninja guys surrounded the car—Secret Service agents all dressed in black. Mrs. Bush then got in the car, and they took us to the 'secure location' you've heard about.... Many of the women on our staff are quite young. Some were crying; others, you could see the shock on their faces. Mrs. Bush was worried about them. She was trying to show by example that everything was going to be OK. She was also concerned about the staff we'd left behind at the White House....About 1:30 p.m., we were escorted back to the White House to get our purses and keys. And we got the pets, Spot, Barney, and I think India came too. She's the cat. That was the first time I felt afraid. I remember seeing a couple of empty strollers near the East Wing entrance. They must have belonged to visitors who were on a White House tour that morning....Anyway, we went back to where Mrs. Bush was. At about 4:30 p.m., we returned to the White House one final time that day. After we showed our IDs, the agent said, 'Thank you, ladies, have a nice day!' I know it's just an automatic response, but it didn't make sense. I said, 'I think it's too late for that.' Then it was time to go home." See "Voices of 9-11: 'A Cacophony of Information,'" *National Journal*, August 31, 2002, http://nationaljournal.com/911-anniversary/voices-of-9-11-20020831 (accessed November 17, 2012); *Dead Certain: The Presidency of George W. Bush*, p. 141.

15. *Spoken from the Heart*, p. 202; Bob Woodward, *Bush at War*, p. 15; *Dead Certain: The Presidency of George W. Bush*, p. 141.

16. *Spoken from the Heart*, pp. 202–203.

17. *Dead Certain: The Presidency of George W. Bush*, p. 141.

18. *Decision Points*, p. 132.

19. Mission Essential Personnel (MEP) Press Release, Mission Essential Personnel Hires Seasoned White House Official as Chief of Staff, September 29, 2009.

20. DOE, Continuity Programs, DOE Order O 150.1, May 8, 2008, p. I-10.
21. FEMA director Joe Allbaugh, who in theory was the man "in charge of" continuity or at least the director of the agency theoretically in charge, was also at a conference in Montana. "Allbaugh, who didn't have a cell phone, knew nothing....As the FEMA director walked through the lobby after breakfast, Fugate stopped him to ask if he knew what was going on in New York. Allbaugh shrugged. Fugate then told his deputy at the other end of the phone, 'I'm handing you over to the director of FEMA—brief him.' He then pressed the receiver into Allbaugh's hand"; *Disaster: Hurricane Katrina and the Failure of Homeland Security*, p. 74.
22. *Cheney: The Untold Story of America's Most Powerful and Controversial Vice President*, p. 335. See also *Dead Certain: The Presidency of George W. Bush*, p. 139; *No Higher Honor: A Memoir of My Years in Washington*, pp. 72–73; *Known and Unknown: A Memoir*, p. 338.
23. *Decision Points*, pp. 128–134; The White House, Office of the Press Secretary, Internal Transcript, Interview of General Mark V. Rosenker, Director of the White House Military Office, by CBS, August 29, 2002.
24. *24 Hours Inside the President's Bunker: 9-11-01 The White House*, p. 35; "Voices of 9-11: 'A Cacophony of Information,'" *National Journal*, August 31, 2002, http://nationaljournal.com/911-anniversary/voices-of-9-11-20020831 (accessed November 17, 2012).
25. Elisabeth Bumiller, "Inside the Presidency: Few outsiders ever see the President's private enclave," *National Geographic*, January 2009; http://ngm.nationalgeographic.com/print/2009/01/president/bumiller-text (accessed November 18, 2012).
26. *Decision Points*, p. 126.
27. *Dead Certain: The Presidency of George W. Bush*, p. 141.
28. The White House, Office of the Press Secretary, Internal Transcript, Interview of General Mark V. Rosenker, Director of the White House Military Office, by CBS, August 29, 2002.
29. See in particular the account of the Air Force One pilot, National Museum of the United States Air Force, Wings and Things Guest Lecture Series, Air Force One: Zero Failure, presentation of Col. (Ret.) Mark W. Tillman, n.d. (2009). Condoleezza Rice says that the reason Air Force One moved on from Barksdale was that "we had insufficient secure communications there"; *No Higher Honor: A Memoir of My Years in Washington*, p. 76.
30. *Decision Points*, pp. 130–131; *Dead Certain: The Presidency of George W. Bush*, p. 142.
31. Bill Kelly, NET News, "Military insiders recall Bush's 9/11 stop at Stratcom," KVNO News, September 7, 2011; http://www.kvnonews.com/2011/09/military-insiders-recall-bushs-911-stop-at-stratcom/.

32. Howard Wilkinson, "Real-life 'West Wing' drama: Indian Hill native at Bush's side," *Cincinnati Enquirer*, Monday, January 20, 2003; http://www.enquirer.com/editions/2003/01/20/loc_hagin.html (accessed November 18, 2012).

33. Howard Wilkinson, "Real-life 'West Wing' drama: Indian Hill native at Bush's side," *Cincinnati Enquirer*, Monday, January 20, 2003; http://www.enquirer.com/editions/2003/01/20/loc_hagin.html (accessed November 18, 2012). Mike Allen, "Hagin Leaving the White House," *Politico*, July 3, 2008; http://www.politico.com/news/stories/0708/11507.html (accessed November 18, 2012); *Dead Certain: The Presidency of George W. Bush*, p. 144.

34. "At 10:11 a.m., on the morning of September 11, 2001, Deputy National Security Advisor Stephen Hadley notified the White House Situation Room that 'Continuity of Government and Continuity of Presidency programs' were in effect"; *24 Hours Inside the President's Bunker: 9-11-01 The White House*, p. 57. See also *911 Commission Report*, pp. 35–36.

35. *In My Time: A Personal and Political Memoir*, p. 4.

36. Tim Dickinson, "The Ten Worst Members of the Worst Congress Ever," *Rolling Stone*, November 2, 2006; http://www.rollingstone.com/politics/news/the-ten-worst-members-of-the-worst-congress-ever-20120112 (accessed November 18, 2012).

37. *Cheney: The Untold Story of America's Most Powerful and Controversial Vice President*, pp. 336–337, 340–341.

38. *24 Hours Inside the President's Bunker: 9-11-01 The White House*, pp. 66–68.

39. Dick Armey, who also went to Andrews and then to the undisclosed location with Hastert, recalled: "We were escorted to an office, and we were impressed with how nice the office looked. The speaker asked me if I saw anything curious. I looked, and there was the presidential seal. Somebody had put us in there by mistake. The speaker called and said somebody had made a mistake, and we were moved to another room." See "Voices of 9-11: 'A Cacophony of Information,'" *National Journal*, August 31, 2002, http://nationaljournal.com/911-anniversary/voices-of-9-11-20020831 (accessed November 17, 2012).

40. *In My Time: A Personal and Political Memoir*, p. 6; *Disaster: Hurricane Katrina and the Failure of Homeland Security*, p. 45.

According to an account by then-senator Joe Biden: "I heard that some congressmen and senators were over at the police headquarters by the Monocle restaurant. I asked where [Tom] Daschle was, where the leadership was. I got a private briefing upstairs. They had already briefed Daschle and others, and said they should go to a secure bunker. I called and said, 'Tom, don't go. Don't do that. Stay here.' He explained that he felt that since others were doing it, he was obliged to. He didn't think he should. Byrd refused to go, God love him, which I loved"; "Voices of

9-11: 'A Cacophony of Information,'" *National Journal*, August 31, 2002, http://nationaljournal.com/911-anniversary/voices-of-9-11-20020831 (accessed November 17, 2012).

A few sources report incorrectly that Byrd was also evacuated when he was not; see, e.g., *Angler: The Cheney Vice Presidency*, p. 156.

41. *24 Hours Inside the President's Bunker: 9-11-01 The White House*, p. 70.

42. *No Higher Honor: A Memoir of My Years in Washington*, p. 76.

43. Rick Martinez, KFSN (Fresno, CA), "Former White House official talks about 9/11," Tuesday, September 6, 2011; http://abclocal.go.com/kfsn/story?section=news/education&id=8344254 (accessed November 19, 2012).

44. *Dead Certain: The Presidency of George W. Bush*, p. 143.

45. John Ashcroft on September 11, 2001, Salem Radio Network, September 9, 2011; on YouTube ("John Ashcroft reflects with Janet Mefferd on his experiences the day the United States came under attack by al-Qaeda"); http://www.youtube.com/watch?v=GC-GytLiDQ4 (accessed November 19, 2012).

46. *24 Hours Inside the President's Bunker: 9-11-01 The White House*, pp. 84–86.

47. Barbara Bush, *Reflections: Life After the White House*, p. 389.

48. Richard Myers and Malcolm McConnell, *Eyes on the Horizon: Serving on the Front Lines of National Security*, p. 153.

49. *Eyes on the Horizon: Serving on the Front Lines of National Security*, p. 153. See also *Angler: The Cheney Vice Presidency*, p. 157.

50. The Office of Army Reserve History wrote: "Despite the attack, command and control of the nation's armed forces never lapsed. The Chief of the Army Reserve, Lieutenant General Thomas J. Plewes, was working in his office in the Pentagon when the attack occurred. Key defense leaders, including General Plewes, participated in the building's evacuation before they were whisked away to Site R, also known as the Alternate Joint Communications Center, a secure location on the Maryland-Pennsylvania border. For a time, General Plewes was the ranking military official at the site, considered to be the 'back up' command and control center for the Pentagon." Quoted at the most excellent About Camp David blog, Raven Rock Mountain Complex, Tuesday, August 23, 2011 (last updated: 11/14/2012); http://aboutcampdavid.blogspot.com/2011/08/raven-rock-mountain-complex.html (accessed November 19, 2012).

51. *Known and Unknown: A Memoir*, p. 338.

52. "Amid the hectic activity and confusion," the official army history reads, "the Army Operations Center staff removed Secretary White, despite his objection, to a remote location. Later, the staff realized that his relocation had not been required by the situation in accordance with contingency plans. The evacuation of Secretary White left General Keane in charge at the Pentagon for the remainder of the day"; Department of the Army Historical Summary, Fiscal Year 2001, p. 57.

53. Michael K. Bohn—McClatchy Newspapers, "Former staffers remember the White House Situation Room on 9/11," *Bellingham Herald*, August 29, 2011; http://www.bellinghamherald.com/2011/08/29/2144159/the-dead-list -former-staff-members.html; Scott Thurman, "Inside the Situation Room and with the president on Sept. 11," ABC News Channel 8 (WJLA-TV), September 11, 2011; http://www.wjla.com/articles/2011/09/inside-the -situation-room-and-with-the-president-on-sept-11-66269.html; *Dead Certain: The Presidency of George W. Bush*, p. 140.

54. *Dead Certain: The Presidency of George W. Bush*, p. 142; *24 Hours Inside the President's Bunker: 9-11-01 The White House*, p. 76.

55. *24 Hours Inside the President's Bunker: 9-11-01 The White House*, p. 80.

56. *Cheney: The Untold Story of America's Most Powerful and Controversial Vice President*, pp. 345–346.

57. *In My Time: A Personal and Political Memoir*, pp. 10, 329.

CHAPTER TWELVE: EXECUTIVE AGENTS

1. DC press release, Mayor Gray Taps Christopher T. Geldart to Direct Homeland Security and Emergency Management Agency, May 24, 2012. After a stint in the marine corps, Geldart worked a number of homeland security jobs, including serving during the Bush administration as director of the National Capital Region Coordination Office of FEMA.

2. Press release, New York State Division of Military & Naval Affairs (via readMedia), "Fredericksburg Virginia Resident Named Adjutant General of the DC National Guard," June 7, 2012; http://readme.readmedia.com/ Fredericksburg-Virginia-Resident-Named-Adjutant-General-of-the -DC-National-Guard/4154987 (accessed June 9, 2012).

3. NGB, Domestic JTF Commander Handbook, 2011, p. 81.

"When DCNG assistance is needed, the Mayor must coordinate the request through the Commanding General of the DCNG. The Commanding General notifies the Under Secretary of the Army of the request and its nature. The Under Secretary consults with the Attorney General and the Secretary of Defense on the request. The Attorney General establishes policies to be observed by military forces in the event they are used for Military Support to Civil Authorities in the District. If approved by the Under Secretary of the Army, the Commanding General advises the Mayor of the decision and commits resources as necessary to assist within the parameters established by the Under Secretary and the Attorney General"; District Response Plan, August 2011, p. 21.

4. The National Capital Region was originally defined in the National Capital Planning Act of 1952 (Title 40, US Code, Sec. 71 (b)). Title 10, United States Code, Section 2674 (f)(2) provides the following definition: The term "National Capital Region" means the geographic area located within the boundaries of (A) the District of Columbia, (B) Montgomery and

Prince Georges Counties in the State of Maryland, (C) Arlington, Fairfax, Loudoun, and Prince William Counties and the City of Alexandria in the Commonwealth of Virginia, and (D) all cities and other units of government within the geographic areas of such District, Counties, and City. The following local governments are participating components of the NCR although they are not explicitly named in Title 10, United States Code, Section 2674(f)(2): the cities of Fairfax and Falls Church in the Commonwealth of Virginia; and the cities of Bowie, College Park, Gaithersburg, Greenbelt, Rockville, and Takoma Park in the state of Maryland.

5. According to the DHS, "coordination of key homeland security functions, particularly infrastructure protection, requires coordination beyond the NCR"; DHS, National Capital Region Coordination: First Annual Report to Congress, p. 14.

6. Section 7302(a)(7) of the Intelligence Reform and Terrorism Prevention Act of 2004 (Pub. L. 108-458), December 17, 2004, amended the definition of the National Capital Region to include Clarke, Fauquier, and Stafford Counties in the Commonwealth of Virginia, and Frederick, Howard, Anne Arundel, Calvert, and Charles Counties in the state of Maryland, and all municipalities within those counties. However, the Homeland Security Act of 2002 limits the purview of the NCRC's oversight and coordination function within the boundaries of the NCR as defined under section 2674(f)(2) of Title 10, United States Code.

7. Assets at Fort Detrick and Fort Meade in Maryland and Fort A.P. Hill and the Quantico marine corps bases in Virginia, even though they are outside the NCR, are also considered part of the catastrophic war plan for JFHQ-NCR; see JFHQ-NCR PowerPoint Briefing, Joint Force Headquarters National Capital Region (JFHQ-NCR), n.d. (31 Jan PGC (Rev. 1)) (2005), obtained by the author.

On December 8, 2004, the US House and Senate approved a measure that enhanced the power of the District of Columbia, Maryland, Virginia, and counties and municipalities within the National Capital Region to enter into interstate mutual aid agreements for the provision of emergency and other public services. The new measure, which was passed as part of the Intelligence Reform and Terrorism Prevention Act of 2004, resolved the problem of legal liability that can result when emergency personnel in the NCR provide assistance outside their local jurisdictions.

A new Memorandum of Understanding between DC, MD, and VA was signed on July 15, 2004, relating to JTF-NCR; and an MOU between DC, DE, MD, WV, PA, and VA was signed on May 19, 2005. Fort Hamilton in New York is included in the Military District of Washington (MDW) organization. The South Carolina National Guard is responsible for providing a ground-based air defense unit to protect Washington, DC.

8. JFHQ-NCR PowerPoint Briefing, Joint Force Headquarters National Capital Region (JFHQ-NCR), n.d. (31 Jan PGC (Rev. 1)) (2005) [January 31, 2005], obtained by the author.
9. DHS, National Capital Region Coordination: First Annual Report to Congress, p. 2.
10. The NCRC officially began operations on March 9, 2003, with the mission to oversee and coordinate regional homeland security in the NCR. The Office of National Capital Region Coordination (NCRC) was established by Public Law 107-296, Sec. 882, the Homeland Security Act of 2002. Specifically, the act gave NCRC the responsibility of:

   - Overseeing and coordinating federal programs for and relationships with state, local, and regional authorities in the NCR;
   - Coordinating the activities of the Department of Homeland Security (DHS) relating to the NCR;
   - Providing state, local, and regional authorities in the NCR with information, research, and technical support to assist in efforts to secure the homeland, and coordinating with these authorities and the private sector on terrorism preparedness efforts to ensure adequate planning, information sharing, training, and execution of domestic preparedness activities;
   - Developing a process for receiving meaningful input from state, local, and regional authorities and the private sector in the NCR to assist in the development of the homeland security plans and activities of the federal government; and
   - Serving as a liaison between the federal government and state, local, and regional authorities and the private sector in the NCR to facilitate access to federal grants and other programs.

11. CJCS Message, Subject: Establishment of Joint Force Headquarters-National Capital Region, EXORD, DTG 202330ZJUN03 (June 20, 2003), obtained by the author.

   The Joint Force Headquarters is responsible for protecting the District of Columbia and the neighboring counties and cities of Maryland and Virginia, including Arlington, Loudoun, Fairfax, and Prince William Counties; and the cities of Alexandria, Fairfax, Manassas, and Manassas Park in Virginia; as well as Montgomery and Prince Georges Counties in Maryland; NGB, Domestic JTF Commander Handbook, 2011, p. 82.
12. Hawrylak was appointed on April 29, 2007, as deputy commander both of the JFHQ-NCR and its peacetime headquarters, the US Army Military District of Washington (USAMDW).

13. The website of the JFHQ-NCR states that the command "is USNORTH-COM's 'eyes and ears' for NCR situational awareness and relevant common operating picture. Partnered with other federal, state, county, and city governmental agencies, personnel from the JFHQ-NCR are prepared to respond when called upon for assistance. As a proud partner in homeland defense, JFHQ-NCR will augment civil responders when necessary. The DOD will respond when asked with JFHQ-NCR as a willing, subordinate partner and advisor." http://www.jfhqncr.northcom.mil/ (accessed March 12, 2009).

14. About Joint Force Headquarters National Capital Region; http://www.mdw.army.mil/jfhq-ncr.htm (accessed June 11, 2012).

15. The Pentagon Reservation is defined in the Code of Federal Regulations (Title 32, Code of Federal Regulations, Part 234, Sec. 234.1) as: "area of land and improvements thereon, located in Arlington, Virginia, on which the Pentagon Office Building, Federal Building Number 2, the Pentagon heating and sewage treatment plants, and other related facilities are located. Pursuant to 10 U.S.C. 674, the Pentagon Reservation also includes the area of land known as Raven Rock Mountain Complex (RRMC), located in Adams County, Pennsylvania, and Site C, which is located in Washington County, Maryland, and other related facilities. The Pentagon Reservation shall include all roadways, walkways, waterways, and all areas designated for the parking of vehicles."

16. *Angler: The Cheney Vice Presidency*, pp. 135–136.

17. *Cheney: The Untold Story of America's Most Powerful and Controversial Vice President*, p. 333.

18. When signing the 2008 National Defense Authorization Act, which included the provision to repeal Enforcement of the Laws to Restore Public Order, the Bush Administration said: "The Administration opposes section 1022, which could be perceived as significantly restricting the statutory authority for the President to direct the Secretary of Defense to preserve life and property, and would imprudently limit the President's authority to call upon the Reserves. Such a result would be detrimental to the President's ability to employ the Armed Forces effectively to respond to the major public emergencies contemplated by the statute; Executive Office of the President, Office of Management and Budget, Statement of Administration Policy: S.1547—National Defense Authorization Act for Fiscal Year 2008, July 10, 2007.

  Haynes also tried to torpedo congressional efforts to restore the Insurrection Act and a seeming balance between the federal government and the states after Hurricane Katrina.

  Senator Patrick Leahy and Senator Christopher "Kit" Bond introduced Senate Bill 513 on February 7, 2007, to repeal the Enforcement of Laws to Restore Public Order and revive the previous Insurrection Act. Senate Bill 513 was never enacted, though the essence of the bill made its way into the 2008 NDAA, which was enacted in January 2008.

DOD General Counsel William J. Haynes II drafted a letter to the chairman of the Senate Armed Services Committee stating the following: "If this legislation [Senate Bill 513] is enacted, it would affect the Department detrimentally by revoking a congressionally granted authority for the President to direct the Secretary of Defense to preserve life and property by limiting the president's authority to call upon the Reserves to restore order, repel invasions or suppress rebellions."

19. IDA, Federal Civil Defense Organization: The Rationale of Its Development, Study S-184, January 1965, p. 23.

20. For example, from 1951 to 1953, President Truman's budget requested $1.5 billion for civil defense, but congressional appropriations totaled only $153 million—90 percent less than requested.

21. IDA, Federal Civil Defense Organization: The Rationale of Its Development, Study S-184, January 1965, p. 36.

22. DHS, Civil Defense and Homeland Security: A Short History of National Preparedness Efforts, September 2006, p. 14.

23. Amanda Ripley, "Why Disasters Are Getting Worse," *Time Magazine*, September 3, 2008; Ker Than, "Scientists: Natural Disasters Becoming More Common," LiveScience.com, October 17, 2005; http://www.livescience.com/414-scientists-natural-disasters-common.html (accessed May 4, 2012).

According to the Center for Research on Epidemiology of Disasters (CRED) in Brussels, the total of natural disasters reported each year—those killing 10 or more people—has been steadily increasing in recent decades, from 78 in 1970 to 348 in 2004. The Worldwatch Institute says that the average number of disasters throughout the 1980s was 400. This increased to 630 in the 1990s, and to 730 in the decade 2000–2009 (Worldwatch Institute, Natural Disasters Becoming More Frequent, n.d. (accessed May 4, 2012); http://www.worldwatch.org/node/5825.

While natural geologic disasters, such as volcanic eruptions, earthquakes, and avalanches, have remained steady, hydrometeorological disasters—droughts, tsunamis, hurricanes, typhoons, and floods—have significantly increased since the 1980s, accounting for about two-thirds of the increase.

One could additionally make the bureaucratic observation that another reason why there was a perception of an increase in natural disasters was that agencies such as CRED and the US Agency for International Development (AID) began record-keeping and thus actively looking for them.

24. FEMA absorbed the Federal Insurance Administration, the National Fire Prevention and Control Administration, the National Weather Service Community Preparedness Program, the Federal Preparedness Agency of the General Services Administration, and the Federal Disaster Assistance Administration activities from the Department of Housing and Urban Development, combining them into a single independent agency.

CHAPTER THIRTEEN: PULL TO PUSH

1. His letter stated that "while the [Posse Comitatus] Act does not apply to the National Guard while under the control of the governor, the command and control of such forces…presents its own problems.

    "The use of the National Guard under title 32, US Code, presents the federal government with a situation in which the federal government is expected to provide funding while leaving command and control to the States. The Insurrection Statutes found in chapter 15 of title 10, US Code, do bypass the Posse Comitatus Act, but they were enacted…to deal with primarily different situations." Senator Warner goes on to recommend that DOD review the Insurrection Statutes and those statutes governing the federalization of the National Guard with a view toward amending them. He said he would be looking into "the entire legal framework governing a President's power to use the regular armed forces to restore public order in…a large-scale, protracted emergency"; Senator John Warner, Letter to US Secretary of Defense Donald Rumsfeld, September 14, 2005, obtained by the author.

    Two days prior, the senator spoke on the Senate floor and argued that the *Posse Comitatus* Act needed to be changed to better meet "a contingency of the nature we have experienced"; *Congressional Record*, S9945–47 (daily edition, September 13, 2005) (Remarks of Senator Warner). "I believe the time has come that we reflect on the Posse Comitatus Act." He advocated giving the president and the secretary of defense "correct standby authorities" to manage disasters; see also AP (Robert Burns), Bush: Boost military role in domestic emergencies, September 17, 2005.

2. AP (Robert Burns), Bush: Boost military role in domestic emergencies, September 17, 2005.

3. *Katrina's Secrets: Storms after the Storms*, p. 255.

4. The White House, President Discusses Hurricane Relief in Address to the Nation, Jackson Square, New Orleans, Louisiana, September 15, 2005.

5. Memorandum, Rumsfeld to Myers, USG's Ability to Deal with Catastrophic Events—Natural or Terrorist, September 20, 2005, classified secret.

6. Though it is impossible to prove that the amendment was DOD (or White House) authored, more than one inside military author so refers to it: See Caroline Ross Prosch, "Getting to One from Title 10 + Title 32: Unity of Effort in the Homeland," Naval Postgraduate School, September 2011, pp. 29–31; Ludwig J. Schumacher, "Dual Status Command for No-Notice Events: Integrating the Military Response to Domestic Disasters," *Homeland Security Affairs*, vol. 7, article 4 (February 2011).

7. The Federal Response to Hurricane Katrina: Lessons Learned, February 23, 2006, pp. 66–67.

Notes

8. Statement of Daniel J. Kaniewski, Deputy Director, Homeland Security Policy Institute, the George Washington University, before the House Committee on Homeland Security Subcommittee on Emergency Communications, Preparedness, and Response, "PKEMRA Implementation: An Examination of FEMA's Preparedness and Response Mission," March 17, 2009.

9. The Federal Response to Hurricane Katrina: Lessons Learned, February 23, 2006, pp. 66–67.

10. The Federal Response to Hurricane Katrina: Lessons Learned, February 23, 2006, p. 10.

11. Rumsfeld wrote: "DHS was established with little, if any input from anyone outside a small circle of White House aides and congressional staffers. The first I heard of the plan was a phone call from White House Chief of Staff Andy Card in early 2002, the night before it was announced publicly." *Known and Unknown: A Memoir*, p. 617.

    The decision was communicated to President Bush's Cabinet secretaries, including those immediately affected, only hours before he addressed the nation on June 6; Brookings, Assessing the Department of Homeland Security, pp. 1–14. See also DHS, Addressing the 2009 Presidential Transition at the Department of Homeland Security, pp. 7–9.

    See The White House, Remarks by the President in Address to the Nation, June 6, 2002. For the creation of the department, see, in particular, the summary by Richard S. Conley, assistant professor, Department of Political Science, University of Florida, The War on Terrorism and Homeland Security: Presidential and Congressional Challenges, Paper prepared for the Conference "Assessing the Presidency of George W. Bush at Midpoint: Political, Ethical, and Historical Considerations," University of Southern Mississippi, Gulfport, November 22–23, 2002; Allison Mitchell, "New Anti-Terrorism Agency Faces Competing Visions," *New York Times*, June 14, 2002, p. A27; Associated Press, "Access to Intelligence at Homeland Security Main Sticking Point in Congress," June 21, 2002; Fred Hiatt, "Truman's Rose-Colored Reforms," *Washington Post*, July 15, 2002, p. A17.

12. "The PFO assigned to Katrina, FEMA director Mike Brown, was relieved seven days into the incident under severe criticism and replaced by USCG Vice Admiral Thad Allen. With essentially a leadership vacuum prior to this point, individual DOD and USCG commanders, in the absence of a pull from an organized DHS/FEMA or state command structure, eventually pushed independently, along with state NG troops and other agencies"; Commander Darren J. Hanson (USN), Unity of Command: An Answer to the Maritime Homeland Security Interagency Quagmire, 2008, p. 9.

13. Senate Committee on the Armed Forces, National Defense Authorization Act for Fiscal Year 2007: Hearing on H.R. 5122, June 12, 2006.

14. Former Governor Ruth Ann Minner spoke on behalf of the National Governors Association and said, "We have serious concerns over the repeated lack of consultation between the Department of Defense and the governors." See Caroline Ross Prosch, "Getting to One from Title 10 + Title 32: Unity of Effort in the Homeland," Naval Postgraduate School, September 2011, pp, 29–31.

15. Lieutenant Colonel Paul J. Sausville, DOD Response to Natural Disasters—Why the National Guard Is Off Limits, New York Army National Guard, Army War College, 2008, pp. 17–18.

16. John Warner National Defense Authorization Act of 2007, Public Law 109-364, 109th Cong., 2d sess. (October 17, 2006), Section 1076, "Enforcement of the Laws to Restore Public Order."

17. Lieutenant Colonel Paul J. Sausville, DOD Response to Natural Disasters—Why the National Guard Is Off Limits, New York Army National Guard, Army War College, 2008, p. 21.

    In an address before the House on May 22, 2007, Representative Ron Paul (R-TX) cited "the changes made to the Insurrection Act of 1807 and to Posse Comitatus by the Defense Authorization Act of 2007." Because of that act, warned Paul, "martial law can be declared not just for 'insurrection' but also for 'natural disasters, public health reasons, terrorist attacks or incidents' or for the vague reason called 'other conditions.'"

18. Transcript: Sen. Graham Talks Costs on "FNS," FoxNews.com, published September 19, 2005; Fox News Sunday, September 18, 2005; http://www.foxnews.com/story/0,2933,169708,00.html (accessed June 5, 2012).

19. Caroline Ross Prosch, "Getting to One from Title 10 + Title 32: Unity of Effort in the Homeland," Naval Postgraduate School, September 2011, pp. 29–31; Major Mark M. Beckler, US Army National Guard, Insurrection Act Restored: States Likely to Maintain Authority Over National Guard in Domestic Emergencies, SAMS Monograph, 2008, pp. 38–40.

20. "By changing the language in the Insurrection Act, Congress has explicitly acknowledged that the unrest may be the result of emergencies other than insurrection: natural disaster, epidemics, terrorism, etc. It would have been difficult to define any looting and other lawless behavior in New Orleans as an insurrection." Randall Jackson, Senior Legal Research Associate, CIP Program, George Mason University, "The Insurrection Act (Title 10, US Code, sections 331–335) and the John W. Warner Defense Authorization Act of 2006 (PL109-364)," The CIP Report, September 2006.

21. The New York Times editorialized: "Beyond cases of actual insurrection, the President may now use military troops as a domestic police force in response to a natural disaster, a disease outbreak, terrorist attack or to any 'other condition'"; Editorial, "Making Martial Law Easier," New York

Times, February 19, 2007. Of course, the president already had this power. See also Jeff Stein, "Fine Print in Defense Bill Opens Door to Martial Law," CQ.com [*Congressional Quarterly*], December 1, 2006.

22. Martha Derthick, The Transformation That Fell Short: Bush, Federalism, and Emergency Management, Nelson A. Rockefeller Institute of Government, August 2009, p. 19.

23. In February 2007, Chertoff issued a memorandum referred to as the "One DHS" memorandum, setting out a strategy to create a DHS "brand," unify the department across all DHS component agencies, and improve information sharing.

24. DHS, A National Response Framework (NRF), January 8, 2008.

25. DHS IG, FEMA's Management of Corrective Actions and Lessons Learned from National Level Exercises, OIG-12-118, September 2012, p. 3.

26. DHS IG, DHS' Progress in Federal Incident Management Planning, February 2010, pp. 1–2.

27. Five Years Later: Lessons Learned, Progress Made, and Work Remaining from Hurricane Katrina, S. Hrg. 111-1007, p. 113.

28. DHS, National Response Framework List of Authorities and References (Draft), September 2007, p. 1.

29. NRF, pp. 4–5; FEMA Pub 1, 2010, p. 12.

Chapter Fourteen: Dual Command

1. The White House, Office of the Press Secretary, Executive Order 13528—Establishing Council of Governors, January 11, 2010.

2. The National Guard Empowerment Act of 2007 recommended that the Pentagon "engage with the community of governors to work out an understanding of unity of effort during domestic terrorist events and public emergencies." The National Guard Act was part of the National Defense Authorization Act of 2008. President Obama issued Executive Order 13528, Establishing Council of Governors, on January 11, 2010, creating the Council of Governors and describing its function.

3. For Katrina's fifth anniversary, Congress held a special hearing to review the disaster and the progress made since. Louisiana senator Mary L. Landrieu offered thanks: "We will always be grateful to our first responders who saved so many lives, our firemen, our police officers, the Coast Guard, the National Guard, the Cajun armada of ordinary citizens and individuals who traversed the floodwaters in skiffs and airboats to ferry distressed citizens to safety. We are grateful to the hundreds of thousands of volunteers who have provided relief to help build our communities and we are thankful to the American people for their generosity, their prayers, and their investment in this region's recovery." Not a word about the federal military. See Five Years Later: Lessons Learned,

Progress Made, and Work Remaining from Hurricane Katrina, S. Hrg. 111-1007, pp. 2–3.

4. Naval Postgraduate School, Center for Homeland Defense and Security, Monterey, CA, "Stockton Outlines 'Unity of Effort,'" March 2010.

5. Quoted in Randall Jackson, Senior Legal Research Associate, CIP Program, George Mason University, "The Insurrection Act (Title 10, US Code, sections 331-335) and the John W. Warner Defense Authorization Act of 2006 (PL109-364)," *CIP Report*, September 2006.

6. Hurricane Katrina: The Defense Department's Role in the Response, S. Hrg. 109-813, pp. 13–14.

7. "There has been an extended discussion since [Katrina]...regarding how National Guard forces conduct operations in conjunction with active duty forces deployed pursuant to requests for assistance by states. The National Guard can be recalled by the Governor under Title 32 USC, while recall for duty under the Department of Defense falls under Title 10 USC. In addition, there is limited authority for DOD to call up Regular Reservists if needed," Thad Allen wrote of the first meeting. See iCommandant, Web Journal of Admiral Thad Allen, Council of Governors...an historic day, Tuesday, February 23, 2010.

8. Letter, Secretary of Defense Robert Gates to the Honorable Chris Gregoire, February 11, 2011.

9. Department of the Army, FM 3-28, Civil Support Operations, August 20, 2010.

10. The arrangement follows from the Memorandum of Agreement between the State of Pennsylvania and the federal government for the Summit of G-20 Leaders, held in September 2009:

> In the event that a mission tasking conflict cannot be resolved, the dual-status commander should consult with a judge advocate from both the Federal chain of command and the State chain of command. While the conflict is being resolved, the dual-status commander will continue to execute his federal missions, and will continue to execute those State missions in areas not subject to the conflict.

> Quoted in Colonel John T. Gereski, Jr.; Director of Operations Law, US Northern Command; and Lieutenant Colonel Christopher R. Brown, Professor of Law, International & Operational Law Department, Judge Advocate General's Legal Center and School, US Army; "Two Hats Are Better Than One: The Dual-Status Commander in Domestic Operations," *Army Lawyer*, June 2010, p. 81.

11. DOD Directive 5105.83, National Guard Joint Force Headquarters—State (NG JFHQs-State), January 5, 2011, p. 14.

12. DOD Directive 5105.83, National Guard Joint Force Headquarters — State (NG JFHQs-State), January 5, 2011.

13. As of October 1, 2003, the State Area Commands (STARCs) were disbanded and replaced by the JFHQs. The JFHQs are nondeployable organizations. The adjutant general of each state commands the organizations.

14. NGA Policy Statement, HHS-03. Army and Air National Guard, Winter 2009 Meeting.

15. "Working closely with congressional allies and largely bypassing DOD, the National Guard sought and received congressional authorization to establish 10 CSTs [civil support teams] in 1999"; Paul McHale, "Critical Mismatch: The Dangerous Gap Between Rhetoric and Readiness in DOD's Civil Support Missions," Heritage Foundation SR-115, August 13, 2012.

    The story of the domestic foray into WMD consequence management is told in *Top Secret America*, pp. 120–22.

16. In late 2009, Secretary of Defense Gates announced the creation of 10 National Guard HRF units over the recommendations of NORTH-COM's commander, General Renuart. NORTHCOM favored a continuance of three federal-level CCMRFs and a reduction in state-level CERFPs. See Potential Standards and Methods for the National Guard's Homeland Response Force, 2011, pp. 28–29.

17. Jeffrey W. Burkett, "Command and Control: Command and Control of Military Forces in the Homeland," Civil Support and the US Army Newsletter, no. 10-16, December 2009, p. 20.

18. "As an organizational arm of the Defense Department, each individual Joint Forces Headquarters can be federalized. A Joint Force Headquarters-State (JFHQ–State) is organized within each State. The JFHQ–State is responsible for the manning, equipping, and training of ARNG [Army National Guard] units during pre-mobilization. As directed by FORSCOM and First Army and as coordinated by NGB, the JFHQ is responsible for providing increased levels of support to federalized units and moving federalized units to the mobilization station or port of embarkation. The JFHQ–State is also capable of providing some installation support, family support, and mobilization support to other RC units within the State upon declaration of a national emergency. The JFHQ–State continues to provide support to non-federalized ARNG units within the State. Upon mobilization, the gaining numbered Army or COCOM assumes command and control of federalized ARNG units. If the JFHQ–State is federalized for a domestic Homeland Defense mission, it will fall under the command and control of the respective geographic COCOM." See How the Army Runs, p. 116.

19. Answers to Questions by Admiral James Winnefeld; Nominations before the Senate Armed Services Committee, Second Session, 111th Congress, S. Hrg. 111-896, 2010, p. 197.
20. National Guard Bureau, 2009 Posture Statement, p. 4.
21. The National Defense Authorization Act (NDAA) of 2012 (signed into law December 31, 2011); Opening Remarks by General Craig R. McKinley, Chief, National Guard Bureau, Before the Advisory Panel on Department of Defense Capabilities for Support of Civil Authorities After Certain Incidents, March 17, 2010.
22. Mark Thompson, "The Changing of the Guard," Battleland Blog (*Time Magazine*), January 4, 2012; http://battleland.blogs.time.com/2012/01/04/the-changing-of-the-guard/ (accessed June 7, 2012).
23. Remarks of Senator Leahy on the National Guard Empowerment Provisions Included in the National Defense Authorization Act, December 15, 2011.
24. Joint Action Plan on Developing Unity of Effort, n.d. (2011), obtained by the author. See also letter to Leon Panetta from Governor Terry E. Branstad, Governor Christine O. Gregoire; cochairs, Council of Governors, March 5, 2012; letter to Chairman [Carl] Levin, Ranking Member McCain, Chairman [Buck] McKeon, and Ranking Member Smith; letter from Governor Terry E. Branstad, Governor Christine O. Gregoire; cochairs, Council of Governors, August 18, 2011.

    The 2004 National Defense Authorization Act amended US Code Title 32, Section 325 (32 U.S.C. § 325), to allow a National Guard officer to retain his or her state commission after ordered to active duty (Title 10). The statutory change allows for a National Guard officer familiar with the state and local area of operations (AO) to serve in both a federal and a state status to provide unity of effort for federal and state chains of command. Command authorities for both federal and state chains of command are mutually exclusive. Additionally, the statute requires both presidential authorization and a governor's consent to the establishment of a dual status commander. Under this statute, dual-status JTF commanders were established for a number of planned events (but not during any crisis): the 2004 Group of Eight (G-8) Summit, the 2004 Democratic and Republican conventions, Operation WINTER FREEZE (2005-2006), the 2008 Democratic and Republican conventions, and the 2009 G-20 Pittsburgh Summit (PITTSUM).

    In addition, US Code Title 32, Section 315 (32 U.S.C. § 315), allows a regular officer, i.e., an active-duty officer (Title 10), to receive a state commission from a governor without giving up his or her regular commission to provide unity of effort over both Title 32 and Title 10 personnel. 32 U.S.C. § 315 was used to appoint a Title 10 officer as a dual status commander for the 2010 National Scout Jamboree.

According to the Council of Governors: the law "provides for a commissioned officer of the Regular Army or the Regular Air Force to be appointed as a dual status commander. Such consent can be granted or withheld in the sole and unrestricted exercise of the governor's discretion as a State's commander-in-chief. A federal military officer is eligible for appointment as a dual status commander only if the governor voluntarily grants the officer a commission in the state's National Guard...and then consents to appointment of the officer as a dual status commander"; Letter to All Governors, from the Council of Governors, Subject: Joint Action Plan on Developing Unity of Effort, November 23, 2010.

25. On April 14, 2011, President Obama delegated functions and authorities to the secretary of defense to authorize Title 10 Active Duty and Title 32 National Guard officers to accept a dual status command authority over both Title 10 and Title 32 military members. See also Caroline Ross Prosch, "Getting to One from Title 10 + Title 32: Unity of Effort in the Homeland," Naval Postgraduate School, September 2011, pp. 80–81.

26. Letter to all Governors, from Governor James H. Douglas, Governor Christine O. Gregoire; cochairs, Council of Governors, October 1, 2010.

27. James P. Harvey, Not in Our Own Backyard: Posse Comitatus and the Challenge of Government Reorganization, The Counterproliferation Papers, Future Warfare Series No. 42, Air University, September 2007, p. 24.

28. Major Nicholas K. Dall, USA; The Department of Defense Chemical, Biological, Nuclear and High Yield Explosive Response Enterprise: Have We Learned the Lessons to Ensure an Effective Response?, A thesis presented to the Faculty of the US Army Command and General Staff College, October 6, 2011, p. 70.

29. "In order to carry out their homeland defense and homeland security responsibilities, governors must retain command and control over the domestic use of their own National Guard forces and supporting National Guard forces from other states operating within the supported governor's state or territory. For the same reasons, when a Dual Status Command has not been established under 32 USC 325, governors, acting through their Adjutants General and Joint Force Headquarters-State, must have tactical control over all Title 10 active duty and reserve military forces engaged in domestic operations within the governor's state or territory. Exceptions to this are: (1) if the application of lethal military force is required to repel an invasion or attack against the United States; and/or (2) if National Guard forces in state active duty or Title 32 status are being used to resist a lawful order of the executive or judicial branch of the federal government. In these two instances, a governor's tactical control of Title 10 military forces would be inappropriate and federal activation of the governor's National Guard forces under Title 10 USC for domestic operations should be authorized. Unless or until governors are given tactical control over

Title 10 active duty and reserve military forces engaged in domestic operations within their state or territory, governors support the congressional rejection of provisions to change the Insurrection Act to allow the President to call-up and domestically deploy federal reservists during the response to a domestic event"; NGA Policy Statement, HHS-03. Army and Air National Guard, Winter 2009 Meeting.

30. The dual status commander will be a National Guard officer except for responses in an area of exclusive federal jurisdiction such as a federal military installation; Memorandum to All Governors, from Governor Terry E. Branstad, Governor Christine O. Gregoire; cochairs, Council of Governors, March 11, 2011.

31. National Guard Domestic Operations Manual, Final Draft, with Change 2 incorporated, Draft Version 1.9 of December 21, 2010, p. 4; obtained by the author.

CHAPTER FIFTEEN: MARCHING ORDERS

1. On March 30, 2011, President Obama promulgated PPD-8 to update and replace HPSD-8 "National Preparedness," 2003, and its Annex I (2007), with the exception of paragraph 44 in Annex 1. Separately, PPD-8 complements HSPD-5 (2003), which remains in effect.

2. The White House, Presidential Policy Directive 8 (PPD-8), National Preparedness, March 30, 2011.

3. The White House, *US National Security Strategy*, May 2010.

4. DOE, Energy Emergency Preparedness Quarterly, vol. 1, issue 1, January 15, 2012.

5. Just three months after becoming NORTHCOM's fourth commander, in 2010, Admiral James A. Winnefeld, Jr., found what he said was a "command growing out of the insecurity of adolescence—with all of the promise and well-intended misapplications of ego that involves—and into the security of adulthood." Admiral James A. Winnefeld, Jr., Commander, NORAD and USNORTHCOM, [corrected] transcript of remarks to 132nd General Conference of the National Guard Association of the United States, Austin Convention Center, Austin, TX, Sunday, August 22, 2010.

6. FEMA, Hurricane Sandy Timeline, n.d. (2012); http://www.fema.gov/hurricane-sandy-timeline (accessed November 26, 2012).

7. The White House, Office of the Press Secretary, Ongoing Response to Hurricane Sandy, November 15, 2012; The Ongoing Response to Hurricane Sandy photo gallery; http://www.whitehouse.gov/issues/hurricane/sandy (accessed December 14, 2012).

8. Armed Forces Press Service, "Pentagon Provides Sandy Response Update," November 9, 2012, National Guard Bureau, Army Sergeant 1st Class Jim Greenhill, "12,000 National Guard members helping 11 states

recover from Hurricane Sandy," November 30, 2012; Navy News Service, Lieutenant John Ripley, US Navy Public Affairs, "Grateful Sailors Wrap Up Hurricane Sandy Relief Efforts," Story Number: NNS121115-08, Release Date: 11/15/2012 2:34:00 p.m. [November 15, 2012].

9. The National Defense Authorization Act of 2012 "streamlined" the process for Federal Reserve forces to mobilize in support of relief efforts within local communities. NORTHCOM didn't need the consent of any state to activate quartermaster and engineer units from Florida and North Carolina. *Army News* (Major Angel Wallace), "Army Reserve assets activated in support of relief efforts," November 3, 2012.

10. National Guard Bureau, Army Sergeant 1st Class Jim Greenhill, "12,000 National Guard members helping 11 states recover from Hurricane Sandy," November 30, 2012.

11. NORAD and USNORTHCOM Public Affairs, US Northern Command's Support to Hurricane Sandy, October 29, 2012.

12. Those visitors to New York and New Jersey, by the author's count, include Army General Frank Grass, the chief of the National Guard Bureau; Army General Raymond T. Odierno, army chief of staff; Admiral Jonathan Greenert, chief of naval operations; General James F. Amos, commandant of the marine corps; Army General Charles H. Jacoby, Jr., commander of NORTHCOM; Lieutenant General Thomas P. Bostick, commanding general, Army Corps of Engineers; Lieutenant General William E. Ingram Jr., director of the Army National Guard; Major General Kendall P. Cox, Army Corps of Engineers deputy commanding general for military and international operations; Lieutenant General William Caldwell IV, commanding general, US Army North (Fifth Army); Navy Vice Admiral Mark Harnitchek, DLA director; Major General Charles Gailes, US Army North's senior representative to FEMA; Major General Kenneth S. Dowd, DLA director of operations; Major General William D. Razz Waff, commanding general of the Army Reserve's 99th Regional Support Command; Rear Admiral Michael P. Tillotson; Deputy Commander of the Joint Coordination Element (JCE), Navy Expeditionary Combat Command (NECC); and Air Force Brigadier General Giovanni Tuck, DLA energy commander.

The Coast Guard visitors included Admiral Bob Papp, commandant of the Coast Guard; Vice Admiral John Currier, vice commandant of the Coast Guard; Coast Guard Vice Admiral Robert C. Parker, Atlantic Area commander; Rear Admiral Richard T. Gromlich, director of operational logistics; and Rear Admiral Daniel Abel, commander, 1st Coast Guard District.

13. The only hiccup in the preelection government virtuosity was a slight wording error on the FEMA website, where it was announced that the

"US National Guard" had positioned more than 61,000 personnel along the eastern seaboard, and then that the Guard was coordinating with state authorities. Of course, there is no "US National Guard," and the number is wrong because 61,000 refers to the number of units located within the affected area. And it would be in error to say that *the* Guard was coordinating with state authorities when in fact the Guard is subordinate to state authorities. But still, it is an interesting error.

14. Army News Service, Army North, Randy L. Mitchell, Public Affairs Officer, Region II Defense Coordinating Element, "Extraordinary Coordination, Cooperation Key to Hurricane Sandy Response," November 19, 2012.

15. DHS, Moving Towards Credentialing Interoperability: Case Studies at the State, Local, and Regional Levels, July 2010, p. 3.

16. Hurricane Katrina: A Nation Still Unprepared, p. 296.

17. Homeland Security Presidential Directive 12 (HSPD-12), Policy for a Common Identification Standard for Federal Employees and Contractors, August 24, 2004.

18. The National Institute of Standards and Technology (NIST) of the Department of Commerce was tasked with producing a standard for secure forms of identification in accordance with HSPD-12. NIST published Federal Information Processing Standard Publication 201 (FIPS 201), Personal Identity Verification (PIV) of Federal Employees and Contractors, on February 25, 2005, the first of standards. Public Law 110-53, The Implementing Recommendations of the 9/11 Commission Act of 2007, mandated the need for a standard for first responder credentialing. Additional requirements for Federal Information Security Management were established in Presidential Memorandum M-11-33.

19. DHS, NIMS Guideline for the Credentialing of Personnel, July 2011, p. 2.

20. As of September 1, 2011, a total of 3.9 million smart credentials were issued to people under the Pentagon's purview, including 549,000 contractors; DOD, HSPD-12 Implementation Status Report, September 2012. A total of 10.9 million military-affiliated personnel are eligible for the military ID card, separate from the Common Access Credential, as of September 2012.

Some 5.1 million credentials were issued to federal civilians and contractors, about half the 12 million nonmilitary cards the government estimated were needed to cover this group. See IDManagement.gov, "HSPD-12 Summary, as of 1 September 2011"; http://www.idmanagement.gov/pages.cfm/page/HSPD12-Summary (accessed April 23, 2012).

21. Statement of Stephen Sadler, Deputy Assistant Administrator, Transportation Threat Assessment and Credentialing, Transportation Security Administration, before the House Committee on Homeland Security, Subcommittee on Transportation Security: "H.R. 1690, The MODERN Security Credentials Act," May 3, 2011.

22. DHS, First Responder Capstone IPT: Delivering Solutions to First Responders, May 2009, p. 9. The 2002 National Homeland Security Strategy, p. x, stated that there were "nearly three million state and local first responders." US HLS-HLD Markets—2011-2014, p. 68, refers to 2.6 million first responders at the state, county, and city levels, including police officers, sheriffs, firefighters, medics, and emergency room personnel. The United States has approximately 750,000 law enforcement officers and 430,000 corrections officers (some overlapping with law enforcement).

Secretary of the Army Thomas E. White referred to "11 million first responders in this country that have the primary duty to deal with emergencies"; DOD, Secretary Rumsfeld Media Availability with Secretary White (Media availability with Secretary of the Army Thomas E. White), October 11, 2001.

23. Section 335 of the 2009 National Defense Authorization Act and a 2008 Defense Science Board Report recommendation that the Department of Defense take actions to "island" installations from the commercial electric power grid; Report of the Defense Science Board Task Force on Department of Defense Energy Strategy, "More Fight—Less Fuel," February 2008.

24. Perhaps nothing exemplifies the drive for greater resiliency and survival more than the military's embrace of renewable energy. The military has for a long time been attuned to its rising fuel costs, but these days the focus is on building an independent power base—literally—taking advantage of its abundance of land, financial resources, and national goodwill to embrace stewardship of the environment and savings for a commendable goal. In April 2012, the White House announced that the Department of Defense was making one of the largest commitments ever to clean energy, with a goal of three gigawatts of production on military installations by 2025. In 2012 alone, solar arrays were started or installed on military bases in Alabama, Arizona, California, Colorado, Hawaii, Massachusetts, New Jersey, New Mexico, and Utah, adding to projects already operating in a half dozen states, some of the largest in the country. In one year, the army added more renewable power than the combined total from all previous years. The air force topped 130 separate solar, wind, waste-to-energy, and landfill gas projects. The model marine corps base at Twenty Nine Palms, California, in the Mojave Desert, where solar, wind, fuel storage, cogeneration, and intelligent monitoring are building an austere microgrid, was well on its way to being able to unplug from the public utility if needed.

See Army News Service, Dennis K. Bohannon, ASA IE&E, "Army leaders break ground on $9.6 million solar power project," August 18, 2012; Army News Service, Nathan Pfau, *Army Flier* Staff Writer, "Fort

Rucker Facility Goes Net Zero Energy," November 15, 2012; Air Force News Service, "Large Solar Array Planned for Davis-Monthan AFB," posted August 19, 2012; updated November 5, 2012; Army Public Affairs, Energy Initiatives, "STAND-TO!" Edition: October 26, 2012; *Navy Live*, Jeremy Johnson, "Action Moves Navy in Hawaii to Greater Energy Security," October 22, 2012; Army News Service, Ms. Miriam U. Rodriguez (ATEC), "White Sands Breaks Ground on Army's Largest Solar Array," April 26, 2012; Army News Service, Brian Clark, Presidio of Monterey Directorate of Public Works, "New Solar Array Does Heavy Lifting at Presidio Fitness Center," August 24, 2012; Testimony of the Honorable Paul Stockton, Assistant Secretary of Defense Homeland Defense and Americas' Security Affairs, Before the Subcommittee on Energy and Power, Committee on Energy and Commerce, United States House of Representatives, May 31, 2011.

25. The island—literally and figuratively—attempts to fortify the military at home from the fragility and the messiness of America. The warriors form a healthy, ready, and superior exemplar for the land of the fat. As Rich Haver, former special assistant for intelligence to Donald Rumsfeld, told a military audience, there should be "incentives for military families to prepare for a catastrophic event." How can military personnel protect the nation if they cannot protect themselves or their families? he asks. Rich Haver, presentation at "IN THE DARK," Military Planning for a Catastrophic Critical Infrastructure Event, p. 19.

The website Ready Army (http://www.acsim.army.mil/readyarmy/) provides military families with information on how to provide for their own survival for a short period. The information is aimed toward deployed soldiers so they can have a degree of confidence that their families are protected and safe.

26. Army PowerPoint Briefing, Energy Security for Enduring Operations, Joe Sartiano, Power Surety Task Force, n.d. (2008); obtained by the author. See also Testimony of the Honorable Paul Stockton, Assistant Secretary of Defense Homeland Defense and Americas' Security Affairs Before the Subcommittee on Energy and Power, Committee on Energy and Commerce, United States House of Representatives, May 31, 2011; Office of the Assistant Secretary of Defense for Homeland Defense and Americas' Security Affairs, DCIP News, vol. 1, issue 2, November 2009.

27. Department of the Army, FM 3-28 (Final Approved Draft), Civil Support, June 29, 2010, p. 3-21; Nominations before the Senate Armed Services Committee, Second Session, 111th Congress, S. Hrg. 111-896, 2010, p. 200.

28. The Communications Bridge: Planning and Implementing Strategic Communications for Operation Enduring Freedom and Beyond, 2003, pp. 2–3; National Guard Bureau 2013 Posture Statement, p. 12.

29. Testimony of the Honorable Paul Stockton, Assistant Secretary of Defense for Homeland Defense and Americas' Security Affairs, Before the Subcommittee on Energy and Power, Committee on Energy and Commerce, House of Representatives, May 31, 2011.

"The traditional boundary between tactical and sustaining base activities are [sic] disappearing as the installation power projection platforms assume an increasing role in the sustainment, support and the welfare of deploying operating forces as information technology (IT), rapid transportation and improved management techniques enables more consolidated installation activities and 'reach-back' to the installations for deployed forces"; How the Army Runs, 2011–2012, p. 32.

30. The February 2003 *National Strategy for Physical Protection of Critical Infrastructure and Key Resources* highlighted not just destroying or disabling critical infrastructures but also the potential to *exploit* critical infrastructures to ill effect. See National Strategy for Physical Protection of Critical Infrastructure and Key Resources, February 2003, p. viii; Office of the Assistant Secretary of Defense for Homeland Defense and Americas' Security Affairs, DCIP News, vol. 1, issue 2, November 2009; William Bryan (Director CIP/OASD (HD)), briefing to the Intelligence Surveillance and Reconnaissance Conference, August 19, 2003; OASD (HD), Functional Responsibilities Document (FRD), September 10, 2003.

In a draft DOD Directive 3020.ff, Defense Critical Infrastructure Program (DCIP), October 2004, the Office of the Assistant Secretary of Defense for Homeland Defense proposed to define mission assurance as:

A process to ensure that assigned tasks or duties can be performed in accordance with the intended purpose or plan. It is a summation of the activities and measures taken to ensure that required capabilities and all supporting infrastructures are available to the DOD to carry out the National Military Strategy. It links numerous risk management program activities and security related functions—such as force protection; antiterrorism; critical infrastructure protection; information assurance; continuity of operations; chemical, biological, radiological, nuclear, and high-explosive defense; readiness; and installation preparedness—to create the synergistic effect required for DOD to mobilize, deploy, support, and sustain military operations throughout the continuum of operations.

The DOD IG later noted: "The language of the draft is confusing, describing mission assurance alternately as an activity leading to readiness and as a necessary state for successful military operations. It lists readiness as a complementary or subordinate risk management or security-related function." See DOD IG, Evaluation of Defense Installation Vulnerability Assessments, p. 10.

31. As an example, even today, one study notes that "human developments near military land increasingly reduce places where wildlife can live and pushes more animals onto military land as a refuge of last resort," lamenting as an example that the presence of the endangered red-cockaded woodpecker at Ft. Bragg, North Carolina, forced a part of the base to be off-limits to military operations. National Academy of Public Administration, Strengthening National Defense: Countering Encroachment through Military-Community Collaboration, A Report of a Panel of the National Academy of Public Administration, for the US Department of Defense, Office of Economic Adjustment, September 2009, p. 5.

32. DOD New Release, Ribbon-Cutting Ceremony Marks First DOD-California Buffer Zone Agreement, No. 014-06, February 17, 2006; National Academy of Public Administration, Strengthening National Defense: Countering Encroachment through Military-Community Collaboration, A Report of a Panel of the National Academy of Public Administration, for the US Department of Defense, Office of Economic Adjustment, September 2009, p. V.

33. NORTHCOM/NORAD PowerPoint Briefing, NORAD: Moving Forward with Risk Reduction, Lieutenant Colonel Bryan Miller, NORAD J35W, November 19, 2009, obtained by the author; National Academy of Public Administration, Strengthening National Defense: Countering Encroachment through Military-Community Collaboration, A Report of a Panel of the National Academy of Public Administration, for the US Department of Defense, Office of Economic Adjustment, September 2009, p. 5.

34. "Prior to 9/11," the Defense Department says, "no significant CONUS [continental United States] threat had been identified, and DOD focused protection and assurance activities OCONUS [outside the continental United States]." The Joint Staff's Counterterrorism Division, J-34, was created after the Khobar Towers attack of 1996. See Responding to Terror: A Report of the US Army War College Consequence Management Symposium, August 21–23, 2001, pp. 27–28.

35. The definition of "force protection" was originally articulated in Joint Pub 3-07.2, Joint Tactics, Techniques, and Procedures (JTTP) for Antiterrorism, June 1993: "a security program designed to protect military members, civilian employees, family members, facilities, and equipment in all locations and situations. This is accomplished through planned and integrated application of combating terrorism, physical security, operations security (OPSEC), personal protective services, supported by intelligence, counterintelligence, and other security programs."

36. DOD IG, Evaluation of Defense Installation Vulnerability Assessments, p. 14.

37. Statement of Work, RFQ M67001-12-Q-0020, Mass communication system, Attachment 1, October 20, 2011.

38. JCS, Antiterrrorism, JP 3-07.2, November 2010, p. viii.

   DOD Directive 2000.12, DOD Antiterrorism/Force Protection (AT/FP) Program, April 13, 1999, concentrated on the protection of personnel and reflected the prevalent attitude that terrorism occurred outside the United States. Part of the new force protection is the military plan for "islanding" assets on military installations.

39. The mission assurance program, the National Guard says, "is designed to educate civilian agencies in basic force protection and emergency response; develop relationships between first responders, owners of critical infrastructure, and National Guard planners in the states; and to deploy traditional National Guard forces in a timely fashion to protect the nation's critical infrastructure....During 2005, the National Guard trained six Critical Infrastructure Program—Mission Assurance Assessment Detachments to conduct vulnerability assessments. The National Guard plans to train four additional detachments in 2006 to cover the four remaining Federal Emergency Management Agency Regions. The MAA teams' pre-crisis preparatory work facilitates the National Guard in continuing its time-honored tradition of preventing attacks, protecting and responding when necessary in defense of America at a moment's notice." See National Guard Bureau, 2007 Posture Statement, p. 22.

40. DOD, Developing a Comprehensive and Integrated Vulnerability Assessment Methodology for the Defense Department's Critical Infrastructure Protection (CIP) Program, A Report Supporting CIP Program Outreach and Education, December 12, 2003, pp. 19–21.

41. Military Operations Research Society (MORS) Workshop, Optimizing Investments in Critical Infrastructure Protection, November 15–18, 2010, Arlington, VA, Working Group 4 (WG4), Nexus of National Security and Homeland Security; Lawrence P. Farrell Jr., "To Improve Cyber-Security, US Needs Cohesive Public-Private Partnership," National Defense Magazine, February 2011.

42. Office of the Assistant Secretary of Defense for Homeland Defense and Americas' Security Affairs, DCIP News, vol. 1, issue 2, November 2009.

43. National Academy of Public Administration, Strengthening National Defense: Countering Encroachment through Military-Community Collaboration, A Report of a Panel of the National Academy of Public Administration, for the US Department of Defense, Office of Economic Adjustment, September 2009, p. 3.

44. NDIA, 2009 Biometrics Conference "Strategies for Implementing HSPD-24," meeting minutes, p. 5.

45. DOD PowerPoint Briefing, HSPD-12 and Personnel Identity Protection Force Protection Systems (DBIDS), Defense Manpower Data Center, January 2005, obtained by the author.

46. DOD Instruction (DODI) 2000.12, DOD Antiterrorism (AT) Program, March 1, 2012.

    DOD-affiliated personnel are defined as "DOD active and reserve personnel, DOD civilian employees, retired military and DOD civilian employees, contractors and their employees, inactive reservists, National Guard members, family members of active duty and civilian personnel, persons residing on or having access to DOD facilities, persons under consideration for DOD employment, and former DOD employees and contractors"; DOD Instruction (DODI) 5240.26, Countering Espionage, International Terrorism, and the Counterintelligence (CI) Insider Threat, May 4, 2012, p. 13.

47. Number of retirees as of 2010; DOD, Statistical Report on the Military Retirement System Fiscal Year 2010, May 2011.

48. "In almost a decade of sustained combat, more than 1.1 million Soldiers have deployed to combat, impacting not only the Soldiers, but their families as well. Additionally, 30,000 Civilians have deployed into harm's way. Over 4,000 Soldiers have sacrificed their lives leaving over 25,000 surviving family members. More than 28,000 have been wounded, 7,500 of whom require long term care"; How the Army Runs 2011–2012, p. 2.

49. The total number of veterans in the United States is 22.3 million veterans as of 2010; US Census Bureau, 2006–2010 American Community Survey. About 2 million of those are military retirees, that is, people granted full base access and privileges.

50. JCS, *Guardian Antiterrorism Journal*, Fall 2011, vol. 13, issue 3, p. 1.

51. Secretary of Defense Memorandum, Follow-on Action on the Findings and Recommendations of the DOD Independent Review Related to the Ft. Hood Incident, January 29, 2010; Fort Hood Army Internal Review Team: Final Report, August 4, 2010, p. 11.

52. Vice Chief of Staff of the Army Memorandum, Fort Hood Army Follow-on Internal Review Tasking Memo, April 19, 2010.

53. All Army Message, ALARACT 322/2009, Force Protection, DTG 231751Z NOV 09 [November 23, 2009].

54. The Army "enhanced pre-screening process for certain categories of foreign nationals and United States persons with significant foreign loyalties and connections (i.e., Soldiers enlisting into Military Occupational Specialty (MOS) 09L Interpreter/Translator, MAVNI, contract linguists and cultural role players)." The Army then developed and "improved business processes and procedures related to the background vetting process." See Fort Hood: Army Internal Review Team Final Report, p. 53.

55. Department of the Army, AR 381–12, Threat Awareness and Reporting, October 4, 2010, p. 10. The regulation replaces AR 381-12, Subversion and Espionage Directed Against the Army (SAEDA), January 15, 1993.

56. Department of the Army, AR 380–67, Personnel Security Program, Rapid Action Revision (RAR) Issue Date: August 4, 2011, p. 62. Even when religion is explicitly mentioned, the regulation steers clear of Islam:

> Types of questions regarded as improper or irrelevant in security investigations unless relevancy to the investigation is established...
>
> a. Religious matters.
>   (1) Do you believe in God?
>   (2) What is your religious preference or affiliation?
>   (3) Are you anti-Semitic, anti-Catholic or anti-Protestant?
>   (4) Are you an atheist or an agnostic?
>   (5) Do you believe in the doctrine of separation of church and state? (p. 64)

57. Navy Recruiting Command, Military Accessions Vital to the National Interest (MAVNI) Pilot Program COMNAVCRUITCOMINST 1133.13, August 14, 2009.

58. FBI National Press Office Statement, "Investigation Continues into Fort Hood Shooting," November 11, 2009.

59. Peter Huller, "Intelligence Preparation of the Garrison Environment (IPGE)," JCS, *Guardian Antiterrorism Journal*, Fall 2011, vol. 13, issue 3, pp. 10–15. Force protection indicators, the author says, include: "politics, civilian press, local population, and demographics." Radical groups use venues such as "universities, religious centers, and the Internet to recruit and to plan operations," the Joint Chiefs advise. "Knowing, for example, that radical extremist groups are recruiting in your AI [area of interest] may explain a report of a Soldier suddenly exhibiting unusual behavior consistent with insider threat behavior." Activist groups, even those "opposed to military construction on the installation for some reason," are suspect, and "ignorance of them can be dangerous." Mission assurance necessitates use of the "full range of garrison sensors"—military police, contract security guards, military personnel, family members, and contractors.

60. Richard R. Dickens, Negotiable Collateral Damage: Civil Liberties Versus National Security in Times of Threat, A Thesis Presented to the Faculty of the School of Advanced Air and Space Studies, Air University, Maxwell AFB, Alabama, June 2011.

CONCLUSION: MARTIAL LIFE

1. Andrew Freedman for Climate Central, part of the Guardian Environment Network, "NOAA: 2012 to rank as second costliest US year since 1980," *Guardian* (UK), December 21, 2012.

2. DHS, FY 2013 Budget Request and Supporting Information: Office of Health Affairs, p. 2261; Department of Homeland Security (DHS) Funding Opportunity Announcement (FOA), Catalogue of Federal Domestic Assistance (CFDA) Number 97.091, CFDA Title: Homeland Security BioWatch Program, 2012; EPA OIG, Evaluation Report, EPA's BioWatch Role Reduced, Report No. 10-P-0106, April 20, 2010; Nancy S. Bush, "BioWatch: Case for Change of Traditional Leadership to Improve Performance," master's thesis, Naval Postgraduate School, September 2009, p. 3; National Academy of Sciences, BioWatch and Public Health Surveillance: Evaluating Systems for the Early Detection of Biological Threats: Abbreviated Version, 2009, p. 2; Spencer S. Hsu, "Costly Weapon-Detection Plans Are in Disarray, Investigators Say," *Washington Post*, July 16, 2008, p. A15; DHS OIG, DHS' Management of the BioWatch Program, OIG-07–22, January 2007; EPA OIG, Evaluation Report, EPA Needs to Fulfill Its Designated Responsibilities to Ensure an Effective BioWatch Program, Report No. 2005–P–00012, March 23, 2005; EPA OIG, Evaluation Report, EPA's Homeland Security Role to Protect Air from Terrorist Threats Needs to Be Better Defined, Report No. 2004–M–000005, February 20, 2004.

3. Homeland Security Watch, Arnold Bogis, "Being sent to the minors can be a good thing—even in homeland security," March 19, 2012; http://www.hlswatch.com/index.php?s=DNDO (accessed May 17, 2012); Opening Statement of Warren M. Stern, Director, Domestic Nuclear Detection Office, Department of Homeland Security, Before the House Committee on Science, Space, and Technology, Subcommittee on Technology and Innovation Research and Development Priorities and Strategic Direction, March 15, 2011; DHS, IT Program Assessment, DNDO-Joint Analysis Center Collaborative Information System (JACCIS), n.d. (2009); GAO, Combating Nuclear Terrorism: DHS's Program to Procure and Deploy Advanced Radiation Detection Portal Monitors Is Likely to Exceed the Department's Previous Cost Estimates (Letter Report to Congressional Requesters), September 22, 2008; DNDO, Cost Benefit Analysis for Next Generation Passive Radiation Detection of Cargo and the Nation's Border Crossings, May 30, 2006; GAO, Combating Nuclear Smuggling: DHS Has Made Progress Deploying Radiation Detection Equipment at US Ports of Entry, but Concerns Remain, GAO-06-389, March 22, 2006; "Detecting Nuclear Weapons and Radiological Materi-

als: How Effective Is Available Technology?", Opening Statement of Mr. Vayl Oxford, Acting Director, Domestic Nuclear Detection Office, Department of Homeland Security, Before House Homeland Security Committee Subcommittee on Prevention of Nuclear and Biological Attack, Subcommittee on Emergency Preparedness, Science, and Technology, June 21, 2005.

4. DOD IG, Review of the Department's Preparation to Respond to a WMD Incident, May 2010; DOJ IG, The Federal Bureau of Investigation's Weapons of Mass Destruction Coordinator Program, Audit Report 09-36, September 2009.

5. FEMA, Continuity Evaluation Tool: Version 6, n.d. (2009).

"A critical part of the planning we're doing now with respect to the possibility of a pandemic is in fact making sure government agencies have reviewed and our [sic] strengthening their continuity of operation plans. Part of that means identifying essential workers, and also figuring out who could work from home. And obviously the ability to do that depends on the availability of a significant IT structure and the ability to have people do some of their work using home computers"; Remarks by Department of Homeland Security Secretary Michael Chertoff at the US News & World Report Emergency Preparedness Health Summit, National Press Club, April 18, 2006.

6. "The imagination can take us anywhere," writes Chuck Baldwin, pastor and founder of Crossroad Baptist Church in Pensacola, "but it is not a little disconcerting when the same federal government that is building these internment camps begins categorizing Christians, conservatives, people who support the Second Amendment, people who oppose abortion and homosexual marriage, people who oppose the North American Union and the New World Order, people who oppose the United Nations and illegal immigration, and people who voted for Ron Paul or Chuck Baldwin as 'extremists,' or 'potential dangerous militia members.' Anyone knows that before a government can begin persecuting and imprisoning large groups of people, they must first marginalize them." See Chuck Baldwin, "Why Are Internment Camps Being Built?," NewsWithViews.com, August 11, 2009; http://www.newswithviews.com/baldwin/baldwin527 .htm (accessed December 18, 2012).

7. Admiral James A. Winnefeld, Jr., Commander, NORAD and NORTHCOM, [corrected] transcript of remarks to 132nd General Conference of the National Guard Association of the United States, Austin Convention Center, Austin, TX, Sunday, August 22, 2010.

8. Quoted in Sandra I. Erwin, Stew Magnuson, Dan Parsons, and Yasmin Tadjdeh, "Top Five Threats to National Security in the Coming Decade," *National Defense*, November 2012.

9. JCS, *National Military Strategy 2011*, February 2011, p. 2.

10. Lieutenant General Russel Honoré, my exemplar of the rousing and sensitive leader and a soldier for thirty-four years, makes a similar martial slip in his autobiography: Hurricane Katrina, he wrote in the opening paragraph, "moved into position to attack the Gulf Coast with all the precision of a well-planned and well-coordinated military assault." Hurricane as war: most Americans would skip right over that paragraph and hardly see it as menacing, especially from an upstanding man who would become a genuine star of the sordid episode. "The art of warfighting," Honoré continued: readiness, improvisation, leadership.

    The military certainly exemplifies leadership, but it is a peculiar type of leadership. At the moment of greatest tension in New Orleans, soldiers arrived at the convention center to evacuate some 25,000 stranded citizens. Television cameras rolling, they jumped off trucks with rifles drawn, and Honoré started moving down the line, yelling at them to put their guns away, reminding them that they were in the United States and not in Iraq.

    That evening, Major General Bennie Landreneau, commander of the Louisiana National Guard, asked to meet Honoré at the Superdome, helicoptering down from Baton Rouge for the one-on-one. The two brothers in arms had worked closely together; Landreneau was well aware that Honoré's force of personality and level head had helped save Louisiana from federal takeover.

    "You can't tell my soldiers what to do," Landreneau said to Honoré with an edge in his voice when they met. It might seem like the most petty of reactions, two senior officers in a pissing match over a minor and potentially life-saving order while Rome burned; but it was National Guard versus Big Army; state versus federal; even constitutional versus XYZ.

    Survival: How a Culture of Preparedness Can Save You and Your Family from Disasters, p. 133.

11. DOD, Population Representation in the Military Services 2011; Appendix B, Active Components, 2012; http://prhome.defense.gov/RFM/MPP/ACCESSION%20POLICY/PopRep2011/download/download.html (accessed January 2, 2013).

12. On January 29, 2009, DOD issued a new DOD Directive (DODD), 1404.10, DOD Civilian Expeditionary Workforce. This new directive reissued the previous DODD 1404.10, Emergency-Essential (E–E) DOD U.S. Citizen Civilian Employees (dated April 10, 1992), under a new title to establish the policy through which an appropriately sized subset of the DOD civilian workforce is pre-identified to be organized, trained, and equipped in a manner that facilitates the use of its capabilities "for operational requirements"—in other words, civilian adjuncts of those in uniform, performing identical missions on the battlefield.

13. National Guard Bureau, 2008 Posture Statement; http://www.ng.mil/features/2008PostureStatement/scherling.html (accessed April 29, 2012).

    The prevailing regulation says that the National Guard Bureau provides "situational awareness of the activities of the non-Federalized National Guard to the Office of the Secretary of Defense, the CJCS and the Joint Staff, appropriate combatant commanders, and the Services, in order to facilitate deliberate and crisis action joint military planning and contingency operations," and serves "as the channel of communication for all DOD elements to and from the National Guard of the Several States (the non-Federalized National Guard)." See NGB Memorandum 10-5/38-101 (PROVISIONAL), July 1, 2003, p. 5.

14. *Survival: How a Culture of Preparedness Can Save You and Your Family from Disasters*, pp. 3–4.

INDEX

About the Author

William M. Arkin is an independent writer and one of America's premier military experts, having first served in army intelligence in West Berlin during the Cold War and since then working on national security matters in nongovernment organizations and activist groups, journalism, government, and academia. He has written more than a dozen books, consulted for the military and the United Nations, briefed hundreds of top military, intelligence, and government officials, and been a part of countless exposés. Few can match the breadth of his experience, whether revealing government secrets or working in war zones to evaluate the nature of modern warfare. Working for the *Washington Post*, he conceived and coauthored the landmark *Top Secret America* investigation, and he cowrote the national bestseller of the same name with colleague Dana Priest. He lives in Vermont.